FAMILY LAW REFORM NOW

This collection provides a snapshot of big ideas in family law reform.

The book asks: if you could change one part of family law, what would it be? This deceptively simple question is answered by 10 family law experts and debated within the volume by expert respondents.

The book puts the proposal first, forcing authors (and their respondents) to critically engage with what family law should look like, and where the development of law is needed to address the changing landscape of family life. Cultural and religious plurality, the use of technology, and changes in societal attitudes have all had an impact on the continuing evolution of families. As a consequence, the law has some complex challenges to address in its attempt to regulate familial diversity.

This book is an invaluable resource for scholars of family law, practitioners, policymakers, or anyone more broadly interested in family law reform, and serves as a pair to Hart Publishing's landmark Criminal Law Reform Now.

Family Law Reform Now

Proposals and Critique

Edited by
Charlotte Bendall
and
Rehana Parveen

• HART •
OXFORD • LONDON • NEW YORK • NEW DELHI • SYDNEY

HART PUBLISHING

Bloomsbury Publishing Plc

Kemp House, Chawley Park, Cumnor Hill, Oxford, OX2 9PH, UK

1385 Broadway, New York, NY 10018, USA

29 Earlsfort Terrace, Dublin 2, Ireland

First published in Great Britain 2024

A catalogue record for this book is available from the British Library.

A catalogue record for this book is available from the Library of Congress.

Library of Congress Control Number: 2024944191

ISBN: HB: 978-1-50996-218-1
ePDF: 978-1-50996-220-4
ePub: 978-1-50996-219-8

Typeset by Compuscript Ltd, Shannon

FOREWORD

If you could change one thing in family law, what would it be? Would your focus be on reforming the rights of children, the responsibilities of adults for children and other family members, on the legal framework that formally constructs and deconstructs adult relationships, on money, property, how disputes are addressed, or something else? This collection gives us much food for thought across all of these areas. It also provides a lens through which we can view our society – to explore how much it has changed since the law was last reformed, and in what ways, and how our legal frameworks capture and further current understandings of our social realities. This ambitious collection, which reflects the law reform objectives of the Family Law Reform Now initiative involving the editors and various contributors, provides many such insights.

The chapters in this collection have been developed through an interactive process following a three-day conference led by Charlotte Bendall and Rehana Parveen at the University of Birmingham, attended by the Law Commission of England and Wales. The series of events that has brought contributors together to develop their reform proposals has been financially supported by Birmingham Law School and the Society of Legal Scholars. The outputs of the conference and subsequent work give us much to think about as regards the current state of family law and in what ways it may be improved.

Chapters in the collection examine the legal provisions that govern coupling up whether formally or informally, the process of uncoupling and provisions that govern fairness in this regard, parenting, grandparenting, and adult and children's rights. They consider the rights of children (Anne Barlow and Jan Ewing, 'A Review of Children's Rights When Parents Live Apart', with Helen Stalford as respondent) and public funding via legal aid support for contested cases involving children (Mavis Maclean, 'The Case for a Legal Support for Children Bill, to Swiftly Reinstate Legal Aid for Those at Risk of Harm or Neglect', with Mandeep Dyal as respondent). They explore new dilemmas as a result of assisted reproduction (Alan Brown and Katherine Wade, 'Reform of the Legal Framework for Origin Information in Assisted Reproduction', with Kirsty Horsey as respondent) and ways in which the registration of births could be reformed (Craig Lind, Philip Bremner and Maria Moscati, 'Legal Parenthood and Birth Registration: Time to Respond to Diversity in Family Formation?', with Julie McCandless as respondent).

They examine family property (Sharon Thompson, 'A New Law of Family Property', with Alison Diduck as respondent) and financial provision on divorce (Ruth Deech, 'Reform of Financial Provision on Divorce', with Nicholas Mostyn as respondent) and when cohabitants split up (Andy Hayward, 'Cohabitation Reform in England and Wales: Time for Action', with Rob George as respondent). They also explore the interaction of religion and the law in the context of marriage (Russell Sandberg, 'The Adult Intimate Relationships Bill', with Simran Kalra as respondent) and potential reform around the grounds on which annulment is available (Alexander Maine, 'Nullity Reform: Redefining Marriage', with Gillian Black as respondent).

The collection also addresses grandparents in family law (Samantha Davey, 'Grandparent and Kinship Carers Act or Granny "Annex"? Waiting for the Government', with Felicity Kaganas as respondent), where many consider there to be underdeveloped legal protections given grandparents' pivotal roles within many families. In addition, there are two overarching chapters, the introduction by the project leads and book editors, Charlotte Bendall and Rehana Parveen, along with Nicholas Hopkins and Andrew Bazeley from the Law Commission. Final reflections are provided by solicitor Joe Ailion, who pulls together all these fascinating threads. All of the chapters integrate an exposition and review of the current legal position, the law-reform proposal and its justification. Each critiques the way in which the law currently serves our diverse and changing society and provides a proposal, or proposals, for how the law might be reformed, with evidence as to why such amendments are timely. An important feature of this collection is that each chapter has a corresponding response from another expert or experts in the field. These contributions add nuance, critique and allow for additional reflection. They are a counter-point to and/or a reinforcement of each of the proposals and their justification, giving insights into issues that would need to be addressed were the proposals to be taken forward.

All of the contributions give us valuable insights, whether, for example, by presenting the case for cohabitation reform in England and Wales, or proposing a strengthening of the focus on children's rights and voices within legal processes that affect them. In the former reform proposal, Andy Hayward notes that adult cohabitation is the fastest-developing way for adults to arrange their relationships, rather than formal marriage, and yet there has been no substantial meaningful legislative reform to address the dissolution or breakdown of these forms of relationships. This leaves a substantial risk of relationship-generated disadvantage, particularly given the prevalence of the common law marriage myth. This area was reviewed by the Law Commission in 2002, which brought forward proposals, most of which remain unadopted. Hayward argues that it is timely to review our legislative framework, looking to the experience of other similar jurisdictions that have introduced legislation in the context of cohabitation to provide an evidence base upon which we may draw.

In the latter proposal, for example, Anne Barlow and Jan Ewing argue that 30 years on, the ground-breaking nature of the Children Act 1989 needs to be built upon to provide greater focus on children's rights, rights that are guaranteed in Article 12 of the United Nations Convention on the Rights of the Child. They argue that, whereas the Children Act 1989 broke the mould by focusing on the welfare of children and requiring their welfare to be the paramount consideration in family legal proceedings, it is now time to engage with the specific rights of children as foundational to the assessment of a child's welfare, giving effect to and thus strengthening the voice of the child in private law child-arrangement contexts (amongst others). This would add further weight to the interests of children being firmly considered as distinct from the interests of their parents, giving effect to the paramountcy principle albeit in a different way. Their proposal also provides that there be careful consideration as to how children's rights are protected, and children's voices properly heard, during negotiations, including mediation and solicitor or party negotiations. This would seek to ensure that rather than – as the risk is now – children's interests being left to be determined by parents, who may be of the view that their children's best interests are what they consider their own views to suggest, children should be considered as individual rights-holders whose interests require separate consideration.

These two examples of what lies within are simply a small window on what this collection holds for the reader. I very much hope that you enjoy the insights in this collection as much as I have. Thank you to all involved for their proposals, their reflections and responses, for the generosity of the funders who made the conference possible, and for the Law Commission's active involvement in this wonderful project.

Lisa Webley
Birmingham Law School
January 2024

ACKNOWLEDGEMENTS

The editors wish to thank all authors within this collection for their generous time contributions to Family Law Reform Now, both in producing their written pieces and, in many cases, in presenting their work at the associated conference held in 2021. Further thanks go to the Society of Legal Scholars and the College of Arts and Law at the University of Birmingham for their financial contributions towards that conference. Finally, we wish to express our appreciation to Iulia Mirzac for her research assistance, to John Child, and also Verity Stuart at Hart Publishing, for their constant support and patience, and to the copy editor Catherine Minahan.

CONTENTS

LIST OF CONTRIBUTORS

Joe Ailion is an Associate at Brabners LLP. Joe specialises in family law, particularly in private children matters, fertility law and financial matters on divorce. Joe is passionate about progress and reform in family law, both legally and for the experience of practitioners on the ground. He sits on the steering committee of the Family Law Reform Now Network. Joe also sits on Resolution's Wellbeing committee.

Professor Anne Barlow, FAcSS, is Professor of Family Law and Policy at the University of Exeter Law School. She has led a number of funded socio-legal research projects on aspects of family law and justice, including *Mapping Paths to Family Justice* and *Healthy Relationship Transitions*. She was a member of the Government's Task Force on Family Mediation (2014) and co-authored *Mapping Paths to Family Justice: Resolving Family Disputes in Neo-Liberal Times* (London, Palgrave, 2017), awarded the Hart-SLSA book prize 2018.

Andrew Bazeley is a Lawyer at the Law Commission of England and Wales. He joined the Commission in 2022, initially working on the final stages of the project recommending reforms to surrogacy law, and has since led on the project on burial, cremation and new funerary methods. Prior to joining, he worked for 14 years in public policy, research and advocacy across Parliament, local government and the charity sector.

Dr Charlotte Bendall is an Associate Professor at Birmingham Law School, University of Birmingham, UK. She is the co-editor of this collection, and leads jointly on the Family Law Reform Now network, together with Rehana Parveen. She has published on various family-related issues to date, including: civil partnership dissolution; relationship finances; divorce; shared parental leave; and grandparents seeking contact with grandchildren. She is the co-convenor of the family law and policy stream at the Socio-Legal Studies Association's annual conference.

Professor Gillian Black is Professor of Scots Private Law at the University of Edinburgh. Her primary research interest is in the broad field of family law, with a particular focus on adult relationships and on the parent/child relationship She is currently a Commissioner at the Scottish Law Commission, leading a review of civil remedies for domestic abuse.

Dr Philip Bremner is a Lecturer in Family Law at the Dickson Poon School of Law, King's College London. Philip undertook an ESRC-funded socio-legal PhD at the University of Exeter under the supervision of Professor Anne Barlow on the legal recognition of gay and lesbian co-parenting arrangements. His subsequent research has focused on family formation through surrogacy and other aspects of LGBTQ+ families. Philip is currently the treasurer, and co-convenor of the family law and policy stream, of the Socio-Legal Studies Association.

Dr Alan Brown is a Senior Lecturer in Private Law at the University of Glasgow. His research interests are primarily in the field of family law, focusing on the construction of the family and parenthood within the law, particularly in the context of assisted reproduction, surrogacy, and non-traditional families. His monograph, *What is the Family of Law? – The Influence of the Nuclear Family* was published by Hart Publishing in February 2019.

Dr Samantha Davey is a Lecturer in Law at the University of Essex where she is the module director for family law. She has authored three books: *Family Law* (London, Red Globe Press, 2020), *A Failure of Proportion: Non-Consensual Adoption in England and Wales* (Oxford, Hart Publishing, 2020) and, most recently, *Grandparents and the Law: Rights and Relationships* with Dr Jaime Lindsey (Oxford, Hart Publishing, 2023). She is the project lead for the 'Supporting Families' project, which is part of the Family Law Reform Now network.

Baroness Ruth Deech, DBE KC is a crossbench peer in the House of Lords. She taught family law at Oxford University and was Principal of St Anne's College and Gresham Professor of Law. She served on many public bodies, including the Human Fertilisation and Embryology Authority, the BBC Board, the Rhodes Scholarships and the Mandela-Rhodes Foundation, the Bar Standards Board and the Law Commission Board, and she was the first Independent Adjudicator for Higher Education.

Professor Alison Diduck is Professor of Law at UCL, London, UK. She teaches and researches in family law and gender and the law, and has published extensively in these areas.

Dr Mandeep Dyal is a barrister at Cornwall Street Barristers, England. She has been a member of Cornwall Street Barristers since 2009. She practises in the field of family law and specialises in private law children cases. In 2014, she completed her PhD in Law and Medicine at the University of Birmingham.

Dr Jan Ewing is Assistant Professor in Family Law at The University of Cambridge, UK. She conducts empirical research on improving children's access to and enforcement of their rights on parental separation, particularly when parents agree matters without recourse to the court.

Professor Rob George is Professor of Law and Policy and University College London and a Barrister at Harcourt Chambers. He is co-author of *Family Law: Text, Cases, and Materials*, 5th edn (Oxford, Oxford University Press, 2023) and has previously published on post-separation financial disputes in relation to married and unmarried couples, alongside his main interest in the law relating to children.

Dr Andy Hayward is an Associate Professor in Family Law at Durham Law School, Durham University, UK. His research focuses on domestic and comparative family law, especially the legal regulation of adult interpersonal relationships. With Professor Jens Scherpe, he published *The Future of Registered Partnerships* (Cambridge, Intersentia, 2017) and *De Facto Relationships: A Comparative Guide* (Cheltenham, Edward Elgar, forthcoming). In 2021, he was appointed Special Advisor to the UK Parliament's Women and Equalities Committee for their Rights of Cohabiting Partners Inquiry.

Professor Nicholas Hopkins is Commissioner for Property, Family and Trust Law at the Law Commission of England and Wales. He was appointed in 2015 and has led on projects including enforcing family financial orders, weddings and surrogacy, and the Commission's current scoping report on financial remedies following divorce or dissolution. Prior to the Commission, he was an academic for over twenty years. He holds a Chair in Law at Reading University and is an Honorary Bencher of Middle Temple.

Professor Kirsty Horsey is Professor of Law at Kent Law School, UK. Her research interests lie primarily in the regulation of surrogacy, other forms of assisted human reproduction and genetic technologies. She is particularly interested in where these areas overlap and intersect with issues in family law, especially the concept of legal parenthood. Her long-term research project focuses on reform of the UK's laws on surrogacy.

Professor Felicity Kaganas is Professor of Law at Brunel University London, UK. She teaches family law and children and the law. Her research focuses on those areas of the law and she has published extensively. She is joint author (with Professor Alison Diduck) of three editions of *Family Law, Gender and the State* (Oxford, Hart Publishing).

Dr Simran Kalra is a Lecturer in Law at the University of Leicester. She was awarded a PhD in Law at the Dickson Poon School of Law King's College London (2023). Her departmentally funded research examined the plurality of adult unions within the overlapping English and Islamic legal orders in England. Embedded in socio-legal methods, her work reconciles the theoretical frameworks of legal pluralism and legal consciousness. She has previously taught at SOAS and UCL as a teaching fellow.

Craig Lind taught at the University of the Witwatersrand (until 1989) and the University of Wales in Aberystwyth (until 1998), and he was a Senior Lecturer in Law at the University of Sussex in Brighton until he retired in 2020. He taught (amongst other subjects) family law and constitutional law. His major research interests lie in the areas of family law and sexuality and have a strong cultural focus and a comparative slant.

Professor Mavis Maclean, CBE, St Hilda's College and Department for Social Policy and Intervention, Oxford, Honorary Bencher Middle Temple, was for many years Academic Adviser to the Lord Chancellor. She co-edits the *Journal of Social Welfare and Family Law*, and has edited many volumes for the Hart International Institute for the Sociology of Law series, including *What Is a Family Justice System For?* in 2022. She has carried out empirical research on the work of family lawyers, mediators, the judiciary, and the advice sector following the Legal Aid, Sentencing and Punishment of Offenders Act 2012.

Dr Alexander Maine is a Senior Lecturer at The City Law School, University of London. He is Co-Editor of the Edward Elgar *Research Handbooks on Gender and the Law* and Reviews Editor for the *International Journal of Gender, Sexuality and Law*. His research focuses on the interplay of law and sexuality, particularly relationship recognition.

Dr Julie McCandless is a Senior Lecturer in Law at the University of Kent, UK. She teaches and researches in the fields of family and healthcare law. Her current research is a socio-legal exploration of birth registration law and exclusion. She co-directs the Research Centre for Sexuality, Race and Gender Justice and is on the Editorial Board for the peer-reviewed open-access journal, *feminists@law*.

Dr Maria Federica Moscati is Reader in Law and Society at University of Sussex. Her main research interests lie in issues relating to dispute resolution, access to justice, comparative family law, children's rights, sexuality, reproduction and health, and their intersection. She is an Italian advocate, trained mediator and co-director of the Centre for Cultures of Reproduction, Technologies and Health at the University of Sussex.

Sir Nicholas Mostyn was a High Court judge from 2010 until 2023. Although assigned to the Family Division, where he tried cases of the utmost seriousness across the full spectrum of family law, he was additionally authorised to sit in the Administrative Court, where he did about one-third of his work, hearing complex judicial reviews, Human Rights Act challenges and regulatory appeals. He was diagnosed with Parkinson's disease in 2020, and has decided to resign early in order to try to guarantee as many good years of retirement as possible before the condition takes its grip.

Dr Rehana Parveen is a former family law solicitor and currently an Associate Professor at Birmingham Law School. She teaches on a wide range of modules, including Family Law, Decolonising Legal Concepts, Legal Skills & Methods, and Equity & Trusts. Rehana's research interests are in investigating the developing relationships between English Family Law and Islamic Family Law, and how women navigate these interacting frameworks including their use of sharia councils. More recently, Rehana has been exploring how legal concepts and structures may be decolonised to place them within their social, historical, political and postcolonial context.

Professor Russell Sandberg is Professor of Law at Cardiff University, Wales. His research interrogates the interactions between law and the humanities, with particular emphasis on history and religion. He is author of *Religion and Marriage Law: The Need for Reform* (Bristol, Bristol University Press, 2021).

Professor Helen Stalford is a leading expert in children's rights with a particular interest in children's participation in and experience of justice proceedings. She was a co-lead on the seminal AHRC-funded project, *Rewriting Children's Rights Judgments: From Academic Vision to New Practice* (Oxford, Hart Publishing, 2017) and has completed a number of empirical projects with children as peer researchers. She has acted as consultant to the European Commission, the EU Fundamental Rights Agency, the Council of Europe and UNICEF on a range of projects relating to children's enforcement of their legal rights.

Professor Sharon Thompson is Professor in the School of Law and Politics at Cardiff University, Wales. Her research specialises in adult relationships, with particular focus on power, inequality and the gender of money. To date, she has published two monographs: *Prenuptial Agreements and the Presumption of Free Choice* (London, Bloomsbury, 2015) and *Quiet Revolutionaries: The Married Women's Association and Family Law* (London, Bloomsbury, 2022).

Dr Katherine Wade is a Lecturer in Family Law at the University of Bristol, UK. Her research is at the intersection of medical law, family law and children's rights. She is particularly interested in surrogacy and gamete donation from a children's rights perspective. She is Principal Investigator on a project called 'Children's Voices in Surrogacy Law', which collects and analyses the views of children on surrogacy law reform, with a view to influencing domestic and international law and policy reform.

Introduction

NICHOLAS HOPKINS, ANDREW BAZELEY,
CHARLOTTE BENDALL AND REHANA PARVEEN

This collection, and the proposals contained within it, largely emanates from a conference held by the newly established Family Law Reform Now network, at which participants were asked to address the question 'If you could change one thing in family law, what would it be?' The proposals presented at that conference were predominantly geared towards influencing the priorities of the Law Commission, a body charged with reviewing the law of England and Wales and recommending change where it is needed.

By way of some contextualisation of the Law Commission's work within this area, the Commission's first programme of law reform, published in 1965, envisaged establishing 'a new branch of the law embracing all matters which directly affect the family as such, whether they concern property, status or otherwise' and the 'eventual enactment of a code of family law'.[1] While Baroness Hale was right to question whether the Commission did in fact invent family law,[2] it has certainly had a vital role in reforming it. The single code envisaged at that time did not eventuate, but a number of the key statutes that govern the field have.

The Commission's focus around reform in recent decades has changed. The early years of its work featured the sweeping-away of what appeared archaic features of the law as it stood: remedies against the jactitation of marriage,[3] restitution of conjugal rights,[4] or breach of promise of marriage,[5] for example. Now, its work seeks to keep pace with the continuously changing nature of family life, and to ensure that past reforms that the Commission has led remain fit for purpose.

This introduction sets out, in an inexhaustive manner, some of the ways in which families have changed since the Commission's formation in 1965, and

[1] Law Commission of England and Wales, *First Programme of the Law Commission* (1965).

[2] B Hoggett, 'Family Law Reform: Where will it end? (1992) 3 *King's College Law Journal* 64.

[3] Derived from the Latin 'jactitare' meaning 'to boast', and which petitioned the court to order that the respondent cease and desist from 'wilfully and without the consent of [the] petitioner … boasting that he is the husband of [the] petitioner'. Law Commission of England and Wales, *Jactitation of Marriage* (1971) Working Paper No 34.

[4] Law Commission of England and Wales, *Proposal for the Abolition of the Matrimonial Remedy of Restitution of Conjugal Rights* (Law Com No 23, 1969).

[5] Law Commission of England and Wales, *Breach of Promise of Marriage* (Law Com No 26, 1969).

ways in which they are continuing to change in the present day. We consider the Commission's role in enabling the law to respond to those changes.

As King LJ has noted, 'it is unnecessary to resort to statistics or research in order to appreciate' the changes in our society in recent decades. Data are a useful indicator of changes in society, but the position is often more nuanced. Statistics can capture only so much of the diversity of modern families. As King LJ went on to say:

> These changes have led to the current acceptance of an infinite variety of forms of family life of which single sex, single person and so called 'blended families' are but examples.[6]

She was also right to suggest that the law has sometimes struggled to keep up with these changes,[7] although the Commission has sought to help the law to keep pace.

I. Marriage and Civil Partnership

The making and unmaking of families through marriage, civil partnership, cohabitation and divorce have been significant concerns of the Commission. Marriage is on the wane. In 1965, 371,127 marriages took place in England and Wales; after peaking in the early 1970s, this fell to 219,850 in 2019, the lowest number since 1893.[8] Of these, 6,728 were of same-sex couples, following the introduction of the Marriage (Same-sex Couples) Act 2013.

How people marry has changed significantly, too. In 1965, more than two-thirds of marriages were celebrated in religious, rather than civil, ceremonies, but by 2019 this had fallen to just one-fifth. The shift away from predominantly Christian patterns of worship towards greater diversity of faiths, those of no faith and those who hold non-religious beliefs, such as humanists, is poorly served by the law's sharp distinction between religious and civil marriage.[9]

Alongside marriage, since 2004, civil partnerships have been a route for same-sex couples and, following *R (Steinfeld and Keidan)*,[10] mixed-sex couples, to have their relationships recognised by the law. The popularity of civil partnerships fell for same-sex couples after the introduction of same-sex marriage in 2014, while conversely, take-up among mixed-sex couples was swift[11] – suggesting that civil partnerships have indeed 'become a more meaningful concept to a wider part of society than perhaps was originally intended'.[12] For the most part, though, the big

[6] *XX v Whittington Hospital NHS Trust* [2018] EWCA Civ 2832, [2018] WL 06621444 [101] (King LJ).
[7] ibid.
[8] ONS, 'Marriages in England and Wales: 2019'.
[9] Law Commission of England and Wales, *Celebrating Marriage: A New Weddings Law* (Law Com No 408, 2022) para 1.30.
[10] *R (Steinfeld and Keidan) v Secretary of State for International Development* [2018] UKSC 32.
[11] ONS, 'Civil partnership formations' (2022).
[12] 'Civil Partnerships: a case for reform' (2018) 63 *Scottish Private Client Law Review* 1.

shift has not been from marriage to civil partnership but rather to cohabitation and single life,[13] although the experience of couples who undergo a religious-only marriage (without legal status) blurs the line between these statuses.[14]

The Commission has been responsive to many of these trends. In 2022, it published a landmark report on the law on weddings,[15] making recommendations that would give couples greater choice on where and how they get married within a simpler legal framework that focused on regulation of the officiant, not the building. The scheme would enable religious and inter-faith ceremonies to be held outside places of worship and enable the Government to integrate officiants from non-religious belief organisations and independent celebrants into a single scheme. Indeed, this report was not the first time that the Commission had considered the issue of weddings law. Its 1973 *Report on Solemnisation of Marriage in England and Wales*[16] took a somewhat different tack, recommending maintaining the restriction to prescribed buildings and advocating a universal set of civil preliminaries to marriage. As against this, the recent review ultimately stopped short of recommending universal civil preliminaries. While acknowledging the potential advantages of such a scheme, the Commission accepted that the question ultimately raised wider constitutional issues, given the Church of England's position as the established Church, with the King as its Supreme Governor.[17]

In some cases, reforms to marriage law that the Commission has recommended have had consequences further down the line. The 1970 report on nullity of marriage recommended that marriages without valid consent be voidable not void, for a mix of technical and substantive reasons.[18] Cretney traces the problem now described as 'predatory marriage' to this reform.[19] The issue of predatory marriage has come into sharp focus in recent years, particularly though the work of Predatory Marriage UK.[20] How the law protects vulnerable adults from financial abuse is an increasing concern, and one that has wide-reaching consequences, including within family law. The Commission's recommendations on reform of weddings law also seek to ensure that a person's capacity to marry is properly assessed and make it easier for those concerned about a vulnerable adult to

[13] S Hunt, 'Major demographic trends' in S Hunt (ed), *Family Trends: British families since the 1950s* (London, National Family & Parenting Institute, 2009), 1.

[14] A Barlow, 'Modern Marriage Myths: the Dichotomy Between Expectations of Legal Rationality and Lived Law' in RC Akhtar, P Nash and R Probert (eds), *Cohabitation and Religious Marriage: Status, Similarities and Solutions* (Bristol, Bristol University Press, 2020) 39.

[15] Law Commission of England and Wales, *Celebrating Marriage: A New Weddings Law* (2022) HC 557.

[16] Law Com No 53, 1973.

[17] Law Commission of England and Wales, *Celebrating Marriage: A New Weddings Law* (Law Com No 408, 2022) paras 3.22–3.26.

[18] Law Commission of England and Wales, *Report on Nullity of Marriage* (Law Com No 33, 1970) paras 12–15.

[19] S Cretney, *Family Law in the Twentieth Century: A History*, 2nd edn (Oxford, Oxford University Press, 2005) 87.

[20] At www.predatorymarriage.uk.

discover when notice to marry is given.[21] The Commission is also considering the issue in its current review of the law of wills, as the longstanding rule that marriage revokes a will appears to incentivise predatory marriage.[22]

II. Divorce

The trickle of divorces in the decades preceding the Commission's establishment, with around 1,000 granted each year, became a tide of tens of thousands in the subsequent decades, as legal reform and social change went hand in hand. The rate then steadily fell, levelling out at around eight or nine divorces per 1,000 married people by the mid-2010s.[23]

Overall rates disguise particular recent trends: for example, marriages entered into in the 2010s are almost half as likely to result in divorce after five years as those entered into the 1980s or 1990s;[24] rates of divorce among people over 65 have increased whilst overall rates have fallen;[25] or shifts in the economics of divorce, with, at the turn of the century, women who are graduates becoming less likely to divorce than women without educational qualifications, reversing the trend of previous decades.[26]

Reforming divorce law was one of the first major contributions of the Law Commission: its publication in 1966 of *The Field of Choice*,[27] a response to the Archbishop of Canterbury's Working Group report *Putting Asunder*,[28] precipitated a negotiated settlement with the Church of England[29] that resulted in the Divorce Reform Act 1969, later consolidated (along with other Commission reforms) into the Matrimonial Causes Act 1973. The recent Divorce, Dissolution and Separation Act 2020 may not have the same seismic effect on the number of divorces granted as reform in the 1970s, but it is a significant change in the nature of how divorce is understood – and it is welcome to see much of the scheme in the Commission's 1990 Report *Grounds for Divorce*[30] implemented, if a little late.[31]

[21] Law Commission of England and Wales, *Celebrating Marriage: A New Weddings Law* (Law Com No 408, 2022) para 3.36.

[22] Law Commission of England and Wales, *Making a Will: A Supplementary Consultation Paper* (Law Com No 260, 2023).

[23] ONS, 'Divorces in England and Wales: 2021 data tables, Worksheet 1' (2021).

[24] ibid.

[25] ONS, 'Marriage and divorce on the rise at 65 and over' (2017).

[26] S Hunt, 'Major demographic trends' in S Hunt (ed), *Family Trends: British families since the 1950s* (London, National Family & Parenting Institute, 2009) 1, 22.

[27] Law Commission of England and Wales, *Reform of the Grounds of Divorce, the Field of Choice* (Law Com No 15, 1966).

[28] Church of England Group on Divorce Law, *Putting Asunder: A divorce law for contemporary society: The report of a group appointed by the Archbishop of Canterbury in January 1964* (SPCK, 1966).

[29] Cretney (n 19) 364.

[30] Law Commission of England and Wales, *Family Law: Grounds for Divorce* (Law Com No 191, 1990).

[31] Baroness Hale, lead Commissioner for the 1990 report, has remarked that the 2020 Act is 'remarkably similar to, but even more radical than [the scheme in the 1990 report] … Its time has

In terms of the financial impacts of divorce, these are notably not even – research using data from the early 1990s found a gender gap in real income for separating wives, compared with the income of separating husbands,[32] a disparity that continues to the present day.[33] The Law Commission's consolidating legislation, the Matrimonial Causes Act 1973 (as amended by the Matrimonial and Family Proceedings Act 1984, which arose from another Commission report[34]) remains the primary statute governing the financial remedies available on divorce. The question of 'who gets what' after a union is ended is a difficult one: it has been the subject of numerous Commission reports,[35] with recent work resulting in guidance on the meaning of financial needs.[36] In 2023, the Commission began a review to determine whether there are problems with the current framework that require law reform, and what the options for reform might look like (see Alison Diduck's response to chapter 6 for another view on that question). The Commission's current work may provide the basis for a full review and future financial remedies reform.[37]

Many couples may seek to contract out of the financial rules on divorce through marital property agreements, including pre-nuptial agreements. Although estimates for the prevalence of marital property agreements are scarce, one organisation has suggested that one-fifth of marriages conducted in the last 20 years may have included some form of agreement, however informal.[38] Polling data also find that more Britons view pre-nuptial agreements as a good idea than a bad one, with high-earning women the most likely to approve.[39] The law remains as set down in *Radmacher v Granatino*,[40] with the uncertainty that entails. The Commission's draft report set out a scheme with procedural safeguards that would enable certain

come.' B Hale, 'Foreword' in J Miles, D Monk, R Probert (eds) *Fifty Years of the Divorce Reform Act 1969* (Oxford, Hart Publishing, 2022) viii.

[32] S Jarvis and S Jenkins, 'Marital splits and income changes: Evidence from the British Household Panel Survey' (1999) 53(2) *Population Studies* 237.

[33] E Hitchings et al, *Fair Shares? Sorting out money and property on divorce* (2023) Nuffield Foundation at www.nuffieldfoundation.org/wp-content/uploads/2021/03/Fair-Shares-report-final.pdf; D de Vaus et al, 'The economic consequences of divorce in six OECD countries' (2015) Australian Institute of Family Studies Research Report No 31.

[34] Law Commission of England and Wales, *The Financial Consequences of Divorce* (Law Com No 112, 1981).

[35] *Report on Financial Provision in Matrimonial Proceedings* (Law Com No 25, 1969); *Orders for Sale of Property under the Matrimonial Causes Act 1973* (Law Com No 99, 1980); *Financial Relief after Foreign Divorce* (Law Com No 117, 1982). The related issue of ensuring effective enforcement of orders once made is addressed in the Law Commission's report on *Enforcement of family financial orders* (Law Com No 370, 2016).

[36] Law Commission of England and Wales, *Matrimonial Property, Needs and Agreements* (Law Com No 343, 2014).

[37] Law Commission of England and Wales, 'Review to examine 50-year-old laws on finances after divorce and the ending of a civil partnership', press release (4 April 2023).

[38] Marriage Foundation, '1 in 5 couples married since 2000 may have some form of prenup in place, finds first-ever research on the subject', press release (29 August 2021).

[39] M Smith, 'Are pre-nuptial agreements unromantic' (2023) at yougov.co.uk/topics/society/articles-reports/2023/03/15/are-pre-nuptial-agreements-unromantic.

[40] *Radmacher v Granatino* [2010] UKSC 42.

nuptial agreements to have binding effect, but it has not been taken forward.[41] In chapter 7, Baroness Deech argues that a lack of principle and excessive judicial discretion result in the state of uncertainty the law finds itself in on matters such as pre-nuptial agreements.

III. Cohabitation

Cohabitation has been on the rise even in the short time for which reliable statistics have been available.[42] In 2002, 4 million adults cohabited in England and Wales, rising to 6.3 million in 2020.[43] Today, for every 10 married people, there are three people who are cohabiting, and 15 per cent of families with children cohabit compared to 7 per cent in 1996.[44] Some scholars argue that we are in the midst of a second demographic transition towards cohabitation and marriage as socially indistinguishable.[45] It remains the case, however, that insufficient legal protection is available to cohabitees at the end of their relationships. The Commission's recommendations on the financial consequences of relationship breakdown between cohabitees[46] have sought to resolve that position in a way that ensures that cohabitation and marriage remain legally distinguishable, an approach recently endorsed by the Women and Equalities Committee.[47]

In its 2007 report, the Commission recommended the creation of an opt-out scheme of financial relief for cohabitant couples who had a child together or had lived together for a minimum number of years, with remedies based on each party's contribution to the relationship.[48] The Government did not take forward

[41] Law Commission of England and Wales, *Matrimonial Property, Needs and Agreements* (Law Com No 343 2014), Appendix A.

[42] Data prior to the early 2000s were inconsistent. M Murphy, 'The evolution of cohabitation in Britain, 1960–95' (2000) 54 *Population Studies* 43.

[43] ONS, Table 4: Living arrangements by age group and sex for all persons, England and Wales, 2002 to 2020 at www.ons.gov.uk/peoplepopulationandcommunity/populationandmigration/populationestimates/bulletins/populationestimatesbymaritalstatusandlivingarrangements/2020.

[44] Analysis of ONS, 'Families and households 2021, Table 4: Dependent children in families by family type, United Kingdom, 1996 to 2021' (2021) at www.ons.gov.uk/peoplepopulationandcommunity/birthsdeathsandmarriages/families/bulletins/familiesandhouseholds/2021.

[45] K Kiernan, 'The rise of cohabitation and childbearing outside marriage in Western Europe' (2001) 15 *International Journal of Law, Policy and the Family* 1, 3; R Lesthaege, 'The second demographic transition: Cohabitation' in W Kim Halford and F van de Vijver (eds), *Cross Cultural Family Research and Practice* (Amsterdam, Elsevier, 2020) 103; for a critique see B Zaidi and S Morgan, 'The Second Demographic Transition Theory: A review and appraisal' (2017) 43 *Annual Review of Sociology* 473.

[46] The Law Commission of England and Wales, *Cohabitation: The Financial Consequences of Relationship Breakdown* (Law Com No 307, 2007). For recommendations in respect to the death of a cohabitant, see *Intestacy and Family Provision Claims on Death* (Law Com No 331, 2011), pt 8.

[47] House of Commons Women and Equalities Committee, *The Rights of Cohabiting Partners: Government response to the Committee's Second Report, Third Special Report of Session 2022–23* (2022) HC 766, para 63.

[48] The Law Commission of England and Wales, *Cohabitation: The financial consequences of relationship breakdown* (Law Com No 307, 2007).

those recommendations at the time.[49] In response to the Women and Equalities' Committee's support for them, the Government has stated that reform of cohabitation law would need to build on proposed reforms to financial provision on divorce, and would require fresh consultation.[50] The position in England and Wales remains in sharp contrast to the position in Scotland, where proposals for cohabitation reform in the Scottish Law Commission's 1992 *Report on Family Law*[51] were implemented in sections 25–30 of the Family Law (Scotland) Act 2006, and are sufficiently mature to have been the subject of further review three decades on from the report.[52] The opt-out scheme is more fully explored by Andy Hayward in chapter 10, where he argues in favour of increased legal protections for unmarried couples and addresses some of the political challenges that remain as obstacles to reform.

IV. Children

Now, as in the 1990s, around 9 million children live in families where the adults are a married couple, and a little under 3 million live in lone-parent families.[53] However, factoring in the increase in children living in cohabiting families, second and blended families, and increasing numbers and visibility of LGBT+ families, the families that children live in today are quite different from those even a few decades ago, let alone in the 1960s. How the state interacts with children is changing too. The number of children who require the support of child social services is stark, with 404,310 children in 2021 identified by local authorities as 'children in need' under section 17 of the Children Act 1989, an increase of 7 per cent since 2013.[54] The reach of private family law is significant too, with around 50,000 cases begun in the family courts each year.[55]

The main statute in the area of child law remains the Children Act 1989, one of the great achievements of the Law Commission. Concepts that we now take for granted, such as a unified concept of parental responsibility, or the non-intervention principle, came out of the series of Working Papers published for consultation by the Commission between 1985 and 1987.[56] As Stephen Cretney notes, the draft

[49] Law Commission of England and Wales, 'Statement on the Government's response to the Law Commission report "Cohabitation: The Financial Consequences of Relationship Breakdown"', 6 September 2011 at s3-eu-west-2.amazonaws.com/lawcom-prod-storage-11jsxou24uy7q/uploads/2015/03/20110906_Statement_on_Govt_response.pdf.

[50] House of Commons Women and Equalities Committee (n 47).

[51] Scottish Law Commission, *Report on Family Law* (Scot Law Com No 135, 1992).

[52] Scottish Law Commission, *Report on Cohabitation* (Scot Law Com No 261, 2022).

[53] Analysis of ONS (n 44).

[54] Department for Education, 'Characteristics of children in need, Reporting year 2022' (2022).

[55] Ministry of Justice, 'Family Court Statistics Quarterly: October to December 2022' (2023).

[56] Law Commission of England and Wales, *Guardianship* (1985) WP 91; *Custody* (1986) WP 96; *Care Supervision and Interim Orders in Custody Proceedings* (1987) WP 100; *Wards of Court* (1987) WP 101.

Bill published alongside the eventual report[57] avoided 'paying excessive respect to a rigorous interpretation of its terms of reference'[58] by taking the opportunity to demonstrate how the Commission's recommendations on private child law could be incorporated into one legislative code with the work of the Government's own *Review of Child Care Law*,[59] which had addressed the public law aspect.

The Act was revolutionary, although its passage into law was given impetus not solely by the Commission's view that the law needed reform, but also by a number of high-profile cases of child abuse. Such cases occur all too frequently today, and the work to limit them is not solely the preserve of the law, but family law reformers must continue to ask how the law can best serve the interests of children. A number of contributors to this collection ask those questions, and the Commission's 13th Programme of Law Reform identified a number of difficulties with the 1989 Act's workings on which it would welcome a chance to work[60] (and some of which may be addressed by the work the Commission has been asked to conduct on the law on disabled children's social care[61]).

V. Becoming a Parent

The ways in which people become parents are also changing, with the inception of in vitro fertilisation (IVF) in the late 1970s and the increasing recognition of surrogacy as a way of building a family. Since data on IVF births began to be recorded by the newly established Human Fertilisation and Embryology Authority in 1992, we have seen a nearly fourfold increase in donor conception, to 4,016 births in 2019.[62] The number of children born through surrogacy, when a woman (the surrogate) carries a child with the intention that another couple or individual (the intended parents) will be the child's legal parent(s), has also risen, with 435 parental orders granted in England and Wales in 2021.[63]

[57] Law Commission of England and Wales, *Review of Child Law: Guardianship and Custody* (Law Com No 172, 1988).

[58] Cretney (n 19) 710.

[59] Department of Health and Social Security, *Review of Child Care Law: Report to ministers of an interdepartmental working party* (September 1985).

[60] Law Commission of England and Wales, *Thirteenth Programme of Law Reform* (Law Com No 377, 2017) para 4.47.

[61] Law Commission of England and Wales, 'Law Commission invited to review legislation on social care for disabled children' (20 April 2023) at www.lawcom.gov.uk/law-commission-invited-to-review-legislation-on-social-care-for-disabled-children.

[62] Human Fertilisation and Embryology Authority, 'Trends in egg, sperm and embryo donation 2020: underlying dataset' (2022) at www.hfea.gov.uk/about-us/publications/research-and-data/trends-in-egg-sperm-and-embryo-donation-2020/.

[63] Ministry of Justice, Family Court Statistics Quarterly – Family Court Tables January to March 2022 (June 2022) Table 4: Number of orders and children involved in Public and Private law (Children Act) applications made in the Family courts in England and Wales, by type of order, annually 2011–2021 and quarterly Q1 2021–Q1 2022, at www.gov.uk/government/statistics/family-courtstatistics-quarterly-january-to-march-2022 (last visited 23 March 2023). The actual number of surrogacies is

The Law Commission's most recent family law publication, *Building Families Through Surrogacy: A New Law*,[64] a joint report with the Scottish Law Commission, has sought to address the gap in the current law between the intentions of all parties entering into a surrogacy arrangement and the legal parental status of the child at birth. The Commission has recommended the creation of a new pathway that, following pre-conception screening and safeguarding checks, will enable the intended parents to become the legal parents on the birth of the child, where that remains the intention of the surrogate. Overall, the recommendations are designed to ensure that the best interests of the child are put at the heart of surrogacy law.[65]

VI. What is a Family, what is Family Law?

The issues explored above are more frequently trodden ground for family lawyers and family law reformers, but they are not the only ways in which families are transforming in the 2020s. Baroness Hale's time as Commissioner was noted for drawing new topics under the umbrella of family law, such as domestic violence.[66] The Commission's current work continues that momentum, with consideration of the question of the wishes of the individual and the family following death, issues that have come to the fore with the growth of second and blended families.[67]

In its first programme, the Commission thought that its family law reform work would address all matters affecting the family, 'property, status or otherwise'. Its recent and forthcoming work, encompassing financial remedies on divorce, legal parental status in surrogacy and the deceased's wishes following death, arguably fits those categories, as well as demonstrating the mix of iterative improvement and reform at the cutting edge of societal development that has characterised the Commission's work since its beginning.

The way in which the Commission works has also developed since its inception, with a now-familiar model of wide-ranging public consultation, including close engagement with academia, informing its programmes and projects. The interplay of its programmes with the innovative research happening within the academy is now, as ever, deeply important to how the Commission works.

likely to be higher, as not all surrogacy teams may be aware of the need to apply for a parental order, as exemplified in *X v Z (Parental Order Adult)* [2022] EWFC 26.

[64] Law Com No 411, 2022.

[65] G Black and N Hopkins, 'Building Families Through Surrogacy: placing the child at the heart of surrogacy law' (2023) *Child and Family Law Quarterly* 3.

[66] B Hoggett, 'Family Law Reform: Where will it end? (1992) 3 *King's College Law Journal* 64. Notably, the second phase of the Scottish Law Commission's current project on 'Aspects of Family Law' includes a review of civil remedies for domestic abuse, see Scottish Law Commission, 'Aspects of family law' at www.scotlawcom.gov.uk/law-reform/law-reform-projects/aspects-of-family-law.

[67] These issues are being considered as part of the project on Burial, Cremation and New Funerary Methods; see at https://lawcom.gov.uk/project/burial-cremation-and-new-funerary-methods/.

This collection reflects a continuation of that dialogue between the Commission and academia, as well as bringing Parliament and legal practice communities into the debate. It acknowledges that, whilst the Commission has, as noted, performed a highly significant role in ensuring that the law remains up to date, families continue to evolve, and consequently there is more still to be done.

VII. Outline of the Collection

This book begins with five proposals relating to the law around children, followed by five concerning the law around adult relationships. Following each proposal is a response that 'speaks' to that proposal, addressing, for instance, ways in which the 'respondent' considers the proposal might best be developed, or factors they feel the original 'proposer' should take into account.

In chapter 1, Anne Barlow and Jan Ewing consider the arrangements for children when parents live apart, as governed by the Children Act 1989. This Act is still widely regarded as a successful piece of legislation but, 30 years on, the authors argue that it remains focused on children's welfare through the paramountcy principle (section 1(1)), rather than any explicit acknowledgment of children's rights, particularly in the private family law context. There has been no formal assessment of how well the 1989 Act guarantees the rights accorded to children under Article 12 of the United Nations Convention on the Rights of the Child (UNCRC). Given recent developments, they suggest that this is a critical moment for the Law Commission to examine whether the 1989 Act adequately protects the rights and facilitates the voice of the child in private law child arrangement disputes in processes both in and out of court, as envisaged by Article 12 UNCRC. Barlow and Ewing state such a review would be particularly timely given recent family law developments that have resulted in: (i) strong encouragement of out-of-court dispute resolution (particularly mediation) in child arrangement cases in England and Wales following the Legal Aid, Sentencing and Punishment of Offenders Act (LASPO) 2012, where children have little or no agency; (ii) the repeal of section 41 of the Matrimonial Causes Act 1973 and the loss of any requirement for the court to consider the proposed arrangements for children on divorce; (iii) developments internationally to promote children's rights through the UNCRC and which the UK has ratified; and (iv) the move in other UK nations to adopt the UNCRC principles in domestic legislation, potentially leaving children in England with fewer rights than their counterparts in Wales and Scotland.

As part of their arguments, Barlow and Ewing refer to the Family Solutions Group (FSG) report (2020) *What about me?*, which has also called for a reframing of support for families following parental separation. In particular, they describe the FSG report as looking to realise holistic support that ensures that children's voices are facilitated and heard not only in court but also in out-of-court processes, where they argue many child arrangements are agreed between parents with little heed to children's wishes and feelings or, in some situations, the Children Act welfare threshold.

Barlow and Ewing argue that there is a critical role for the Law Commission to play in scoping out whether England needs a children rights framework to protect children's welfare in the new family justice landscape.

Helen Stalford, in her response, reaffirms the value of participation in family decision-making. Further, Stalford supports the application of Article 12 UNCRC and children's participation rights in mediation to avoid 'edging out' children, both legally and procedurally, from private family decision-making, and argues that the commitment to reading children's rights should be included in parental responsibility and welfare considerations too.

In chapter 2, Craig Lind, Philip Bremner and Maria Moscati consider the issue of legal parenthood and birth registration. In recent decades, the system of birth registration has been challenged by increasing diversity in family formation, but its underlying functions have not been scrutinised by law reformers. Lind et al argue that the time is ripe for the Law Commission to undertake a thorough review of the birth registration system in England and Wales. They assert that, were a review of birth registration to be undertaken, reform could yield a more principled and efficient birth register that would provide for the dignity of all families, and all family members. Such a project might aim to identify the appropriate principles of birth registration (as considered within the chapter) and to reform the system so that those principles are met. Lind et al further proceed to recommend a two-part register in which basic birth-related information, necessary to the state and open to public scrutiny, is collected in a 'core' birth register, with more detailed information, material to the private interests of individuals who have (or will have) rights to that information, stored in a 'supplementary' section of the register. In response, whilst Julie McCandless agrees with Lind et al's call for a 'first instance' reconsideration of the purpose of the birth registration system in society, she suggests an enlarged focus, beyond the important challenges for birth registration incurred by family diversity, reproductive developments and modern understandings of gender. She argues that we need to think creatively about how to approach a law reform project on birth registration so that we can figure out its current and future role in society, particularly in terms of societal inclusion and belonging. McCandless draws on Jess Smith's research on registration and her socio-legal methodology of movement as a potential way of enlarging this focus. She also puts forward the prefigurative law reform idea of imagining our society without a birth registration system, to help to figure out what we might want it to achieve. Finally, McCandless urges caution around notions of a 'core' and 'supplementary' birth register by drawing attention to the interrelationship between law and registration, and registration's perceived role in materialising the legal imaginary.

In chapter 3, Alan Brown and Katherine Wade address the legal framework for origin information in assisted reproduction. Assisted reproductive technologies can lead to the separation of genetic, gestational and social parenthood. This, they say, raises questions regarding how the law should regulate information about genetic, gestational and 'intention-based' origins. Moreover, currently, they highlight, there is inconsistency within the law governing origin information in different regulated assisted reproductive technologies: gamete donation; surrogacy; and mitochondrial replacement therapy. Their chapter adopts a children's rights-based approach, setting out recommendations for reform relating to: (i) *which* information should be collected about *which* individuals; and (ii) *whether*, *when* and *how* this information could be accessed. Brown and Wade make suggestions both around who should control the release of information and the manner in which that information should be released, arguing in favour, for instance, of an overarching system for origin information across reproductive contexts and, to this end, a national registry for the collection and retention of origin information, to be maintained by the Human Fertilisation and Embryology Authority. Their focus is on streamlining the current system for origin information for different assisted reproductive technologies. In response to that proposal, whilst Kirsty Horsey recognises the arguable desirability of origin information's being made available, she expresses reservations around whether it should be the mandate of the state to disclose such information as is collected and stored. We must decide, she says, what value we place on identity/origin information, as well as what identity 'means' (which may be different things to different people). Specifically, she contends that Brown and Wade's proposal raises potential issues related to privacy, the practicalities of telling and comparisons between methods of conception, and risks the (over) geneticisation of familial relationships.

In chapter 4, Samantha Davey submits that the Children Act 1989, as it stands, does not provide sufficient protection to the rights of grandparents and kinship carers. Grandparents, and other non-parental attachment figures, lack procedural and substantive legal rights within English law. This, she suggests, leads to difficulty in protecting the relationship between children and non-parents when children are taken into care, or when parents choose to terminate these relationships. Whilst challenges of this nature are often faced by grandparents, they are representative of challenges encountered by other blood-family members and step-relatives. Reform, Davey argues, could be achieved via the enactment of a Grandparents and Kinship Carers Act, which would amend three essential provisions of the Children Act 1989. First, she proposes that the welfare checklist under section 1(3) of the Children Act should be amended to make specific reference to the interests of 'relatives', such as grandparents, in line with section 1(4)(f) of the Adoption and Children Act 2002. Second, she considers that the language of the Children Act 1989 could be amended – to be more inclusive of those closely involved in children's lives, such as grandparents – by amending 'parental responsibility' and replacing it with 'welfare responsibility'. Finally, she asserts that section 10 might be amended to remove the leave requirement for grandparents. In response to Davey's proposal, Felicity Kaganas points to a lack of evidence that the law is denying grandparents the relationship with their grandchildren that they might want. She also questions the evidence that the grandparent/grandchild relationship is important for children's well-being in general, as against that simply for specific children. Whilst symbolic legislation may well strengthen the position of grandparents in intergenerational disputes, Kaganas expresses concern that it may also have adverse real-life consequences, especially for mothers and children.

In chapter 5, Mavis Maclean discusses the need for legal support where children are involved in 'cross-over' cases. LASPO 2012 removed from the scope of public funding access to a lawyer in family matters arising from individual decision-making. This included matters where the state was not involved, keeping only cases that sit close to the criminal law, such as domestic abuse and child-protection cases, where the state has a clear interest in protecting the citizen. Yet Maclean stresses that family matters are far from clear-cut. A difficult contact dispute between separated parents may well include elements of abuse, such as coercive control, which are difficult for the layman to work with. Women and children, she emphasises, may not be safe without access to legal help. Maclean seeks change within the criteria for access to publicly funded legal help to include all contested matters where there is a safeguarding question about the children. Further, she makes a case for easing the means test for access by excluding inaccessible capital assets, such as a house bought on a mortgage in joint names. The legal support provided, she asserts, should include face-to-face provision by a solicitor of information, written advice and support in taking the next steps. Mediation could also play a larger part if mediators who are also practising lawyers were enabled to offer this kind of support. In response, Mandeep Dyal agrees that legal aid in private law children matters should be extended to 'cross-over' cases, but she argues that consideration should be given to extending it to cover *all* private law children cases. The basis of her assertion is that the extension of legal aid would, in itself, arguably result in financial benefits: a reduction in the number of litigants in person in the family court; and the prevention of some 'cross-over' cases from descending into costly public law care proceedings. Reducing the prevalence of these two could help courts to deal with cases more expeditiously, utilising fewer resources. As such, she feels that Maclean's proposal may be too modest, and that there may be scope for it to be expanded further.

In chapter 6, Sharon Thompson raises a need to reconsider the law around family property. However, she highlights the complexity of reforming this area, and stresses that providing a clear basis for reform must not mean compromising the concepts of equality and fairness that are important when determining financial remedies. As a result, she says, it could be useful to explore alternatives by shifting attention away from the point of separation. One potential route to reform could therefore be to review the rules for determining property ownership *during* marriage. The Law Commission's 1988 proposals could, Thompson believes, provide an interesting launchpad for further research into the matter, obviously bearing in mind that the social, legal, economic and political context of family life is different in the current day. The intention of such reform would not be to undermine party autonomy but to *facilitate* it, by reflecting the reality of how parties manage property during the relationship. This would neither cure all of the current problems with this area of law, nor negate the need for reform of the financial consequences of divorce. Indeed, the road to comprehensive reform of this area may well be a lengthy and sinuous process. Yet a new law of family property that provides clearly defined rights *during* the marriage could, Thompson argues, be beneficial, potentially resolving (or at least alleviating) some disputes over property that could otherwise become intractable on relationship breakdown. It could encourage transparency, clarify property ownership during the relationship, reflect parties' expectations and, importantly, reduce uncertainty on divorce. Thompson stresses that, particularly in light of cuts to legal aid, couples need to be able to bargain in the shadow of the law effectively, and should not have to wait until relationship breakdown to understand questions of property entitlement. The clarity that such reform could provide might also, she says, supply justification for legislative reform of marital property agreements, whereby parties wishing to depart from rules of co-ownership could do so by private agreement. Nevertheless, reform of such agreements without consideration of broader reform proposals would, Thompson perceives, be a missed opportunity to clarify questions of property ownership throughout the relationship; questions to which couples entering marital property agreements need to know the answers in order to make informed decisions about how to distribute their assets. In response, Alison Diduck argues that, in light of family law's separate property rhetoric, creating any form of a community property system would not be accepted in England and Wales. Thompson's proposal to create a system of beneficially co-owned property within the relationship aims to try to do something different to redress inequalities and women's property insecurity during marriage and cohabitation. Whilst feeling that this aim is admirable, Diduck emphasises that the assumptions upon which the proposal relies about the 'partnership of equals' are too often belied by the gendered realities of domestic living. Evidentiary and gender issues regarding the proposed opt-out in particular may further, she perceives, limit the proposal's ability to achieve its goal.

In chapter 7, Ruth Deech also considers the need for reform of financial provision on divorce, which, in her view, would bring English law into line with the principles of the law in Scotland, most of Western Europe, North America, Australia and New Zealand. Baroness Deech argues that this would make English law more certain, with fairer principles and minimising the need for judicial discretion. The approach she advocates would include support for pre-nuptial agreements, equal division of matrimonial property, limited spousal support and extended support for children up to the age of 21 years. As a result, Deech states, this would save legal costs, preserve assets for the children and assist settlement. It would additionally bring financial provision law into harmony with the new no-fault divorce law. If a new divorce law aims to minimise bitterness and stress, those elements should not remain in financial provision law. The current law has not been reviewed for 50 years, during which time, Deech argues, the statutory provisions have almost vanished under layers of judicial discretion and changes of direction, which have exacerbated uncertainty and expense. She takes the view that there are also changes in society in relation to the status of women and family relationships that need to be reflected, as they have been in so many other jurisdictions. Deech states that the argument against this reform, namely that the financial position of women in England is weak, is not borne out by statistics, and is confident that this reform would be welcomed by the public. The Law Commission is currently assessing the reform options for the laws governing finances on divorce and the ending of a civil partnership. Deech's chapter suggests a possible approach in this respect.

In his response, Nicholas Mostyn argues that the lack of democratic input into our judge-made system is a major deficit. He advocates for greater research to understand why so many divorces do not give rise to financial claims, meaning that presumably those couples are resolving financial matters without making use of the legal system. Even with cases that do come before courts where a final order is made, Mostyn takes the view that there is a lack of transparency as to the principles on which the final division of assets was decided. Whilst Mostyn does not disagree with the suggestions made by Deech, he argues that reform must be foregrounded in a statistical analysis of the shape, size and objectives of the cases dealt with at the coalface, and asks whether some of the assumptions that underpin Deech's proposals are borne out by the evidence. Finally, Mostyn points out that the judicial attitudes that underpin current decision-making are firmly rooted in an earlier time and are often paternalistic and patriarchal. He concludes that whilst he fully supports, in principle, Deech's campaign for change, it must be based on evidence and not tropes gathered from a handful of unrepresentative big-money cases.

In chapter 8, Russell Sandberg considers the limitations of the current law regulating adult relationships, particularly when it comes to marriage. Drawing upon and developing his book, *Religion and Marriage Law: The Need for Reform*, he argues that the law regulating intimate adult relationships is currently archaic, overly complex and discriminatory, especially in how it applies to religion or belief organisations. He proposes the need for a new legislative framework – the Adult Intimate Relationships Bill – which would consolidate, modernise and reform the current legal framework.

Sandberg's proposal for reform of marriage laws would include moving from a system of marriage laws that regulates buildings to one that regulates officiants, as recommended by the Law Commission's review of weddings law. This would remove current legal requirements that he argues indirectly discriminate against some religions by mandating that religious marriages must take place in a place of worship in order to become legally binding. His approach would also enable wedding ceremonies conducted by belief organisations, such as Humanists UK, and independent celebrants to be legally binding for the first time. However, unlike the Law Commission recommendations, Sandberg's chapter proposes that the nominating organisation would not be limited to religion or belief organisations.

Sandberg states that these changes would still be insufficient, since there would still be some unregistered religious marriages – and some of these would not result from a voluntary and witting choice by both of the parties. This, he argues, could be remedied by providing an opt-out system of cohabitation rights on separation, allowing ex-cohabitants to seek a financial order where they have suffered a financial detriment. The Adult Intimate Relationships Bill would therefore not only regulate formalised adult relationships but would also provide some recognition of functional relationships.

Simran Kalra, in her response, recognises that Sandberg's proposal deals with both extending marriage provisions and reforming the regime for cohabitation rights. Whilst Kalra accepts that reforms in both these areas are urgently needed, her response explores how the law conceives of individuals in intimate relations and whether the reforms go far enough in addressing power dynamics. Relying on narrative interviews from her own field work, Kalra explores relationship progression within specific Muslim diaspora communities in England, and has sought to understand how law, religion and social practices have been used by women in securing their rights. Additionally, Kalra explores a new form of family relations: living apart together. Despite living separately, couples in such relationships may share intimacy and contribute to each other's lives, both financially and emotionally, highlighting the challenges and diversity in the varied types of intimate adult relationships that may be formed. In light of the narrations that Kalra explores, she argues that Sandberg's proposals conceive of individuals as autonomous and equal agents. Thus, the law would not take account of emotional manipulation and disparate interests. Rights regimes that depend on voluntariness are embedded in principles of autonomy. Opt-out mechanisms can reinforce socially produced inequalities and create opportunities for coercion or manipulation. Ultimately, Kalra takes the view that though there may be many merits in Sandberg's proposals, reform needs to go further. Rather than the prioritising of legal bureaucracy by the law, it needs to prioritise lived realities as a means of assessing rights claims.

In chapter 9, Andy Hayward focuses on cohabitation as the fastest-growing family form in the United Kingdom. Hayward recognises that couples are choosing not to formalise their relationships for a variety of different reasons. However, following relationship breakdown, cohabitants cannot benefit from the structured judicial discretion available to spouses and civil partnerships, and must have any entitlement determined using general principles of property, trusts and contract law. This antiquated framework creates the potential for relationship-generated disadvantage, which is a problem exacerbated by the prevalence of the erroneous belief among the population that simply living together generates legal protections (the so-called 'common law marriage myth').

Hayward's chapter aims to reignite interest in increasing the level of protections afforded to cohabitants upon relationship breakdown in England and Wales. This important issue was previously reviewed by the Law Commission in 2002 in its *Sharing Homes* project, and later in 2007, culminating in its more comprehensive report, *Cohabitation: The financial consequences of relationship breakdown*. However, the recommendations in that report have not been implemented to date.

Hayward's proposal seeks to revisit reform potential in this area, with a specific focus placed on various frameworks that could be adopted in England and Wales. Drawing upon comparative law insights, he argues that the Law Commission should consider a range of different legal responses to cohabitation, ranging from a compensation-style claim akin to the Scottish and Irish systems to a de facto regime operating in a more automatic fashion, similar to those used in Canada, Australia and New Zealand.

In his response, Rob George states there is general consensus that reform of the law regulating post-separation financial issues between former cohabitants is an urgent issue. George argues that the most principled and pragmatic solution is to incorporate cohabitants within the existing regime for former spouses and civil partners. Rather than introduce a new, complex and unpredictable regime specifically for cohabitants, George proposes that the existing law be extended, with judges trusted to take account of the circumstances of the relationship (including the fact of not having married, and the reasons for that) as part of their overall assessment of fairness.

In chapter 10 of this collection, Alexander Maine explores the current English legal framework for annulment of marriage. Section 11 of the Matrimonial Causes Act 1973 stipulates the grounds on which a marriage may be void owing to some defect in its creation; and section 12 of the Matrimonial Causes Act 1973 stipulates the grounds on which a marriage may be voidable owing to some defect in its operation, and therefore vulnerable to a decree of nullity. He argues that these categories render marriage problematic, in the imposing of discriminatory standards that give a party an 'out' from marriage if their partner does not fit within the traditional mononormative and cisnormative roles of marriage. If a party's new wife is pregnant by someone else, if their new husband has a communicable venereal disease or if their partner is transgender, a marriage is vulnerable to a decree of nullity. The inapplicability of consummation to same-sex marriage further demonstrates the confusion that section 12 creates. Ultimately, in Maine's view, these categories tell us about the exclusionary nature of marriage and the attempt to recreate a perfect standard of marriage. Maine's chapter makes the case for reform of the law of nullity, considering much of it to be unnecessary in the age of no-fault divorce.

In her response to Maine's chapter, Gillian Black draws out the differences between the English law of nullity and that of Scotland as a way of assessing Maine's proposals for reform. Black agrees that modernising nullity and removing outdated grounds, such as non-consummation or impotence in Scotland and, additionally, venereal disease, pregnancy or interim/full gender recognition certificates in England, are essential in order to better reflect contemporary attitudes to marital relationships. Where Black differs from Maine is on the law's role when it comes to consent and capacity. Whereas Maine favours keeping those grounds for avoiding a marriage, Black argues they are so fundamentally important that lack of consent or capacity should render a marriage void. In addition, Black suggests that any reforms that permit polyamory or polygamous unions need to be approached with caution, particularly as their unintended consequences may be to expose parties, particularly women, to exploitative or subservient relationships.

This collection of proposals and responses to reform ends with a concluding chapter from Joe Ailion, a family law solicitor in practice and at the coalface of family law. Ailion reflects on developments in family law, the relationship between academia, practitioners and law reform, and the ways in which law reform impacts the daily life of a practitioner. Ailion recognises the inconvenience of reform for practitioners but, importantly, he stresses the significant role that practitioners play as the 'eyes and ears on the ground' in addressing challenges that are experienced by our diverse communities and coming before our courts. Ailion gives the example of the most recent changes to divorce law as a clear example of the ways in which family law practitioners and academics can support one another in effecting reform: as Ailion points out, practitioners informed academia; academia emboldened practitioners. The matter came to a head in a test case in which both voices were heard in tandem. The result was legislative amendment and a huge and long-awaited step forward for family justice. Ailion recognises that this alignment of all the different factions is not always possible, but it does allow him to reflect on the key strategies that those collaborating for reform can actively and consciously adopt in order to effect change.

1

A Review of Children's Rights when Parents Live Apart

ANNE BARLOW AND JAN EWING

I. Introduction

Arrangements for children when parents live apart are governed by the Children Act 1989 (CA 1989 or 'the 1989 Act'). This Act is still widely regarded as a successful piece of legislation. However, over 30 years on, it remains focused on children's welfare through the paramountcy principle (section 1(1)) rather than any explicit acknowledgement of children's rights, particularly in the private family law context. No formal assessment has been undertaken of how well the 1989 Act guarantees the rights accorded children under Article 12 of the United Nations Convention on the Rights of the Child (UNCRC) when parents separate. Given recent developments, it is suggested that this is a critical moment for the Law Commission to examine whether the 1989 Act adequately protects the rights and facilitates the voice of the child in private law child arrangement disputes in processes both in and out of court, as envisaged by Article 12 of the UNCRC. Such a review would be particularly timely given recent family law developments, which have resulted in (i) strong encouragement of non-court dispute resolution (particularly mediation) in child arrangement cases in England and Wales following legal aid changes in 2013, where children have little or no agency; (ii) the repeal of section 41 of the Matrimonial Causes Act 1973 (MCA 1973) and the loss of any requirement for the court to consider the proposed arrangements for children on divorce; (iii) developments internationally to promote children's rights through the UNCRC, which the United Kingdom (UK) has ratified; and (iv) the move in other UK nations to adopt the UNCRC principles in domestic legislation, potentially leaving children in England with fewer rights than their counterparts in Wales and Scotland.

The Family Solutions Group (FSG) report[1] has called for a reframing of support for families following parental separation. In particular, it is looking to realise

[1] Family Solutions Group, *What about me? Reframing Support for Families following Parental Separation* (London, Judiciary UK, 12 November 2020).

holistic support, which ensures that children's voices are facilitated and heard not only in court but also in non-court processes, where many child arrangements are agreed between parents with, in reality, little heed to children's wishes and feelings, or indeed even the Children Act welfare threshold in some situations. This approach has been endorsed both by the President of the Family Division and the more recent report by JUSTICE,[2] which calls for a child participation presumption.

However, we suggest here that there is a crucial role for the Law Commission to play in scoping out whether England needs a children's rights framework to protect children's welfare in the new family justice landscape. As part of this, it should review how well current law protects children's welfare and takes account of their views in child arrangement disputes, both in and out of court, when measured against the expectations of the UNCRC and Article 12 in particular. This would indicate whether the current restriction of the core welfare principle, embedded in section 1 of the 1989 Act, to 'court proceedings' (thereby excluding its application to non-court dispute resolution processes and agreements reached directly between parents) remains appropriate and fit for purpose; whether the concept of parental responsibility in section 3 of the CA 1989 should be amended to specify the duty to take account of children's wishes and feelings in decisions affecting them where possible; and whether the expectations of the welfare checklist (section 1(3)) could be extended to include a child participation presumption that is applied as a benchmark in and out of court.

As part of this, we suggest that now is an appropriate and indeed important time to consult on whether the UNCRC should be formally adopted into the law of England and Wales, to ensure that the position of children following parental separation is safeguarded and their voice in all family dispute resolution processes is appropriately facilitated.

Much has changed since the CA 1989 and the UNCRC were both introduced in 1991, yet little has been done to ensure that more recent changes to family law and procedures align with children's international law rights under the Convention to which the UK is a signatory. At the time of its introduction, it was understood that the 1989 Act, the product of a novel Law Commission project led by (the now) Lady Hale, which codified much of public and private child law in England and Wales, enshrining the 'paramountcy principle' (section 1(1)), would satisfy requirements of the newly ratified UNCRC. This principle made a child's welfare the court's paramount consideration when determining matters relating to their upbringing, going beyond Article 3 UNCRC, discussed in section II. Certainly, the 1989 Act is still regarded by the Law Commission as 'seminal' legislation that has stood the test of time, placing children's welfare at the centre of decisions about them.[3] However, subsequent legislative changes to the way child arrangements

[2] G Douglas, *Improving Access to Justice for Separating Families* (London, JUSTICE, 2022).

[3] See B Hale, '30 Years of the Children Act 1989' (London, Law Commission for England and Wales Scarman Lecture, 2019) at www.lawcom.gov.uk/lectures-talks/30-years-of-the-children-act-1989/.

are made on divorce or separation mean that these are no longer automatically scrutinised by the courts either under the 1989 Act or as part of the parental divorce or separation process. A requirement in the divorce context (under MCA 1973, section 41) for courts to certify that the arrangements for children were satisfactory was removed by section 17 of the Children and Families Act 2014. Section 10(1) of the same Act also prevented applicants in private family law disputes, including child arrangement matters (other than where there was evidence of domestic violence), from issuing proceedings at court unless they had first attended a Mediation Information and Assessment Meeting (MIAM) to assess their suitability for mediation. At the same time, other changes introduced by the Legal Aid, Sentencing and Punishment of Offenders Act (LASPO) 2012, while retaining legal aid for family mediation, withdrew it for legal advice and representation on all private family law matters (excluding domestic violence), to encourage the settlement of child arrangements directly or through mediation. This has left separating parents to make or mediate arrangements between themselves, but without any statutory duty to consult or inform their children about these or indeed check that arrangements are in their best interests, potentially in breach of provisions of Articles 3 and 12 UNCRC. As Murch has observed,[4] to repeal the requirement in section 41 of the MCA 1973 to scrutinise arrangements for children, coupled with the failure to give children a voice within the MIAM procedure introduced by the 2014 Act, is a 'social paradox', especially, we suggest, at a time of growing and compelling national and international research highlighting the emotional fallout for children when parents separate. In the court context, the welfare checklist set out in section 1(3) of the CA 1989, which directs the court to the factors it must consider when applying the paramountcy principle, does include in section 1(3)(a) the child's 'wishes and feelings', to be considered in the light of their age and understanding. Similarly, a requirement for the court to have regard to children's rights to be consulted has, at least in theory, been preserved within paragraph 4.4 of *Practice Direction 12B – Child Arrangements Programme*. At present, while this is supposed to extend to the family mediation context and any agreement reached directly between parents themselves, it is not something of which parents are aware, is rarely upheld in non-court dispute resolution practice and is not enforceable outside of court proceedings. This means children are typically excluded from any consultation or role in the decision-making despite their rights under Article 12 UNCRC to express a view on matters affecting their lives, as discussed in section II. Whilst, within England and Wales, child inclusive mediation (CIM) (where children are directly but separately consulted by a couple's mediator on child arrangements) is an option, this is available only when parents both agree, and provided the mediator is willing and accredited to undertake CIM. In addition, as has been highlighted in the 2020 Ministry of Justice

[4] M Murch, *Supporting Children when Parents Separate: Embedding a Crisis Intervention Approach within Family Justice, Education and Mental Health Policy* (Bristol, Bristol University Press, 2018) 156.

report, *Assessing Risk of Harm to Children and Parents in Private Law Children Cases* ('Harm Report'),[5] pressures and systemic issues within the court system have meant that even within court proceedings, there is a gap between theory and practice. Concerningly, the authors of the report found,

> too often, the voices of children go unheard or are muted in various ways where domestic abuse was raised. A large proportion of children have no direct involvement in the family court process with parents or carers being relied upon to represent their views.[6]

The report goes on to highlight several barriers to children's ability to communicate their views effectively.

This chapter therefore argues that we no longer know how well the current law governing child arrangements in private family law cases sits with our obligations under the UNCRC, particularly, perhaps, with regard to the rights accorded to children under Article 12 to express their views freely in all matters affecting them. In particular, there has been little focus on what the UNCRC means or should mean for children whose parents separate, even though separation is estimated to affect around 280,000 children each year.[7] Whilst the UK's four Children's Commissioners and the Joint Committee on Human Rights have led the process of reporting on UK compliance with the Convention, this has not directly addressed the position of the increasing number of children affected by private family law changes when parents separate. In particular, the policy emphasis on out-of-court, rather than in-court, resolution of such matters has greatly restricted children's right to be heard, with a focus on child-focused rather than child-inclusive mediation as the normative publicly funded process. Added to this, there is no one Minister or government department that takes responsibility for children when parents separate, with different elements falling to the Ministry of Justice, the Department for Work and Pensions, the Department for Education and the Department of Health and Social Care.[8] This results in children's rights falling between different stools, with no department having the control or incentive to grasp the matter and make changes. We therefore suggest that there is a vital role for the Law Commission to play in scoping out both whether the CA 1989 needs reform and whether England, in particular, may need a children's rights framework to ensure that young people's voices are not side-lined in matters that so directly affect their lives and their future. This is especially pertinent at a moment when some of the other UK jurisdictions are moving towards incorporating the UNCRC into domestic law, and would enable comparisons to be drawn

[5] Ministry of Justice, *Assessing Risk of Harm to Children and Parents in Private Law Children Cases: Final Report* (June 2020).

[6] ibid 5.

[7] FSG (n 1) estimated the number of children whose parents separate each year to be approximately 280,000 (see ibid para 54). The figure is difficult to establish accurately, since formal records of the number of children affected by divorce proceedings ceased to be recorded after 2013 and there are no statistics for the number of cohabiting parents whose relationship breaks down.

[8] ibid paras 53 and 56.

from within and beyond the UK. Publication of a Law Commission Scoping Paper would also attract media attention and begin a process of engagement about how the current law serves children, raising awareness, including among young people.

This chapter will first consider the requirements of the UNCRC, reflecting on the potential inconsistencies with domestic law and process in England as compared with approaches in other parts of the UK. It will then look at what statutory changes may be possible, to recognise the importance of children's rights within family law. Despite the fact that the UK is a signatory to the UNCRC, it is open to question whether, in England and Wales in particular, the CA 1989 adequately protects the rights and facilitates the child's voice in private law child arrangement disputes. This, we suggest, is true of processes used both in and out of court when parents separate. In light of research evidence that consistently points to the importance and benefits of giving young people a voice on parental separation,[9] and in the absence of the taking of any direct action by the Children's Commissioner for England on this matter, we argue that this is an important issue worthy of the urgent attention of the Law Commission for England and Wales.

II. What Does the UNCRC Provide?

Although the UK has ratified the Convention, it does not apply directly within domestic law, making it legally binding but not legally enforceable.[10] This leaves the CA 1989 as the principal conduit for children's rights when parents separate in England and Wales. In Scotland, the Children (Scotland) Act 1995 governs this area and takes a very different approach, which acknowledges a more proactive role for children to express their views if they wish to do so. There are, though, formal reporting mechanisms for assessing compliance with the UNCRC. This is delegated to the UN Committee on the Rights of the Child.[11] This monitors progress State Parties are making at five-year intervals, and the UK's last full report on each of the four home jurisdictions was submitted in 2022. As will be discussed, this was not favourably received by the Committee, particularly with regard to respect for children's rights.[12] One specific issue for consideration within the reporting mechanism is progress towards incorporation of the UNCRC into

[9] See 'Hearing the Voice of Children and Young People in Dispute Resolution Processes' in Ministry of Justice, *Report of the Mediation Task Force* (June 2014) at www.familylaw.co.uk/docs/pdf-files/family-mediation-task-force-report.pdf, 40; R Carson et al, *Children and young people in separated families: Family law system experiences and needs* (Melbourne, Australian Institute of Family Studies, 2018); A Barlow and J Ewing, *Children's Voices, Family Disputes and Child-Inclusive Mediation: The Right to Be Heard* (Bristol, Bristol University Press, 2024).

[10] Vienna Convention on the Law of Treaties 1968, Art 26.

[11] These are delegated to the UN Committee on the Rights of the Child, which monitors the progress states are making and to which states report at five-year intervals.

[12] Committee on the Rights of the Child, *Concluding observations on the combined sixth and seventh periodic reports of the United Kingdom of Great Britain and Northern Ireland* (CRC/C/GBR/CO/6–7).

domestic law, following earlier recommendations.[13] Whilst it is recognised that the UNCRC sits alongside other international law rights, and notably the European Convention on Human Rights (ECHR), where the right to respect for private and family life is safeguarded by Article 8, it is the provisions of the UNCRC that are most relevant to how child arrangements are made when parents separate, from the perspective of children. However, ECHR case law is not in tension with the provisions of the UNCRC. In *Nielsen v Denmark*,[14] it was agreed that the ECHR applied to everyone, including children, although there are no special children's rights in that Convention. The later case of *Yousef v The Netherlands*[15] confirmed that where the rights of parents and children conflicted, the rights of children must be the 'paramount consideration'.

Three main UNCRC articles are relevant to the law and procedure governing child arrangements on parental separation. First, there is Article 3, which focuses on the child's welfare; Article 5 then sets out the parental duty to provide guidance to children; and Article 12, which, as a matter of international law, accords rights to children to express their views freely in all matters affecting their lives. Unlike Wales and Scotland, any legislative reform to incorporate Article 12 UNCRC into domestic law in England is likely to be some way off. Yet we suggest that recent criticism, both national and international, of the failure to take children's rights seriously justifies a more immediate approach to enhancing children's rights within England and Wales. Much has been written about the tension in the UNCRC between the need to protect children (Article 3) and the desire to give them a right to a voice appropriate to their age and maturity (Article 12). Within academic literature, this is sometimes characterised as the 'rights v welfare' debate.[16] The juxtaposition of Articles 3 and 12 UNCRC illustrates how children are at first wholly vulnerable and in need of protection, but then develop into young people with views who merit more agency. Article 5 attempts to bridge this gap within the UNCRC. Let us now consider what the UNCRC provisions require, any tensions between them and how domestic law measures up in England and Wales.

Article 3(1) focuses on promoting and protecting children's welfare or best interests. It provides:

> In all actions concerning children, whether undertaken by public or private social welfare institutions, courts of law, administrative authorities or legislative bodies, the best interests of the child shall be a primary consideration.

Arguably, this is a lower test than that provided in section 1(1) of the CA 1989, which clearly makes the child's welfare the paramount consideration. Freeman[17]

[13] See House of Commons and House of Lords Joint Committee on Human Rights, *The UK's Compliance with the UN Convention on the Rights of the Child* (HL Paper 144, HC 1016, 24 March 2015).

[14] *Nielsen v Denmark* (1989) 11 EHRR 175.

[15] *Yousef v The Netherlands* [2000] 2 FLR 118.

[16] See, eg, J Herring, 'The Human Rights Act and the Welfare Principle in Family Law: Conflicting or Complementary?' (1999) 11(3) *Child and Family Law Quarterly* 223.

[17] M Freeman, 'The Human Rights of Children' (2010) 63(1) *Current Legal Problems* 1.

argues that the Convention, in its different provisions, recognises the evolving capacities of children, which he describes as taking them from 'becomings' to 'beings', and Article 3 clearly recognises children's inherent vulnerability and need to be protected before they reach sufficient age, maturity and understanding to express views and make decisions fully for themselves.

Article 5 refers to children's 'evolving capacities' and recognises that a balance needs to be struck between parental and children's rights as they grow up:

> State Parties shall respect the responsibilities, rights and duties of parents … to provide, in a manner consistent with the evolving capacities of the child, appropriate direction and guidance in the exercise by the child of the rights recognised in the present Convention.

When children are very young, they depend on their parents to make decisions for them; but over time, parents have a duty to help their children exercise their own rights responsibly. The Convention sees this as a process, rather than a cliff-edge moment when children go from having no rights at all below the age of majority to full rights at the moment they reach the age of 18. Indeed, this is in line with the *Gillick*[18] principle developed in the case law of England and Wales, according to which a child's agency increases (and parental rights/responsibility diminish) as the child matures, so that their capacity to make decisions should be increasingly respected but may be context-specific, rather than universally achieved during this process of evolving capacities.

However, it is the wording of Article 12 that makes clearer than any provisions in English law that children should have a say in the direction of their lives, providing:

> States Parties shall assure to the child who is capable of forming his or her own views the right to express those views freely in all matters affecting the child, the views of the child being given due weight in accordance with the age and maturity of the child.

As noted, there has been criticism of the fact that, even in court proceedings, children often face barriers to expressing their views freely in private family law cases where the courts will decide child arrangements following an application under section 8 of the CA 1989. Children's views should be ascertained by the ordering of a welfare report by the court under section 7 of the CA 1989, where a Family Court Officer, usually from the Children and Family Court Advisory and Support Service (CAFCASS) will interview the child to ascertain their wishes and feelings. It is noted that this is a permissible way to bring children's views before the court in line with UNCRC, for children capable of forming their own views. Article 12(2) clarifies that a child may be heard 'either directly, or through a representative or an appropriate body in a manner consistent with the procedural rules of national law' to fulfil their Article 12 rights. Thus, in the court context, the mechanisms

[18] *Gillick v West Norfolk and Wisbech Area Health Authority* [1986] AC 112.

for hearing children's voices are in place. However, it is the lack of opportunity given to children to exercise that right routinely in section 8 proceedings, as identified in the 'Harm Report',[19] that is of concern. Other than in the most serious of contested cases, children's views are commonly not sought directly from children. Rather, the court relies on information gathered indirectly by CAFCASS from parents by telephone. The norm is for safeguarding assessments to involve checking if there are records with the police or social services, and then each parent is invited to raise concerns about their children's welfare. In addition, although there is in theory the ability for children to bring section 8 child-arrangement proceedings themselves with the leave of the court,[20] this is rarely exercised in the private law context. This state of affairs would seem to be in breach of Article 12 UNCRC, where a secondhand account of children's views from their parents, and a lack of information enabling children to be aware that they could themselves bring or join proceedings, arguably undermines the exercise and therefore fulfilment of children's rights. Furthermore, in family mediation, whether or not children can participate in the mediation process is subject to the obtaining of the consent of both parents by the mediator.[21] CIM is not the default mediation process, and so few children are given the opportunity to participate; and where they are, it becomes a matter of parental choice. Such a parental gatekeeping approach to children's expression of their views, and thereby getting their voices heard, hardly seems in line with the text of Article 12(1), particularly as UNCRC, General Comment 12,[22] explicitly extends children's Article 12 rights to mediation. Whilst the Family Mediation Council (FMC) Standards Framework for mediation has since 2018 been amended to require parents to be advised that CIM is an opportunity, given that mediation has become the primary means through which parents are expected to settle child arrangement disputes, this seems an area where the law is falling short of providing children with their Article 12 rights, especially in light of the parental duty to enable children to exercise their rights appropriately, as set out in Article 5.

The relationship between Articles 5 and 12 is recognised as having 'special relevance' in the UNCRC's General Comments.[23] These also recognise that children's participation may stimulate the development of the child's evolving capacities.[24] Equally, General Comment 12 states that as the child's capacity evolves, the parent's responsibilities transform from 'direction and guidance into reminders and advice and later to an exchange on an equal footing'.[25] Overall, this chimes with the

[19] Ministry of Justice (n 5).
[20] CA 1989, s 10(8).
[21] Family Mediation Council, *Code of Practice and Guidance* (London, Family Mediation Council, 2018) para 6.6.2.
[22] UN Committee on the Rights of the Child, *General Comment No 12* (2009) T*he right of the child to be heard* (CRC/C/GC/12) para 32.
[23] ibid para 69.
[24] ibid para 79.
[25] ibid para 84.

nuanced approach developed in domestic law through the *Gillick* principle. As Lansdown argues, the concept of 'evolving capacities' embodies the balance in the Convention between 'recognising children as active agents in their own lives, entitled to be listened to, respected and granted increasing autonomy in the exercise of rights, while also being entitled to protection in accordance with their relative immaturity and youth'.[26] Yet we suggest more can be done to fulfil the requirements of Article 12(1) both in and out of court.

Recent research has shown that allowing children to express their views when parents separate is both popular with children and young people, good for their well-being and mental health, and can have a beneficial effect in reducing parental conflict when this is done as part of a CIM process.[27] The FSG (a Subgroup of the Private Law Working Group), which reported to the President of the Family Division in November 2020 in *What about me?*,[28] called for a reframing of support for families following parental separation, with the needs and voices of children placed at the forefront of this reimagined landscape. The JUSTICE report[29] similarly reiterated the need for greater child participation and recommended a presumption of child participation. Whilst to fully achieve a framework of well-signposted services for young people to provide information, consultation and, for the minority who may need it, representation formulated around Article 12 would require holistic support beyond the remit of the Law Commission, some statutory reforms would, we propose, help shift the culture by changing expectations to require that children's voices are facilitated and heard not only in court but also in out-of-court processes.

Lundy has argued that Article 12 is 'one of the most widely cited yet commonly misunderstood of all of the provisions of the UNCRC'.[30] She contends that common abbreviations such as 'the voice of the child' dilute the impact of Article 12 and imperfectly reflect its contents. The four-stage test she advocates to ensure compliance with Article 12 has been adopted by Ireland's Department of Children and Youth Affairs as part of its *National Strategy on Children and Young People's Participation in Decision-Making*.[31] Lundy suggests that an Article 12-compliant offer that allows children to participate meaningfully in decision-making must include 'space' (children must be given the opportunity to express a view), 'voice' (children must be facilitated to express their views),

[26] G Lansdown, 'The Evolving Capacities of the Child' (Florence, UNICEF Innocenti Research Centre, 2005) 3.

[27] A Barlow et al, *Transforming relationships and relationship transitions with and for the next generation: The Healthy Relationship Education (HeaRE) and Healthy Relationship Transitions (HeaRT) Project Report and Key Findings* (Exeter, University of Exeter, 2022); Barlow and Ewing (n 9).

[28] FSG (n 1).

[29] JUSTICE (n 2).

[30] L Lundy, '"Voice" is not enough: conceptualising Article 12 of the United Nations Convention on the Rights of the Child' (2007) 33(6) *British Educational Research Journal* 927, 930.

[31] Department of Children and Youth Affairs, *National Strategy on Children and Young People's Participation in Decision-making, 2015–2020* (Dublin, Government Publications, 2015).

'audience' (the child's view must be listened to) and 'influence' (the child's view must be acted upon, as appropriate). We would suggest that this could be a valuable framework for the Law Commission, against which to judge the Article 12 compliance of any statutory changes it proposes as part of its scoping review.

The Children (Scotland) Act 1995 both gives children the right to express a view in private law child-arrangement proceedings, including where domestic abuse is alleged, and places a broader duty on parents to consult children regarding child arrangements. This shows that it is possible to include statutory provisions to this effect. That something needs to be done within the UK is underlined by the UNCRC Committee's Concluding Observations, published on 22 June 2023 in response to the UK's periodic report, which provide:

> Noting with concern that children's views are not systematically taken into account in decisions affecting them and in national and local decision-making, and underscoring the importance of the availability of age-appropriate information to facilitate child participation, the Committee recommends that the State party:
>
> (a) Ensure the right of all children, including younger children, children with disabilities and children in care, to express their views and to have them taken into account in all decisions affecting them, including in courts and relevant judicial proceedings and regarding domestic violence, custody, placement in alternative care, health care, including mental health treatment, education, justice, migration and asylum.[32]

Children's rights are certainly high up the agenda in some parts of the UK. The Scottish Parliament voted unanimously for the United Nations Convention on the Rights of the Child (Incorporation) (Scotland) Bill to become law so that public authorities in Scotland would have to comply with the UNCRC as a directly applicable part of Scots law. However, this was ruled unconstitutional by the Supreme Court, following a successful challenge by the Westminster Government, arguing the Scottish Parliament did not have the power to take this action independently as a matter of constitutional law.[33] Similarly, Wales-only legislation has already partially incorporated the UNCRC into Welsh domestic law. Although the Rights of Children and Young Persons (Wales) Measure 2011 does not follow the model of incorporation recommended by the UN Committee, and does not ensure that the courts can enforce children's UNCRC rights, it is a statement of intent that is well ahead of the position in England.[34]

Thus, Wales has partially incorporated the UNCRC but has not made it enforceable; and while Scotland intends to embed a child's rights agenda,

[32] Committee on the Rights of the Child (n 12), in response to *Committee on the Rights of the Child, Combined sixth and seventh periodic reports submitted by the United Kingdom of Great Britain and Northern Ireland under article 44 of the Convention, due in 2022* (CRC/C/GBR/6-7).

[33] *REFERENCE by the Attorney General and the Advocate General for Scotland – United Nations Convention on the Rights of the Child (Incorporation) (Scotland) Bill* [2021] UKSC 42.

[34] See further comment in a briefing paper, 'Implementing & monitoring the UN Convention on the Rights of the Child (UNCRC)' (Together (Scottish Alliance for Children's Rights) 2016) at www.togetherscotland.org.uk/pdfs/UNCRC_in_Law_post-briefing_paper_final.pdf.

having unsuccessfully attempted to incorporate the UNCRC in its domestic law, England has yet to embark on a children's rights framework based on the UNCRC. Given the indictment of current law and practice by the UNCRC Committee, action needs to be taken to avoid our current undermining of children's rights. Let us now consider what the Law Commission could recommend in the context of parental separation to better facilitate children's voices and participation, as well as to safeguard their welfare in and out of court in such matters.

III. Reforming the Children Act

When parents separate and are in conflict about the future arrangements for their children, the court has the power to make orders concerning these arrangements in proceedings under section 8 of the Children Act 1989. These orders can decide where the child lives, the time they spend with each parent, whether any specific issues need to be addressed or steps prohibited to promote the child's welfare. Orders can be made if it is in the best interests of the child, applying a combination of the section 1(1) welfare principle[35] and the section 1(3) welfare checklist rather than any explicit acknowledgement of children's rights. However, critically, the welfare principle and checklist are considered as a matter of law only when the matter reaches court, which, in most cases, it will not.

Given the policy shift towards avoiding court in such cases and the lack of scrutiny of children's welfare even on divorce,[36] legislative changes have been 'encouraging' parents to agree their own arrangements for children as much as possible. Court rules were changed to require assessment for mediation before issuing any court proceedings in private family law matters in 2011 (superseded by section 10 of the Children and Families Act 2014, which requires a MIAM). Restrictions to legal aid under LASPO 2012 were also implemented in parallel, which means that from 2013, court proceedings for private law child-arrangement cases are (typically) no longer legally aided, save in instances where there has been provable domestic abuse.

In essence, the only way for children to have a voice (independent of their parents) about child arrangements is through the court, yet access to the court is denied to children unless that is their parents' choice. While mediation can be child-inclusive and should always be child-focused, child-inclusive mediation is contingent on the consent of both parents and the child, and on finding a mediator who can undertake child-inclusive mediation. Indeed, research shows that

[35] Also sometimes referred to as the 'paramountcy principle' or 'the best interests principle'.

[36] The MCA 1973, s 41 was repealed by the Children and Families Act 2014, s 18. However, it used to provide 'In any proceedings for a decree of divorce … the court shall conside – (a) whether there are any children of the family to whom this section applies; and (b) where there are any such children, whether (in the light of the arrangements which have been, or are proposed to be, made for their upbringing and welfare) it should exercise any of its powers under the Children Act 1989 with respect to any of them.'

children are rarely consulted about arrangements when parents separate in non-court dispute resolution, which is often dominated by adult concerns.[37]

All of this, we suggest, invites the question whether we need a children's rights framework to be put in place to comply with Article 12 UNCRC in the context of private family law child arrangements? While we consider the position from the point of view of private family law only, there is scope to consider the position of children more widely in other proceedings affecting their lives.

Despite the legal obligation to uphold young people's UNCRC rights and the evolving understanding of children as social actors, changing rhetoric into the reality of children's meaningful participation in decision-making has been slow.[38] Incorporation of the UNCRC into domestic law is needed to achieve the culture change required. With some justification, the private law context is not seen as a priority for the Children's Commissioner for England, and it is this state of affairs that has led to our call for the Law Commission to undertake a scoping review in the private family law context. While section 2(1) of the Children Act 2004 states that '[t]he Children's Commissioner's primary function is promoting and protecting rights of children in England', section 2(4) goes on to make clear that in discharging this function, the Commissioner must have particular regard to 'the rights of children living away from home or receiving social care'. Thus, the rights of children of parents who are separating are not included as a priority in statute, and neither were they identified as a priority theme by the current Commissioner when undertaking the 'Big Ask' survey of young people.[39] Rather, the clear focus is on children's social care and on services for intact families, alongside bigger social issues such as the environment, education and health. Whereas the Commissioner's recent report[40] does respond to the UN Committee's criticism regarding lack of fulfilment of children's Article 12 rights in the public law and social care context, there is no mention of the need for better representation of children's views in private family law matters.

Yet our research with young people shows that they do want to be able to voice their views to an independent third party in this context, to enable them to express their true feelings rather than tell each parent what they want to hear, and that this is seen as important to their well-being.[41] It may be that the Children Act could be reformed to address these concerns. As noted, in Scotland there are provisions within the Children (Scotland) Act 1995 that do address this in the

[37] See A Barlow et al, *Mapping Paths to Family Justice: Resolving Family Disputes in Neoliberal Times* (Basingstoke, Palgrave Macmillan, 2017).

[38] S Holt, 'A voice or a choice? Children's views on participating indecisions about post-separation contact with domestically abusive fathers' (2018) 40(4) *Journal of Social Welfare and Family Law* 459.

[39] See Children's Commissioner, 'My Priorities' (2024) at www.childrenscommissioner.gov.uk/our-priorities/.

[40] Children's Commissioner, *The state of children and young people's advocacy services in England* (19 December 2023) at https://assets.childrenscommissioner.gov.uk/wpuploads/2023/12/Audit-FINAL.pdf.

[41] Barlow et al (n 27); Barlow and Ewing (n 9).

private law context. For example, section 16 requires the court deciding any matter with respect a child's welfare to 'give him the opportunity to indicate whether he wishes to express his views', taking account of the age and maturity of the child. If the child so wishes, they must be given that opportunity and the court must have regard to their views, with children over the age of 12 being presumed to have sufficient maturity. Section 6 goes further: it obliges a person reaching any major decision that involves fulfilling a parental responsibility to

> have regard so far as practicable to the views (if he wishes to express them) of the child concerned, taking account of the child's age and maturity, and to those of any other person who has parental responsibilities or parental rights in relation to the child (and wishes to express those views).

Given that there are examples of statutory enactments within the UK that go beyond the provisions of the CA 1989 in meeting the requirements of Article 12 UNCRC, and the lack of intended action by the Children's Commissioner for England, we are persuaded that there is a role for the Law Commission of England and Wales to play. In section IV, we will consider our proposal for a Law Commission Scoping Paper to review the CA 1989, to assess, in the current family law landscape, how well the current law protects children's welfare in child-arrangement disputes both in and out of court when measured against the expectations of Article 12 UNCRC. We propose a Scoping Paper as a first step that would consider the extent of any non-compliance and identify potential areas for reform, paving the way for a Consultation Paper and final report.

IV. The Welfare Principle

In contested section 8 proceedings, the welfare principle under section 1(1) of the 1989 Act requires the court to make the child's welfare its paramount consideration. While very much the cornerstone of the CA 1989, the welfare principle has proved surprisingly controversial.[42] Neale criticises it as an adult construct that operates to constrain children's participation in private law proceedings by stressing their vulnerability, failing to disaggregate the needs of the child from those of the parents and recognising children's competence to speak, 'but only in carefully prescribed circumstances and according to adult agendas'.[43] The innate vagueness of the principle allows judges to address adult concerns under the guise of promoting the child's welfare.[44] There is also evidence of parents appealing to

[42] J Herring, 'The welfare principle and the children act: presumably it's about welfare?' (2014) 36(1) *Journal of Social Welfare and Family Law* 14.

[43] B Neale, 'Dialogues with Children: Children, Divorce and Citizenship' (2002) 9(4) *Childhood* 455, 458.

[44] J Fortin, *Children's Rights and the Developing Law*, 3rd edn (Cambridge, Cambridge University Press, 2009).

notions of 'best interests' to promote the parent's agenda when matters settle in mediation.[45]

When proceedings are contested, the court's decision must be considered in the light of the section 1(3) checklist of seven factors to which the court must have regard, which includes the ascertainable wishes and feelings of the child concerned (considered in the light of the child's age and understanding). While reference to the child's wishes and feelings heads the checklist, it is also clear that, as a matter of law, this is just one factor, and those wishes and feelings do not override other welfare considerations in the checklist. The weight to be given to the factors in the checklist will depend on the circumstances of the case, leaving judges free to overrule the child's views if they consider that other prevailing factors outweigh the weight to be given to the child's wishes, or if the judge determines that the child lacks insight into their own needs.[46]

The welfare principle, as currently constructed and applied, fails to adequately protect children's human rights,[47] particularly since most arrangements for children are made without recourse to the court. The child's best interests are seen as being in the domain of the adult decision-making or, in extremis, the court. There is no longer any assessment of the impact of the arrangements on the child, and no attempt whatsoever to take the children's views into account other than through the contested adult versions of what these are, unless and until the matter goes to court and is sufficiently conflicted for a section 7 report to be ordered. We believe that a scoping project by the Law Commission would be an opportune way to consider whether the CA 1989 could be amended to extend the welfare principle beyond court proceedings, so that it applies when parents are attempting direct settlement, mediation or other non-court dispute resolution processes. This would provide a welfare threshold to prevent parents from agreeing to arrangements that are harmful to children. It would also provide a statutory duty to ascertain children's wishes and feelings about arrangements (in accordance with the section 1(3) checklist) in all decisions, however reached (since the direction to do so pursuant to paragraph 4.4 of *Practice Direction 12B* is unenforceable in the absence of proceedings). It would go some way to ensuring that children's Article 12 rights to participate meaningfully in decision-making when parents separate are upheld. Taken together with amendments to parental responsibility that we suggest a Law Commission scoping review should also consider, as discussed in section V, an amendment to the scope of the welfare principle would help to ensure that agreements that are in the best interests of the children are reached in and out of court.

[45] J Smithson et al, 'The "Child's Best Interests" as an Argumentative Resource in Family Mediation Sessions' (2015) 17(5) *Discourse Studies* 609.

[46] Fortin (n 44).

[47] J Fortin, 'A decade of the HRA and its impact on children's rights' (2011) 41 *Family Law Journal* 176.

V. Parental Responsibility

Section 3(1) of the CA 1989 defines parental responsibility as 'all the rights, duties, powers, responsibilities and authority which by law a parent of a child has in relation to the child and his property'. Parental responsibility limits the role of the state in children's lives. It ensures that parents may exercise autonomy over decisions made for their children and protects the family's privacy.[48] However, parenthood is a relational connection between the parent and child. As such, while parental responsibility includes parental rights and duties, it is more than the sum of these and should instead be exercised relationally.[49] We have argued elsewhere that parental autonomy in decision-making when parents separate should be reconceptualised as 'relational family autonomy' to shift the focus onto the need to achieve child-led outcomes that meet the needs of the whole family.[50] To achieve the culture shift needed to realise a more relational approach, one that places children's needs and wishes at the heart of the decision-making process in compliance with their Article 12 rights, we suggest that a scoping project by the Law Commission should consider how parental responsibility might be redefined and understood.

As Fortin has argued, when substituting the old 'parental rights and duties' for 'parental responsibility', the failure of the CA 1989 (and subsequent amendments) to seize the opportunity to impose a duty on parents to consult their children over important matters regarding their future is disappointing.[51] The scoping review we propose could consider ways in which parental responsibility might be extended to include an explicit *duty* for separating parents to consult their children and a *responsibility* to take their children's views seriously. Article 5 UNCRC requires State Parties to 'respect the responsibilities, rights and duties of parents' to provide appropriate direction and guidance to their children. A change to the way in which parental responsibility is conceived would ensure, in turn, that parents *exercise* their responsibilities, rights and duties to provide their child with the direction and guidance to which the child is entitled under Article 5, and *respect* their child's right to participate meaningfully in decision-making, in accordance with Article 12.

VI. Parental Involvement

Introduced in 2014,[52] under section 1(2A) and (6) of the CA 1989, the presumption of parental involvement requires that, provided a parent can be involved in

[48] R George, S Thompson and J Miles, *Family Law, Text, Cases and Materials*, 5th edn (Oxford, Oxford University Press, 2023).

[49] J Bridgeman, 'Parental Responsibility, Relational Responsibility: Caring for and Protecting Children after their Death' in R Probert, S Gilmore and J Herring (eds), *Responsible Parents and Parental Responsibility* (Oxford, Hart Publishing, 2009) 255.

[50] Barlow and Ewing (n 9).

[51] Fortin (n 44).

[52] Children and Families Act 2014, s 11.

their child's life in a way that does not put the child at risk of suffering harm, a court is to presume that that parent's involvement in the child's life will further the child's welfare. The change was enacted to send a symbolic message affirming the importance of fathers when parents separate, and has had little impact on reported decisions[53] or the practice of the lower courts.[54] However, it has reinforced the message that the courts adopt a pro-contact approach, even in cases involving domestic abuse.[55] It also risks putting mothers under pressure to settle without going to court,[56] particularly since many mothers may be acting in a legal advice vacuum following LASPO 2012. Presumptions in favour of contact can work to silence or at least mute the voices of young people when domestic abuse is alleged.[57] Furthermore, presumptions rely on generalisations about what is best for children, rather than considering the needs of the individual child.[58] Presuming to know what is best for children in advance renders hearing from them superfluous.[59] It risks distracting family justice practitioners from considering what might lie behind a child's expressed reluctance to have contact with a parent.[60] Yet hearing from young people and acting upon their views can lead to safer outcomes for them in domestic abuse cases.[61] Section 3 of the Domestic Abuse Act 2021, which came into force on 31 January 2022, specifically provides that a child (under 18 years old) who sees, hears or experiences the effects of domestic abuse and is related to the victim or the suspect is also to be regarded as a victim. Although welcome, this does not ensure that young people's voices will be heard in related section 8 child-arrangements applications. In evidence to a Select Committee in June 2023, the Domestic Abuse Commissioner, Nicole Jacobs, confirmed that her office would be launching 'an oversight mechanism' in three courts in the Autumn of 2023 in response to the recommendations of the 'Harm Report',[62] to look at how domestic abuse is being dealt with in family courts.[63] Judges are beginning to show a willingness to refuse an application for indirect contact in the rare cases in which there have been findings of coercive control at a level that results in the perpetrator's having nothing positive to offer the children.[64] Now is an opportune time to embed children's

[53] F Kaganas, 'Parental involvement: a discretionary presumption' (2018) 38(4) *Legal Studies* 549.

[54] J Harwood, 'Presuming the status quo? The impact of the statutory presumption of parental involvement' (2021) 43(2) *Journal of Social Welfare and Family Law* 119.

[55] ibid; A Barnett, *Domestic abuse and private law children cases: A literature review* (London, Ministry of Justice, 2020).

[56] Kaganas (n 53).

[57] Ministry of Justice (n 5); K Mackay, 'The approach in Scotland to child contact disputes involving allegations of domestic abuse' (2018) 40(4) *Journal of Social Welfare and Family Law* 477.

[58] Neale (n 43); Herring (n 42).

[59] Neale (n 43).

[60] Fortin (n 44).

[61] Holt (n 38); Barlow and Ewing (n 9).

[62] Ministry of Justice (n 5).

[63] *Oral evidence: Government consultation on supporting earlier resolution of private family law arrangements* (19 June 2023) at https://committees.parliament.uk/oralevidence/13327/pdf/.

[64] *F v M (Rev1)* [2023] EWFC 5.

views in decision-making in cases where domestic abuse is alleged, and the Law Commission is well placed to lead a review to achieve this goal.

On 9 November 2020, the Government announced a review of the presumption of parental involvement, focusing 'on the courts' application of the presumption, as well as on the impact on children's welfare of the courts' application of these provisions'.[65] The report of the review has been delayed.[66] However, in any event, there is no indication in the terms of reference that are publicly available that the review will consider how, if at all, the presumption (or proposed legislation that might amend or replace the presumption) will include and be balanced against children's right to be heard in the decision-making when parents separate. It is suggested, given that section 2A of the CA 1989 has amended the welfare principle to provide a presumption that both parents should be involved in a child's life, that it could, and arguably should, be balanced by a duty to consult the child before applying any such presumption. Introducing the presumption of parental involvement alongside the welfare principle without any mention of consulting the child would seem to ride roughshod over Article 12 UNCRC. Notwithstanding the Government's review, there is a need to consider how the child's views might be embedded into child-arrangement decisions, especially when domestic abuse is alleged. We invite the Law Commission to assess how this might be done in its scoping review.

VII. Separate Representation for Children

Article 12 UNCRC protects young people's rights to information, consultation and, for the minority who may need it, representation when parents separate. The FSG recommends that urgent consideration be given to

> laying the requisite court rules to accompany the Adoption and Children Act 2002, s 122 so that private law applications pursuant to the Children Act 1989, s 8 become 'specified proceedings' in which children may be separately represented if needed.[67]

The report further recommends the relaxation of the requirement under section 10(8) of the CA 1989 that children seek the leave of the court to make a section 8 application.[68] We would endorse both recommendations as sensible suggestions to prevent children from becoming locked into arrangements that may no longer suit their needs or be dangerous. We suggest that the scoping review considers how best to ensure that children needing separate representation can secure it.

[65] 'Press release: Child protection at heart of courts review' (Ministry of Justice, 9 November 2020) at www.gov.uk/government/news/child-protection-at-heart-of-courts-review.

[66] In its replies to the Transparency Project's Freedom of Information request in February 2023, the Ministry of Justice indicated that the review would be published 'later this year'. However, as of early January 2024, the review is not yet in the public domain.

[67] FSG (n 1) 38.

[68] ibid 37.

VIII. Conclusion

Taken together, this is a most opportune and appropriate moment to review the position of children's rights in the context of the UNCRC in England. Warning bells have already rung about the plight of children when parents separate, both in court and in non-court dispute resolution processes. These are more fully noted by reports to the President of the Family Division as part of the work of the Private Law Working Group.[69] As a minimum, the position of children when their parents separate seems to fall far short of Article 12 UNCRC due to legislative changes that have radically affected in the way in which we expect child arrangements to be made. Given moves elsewhere to incorporate children's rights more fully into domestic law, recognising them as subjects rather than objects of family law, we suggest that this is also a critical time to consult on whether the UNCRC should be formally adopted into the law of England and Wales, and particularly Article 12, in the private law family separation context.

As we have seen, despite the concerns expressed by the UNCRC Committee in 2023, no person or body has been charged with addressing these for the large numbers of children whose parents separate each year in England. In our view, the Law Commission is ideally placed to carry out such a scoping review and recommend a way forward that is UNCRC-compliant and could go beyond the context of private law family proceedings, if thought appropriate. As the original architects of the CA 1989, which led the way in making family law in England and Wales more child-centred, it seems entirely appropriate that the Law Commission now take the lead in this process to ensure that young people's voices are meaningfully facilitated rather than ignored in this jurisdiction.

[69] ibid; Ministry of Justice (n 5).

Response to Chapter 1

A Review of Children's Rights when Parents Live Apart

HELEN STALFORD

I. Introduction

It is both bewildering and frustrating, for a host of legal, ethical, pragmatic reasons, that we continue to debate whether or not children should be involved in decisions that affect their lives. The legal reasons point to the fact that we are now entering the fourth decade since the UK's ratification of the United Nations Convention on the Rights of the Child (UNCRC); the fourth decade since it accepted to be legally bound to respect, protect and fulfil the rights outlined in that instrument – including adopting or changing laws, policies and procedures with a view to implementing the Convention's provisions.

The latest, insidious way in which children's rights are being undermined, described in the clearest terms by Anne Barlow and Jan Ewing, is the shift to out-of-court settlement of private family disputes. This is the latest example of the vital, statutory baby[1] being thrown out with the bathwater of protracted, costly, inefficient and in many cases traumatic court proceedings.

In this response, I will examine more closely from a children's rights perspective Barlow and Ewing's proposal to affirm the extension of the Children Act (CA) 1989 to out-of-court family proceedings. I will frame this discussion in broader terms of access to justice of which participation is a key element. I will also reflect critically on the potential for statutory protection to achieve better participation of children in mediation, in view of the now abundant empirical evidence on children's actual experiences of private family proceedings.

[1] In the form of the paramountcy principle and corresponding obligation to take into account the ascertainable wishes and feelings of children, commensurate with their age and understanding under s 1(3)(a) of the CA 1989.

II. Mediation as Both a Vehicle and a Blow to Children's Access to Justice

It is irrefutable that the legal,[2] procedural[3] and financial[4] developments described by Barlow and Ewing have systematically edged children out of decision-making in private family law matters, issuing a damning blow not just to children's participatory rights, enshrined in Article 12 UNCRC, but to children's broader right to access justice.

Access to justice is defined as 'the ability to obtain a just and timely remedy for violations of rights as put forth in national and international norms and standards'.[5] The concept of 'access to justice' is a derivation of the right to an effective remedy, enshrined in Article 8 of the Universal Declaration of Human Rights, Article 2(3) of the International Covenant on Civil and Political Rights and Article 13 of the European Convention on Human Rights. Such is the fundamental importance of access to justice to the well-being and development of society that it also features in UN Sustainable Development Goal (SDG) 16.3, which provides that 'the rule of law' should be promoted at the national and international levels, and that 'equal access to justice for all' (that is, adults and children alike) should be ensured.

The UNCRC does not provide a specific right to access justice for children,[6] but the UN Committee states that for children's rights to have real meaning, effective remedies must be available.[7] Indeed, such is the importance of access to justice to the realisation of children's rights that the UN Committee on the Rights of the Child is currently preparing its latest General Comment (No 27) on this very issue.[8] In doing so, the UN Committee has noted:

> A vast majority of children whose rights are violated do not have access to justice and do not receive remedies following violations of their rights or denial of entitlements.

[2] The removal by s 17 of the Children and Families Act 2014 of the requirement (previously under s 41 of the Matrimonial Causes Act 1971) for courts to certify that arrangements for children had been appropriately made as a precondition for granting a divorce.

[3] The introduction by s 10 of the Children and Families Act 2014 of the requirement that parents in family disputes first attend a mediation information and assessment meeting (MIAM) as a precondition for issuing proceedings in court.

[4] The introduction of the Legal Aid, Sentencing and Punishment of Offenders Act 2012 removed private family law out of the scope of legal aid support, save for some narrow exceptions relating to domestic violence or if the applicant could prove that the withholding of legal aid would lead to a violation of their human rights. For an analysis of the impacts of the cuts on children, see Coram Children's Legal Centre, *Rights Without Remedies* (London, Coram, 2018).

[5] T Liefaard, 'Access to Justice for Children: Towards a Specific Research and Implementation Agenda' (2019) 27 *International Journal of Children's Rights* 195.

[6] Although elements of access to justice – such as the right to legal challenge and the right to legal assistance, are provided for children who are detained and in the criminal justice system under Arts 37(d) and 40 respectively.

[7] General Comment No 5, para 24.

[8] Committee on the Rights of the Child, Concept Note: General Comment on Children's Rights to Access to Justice and Effective Remedies (2023) at www.ohchr.org/sites/default/files/documents/hrbodies/crc/gcomments/gc27/2023-01-31-gc27-concept-note.pdf.

> Children's dependent status, their lack of knowledge about their rights and the capacity to claim them as well as the lack of accessible and effective complaints mechanisms at the local level are immediate barriers.[9]

Mediation has important implications for access to justice. In theory, it saves time and money, and is less of a drain on emotional resources compared to court-based litigation.[10] In the post-pandemic world, with courtroom access curtailed and persistent, widespread delays in family cases,[11] mediation plays a more critical role than ever in providing access to justice, such that most countries now consider it beneficial to settle disputes relating to family affairs through mediation rather than by going to court.[12]

Children's rights – including the right to participate – are no less significant and explicit in a mediation context than in court-based proceedings. The UN Committee on the Rights of the Child says as much in its guidance relating to Article 12,[13] as does the extensive international soft-law guidance on 'child friendly justice'.[14] But the extent to which mediation can promote access to justice for all groups affected by a family dispute depends, of course, on the extent to which all groups affected are entitled to be involved in it. The current omission of children from a right to participate in family mediation in England, alongside the omission of any enforceable requirement to place their welfare at the forefront of all decision-making, clearly undermines its potential to act as a vehicle for justice.

To complement Barlow and Ewing's analysis of this, it is important to confront the question as to the likelihood that extending statutory protection to out-of-court mechanisms could remove the current participatory 'block'.

[9] ibid para 1.

[10] There have been various studies in the UK and beyond challenging and testing such presumptions. The most recent addition to the extensive work of Barlow and Ewing is A Barlow, R Hunter and J Ewing, 'Mapping Paths to Family Justice: Resolving Family Disputes Involving Children in Neoliberal Times' in A Kaldal, A Hellner, and T Mattsson (eds), *Children in Custody Disputes* (Cham, Palgrave Macmillan, 2024) 107. See also S Bano and L Webley, 'Family Mediators and Family Mediation: When Norms Collide' [2024] *Oxford Journal of Law and Religion*, rwae003; S Pal, 'Current Focus on Family Mediation in the UK: How Relevant?' (2017) 83(2) *Arbitration: The International Journal of Arbitration, Mediation and Dispute Management* 141; M Maclean and J Eekelaar, *Lawyers and Mediators: The Brave New World for Separating Families* (Oxford, Hart Publishing, 2018).

[11] HM Courts and Tribunals Services Management Information – March 2022 to March 2023 reveals that there were 47,700 outstanding private family law cases, taking an average of 45.7 weeks to be heard; and 13,146 outstanding public family law cases taking an average of 42.3 weeks to be heard.

[12] FRA, *Child-friendly justice – Perspectives and experiences of professionals on children's participation in civil and criminal judicial proceedings in 10 EU Member States* (2015) 47.

[13] General Comment No 12 on The Right of the Child to be Heard, CRC/GC/12 (2009), para 32.

[14] Council of Europe Guidelines on Child Friendly Justice, 2010, assert in the 1st paragraph that they 'deal with the issue of the place and role, and the views, rights and needs of the child in judicial proceedings *and in alternatives to such proceedings*' (emphasis added).

III. To What Extent Would Statutory Protection Achieve Children's Participation and Access to Justice?

Achieving the statutory guarantee of children's participation in out-of-court family proceedings, recommended by Ewing and Barlow, would go some way towards promoting children's voice in mediated decisions, but it certainly would not guarantee it. One only has to examine the now abundant evidence on the implementation of children's existing participatory rights in in-court proceedings, and the emergent evidence in other jurisdictions where child-inclusive mediation is the norm, to see that laws on paper alone fall far short of yielding remedies in practice.

Most of the empirical evidence on children's experience of private family proceedings has been gathered from 2000 onwards, a decade or more since the CA 1989 and the UNCRC came into effect, and much of it during a time when there were significantly fewer impediments to children's participation (including readily available legal aid, advice and representation). The first, seminal empirical studies were conducted by Carol Smart, Bren Neale and Amanda Wade[15] almost 25 years ago. That work – whilst not focused on family justice specifically – indicated that harms to children are likely to arise more from being silenced and not consulted about decisions rather than from the fact of the divorce or separation itself. The suggestion that inadequate execution of procedural justice, including children's statutory participatory rights, causes harm to children is borne out, again and again, in a range of studies subsequently conducted across the globe.[16]

In a recent study, Alice Roe reviewed 45 of the research projects that had directly obtained children's and young people's thoughts on parental separation and/or their experience of court proceedings.[17] All of these studies are remarkably consistent in finding that: children overwhelmingly feel unheard in court proceedings, causing them significant distress; and children consistently indicate that they

[15] C Smart, B Neale and A Wade, *The Changing Experience of Childhood: Families and Divorce* (Cambridge, Polity, 2001).

[16] A few examples of such studies include: R Carson et al, *Children and young people in separated families: Family law system experiences and needs* (Australian Institute of Family Studies, 2018); J Cashmore, P Kong and M McLaine, 'Children's participation in care and protection decision-making matters' (2023) 12(3) *Laws* 49; J Cashmore and P Parkinson, 'Children's and Parents' Perceptions on Children's Participation in Decision Making after Parental Separation and Divorce' (2008) 46(1) *Family Court Review* 91, 94; K Tisdall and F Morrison, 'Children's participation in court proceedings when parents divorce or separate: Legal constructions and lived experiences' in M Freeman (ed) *Law and Childhood Studies: Current Legal Issues*, vol 14 (Oxford, Oxford University Press, 2012) 156; S Kay-Flowers, *Childhood Experiences of Separation and Divorce: Reflections from young adults* (Bristol, Bristol University Press, 2019); C Nelson, *'They Thought it was Safe – But it Wasn't': Recognising Children's Rights as a Means of Securing Children's Safety in Australia's Family Law System* (Sydney, NSW, Whitlam Institute, 2022) 5; L Stafford et al, 'Why having a voice is important to children who are involved in family support services' (2021) 115 *Child Abuse and Neglect* 104987.

[17] A Roe, *Children's experience of private law proceedings: six key messages from research. Spotlight series* (Report for the Nuffield Family Justice Observatory, 2021).

want to be kept better informed about various aspects of the family justice process, which includes a desire for information about who is representing their parents, what the possible outcomes are, who is making the decision, the anticipated length of the process, and when and how they would be able to express their own opinion.

In the same vein, research and jurisprudence have repeatedly confirmed that family justice processes that acknowledge and accommodate children's agency:

(a) lead to more comprehensive and sustainable welfare assessments, and to proceedings that are less protracted and vulnerable to appeal;
(b) facilitate the child's understanding and acceptance of and compliance with decisions made about their living and contact arrangements;
(c) are more likely to support the positive ongoing relationships between children and their parents;
(d) prompt *parents* to pay greater attention to the need to promote and protect their children as independent rights holders.[18]

And yet even a robust statutory framework and consistently strong evidence revealing the consequences of neglecting children's rights in family court proceedings have not led to improved participation. In a very recent study commissioned by the Nuffield Family Justice Observatory, for instance,[19] Hargreaves et al analysed anonymised population-level administrative data on all children involved in a private family law cases where a care arrangements order had been made from 2019–22 (over 67,000 children). Specifically, they examined how and when participation varied at different stages of family proceedings, according to where the case took place and the characteristics of the child. That study found that for almost half of the children involved in private law proceedings (47 per cent), there was no indication that they had participated at all. The majority of those who did participate did so indirectly via a CAFCASS report rather than directly (38 per cent); and older children (teenagers) were less likely to be heard than younger children.

This prompts the question whether mediation, even if supported by a statutory duty to elicit and give due account to children's wishes and feelings when determining what is in their best interests, could overcome some of the barriers to children's participation revealed in existing research? Certainly, studies in Australia, where such a statutory duty to conduct out-of-court resolution in a child-focused and child-inclusive way has been in place since 2006,[20] has evidenced significantly improved outcomes for those children who benefit.[21] Other research, however,

[18] *Marriage of Harrison and Woollard* (1995) 126 FLR 159, 199 (Baker J); A Daly, *Children, Autonomy and the Courts – Beyond the Right to be Heard* (Leiden, Brill Nijhoff, 2017); R Jones, *Children and young people's experiences of participation in private proceedings in the family court*, GSR report no 114/2023 Welsh Government; P Parkinson and J Cashmore, *The Voice of a Child in Family Law Disputes* (Oxford, Oxford University Press, 2008).

[19] C Hargreaves et al, *Uncovering Private Family Law: How often do we hear the voice of the child?* (Report for the Nuffield Family Justice Observatory, 2024).

[20] Family Law Amendment Act 2006.

[21] J McIntosh and L Moloney, 'Child-Responsive Practices in Australian Family: Past Problems and Future Decisions' (2004) 10(1) *Journal of Family Studies* 71; and J McIntosh and C Long, *Children*

has pointed to persistent inconsistencies and tokenism in the way in which such statutory obligations are carried out.[22]

On this point, it is worth returning to Rosemary Hunter's sobering reflection on the power of law alone to effect the changes so desperately needed in children's experiences of family justice:

> We … tend to invest too much faith in law, to imagine that if there is a problem, then law must provide the best kind of answer. But more law is not necessarily the answer. There are real limits to what law can achieve, and sometimes law creates problems rather than solves them. Thus again, rather than automatically reaching for a legal solution to the perceived problem of hearing children's voices in family disputes, we need to consider what other options might be available.[23]

So, if we acknowledge the limitations of statutory provision to improve compliance with children's participatory rights, what direction should family mediation take?

IV. Children's Access to Justice: More than Just a Statutory Exercise

It is helpful to locate the reforms proposed by Barlow and Ewing – and the persistent failure of our family justice system to treat children as equal legal citizens – in the context of wider societal developments in how we understand children and childhood. It is our social and cultural, as much as our legal, perception of what it means to protect and uphold children's rights that requires further scrutiny and redress. Certainly, there appears to be a prevailing gulf between what we, as children's rights advocates and socio-legal researchers, and what the government, the public, parents, and even legal practitioners and judges understand by this.

It has been more than 30 years since scholars seriously challenged the dominance of developmental psychology in shaping presumptions as to the universal, biologically-determined needs and capacities of children. This developmental paradigm validated adult (including parental) control over children who were regarded as inherently immature and vulnerable, and entire systems (health, education, justice) were structured around this paradigm with a view to creating the conditions in which children could be nurtured into full maturity and capacity as adults. It was the early work of sociologists such as Berry Mayall,[24]

Beyond Dispute: A Prospective Study of Outcomes from Child Focused and Child Inclusive Post-Separation Family Dispute Resolution (Final Report issued October 2006).

[22] P Henry and K Hamilton, 'The Inclusion of Children in Family Dispute Resolution in Australia: Balancing Welfare versus Rights Principles' (2012) 20 *International Journal of Children's Rights* 584.

[23] R Hunter, 'Close Encounters of a Judicial Kind: "Hearing" Children's "Voices" in Family Law Proceedings' (2007) 19(3) *Child and Family Law Quarterly* 283.

[24] B Mayall, 'The sociology of childhood in relation to children's rights' (2000) 8(3) *The International Journal of Children's Rights* 243.

Allison James and Alan Prout,[25] and Jens Qvortrup[26] that established a new paradigm of childhood as socially constructed, contextual and highly variable. In doing this, they set a new and bold agenda based on a theorisation of children as social actors, with an emphasis on children as co-constructors of their own lives in the here and now, rather than as mere adults-in-the-making.

Despite the proliferation of research that followed, seeking to directly engage with children's lived experiences and views of the world around them, this shift has evidently not advanced sufficiently beyond the academic endeavour. James and Prout's cautionary observation in 1990 about the impact of viewing children through a developmental as opposed to constructivist lens still rings true today in the context of Barlow and Ewing's proposed reforms:

> [I]n defining children as inferior, as objects essentially of adult socialisation – we depersonalise children. In proposing that we know best the best interests of the child, we deny children's rights. We deny children the right to participate in the structuring of their childhoods. Though we may work to protect children and provide for them, we find it much harder to take children seriously as contributors to social thinking and social policies.[27]

V. Conclusion

In drawing attention to wider, philosophical and attitudinal barriers to enabling children to have a say in family decisions, I am not undermining the importance of the law. Of course, entrenching children's rights obligations in primary legislation provides critical scaffolding for further action.[28] This is all the more important today, as we witness ever-growing threats to our human rights architecture in the UK, including a government-led campaign to repeal the Human Rights Act (HRA) 1998[29] and a senior judiciary that appears less amenable to bringing the UNCRC to bear on its interpretations of domestic law than was previously the case.[30]

[25] A James and A Prout, *Constructing and Reconstructing Childhood*, 1st edn (London, Routledge, 1990).

[26] J Qvortrup, *Childhood Matters: Social theory, practice and politics* (Aldershot, Avebury, 1994) 2.

[27] James and Prout (n 25) 6.

[28] L Lundy, U Kilkelly and B Byrne, 'Incorporation of the United Nations Convention on the Rights of the Child in Law: A Comparative Review' (2013) 21(3) *International Journal of Children's Rights* 442.

[29] The UK Government launched an Independent Human Rights Act Review (IHRAR) into the HRA 1998 in December 2020. See at www.gov.uk/guidance/independent-human-rights-act-review.

[30] The Supreme Court's statements in respect of the status of the UNCRC in the UK in cases such as *R (SC and others) v Secretary of State for Work and Pensions* [2021] UKSC 26 stand in stark contrast to earlier jurisprudence – led by proponents such as Lady Hale and Lord Kerr, in which children's rights were substantially elevated (see, eg, Lady Hale in *Re D (A Child) (Abduction: Custody Rights)* [2006] UKHL 51; and Lord Kerr (dissenting) in *SG R v SSWP* [2015] UKSC 16 [233] et seq), See further H Stalford, K Hollingsworth and S Gilmore, *Rewriting Children's Rights Judgments: From Academic Vision to New Practice* (Oxford, Hart Publishing, 2017) chs 1–3.

But beyond legislative provision is the need for much more concerted efforts to educate parents and justice professionals on the benefits of children's rights-based approaches to decision-making, and on the short-, medium- and long-term harms that are inflicted on children through failure to adopt such approaches. Children and parents alike need to be supported in developing strategies for engaging in conversations that are co-constructive in their everyday family lives. The ability of children and parents to embrace such approaches during the 'crisis talks' of relationship breakdown and separation will no doubt reflect the extent to which such dynamics are accepted and practised as the everyday norm in times of non-crisis. Some empirical studies have pointed to a lot of low-hanging fruit in this regard: more readily available, contextualised information about the family decision-making process, and the range of factors that should be taken into account when reaching decisions, would go some way towards empowering children to make sense of and contribute meaningfully to the process.[31] Encouraging parents and other justice professionals to communicate decisions to children in ways that they can understand is another basic yet highly effective strategy that can be achieved notwithstanding statutory provision.

Ultimately, though, Barlow and Ewing are right in calling for an extension of the Children Act protections to out-of-court family processes as a critical step. We know from the many countries that have incorporated the UNCRC into primary law that cultural and societal change follow: legislative protections lead to a culture of understanding and respect for children's rights,[32] a culture that is evidently so sorely lacking in England at present.

[31] H Stalford, L Cairns and J Marshall, 'Achieving Child Friendly Justice through Child Friendly Methods: Let's Start with the Right to Information' (2017) 5(3) *Social Inclusion* 207.

[32] Lundy, Kilkelly and Byrne (n 28).

2

Legal Parenthood and Birth Registration: Time to Respond to Diversity in Family Formation?

CRAIG LIND, PHILIP BREMNER
AND MARIA FEDERICA MOSCATI

I. Introduction

Birth is an event of both personal and social significance. It establishes a person's earliest personal relationships and, at the same time, marks the beginning of legal personality and inaugurates a person's relationship with a state. The registration of birth therefore engages both personal and social interests. At present, the birth-registration system requires (in addition to some administrative information like the child's NHS number[1]) the name, sex, place, date and time of birth of the child, and the names and places of birth of the parent(s). However, despite widespread recognition and acceptance of the importance of birth registration, there has never been a proper review of the underlying principles of birth registration, nor of the contemporary appropriateness of the current system of birth registration.[2]

In this chapter, we argue that there are several transformations that have occurred in our society – particularly in the last four decades – that justify a thorough reconsideration of the system of birth registration that operates in England and Wales. We argue that a public consultation is needed, in the words of the Law Commission's stated aims, 'to ensure that the law is as fair, modern, simple and as cost-effective as possible'.[3] In identifying the social and political changes that we submit justify a Law Commission project on birth registration, we indicate

[1] See Births, Deaths and Marriages Act 1953, ss 1 and 5; and Registration of Births and Deaths Regulations 1987 (SI 1987/2088), reg 7, sch 2, form 1.

[2] J McCandless, 'Reforming Birth Registration Law in England and Wales?' (2017) 4 *Reproductive Biomedicine & Society Online* 52; MA Crawshaw, ED Blyth and J Feast, 'Can the UK's Birth Registration System Better Serve the Interests of Those Born Following Collaborative Assisted Reproduction?' (2017) 4 *Reproductive Biomedicine & Society Online* 1; J McCandless, 'The Changing Form of Birth Registration' in F Ebtehaj et al (eds), *Birth Rites and Rights* (Oxford, Hart Publishing, 2011) 187.

[3] Law Commission, 'About us' (2023) at www.lawcom.gov.uk/about/.

questions which we suggest the Commission should ask to gauge the necessity for reforming the birth-registration system. While acknowledging that others may answer those questions differently, we suggest that the range of questions themselves impel us towards reform; we think that the Law Commission will be compelled to agree that reform is necessary, urgent, and inevitable. As we proceed to demonstrate the necessity of reforming the birth-registration system, we argue that the system desperately needs a clearer sense of purpose; it needs a clearer enunciation of whose interests it is there to serve and what those interests are. Because of the social changes we elaborate, we suggest functions that we think birth registration should serve now. We conclude this chapter by advancing the outline design of a birth-registration system that we feel would be more defensible in this era of diversity in family life.

In this chapter, we proceed on the basis of the view that a new birth register should differentiate between material recorded because it is information necessary to the state – the 'core register' – and material recorded because the state must retain it to meet the rights of its citizens – the 'supplementary register'. We submit that the birth register currently requires more information than is needed (certainly in any form of 'core register'). Notable in this regard is information about the child's 'sex' and unnecessary detail about the child's parents; the current register's demand to use the gendered nomenclature of 'father' and 'mother' seems to us to be unnecessary. Indeed, we argue that the compulsion to register the person who gives birth at all is to demand more than the functions or principles of registration require. Our system already allows for the registration of a second female parent instead of a father. We take the view that to require any gendering in the identification of parents in the 'core register' is unnecessary. We think that the state has no defensible interest in the gender of either the child or the parents.

Furthermore, the current birth register provides no room for additional information about the child's procreation (even though we already retain some of that information to meet the rights of children to access it later in life).[4] This neglect requires alternative, bureaucratically more complicated processes for the storage of that supplementary information and makes access to that information more complicated. We argue that it would be more convenient and efficient for the collection and storage of this information to be aligned with the birth register.

In the light of all of the flaws in the current birth-registration system, we submit that the 'core register' should contain minimal information, identifying the child and her legal parents, and no other unnecessary or peripheral information. It should remain open to public scrutiny in the way the current register is. The information required in the 'supplementary register', on the other hand, would be a more complex collection of information that either the child or participants in the procreation of that child have or will have a right to access. It is information of a kind that may be changed from time to time (with the vicissitudes of the personal and public politics of procreation and the rights to which those politics give rise).

[4] See Disclosure of Donor Information Regulations 2004 (SI 2004/1511).

The 'supplementary register' should be closed to public scrutiny, accessible only to the particular individuals who have legal rights to its contents, and then only when those rights arise.

We proceed, then, to make these arguments in this chapter, starting with an analysis of the significance of birth registration.

II. The Personal, Political and Cultural Significance of Birth Registration

The birth of an individual has personal, political and cultural significance. The event of our birth, and the social and biological facts surrounding it, although beyond our memory, are key components in the makeup of our individual identities. The event and those facts frame our place in our societies, both at the time of birth and beyond that time into our deepest adulthood; they dictate our ties of kinship.[5] They also frame our personal relationships.[6] However, birth does more than just frame what is personal to us and our identities. It also has political significance.[7] It sets in motion our individual relationships with the states into which we are born. Our claims to citizenship and the rights that are rooted in those claims arise at birth and develop as a consequence of those initial claims. Finally, being born and giving birth are events enveloped in cultural values and traditions that dictate the ways in which we think about and discuss both the facts of birth and the necessity for and method of birth registration. Given this personal, political and cultural importance, it is therefore vital to ensure that our system for recording birth is both rationally defensible and consistent with the legal and political values to which our states adhere.

Our legal system aims to ensure equality for all citizens (irrespective of their diverse individual identities).[8] It also aims to enhance children's rights and their best interests,[9] and to provide access to parenting[10] to people for whom that option was closed in the past. An important element of ensuring consistency with these values is to understand the reasons for the introduction of a system of birth registration in any society. In England and Wales, compulsory widespread birth

[5] For example, when relatives in relation to whom we have rights of succession die, whether or not we have ever had personal relationships with them. See the intestacy rules in Administration of Estates Act 1925, ss 33 and 46.

[6] Here we differentiate between formal family ties as ties of 'kinship', and informal family and friendship ties as 'personal relationships'. See M Sahlins, *What Kinship Is …. And Is Not* (Chicago, IL, University of Chicago Press, 2013) 2; J Carsten, 'Constitutive Knowledge: Tracing Trajectories of Information in New Contexts of Relatedness' (2007) 80 (2) *Anthropological Quarterly* 403.

[7] J McCandless and S Sheldon, 'The Human Fertilisation and Embryology Act 2008 and the Tenacity of the Sexual Family Form' (2010) 73(2) *Modern Law Review* 175; J McCandless, 'The Changing Form of Birth Registration' (n 2).

[8] Equality Act 2010.

[9] Children Act (CA) 1989.

[10] Human Fertilisation and Embryology Acts 1990 and 2008.

registration was introduced in the first half of the nineteenth century in the Births, Deaths and Marriages Act 1836.[11] Scholars have argued convincingly that this introduction of birth registration was part of 'an extensive movement to improve the security of title by the development of institutions to record citizens' claims on property'.[12] This understanding is consistent with, for example, Thomas Cromwell's suggestion that the original reason for the establishment of parish registers in 1538 was to create mechanisms for 'the avoiding of sundry strifes, processes and contentions rising upon age, lineal descent, title of inheritance, legitimation of bastardy, and for knowledge whether any person is our subject or no'.[13] It seems clear to us that birth registration was traditionally concerned with identifying individuals (as subjects of a state, from particular dates – the dates of their birth) and with identifying their parents (so that other individuals in society – as well as the state itself – could have clarity about a person's kinship ties).

From these, we believe, largely uncontroversial original functions of birth registration, two core principles underlying our system of birth registration emerge: (i) the identification of an individual (by name and date of birth); and (ii) the identification of that individual's parents. We take the view – again, we think, uncontroversially – that these two core principles remain defensible in light of our current values.

If the Law Commission were to undertake a project on birth registration, we submit (and we argue more fully during the course of this chapter) that it should conduct a consultation that considers, amongst other things, whether or not these are and should remain the core principles of registration; do they, in other words, remain appropriate to our times? In relation to this question, we submit that there have been significant social and medical changes that might induce respondents to a consultation to think about the issue of birth registration more critically, and to agree that reform is necessary and urgent.

In section III, we explore the social and scientific changes that have complicated the two traditional core principles of registration.

III. Social and Scientific Change and the Birth-Registration System

In this section, we argue that there are two interlocking scientific and social developments that have led to dissatisfaction with the current system of birth

[11] See R Probert, 'Recording Births: From the Reformation to the Welfare Reform Act' in F Ebtehaj et al (eds), *Birth Rites and Rights* (Oxford, Hart Publishing, 2011) 171.

[12] E Higgs, 'A Cuckoo in the Nest? The Origins of Civil Registration and State Medical Statistics in England and Wales' (1996) 11(1) *Continuity and Change* 115, 119. See also E Higgs, 'UK birth registration and its present discontents' (2018) 5 *Reproductive BioMedicine and Society Online* 35.

[13] Quoted in GR Elton, *Policy and police. The enforcement of the Reformation in the Age of Thomas Cromwell* (Cambridge, Cambridge University Press, 1972) 259–60 and cited in Higgs, 'A Cuckoo in the Nest?' (n 12) 121.

registration. In the first place, society has become more accepting of diverse family structures and, in the second, society's attitude to gender and its political and social significance has changed dramatically. Furthermore, medical developments have enabled a range of people – for whom parenting was unavailable before – to have children now, and have, therefore, often complicated the relationship between genetic identity and kinship. We will consider each of these transformations in turn.

A. Family Diversity, Science and Procreation

Society has become open to a wide range of diverse families. Initially, in this jurisdiction, this tolerance of diversity extended to acceptance of adoption.[14] In time, tolerance of unmarried parenthood and parenting,[15] and better appreciation of step parenting, developed.[16] With the advent of medically assisted reproduction, parenting by genetically unrelated social parents has been embraced,[17] and that embrace has more recently been extended to same-sex couples having children using donor gametes,[18] and even to those who involve another person in order to have children (by surrogacy).[19] Lately, we have begun to embrace trans-parenting[20] and, in some other jurisdictions, more than two parents parenting children has been added to the list of diverse family forms accepted and regulated positively.[21]

[14] Adoption of Children Act 1926; Adoption Act 1978; Adoption Act 1988; Adoption and Children Act 2002.

[15] Legitimacy Act 1976; CA 1989; Law Commission, *Family Law, Review of Child Law, Guardianship and Custody* (Law Com No 172, 1988); A Barlow and G James, 'Regulating Marriage and Cohabitation in 21st Century Britain' (2004) 67(2) *Modern Law Review* 143; C Lind and T Hewitt, 'Law and the complexities of parenting: parental status and parental function' (2009) 31(4) *Journal of Social Welfare and Family Law* 391.

[16] By, eg, using the concept of 'children of the family' in the Matrimonial Causes Act 1973 (MCA 1973), in, say, ss 21 and 41 (and defined in s 52).

[17] Human Fertilisation and Embryology Act 1990, ss 27–29.

[18] Human Fertilisation and Embryology Act 2008, ss 42–47.

[19] Human Fertilisation and Embryology Act 1990, s 30; and Human Fertilisation and Embryology Act 2008, s 54. See also Law Commission of England and Wales and Scottish Law Commission, *Building Families through Surrogacy: A New Law* (Law Com No 411 and Scot Law Com No 262, vol 2, 2023).

[20] F Tasker and J Gato, 'Gender Identity and Future Thinking about Parenthood: A Qualitative Analysis of Focus Group Data with Transgender and Non-binary People in the United Kingdom' (2020) 11 *Frontiers in Psychology* 1; S Tornello, RG Riskind and A Babić, 'Transgender and Gender Non-binary Parents' Pathways to Parenthood' (2019) 6(2) *Psychology of Sexual Orientation and Gender Diversity* 232; S Imrie et al, 'Children with Trans Parents: Parent–Child Relationship Quality and Psychological Well-Being' (2021) 21(3) *Science and Practice* 185; M Dierckx and RL Platero, 'The Meaning of Trans* in a Family Context' (2017) 38(1) *Critical Social Policy*, 38, 79–98; S Hines, 'Intimate Transitions: Transgender Practices of Partnering and Parenting' (2006) 40(2) *Sociology* 353. For an overview of research on queer kinship and reproduction, see M Smietana, C Thompson and FW Twine, 'Making and Breaking Families- Reading Queer Reproductions, Stratified Reproduction and Reproductive Justice Together' (2018) 7 *Reproductive Biomedicine & Society Online* 112; M Strathern and S Franklin, 'Kinship and the New Genetic Technologies: An Assessment of Existing Anthropological Research: A Report compiled for the Commission of the European Communities' (Manchester, University of Manchester, 1992) 6.

[21] See, eg, in British Columbia (British Columbia Family Law Act 2011, s 29) and Ontario (*AA v BB*, 2007, ONCA 2). In England and Wales, although we do not accept more than two parents for any child,

Our growing openness to diversity in family structure is supported by an increasing body of empirical work that has found that the formal structure of the family is less important to the welfare of children and positive outcomes for their development than is the quality of the parenting which they experience.[22] In short, what matters most to children and to their success in life is healthy parental relationships (no matter who those parents are), rather than the structure of their families. Growing social acceptance of those alternative structures can therefore only improve matters for them.

The fact that we have become so open to the idea of non-genetically related parents' raising children would have very limited importance for birth registration were it not for a second social development that has accompanied this wider acceptance of diversity in family formation. That second development has seen our society attribute new weight to genetic relatedness. We have begun to recognise the significance of genetics to the personal identity rights of individuals.[23] Two scientific advances in this regard – the advent of a scientific ability to test genetic relatedness and the scientific ability to assist people to have children by using donor gametes – have facilitated a cultural shift; perceptions of genetic relatedness have become a central feature of personal identity, which are understood to be protected by the universal right to respect for private and family life.[24] This has meant that the birth of a child to genetically unrelated parents requires the keeping of information[25] that, in previous eras, had not been necessary and, in any event, seemed impossible.[26]

The law now openly acknowledges a breach between genetic and legal parenthood at birth; the Human Fertilisation and Embryology Act 1990 (HFEA 1990), and its subsequent review and update in the Human Fertilisation and Embryology Act 2008 (HFEA 2008), provided ways in which people could become legal parents

we already accept that more than two people may have responsibility for raising a child: see CA 1989, s 7. See further P Bremner, 'Gay and Lesbian Collaborative Co-Parenting: Recognising Multiple Parents in the Netherlands and the UK' in H Henriksson and K Goedecke (eds), *Close Relations: Critical Studies of Families, and Kinship, and Beyond* (Singapore, IntersentiaSpringer Singapore, 2021) 37; N Surtees and P Bremner, 'Gay and Lesbian Collaborative Co-Parenting in New Zealand and the United Kingdom: "The Law Doesn't Protect the Third Parent"' (2020) 29(4) *Social and Legal Studies* 507.

[22] See, eg, S Golombok, *We are Family: What Really Matters for Parents and Children* (London, Scribe Publications, 2020).

[23] *Re F (A Minor: Paternity Tests)* [1993] 1 FLR 598.

[24] See J Fortin, 'Children's Right to Know their Origins – Too Far, Too Fast? (2009) 21(3) *Child and Family Law Quarterly* 336.

[25] See Royal College of Physicians, Royal College of Pathologists and the British Society of Human Genetics, *Consent and Confidentiality in Genetic Practice: Guidance on Genetic Testing and Sharing Genetic Information* (London, Royal College of Physicians and Royal College of Pathologists, April 2006); R Gilbar, 'Patient Autonomy and Relatives' Right to Know Genetic Information' (2007) 26 *Medicine and Law* 677; C Foster, J Herring and M Boyd, 'Testing the Limits of the "Joint Account" Model of Genetic Information: A Legal Thought Experiment' (2015) 41(5) *Journal of Medical Ethics* 379.

[26] See C Lind, 'Responsible Fathers: Paternity, the Blood Tie and Family Responsibility' in J Bridgeman, H Keating and C Lind (eds), *Responsibility, Law and the Family* (Aldershot, Ashgate, 2008) 191.

without requiring a genetic link between them and their children.[27] The Children Act 1989 (CA 1989), in the concept and management of parental responsibility, had already envisaged a world in which people who were not a child's legal parents could perform parental roles for children.[28] The fact that this divergence between legal parenthood and parental responsibility is overt and known means that we have and are able to store information material to a child's legal, social and biological parentage. Furthermore, our more recent acknowledgement of the right of adults to access information material to their parentage should, we argue, induce us to consider carefully the way, and the place, in which that information is stored. The additional fact that all children can (in theory, at least) test their genetic relatedness to their parents and siblings must, we submit, give us pause to rethink what the register is for (especially as children undertaking these investigations are most likely to discover, as adults, any genetic secrets[29] that their parents might have wished to keep from them). The possibility of uncovering these secrets later in life gives us further reasons to rethink what the birth register is for and what information the birth register should collect and store.

B. Gender, Society and the Birth-Registration System

In this section, we reflect on changes to society's attitude to gender (and particularly to the significance that the state allows to be attached to gender). We suggest that there are now questions relating to the significance of gender in the context of birth registration that the Law Commission urgently needs to investigate in a project on birth registration.

Before we concentrate specifically on the birth register, it is necessary to outline how profound the change is that we have seen in relation to gender equality in our society. The fight for gender equality has been waged, in societies like ours, for over a century. In the context of paid work and other 'public' areas of discrimination, 'formal equality' is now the standard to which we adhere.[30] Paying men and women equally and making employment opportunities equally accessible to women and men is no longer controversial. Yet gender difference (and gender role differentiation) was thought to be necessary and excusable in family relationships for much longer.[31] However, the recognition of same-sex adoption in the Adoption and Children Act 2002 reduced the significance of gender to parenthood. And the advent of legally recognised same-sex marriage in the Marriage (Same Sex Couples) Act 2013, ended gender's signal importance to marriage. The ability of same-sex couples to have children using medically assisted reproduction and

[27] See, in particular, HFEA 2008, ss 35–47.

[28] See, in particular, CA 1989, ss 2–5.

[29] See C Smart, 'Law and the Regulation of Family Secrets' (2010) 24(3) *International Journal of Law, Policy and the Family* 397.

[30] Equality Act 2010.

[31] *Corbett v Corbett* [1971] P 83, [1970] 2 All ER 33; *Wilkinson v Kitzinger* [2006] EWHC 2022 (Fam).

surrogacy on the same basis as different-sex couples, finally meant that discrimination on the grounds of sex or gender, even in the context of family relationships, became inexcusable.[32] It is in this context of a much more profound idea of gender equality that we must consider the appropriateness of the current birth-registration system.

Gender arises in two respects within the birth-registration process: one is in relation to the child identified in the register; and the other relates to the child's parent or parents. In the case of the child, we think that the Law Commission should ask respondents to a consultation whether there are any circumstances in which it is still necessary to record the gender of a child. Whereas, in bygone eras, the gender (or sex) of a citizen had state-sanctioned significance that justified the need to record that information,[33] that significance has disappeared. It is consequently no longer clear that gender is required as part of the core functions of birth registration. Given that requiring it has consequences beyond providing a record of birth, we must be cautious about compelling the information to be recorded and retained, certainly in a register open to public scrutiny. The birth register is a public record that can be accessed by anyone through the General Register Office.[34] As the Final Report of the *Future of Legal Gender Project* notes,

> [r]egistering people with a legal sex, and the expectation that people will have a corresponding legal and social gender, does not just communicate what someone is – that they are this gender or sex. It also helps form their sex and gender status and how they may identify.[35]

We submit that the question of registration of the gender of parents also requires closer critical scrutiny. As *R (McConnell and YY) v Registrar General and Secretary of State for Health and Social Care*[36] so clearly demonstrated, the legal relevance of recording gender is now an issue of seminal importance. In *McConnell*, a trans man had given birth to a child after having obtained a gender recognition certificate. He argued that, as a result of the gender recognition certificate, he was to be treated legally as a man for all purposes and should, therefore, be registered as his child's father. Both the High Court[37] and the Court of Appeal[38] disagreed with McConnell and found that the person who gave birth to the child must be

[32] See R Wintemute, 'Sex Discrimination in *MacDonald* and *Pearce*: Why the Law Lords Chose the Wrong Comparators' (2003) 14(2) *Kings College Law Journal* 267, for a powerful argument that the failure to provide for same-sex marriage was, in fact, gender discriminatory already.

[33] When, for example, same-sex couples could not marry. See also the now repealed MCA 1973, s 11(c).

[34] For procedure see HM Passport Office, 'Official information on births, adoptions, marriages, civil partnerships and deaths in England and Wales' (General Register Office, HM Passport Office, 2023).

[35] D Cooper et al, *Abolishing legal sex status: The Challenge and Consequences of Gender Related Law Reform. Future of Legal Gender Project: Final Report* (London, King's College London, 2022) 16.

[36] *R (McConnell and YY) v Registrar General and Secretary of State for Health and Social Care* [2019] EWHC 2384 (Fam), [2020] 1 FLR 676 [271] (*McConnell*).

[37] ibid.

[38] *R (on application of McConnell) v Registrar General* [2020] EWCA Civ 559.

recorded as the child's mother, regardless of that person's gender. In support of his decision in the High Court, the President of the Family Division reasoned that identifying the person who gave birth to a child in every instance is necessary for a coherent and certain system of birth registration.[39]

It seems to us that this conclusion pre-judges the answers to questions about gender and birth registration that we have yet to ask and to answer in this jurisdiction. At the moment, some cis women, trans men, gender-fluid and non-binary people can give birth.[40] However, it is possible that science may, in the future, make it possible for cis men (and other gender-fluid and non-binary people) to give birth as well. The question the President failed to address was whether or not the need to register the person who gave birth requires registration of that person's gender identity. If a range of people can give birth, why must registration include a gendered registration descriptor of the person who gives birth? Although, until recently, such a question would prompt an obvious binary answer (suggesting that only women could give birth), this is no longer appropriate.[41] We submit that it is time to reflect on how to accommodate these innovations in childbirth within our birth-registration system, and that legislation will be required to repair the registration system that no longer meets our social, political and personal needs. We must reconsider the relationship between birth registration and the information we have (at the time of a child's birth) about the gender of the child's parents. We can choose to record that information, or not to record it. If we choose to record it, we can also choose a method of recording it that is different from the method we currently use. Given the pervasive state policy that now promotes equality irrespective of gender and sexuality, we take the view that it is no longer necessary for the state to know the gender of the parents of any child. As the final report of the *Future of Legal Gender Project* notes:

> In contexts where it is legally important to name physical processes with gendered meanings, this can be done without using an explicitly gendered language (eg gestational or birth parent rather than mother or woman. This recognises that people other than women also become pregnant).[42]

We have argued that the issue of gender and the birth register requires careful reconsideration. Although we have suggested answers to the problem, we know

[39] *McConnell* (n 36) [271]. See further P Bremner, 'Birth registration: "coherent and certain" or "an occasion for exquisite embarrassment and confusion?"' (2020) 42(4) *Journal of Social Welfare and Family Law* 524. See also A Brown, 'Trans Parenthood and the Meaning of "Mother", "Father" and "Parent" – *R (McConnell and YY) v Registrar General for England and Wales* [2020] EWCA Civ 559' (2021) 29(1) *Medical Law Review* 157; A Margaria, 'Trans Men Giving Birth and Reflections on Fatherhood: What to Expect?' (2020) 34(3) *International Journal of Law Policy and the Family* 225; C Fenton-Glynn, 'Deconstructing Parenthood: What Makes a "Mother"?' (2020) 79(1) *Cambridge Law Journal* 34.

[40] See A Alghrani and J Harris, 'Reproductive Liberty: Should the Foundation of Families Be Regulated?' (2006) 18(2) *Child and Family Law Quarterly* 175.

[41] For ethical, social and legal implications, see 'The Future of Human Reproduction' (Future of Human Reproduction, 2023) at https://wp.lancs.ac.uk/futureofhumanreproduction/.

[42] Cooper et al (n 35) 38.

that others in our society may have different views. We think, consequently, that the matter ought to be considered by a dispassionate body whose role it is to make sure that our legal processes are appropriate to our times. That body in this jurisdiction is the Law Commission. It can ask the necessary questions, reflect on the range of answers that people in our society might give to those questions and then propose a way forward in the light of those answers that is appropriately comprehensive.

In section IV, we explore the possibility that the core principles of birth registration that we have identified might, in the light of the transformations discussed here, be insufficiently suited to births in the present era.

IV. Exploring the Possible Deficiencies of the Core Principles of Birth Registration

We have suggested that there are two core principles of birth registration that have remained constant since birth registration was introduced in the nineteenth century, namely, that we register the coming into existence of a child and that we register the child's parents. We will now reflect on the current principles that govern birth registration.

A. Registering the Child

While we accept that registering a child remains a core principle of birth registration, we suggest that the Law Commission should be seeking to ask a number of questions about what a future birth register should reflect concerning the advent of a new person. While naming the child and recording the date of birth seem to us to remain uncontroversial, registering the gender of a child, for example, is no longer self-evidently necessary. We think, therefore, that the Commission should ask respondents to a birth-registration consultation broad or open questions that elicit simple answers, but also encourage reasoned responses that explain those answers. The questions might look something like these:

- What details about a child and the facts surrounding that child's birth should be recorded in the birth register?
- Should the name, place, date and time of birth be recorded?
- Should there be a distinction drawn between information recorded in the child's medical record and information in the birth register? Is it necessary, for example, to record a child's sex, race, disabilities, weight, length (height), eye colour, NHS number, etc, on the birth register?
- Should gendered language be used when storing information about a child on the birth register?

- Should information about the attending medical staff be recorded on the birth register?
- How should we determine whether information is medical information or information necessary to appear on the birth register? What principles should guide this decision?
- What reasons can be given for recording, on the birth register, the information that respondents think should be retained there? [Respondents should be encouraged to be as full and detailed in their reasoning as is possible.]
- Should details about the child be able to be changed later in the life of the child (to record, for example, a new name)?
- If changes were to be permitted, how should they be recorded? Should it be apparent from the birth register that a change had been made?

The Law Commission can then make a judgement about what information it is justifiable, in principle, to retain and what information it is unjustifiable (and, as a result, unnecessary) to retain. It should outline its own preferred principles for including some information on, and excluding other information from, the birth register. In making its judgement, the Law Commission should recommend a coherent set of underlying principles for birth registration. We submit that its recommendation should rationalise the use of gender in the birth-registration system so that it meets clear and justifiable objectives and records information appropriately in distinct publicly and privately accessible parts of the new birth register (as we argue more fully in section V).

B. Registering Parents

Once again, we agree that identifying a child's parents is an important part of birth registration. We think that parents must be registered, because these are the individuals who should bear initial and presumptive responsibility for a child. The state has an interest in knowing who those people are, as do the parents themselves. Being responsible for a child entails rights, powers and duties towards the child, and those should be clearly ascribed to identifiable people.[43] However, registering parents is no longer a simple matter. Questions about who should be registered as parents, and how they should be registered, require more detailed exploration in the current era. Our society has opened itself to a much wider variety of parental nomenclature, and the attribution of that nomenclature to a much broader spectrum of 'parents' than ever before. Socially, we now identify parents as gestational parents, birth parents, genetic parents, would-be parents, adoptive parents, social parents and legal parents (amongst, no doubt, many other descriptors of parent

[43] CA 1989, s 3.

types). We have also altered our view of the (social and legal) significance we wish to attach to that nomenclature. Society now accepts that different-sex couples, same-sex couples, single people and more than two people can, and should, be able to raise children as their own, free from discrimination based on their family design.[44] As a result, while often it may be that our contemporary parental types coalesce in just two people, in a growing number of cases they do not. Several questions therefore arise for the Law Commission to ask of respondents to any consultation on birth registration:

- Who are the parents of a child?
- Which of the parental types (outlined above and, perhaps, outlined in the Law Commission's consultation document) should be registered?
- Should there be a limit on the number of 'parents' who appear on the birth register?
- What is the significance of genetic relatedness to registered parenthood?
- What parental information should the birth register record?
- Should the identities of 'genetic parents' be retained?
- Should the identity of the 'gestational or birth parent' be retained?
- Should the identities of any other 'parents' be retained?
- If genetic parents are to appear on the birth register, should there be a distinction in the way in which the birth register treats:
    - genetic parents who are the donors of gametes in medically assisted reproduction; and
    - genetic parents who participate in procreation in some other way (by, for example, having sex with a birth parent, or by using some other (informal) method of assisted conception)?
- In cases where medically assisted conception has not been the route to parenthood,[45] what should the status and effect be of genetic information that, later in the life of a child, is discovered not to accord with registered parenthood?
- Should any special significance attach to the legal parents at the birth of a child (in so far as the birth register is concerned)? Should the birth register exist to register legal parents only? Or should it also register other 'parents'?
- Which of the other parental designations should be (or should become) legal parents?

[44] Parental responsibility (for the work involved in raising a child) is already available to more than two people (from a very wide range of people) under the CA 1989. See particularly, ss 4, 4A, 10 and 12.

[45] Where the HFEA 1990 or HFEA 2008 has not shifted legal parenthood from the gamete donors to the would-be parents.

- If there is a transfer of legal parenthood at the time of birth, when and how should that transition take place? Should the transition occur before, after or through the mechanism of the birth register? What would the role of the birth register be in relation to that process of transition? Should it record both the legal parents before and after the transition? If so, how should it record the child's parents?
- Should all those 'parents' who respondents think should be registered be registered on the birth register? If so, should the birth register be a more complex, detailed register? Or should additional 'parents' – who respondents think should be recorded – be registered on a separate register?
- Whether on the birth register or a combination of the birth register and some other register(s), how should the different parental types be registered? What parental nomenclature should be used?
- Should there be a specific requirement to register the person who gave birth to the child where that person will not raise the child?[46] Do gestational parents enjoy some special significance? If so, how and where should that significance be recorded?
- What role should gender identification play in the registering of parents? Must parents be registered using gendered language?
- Should the birth register replace the common law presumption of paternity as the most important evidential resource establishing legal parenthood? Should it create presumptions of parenthood (in the way that the current common law presumption of paternity in the case of married women does)?

These questions are not, of course, exhaustive. They are intended to give a taste of what kinds of issues a project on birth registration would entail for the Law Commission. Nevertheless, we think that it is clear from the vast range of questions that, whatever answers the Law Commission might receive, the breadth of issues raised already suggests that reform of our system of birth registration is necessary.

In section V, we explore the possibility that, because of the complexity of these questions, the core principles of birth registration may be insufficient in the current era. We suggest additional questions that the Law Commission should ask in order to recommend a more refined set of principles for birth registration that are better attuned to our times and would serve to frame a better birth-registration system. Identifying contemporary principles of birth registration seems to us to be, to some extent, intuitive. However, some reasons underlying birth registration are only intelligible through an examination of our collective understandings of what is significant about being born into a given society. Such an examination must bear in mind the ways in which rights, duties and responsibilities are

[46] Where a parental order under s 54 of HFEA 2008 is likely to be made.

distributed amongst citizens and the state, and regulated through administrative and judicial agencies.

V. Should the Core Principles Underpinning Birth Registration be Expanded?

We believe that any project the Law Commission launches on birth registration will find broad consensus amongst scholars that the system of birth registration is now seriously defective, and that its underpinning principles are insufficient to the task of remedying those defects. As a result of complications arising from the fracturing of our understanding of parenthood, and profound changes in our attitude towards issues of gender and sexuality, we feel that the Law Commission should conclude that the traditional principles of birth registration are insufficient to frame birth registration in this era of diversity in modes of procreation and styles of parenting. Simply put, they are too broad, and so they fail to provide enough clarity to enable us to frame a focused system of birth registration.

To determine what a more focused set of underpinning principles for birth registration might be, we suggest that the Law Commission asks several questions. These questions should explore birth registration not from the perspective of tradition,[47] but from the perspective of the current social context and contemporary political thinking on the role of the state in the lives of individuals and their family affairs. For that reason, this section proceeds to discuss, first, the interests that we think a birth register should serve and, second, the new core principles that would serve those interests in an age in which diversity in family life is respected.

A. The Interests Served by a System of Birth Registration

In the first instance, then, we think that the Law Commission should ask questions about the interests that the birth register exists to serve, and the ways in which those interests can, in fact, be served by birth registration. We suggest that the Law Commission should be clear in its consultation that, once legitimate interests have been identified that the birth registration system should serve, the system devised to serve those interests should go no further than to do just that.

In setting out its consultation on the issue of interests, the Law Commission should adopt three initial observations that we make about the political context in which birth registration is to operate. First, birth registration is a process conducted under the auspices of the state, engaging the power of the state to extract information that the state requires from individual citizens who are

[47] As we have suggested the current principles do.

obliged to provide it. The information that is required in the birth register is intimate in nature and goes to the heart of what is profoundly personal; it is information that is core to the right to privacy protected in almost every human rights convention.[48] Birth registration – which is, by its nature, coercive – must, therefore, be founded on the most defensible principles available to justify the state in exercising this power to interfere in this most private sphere of the lives of its citizens.

Second, while the state's justifications for registering births may touch on, or reflect, the personal interests of some of those involved in procreation, personal interests are not, in themselves, sufficient justification for the state defensibly to require, and to store, personal information that is private to the individuals concerned. The birth register cannot, and should not, fulfil the demands of anyone who seeks information about the birth of a particular child simply because those demands are made by (however large) a group of people who would simply like to have that information. Individuals must be able to resist a requirement that information be provided to the state simply because a majority in the state would want that information to be recorded. The individual right to privacy, and the fact that it is part of the essence of a democratic society (that the state respects the individual even in the face of the demands of a majority), must be protected.[49]

Third, although the state may not (*qua* state) have an interest in some information surrounding the birth of a child, some of its citizens may have legal rights to that information. It may, as a result, be defensible for the state to store information in order to make meaningful the fundamental or legal rights of those of its citizens who might assert such rights. This is particularly apt in the case of children who, because of their status as children, would be unable to assert their legal entitlements until their maturity later in life enables them to do so.

After its consultation, we think that the Law Commission will conclude that there are two broad interests that should be served by birth registration, and that the state's guardianship of those interests justifies the maintenance of a birth register. The two broad interests are, first, those of the state itself and, second, those of individuals. The state's interest in birth registration arises because it needs to know its citizens so that it can administer the rights and duties of those citizens in relation to the state itself. The interests that individuals have in the birth register are, perhaps, more complex. All citizens in a state have, we suggest, an interest parallel to the state's own interest in the information that the state needs to fulfil its obligations to its citizens. The only individuals who can have interests in birth-related information that lies beyond the information required by the state for its own purposes are the child and the

[48] See, eg, the right to privacy in Art 12 of the Universal Declaration of Human Rights 1949 and Art 17 of the International Covenant on Civil and Political Rights 1966.
[49] ibid.

people involved in that child's procreation. The power of the state to store that (additional) information should only be engaged in the service of those more limited individual interests.

The child's interest in birth-related information is, of course, an intensely personal interest, specific to that child. The information is unavailable to the child at the time of birth because she has no capacity to access that information at that time. The child's interest therefore relies on an objective and reliable system for storing that information so that, when the child has acquired the necessary capacity to access the information, her rights to that information can be effectively exercised. However, we argue that the adults involved in the procreation of a child have a weaker claim against the state to the retention of birth-related information; adults are able to exert a right to access information immediately a child is born. That said, even adults might have a justifiable later claim to access birth-related information (for example, in cases where their ignorance of their involvement in the child's procreation becomes apparent much later). We submit that those individuals may also, later in the child's life, succeed in asserting a rights-based claim to access additional information stored about the birth of a child. In short, then, we think that the state has a duty to store information at and about the birth of a child because some of its citizens (notably, the child) may, at some point later in life, exert a legal right to that information.

B. Contemporary Principles for Birth Registration

On the basis of what we have said so far, concerning particularly the political context in which dramatic social changes surrounding birth have taken place, we proceed, in this subsection, to suggest contemporary principles for birth registration.

We have argued that a system of birth registration must be founded on principles that justify the retention of private information on a public register. We think that these principles must be rooted in the interests that we have suggested a birth register should serve. This subsection is divided into three parts: in the first, we deal with the principles that should underpin the state's decisions to record information for its own purposes; in the second, we discuss the principles that should apply where the state records information on behalf of its citizens who have (or will have) a right to that information; and in the third, we propose a mechanism for two-part registration.

i. Principles Underpinning Birth Registration that Serve State Interests

The state's interest in birth registration gives rise, we suggest, to two underlying principles of registration (which neatly replicate the two principles of birth registration that we have suggested as the principles underlying our current system of registering birth): first, the register must note the coming into existence of a new citizen (by naming the child and recording her time and date of birth); and, second, it must record the identity of her parents (and, through them, her relationship to her wider kinship circle). The state needs this information because it has an interest in, and obligations towards, its citizens. In particular, in relation to its new-born citizens (who are innately vulnerable), it must guarantee appropriate care in their early years and throughout their childhoods. To this end, the state needs to know their parents. It also needs the identity of their parents because it has an ongoing interest in being able to identify the kin relationships of its citizens reliably so that it can administer (and resolve disputes about) the property and other rights of its citizens.

However, these two principles – registering children and registering their parents – have become opaque in the new socio-political context in which they must now apply. They provide no clarity on how the child must be registered (and which information about birth must be stored), nor do they reveal which parents (and what parental details) should be registered. The principles require refinement, therefore, to reveal exactly which information is now required, and how it is to be retained.

In the context of a birth register that simply serves state interests, we feel that the policy context into which children are now being born requires minimal information about the child to be recorded on the birth register. Clearly, information necessary to identify a child as a citizen – such as the child's name and date of birth (to date, the moment of citizenship) – remains necessary. However, we believe that the Law Commission should recommend that it is unnecessary to record a child's gender to meet the state's interests in registration (in the same way as it is unnecessary to record a child's race on the birth register).

For similar reasons, we argue that a birth register that simply fulfils the state's interests in birth registration should register legal parents as the child's parents at birth, without any accompanying gendered nomenclature. These are, after all, the people to whom the state will look to care for the child. No other parental information is, we submit, necessary to meet the state's interests in birth registration.

ii. Principles Underpinning Birth Registration that Serve Individual Interests

We have argued that the state has a duty, at the time of the birth of a child, to regulate the recording and retention of information that the child and others will have a right to access, where that right is not immediately accessible. A third principle of birth registration is, consequently, that the state should record and retain information that it is the right of its citizens to access. In this respect, we think that a much wider range of information may have to be recorded. We already know that children have a right to identifying information about their genetic progenitors. *McConnell* confirms something we might have deduced from the law on adoption,[50] which is that children probably also have a right to identifying information concerning the person who gave birth to them.

We take the view that the collecting and storing of this information belongs, as a matter of administrative efficiency and rationality, with other birth-related information. Our suggestion is prompted by the fact that this information is more easily available at birth than at any other time, and because rights of access to it revolve around conception and birth. Thus, we argue that the fourth principle of birth registration should be that the collection and retention of birth-related information should be conducted in as efficient a manner as possible so that access to it is made as easy as possible. This principle would serve a general democratic principle of efficiency in state administration.[51]

iii. The Necessity for a 'Core' and a 'Supplementary' Birth Register

Because birth-related information, stored to meet the rights of citizens, is sensitive private information, which is not required by the state or by any generality of the citizenry of the state, we suggest that a privacy-protected part of the register has become necessary in which information of this sort should be recorded and stored. For us, a restricted part of the birth register would be the most appropriate place to store material that reveals genetic relationships, gestational relationships and even, potentially, the sex of the child at birth and the gender of the child's parents.

The interests of the state and those of individuals in birth registration are not identical. It is rational, therefore, for there to be two distinct parts to a future register, with each part made appropriate to each of those sets of interests. In the first – which we would call the 'core register' – information essential to the state should be recorded (and should be open to public scrutiny as society at large shares those interests).[52] In the second – which we would call the 'supplementary register' – information that must be accessible to particular citizens should be recorded, and should be open only to those in whom rights to that information vest. The 'core register' would enable the state to fulfil its own obligations to its citizens (and demand fulfilment of their obligations to it), while the 'supplementary register' would enable children and others to access their rights in relation to a

[50] For those adopted on or after 30 December 2005, see Adoption and Children Act 2002, ss 55–65, s 80; and Disclosure of Adoption Information (Post-Commencement Adoptions) Regulations 2005 (SI 2005/888). For those adopted before 30 December 2005, the procedure for tracing a birth record may be found in the Adoption and Children Act 2002, sch 2 and the Adoption Information and Intermediary Services (Pre-Commencement Adoptions) Regulations 2005 (SI 2005/890).

[51] See, eg, the third of the Twelve Principles of Good Democratic Governance of the Council of Europe (Principle of Efficiency and Effectiveness): '12 Principles of Good Democratic Governance' (Centre of Expertise for Good Governance, 2002) at www.coe.int/en/web/good-governance/12-principles#{%2225565951%22:[2]}.

[52] Birth certificates, used for purposes like obtaining access to state education, health services or foreign travel (passports), would be derived from this section of the register.

particular birth more reliably and efficiently. In this way, the state would facilitate the effective access of citizens to their rights.

Having set out our views on the necessity for a Law Commission project on birth registration, and having recommended some matters on which such a project should consult public opinion, we now proceed to our proposal for the kind of birth-registration system we think the Law Commission might advance.

VI. A New Birth Registration System

We have already discussed, at some length, flaws in the current birth-registration system. In this section, we briefly outline some suggestions for an improved birth-registration system. A number of significant features of a reformed register emerge from our arguments in this chapter.

As we have argued that the sex of the child is irrelevant to the fundamental principles of registration, we submit that it should not be required in the 'core register'. However, because we acknowledge the cultural and political significance attaching to sex and gender, and its potential importance as a matter of identity to children themselves, we accept that the 'supplementary register' should continue to offer parents an opportunity to register, in as flexible a way as possible, the sex of children at birth.

We submit that the person who is the most obvious candidate to have the legal duty to register the birth of the child should remain the person who gives birth to the child. We make this suggestion not for moral but for pragmatic reasons. In circumstances of surrogacy or baby adoption, where there are other more obvious candidates on whom that duty might be imposed, it should be shifted to those candidates. Other legal parents should also have the right to register the birth of a child. The registration of parents should be the registration of those people who are already, or will be by the time of registration, the legal parents of the child.

In the 'core register', we have argued that it is unnecessary to record the identity of the person who gives birth to a child. However, we accept that, as a matter of individual identity, that information would be required in the 'supplementary register'. The 'supplementary register' should include any information that our legislators or judges find to be fundamental to the identity of a child. This would include the identity of the person who gave birth to the child and any other (biological or genetic) participants in the child's procreation, where this information is different from information in the 'core register'. We suggest that the legislation establishing a reformed registration system should include amendments to implement this recommendation. The legislation should also provide that information that currently must be stored at the birth of a child (like information about the child's genetic progenitors) should become accessible through the supplementary birth register.

As the gender of parents is not necessary to meet any of the underlying principles of registration, the 'core register' should not, we submit, demand registration of 'mothers' or 'fathers', nor the 'sex' of parents. It should either simply require the registration of 'parent or parents' or it should allow for a more flexible registration of the nomenclature of parenthood (allowing parents, in effect, to choose their own parental classifications). We also take the view that the restriction to registration of no more than two parents should be removed from our birth registration rules. While this limitation may be appropriate for the majority of families, restricting the number of parents to two seems arbitrary in the context of the diverse parenting arrangements that exist. Although concerns must be addressed about the impact of having more parents and the consequences of conflict between parents, there should be a legal mechanism through which all the appropriate social parents can become legal parents. This mechanism would allow more adults to co-exist as legal parents without the need for competition over recognition between potential parents. Further consultation is needed on how this system should operate.

VII. Conclusion

In this chapter, we have argued that the social, scientific and political ground framing parenthood has shifted so dramatically in the last half century that our birth-registration system is no longer adequate to the task of registering births in England and Wales. The current register – which equates to our 'core register' – demands too much information and breaches the fundamental right to privacy that individuals in a democracy should enjoy. What is more, information that it is the right of individuals to access, and which the state (in fostering that right) should administer, is now located in a disparate array of formal and informal registers, records and processes that make accessing that information, at best, cumbersome. We have therefore argued that it is time the birth register was reformed, and that that reform should be commenced by a thoroughgoing Law Commission project on birth registration.

We have argued that the current system of birth registration is unfair because it demands both too much information (that is open to public scrutiny) and too little information (that should not be open to public scrutiny and which it is the right of individuals, notably children, to access). We submit that it is also unfair because it discriminates on the grounds of gender and sexuality; while the process is simple for some, it is not simple for others in the much wider array of families that must register the births of their children today. In that respect, the system is also not modern. It does not provide a simple system of registration that works uniformly well for all who have to register the births of their children. Finally, we have argued that the complex processes and registers that are required to realign parenthood at or soon after the births of children in a growing number of cases, have made the birth-registration system unnecessarily complicated and expensive. We think, therefore, that a project on birth registration is exactly the kind of project that the Law Commission exists to conduct.

In this chapter, we have also tried to aid a future Law Commission project by suggesting a way in which the Law Commission might go about consulting on the future of birth registration, and by recommending an outcome we can imagine from that consultation. We have argued that our proposals for birth registration give the right levels of recognition to the right people and place the responsibilities for children, and the rights in relation to them, in the hands of the right people. Our proposals make for a more stable registration system and eliminate the need for unnecessary additional bureaucratic procedures that might be disruptive and harmful in the lives of children. Of course, we understand that ours will be only a small voice in any future consultation and that the Law Commission might reach other conclusions. However, whatever conclusions it reaches, it would be surprising if it were not to recommend a thorough reform of birth registration (even if its recommendations are not the reform we suggest here). We urge the Commission to engage in such a project at the earliest opportunity.

Response to Chapter 2

Legal Parenthood and Birth Registration: Time to Respond to Diversity in Family Formation?

JULIE McCANDLESS

I. Introduction

Birth registration may seem like a mundane administrative procedure. Routine and, for many, unremarkable. Yet, like childbirth itself, and as the authors of this law reform proposal explain, birth registration is simultaneously vitally personal and deeply political. It is a compulsory state procedure for births in the United Kingdom (UK), with official integration into the country typically necessitating birth-registration documentation from elsewhere. Birth registration is therefore singular in this collection of law-reform proposals for its universal relevance. Birth registration is also the first step in establishing a person's identity for various legal and administrative processes; ones that facilitate access to essential state and societal infrastructure (eg, identity documentation, public healthcare and education, access to social security entitlements, immigration procedures). Given this coercive power, combined with the fact that birth registration records personal details in a publicly accessible register, it is crucial that the birth-registration system is fit for purpose and serves the needs of contemporary society. As scholars of civil registration have observed, registration systems only operate effectively when the populace buys into them due to a mutual exchange with the state, that is formal state recognition in return for legal entitlements and benefits.[1] That the birth-registration system is coming under increasing challenges from the population, including legal challenges, should be concerning to the Government. Birth registration is therefore a highly important issue to have included in this law-reform collection.

[1] K Breckenridge and S Szreter, 'Editors' Introduction: Recognition and Registration: The Infrastructure of Personhood in World History' in K Breckenridge and S Szreter (eds), *Registration and Recognition: Documenting the Person in World History* (Oxford, Oxford University Press, 2012) 1.

There is much to learn from Craig Lind, Philip Bremner and Maria Moscati's proposal. Each time I think about it, another lightbulb flickers. Most of my lightbulbs have been about the supplementary register, but I start my response by discussing the core register dimension of the proposal, then by offering some general observations about conducting a law-reform project on birth registration.

II. The Core Register – Gender, Space and Time

As the authors note, civil birth registration was legally introduced in England and Wales in the early Victorian era, replacing the system of parish registers for the religious rite of baptisms introduced in the Tudor era.[2] A primary driver for both systems was to have a clear record of kinship ties for property rights, inheritance and succession.[3] The authors' proposal does not disrupt this centuries-old function of the birth register and its entanglement with private property rights or hereditary titles. What it does disrupt is the recording of a child's sex/gender,[4] and that of the child's parent(s). When parish registers and civil birth registration were introduced, whether you were someone's son or daughter mattered for these rights, just as it mattered whether someone was a woman or a man for marriage law (more on this below). The state therefore arguably had a legitimate interest in recording this information in a publicly accessible register.

Society has since moved on from a legal preference for male primogeniture for property rights, and even in terms of succession to the British Crown.[5] Male primogeniture endures only for the majority of the 805 hereditary titles and peerages in the UK, including the 92 hereditary peers elected – by their peers – to currently sit in the House of Lords, all of whom are male.[6] Hereditary titles and peerages seem like a minor issue in the grand scheme of things, and most of us may wonder why they are not yet abolished, or at least the sexism of their inheritance rules changed.[7] I am also not suggesting that the state's interest in knowing

[2] R Probert, 'Recording Births: From the Reformation to the Welfare Reform Act' in F Ebtehaj et al (eds), *Birth Rites and Rights* (Oxford, Hart Publishing, 2011) 171.

[3] E Higgs, 'A cuckoo in the nest? The origins of civil registration and state medical statistics in England and Wales' (1996) 11(1) *Continuity and Change* 115.

[4] English law is inconsistent in its use of the terms 'sex' and 'gender'. Furthermore, contestation about the meaning of each term can make their use challenging. I have deliberately used 'sex/gender' because I regard gendered and hierarchical social and institutional processes as interacting with, and giving meaning to, the embodied characteristic traditionally understood as sex. The '/' therefore represents an iterative, rather than a binary, relationship between sex as biology (and fixed) and gender as identity (and flexible).

[5] Succession to the Crown Act 2013.

[6] House of Lords Act 1999.

[7] As well as the sexism of their inheritance rules, hereditary titles and peerages continue to cut against wider developments in family law, as inheritance is not possible in the context of 'illegitimacy', adoption, assisted reproduction and transgender children. See further G Black and SC Agnew, 'The significance of status and genetics in succession to titles, honours, dignities and coats of arms: Making the case for reform' (2018) 77(2) *Cambridge Law Journal* 321.

the sex/gender of the children of hereditary peers should drive policy considerations for the populace at large when it comes to birth-registration reform. However, I wonder if reform of the birth-registration system will be a bit like reform to hereditary peerages, where even quite sensible suggestions fail to gain political traction or disrupt emotional attachments (with the latter being a publicly acceptable presentation of attachments to privilege and power). The Future of Legal Gender Project (FLaG), cited by the authors, demonstrates the emotionally charged terrain that sex/gender and its official recognition and regulation hold in the current milieu.[8] As with proposed reforms to hereditary peerages, the FLaG Project's prefigurative endeavour of decertifying legal gender foregrounded politically charged questions of power, over which there is significant, and increasingly polarised, public disagreement.[9]

Consequently, while the authors' case for why gendered nomenclature should be removed from the core birth register may seem perfectly sound to many, their argument, or that of any future Law Commission project, may not be 'heard' rationally. Of course, just because a reform task may be difficult does not mean it should not be pursued. However, it does raise strategic issues for approaching a law-reform project on birth registration. Although societal transformations relating to sex/gender, family diversity and reproductive science have prompted the most direct challenges to birth registration, and specifically the information recorded,[10] a wider focus for a law-reform project may be preferable – and indeed desirable. The birth-registration system raises important, if rarely discussed, issues of space and time, and how they relate to the construction of personal and collective identity. For example, Jess Smith's recent study develops movement as a

[8] D Cooper et al, *Abolishing legal sex status: The challenge and consequences of gender related law reform. Future of Legal Gender Project: Final Report* (London, King's College London, 2022); and D Cooper, 'A Very Binary Drama: The Conceptual Struggle for Gender's Future' (2019) 9(1) *Feminists@law*.

[9] E Peel and H Newman, '"I Don't Think That's Something I've Ever Thought About Really Before": A Thematic Discursive Analysis of Lay People's Talk about Legal Gender' (2023) 31(1) *Feminist Legal Studies* 121; E Peel and H Newman, 'Gender's Wider Stakes: Lay Attitudes to Legal Gender Reform' (2020) 10(2) *feminists@law*.

[10] There are too many cases to cite in full, and no academic article that analyses the full breadth of challenges to the birth-registration system. In the interests of space, I provide only a small and illustrative sample of recent cases to support the claim. In relation to transgender parenthood, see, eg, *R (on the application of JK) v Registrar General for England and Wales* [2015] EWHC 990 (Admin); *R (McConnell and YY) v Registrar General and Secretary of State for Health and Social Care and Others* [2019] EWHC 2384 (Fam); and *R (on application of McConnell) v Registrar General* [2020] EWCA Civ 559. In relation to female same-sex parenthood, see recent cases, eg, *Osborne v Arnold* [2022] EWHC 1982; *Ms A v Ms J and others* [2022] NICA 3; *A v Bourn Hall Clinic* [2021] EWHC 1750 (Fam); and *M v W* [2019] EWHC 648 (Fam). In relation to re-registering a birth with the biological father's details or changing an original birth certificate to include the biological father's details, see, eg, *X v Y* [2022] EWFC 77; *Aylward Davies v Chesterman* [2022] EWFC 4; *Re L (Declaration of Parentage)* [2022] EWFC 38. There have also been numerous cases involving surrogacy arrangements, as well as a significant series of cases whereby the correct consent forms had not been completed in fertility clinics, with parents required to apply for Declarations of Parentage to enable proper birth registration.

socio-legal method to illustrate the places and spatial imaginaries of registration.[11] In doing so, she investigates much more than the places that are recorded on a birth certificate – for example, the registration district, the place of the child's birth and that of their parent(s), and the mother's usual address – but also evolving relationships between the religious and secular, and the community dynamics of where birth registration takes place. Registration may seem, essentially, to be a process of making lists. It is perhaps therefore instinctive to focus on the textual and what is recorded in the register and certificates. Yet what would happen if our law-reform gaze was broadened, as encouraged by Smith's methodology? What if we focused not so much on core information gathering – although delineating that would be an important part of a wider process – but on the wider role of registration in generating civil society, community, nation and, ultimately, belonging and inclusion/exclusion?

Concerning time, is the six weeks for registering a birth still the right amount of time? Or, more fundamentally, does a 'fixed' and 'snapshot' record of a person's birth and the legal relationships thereof still serve the needs of the state and its citizenry? Would a continually emerging register be more relevant and useful, and how could developments in digital and other technology help to enact this? How does, could or should the birth-registration system interact with the array of other state databases, importantly NHS records?

Taking this wider focus would take the singular emphasis off sex/gender and help shift the law reform lens from looking primarily *backwards* to challenges that have already happened to thinking also about *future-orientated* goals for a birth-registration system. It encourages us to consider what contemporary needs have surfaced for the birth-registration system, and whether we still need it to help us avoid – in the words of Thomas Cromwell – 'sundry strifes, processes, and contentions' relating to age, lineage and property rights.[12] Can this information be gleaned with relative certainty from elsewhere, so that the priorities and justification for the birth registration are otherwise focused? Approaching a birth-registration law-reform project in this way prioritises and expands on the important argument of the authors' proposal, that there needs to be a first-instance consideration of the legitimate interests that a birth registration serves. Only once those interests are clarified can the information to be collected be determined and justified.

The authors' proposal also made me ponder the relationship between law and registration. Despite an oft-cited comment in the Warnock Report that the birth register has 'always been envisaged as a true genetic record',[13] it is commonly

[11] J Smith, *Law, Registration, and the State: Making Identities through Space, Place, and Movement* (London, Routledge, 2023).

[12] Cited in Higgs (n 3) 121.

[13] Her Majesty's Stationery Office (HMSO), *Report of the Committee of Inquiry into Human Fertilisation and Embryology* (London, Department of Health & Social Security, HMSO, 1984) para 4.25.

accepted that the birth register records a child's legal parents.[14] However, birth registration in and of itself does not confer parental legal status. That is regulated by a mix of common law presumptions and legislative provisions. Rather, birth registration creates an official record of that legal status – an easily identifiable mechanism for avoiding contestations over a child's legal kin – and it is an offence to register someone as the legal parent of a child when that is not the case.[15] As well as removing the gendered nomenclature of parents, the authors argue that the birth-registration rules should be changed to permit the recording of more than two parents. While I do not disagree with this, it is important to acknowledge that it is not just the birth registration rules that need to change but the general law relating to parental legal status.[16] This example highlights the interplay between law and registration, whereby legal change may be needed elsewhere to make legal reform of the birth-registration system meaningful. The interplay is also further complicated by the fact that joint birth registration *does* confer parental responsibility under the Children Act 1989 (CA 1989) for legal parents who are not married or in a civil partnership with the child's legal mother.[17] Taking Smith's research approach, this demonstrates an evolving role for the birth-registration system, whereby it does not just *record* legally relevant information but also *enacts* it. Likewise, on every birth certificate the following warning appears: 'A CERTIFICATE IS NOT EVIDENCE OF IDENTITY'. Yet I am routinely asked for my children's birth certificates to prove their identity for access to various entitlements and social goods.[18] Do we therefore need to carefully evaluate how we understand birth registration and what we do with birth certificates? This seems a necessary step in helping us reconsider what birth registration actually *is*, and its relationship with contemporary law and legal processes more widely.

My closing point about the core register relates to gender. Controversial as the idea might prove, the authors' argument that gendered nomenclature be removed from the core register, on the basis that the state has no legitimate interest in knowing this information, seems stronger for parents than for the child being registered. As Alan Brown has shown, the substance of parental legal status is the same whether someone is a mother, father or parent.[19] How a person acquires legal status might differ, depending on their reproductive capacity, the mode of conception and a

[14] See further J McCandless, 'Reforming birth registration law in England and Wales?' (2017) 4 *Reproductive Biomedicine & Society Online* 52; and E Higgs, 'UK birth registration and its present discontents' (2018) 5 *Reproductive BioMedicine & Society Online* 35.

[15] Perjury Act 1911, s 4.

[16] The authors do seem to recognise this implicitly in their suggested 'Registering Parents' consultation questions in section IV.B of ch 2. However, this recognition seems to have fallen away in the recommendations in section VI of ch 2.

[17] CA 1989, ss 4 and 4ZA.

[18] This has included: confirming my spouses' entitlement to shared parental leave from employment, securing nursery places, accessing government-funded free hours for nursery provision, setting up tax-free childcare accounts, applying for passports and securing school places.

[19] A Brown, 'Trans (legal) parenthood and the gender of legal parenthood' [2023] *Legal Studies (Society of Legal Scholars)* 1.

person's sex/gender;[20] but once they are over the 'status threshold', to be a legal mother, a legal father or a legal parent is, in substantive legal terms, the same thing. The introduction of same-sex marriage and opposite-sex civil partnerships might encourage us, as it has the authors, toward a similar argument in terms of quelling the state's legitimate interest in knowing a child's sex/gender. However, there remain differences relating to, for example, consummation requirements for a valid opposite-sex marriage,[21] as well as exemptions for religious institutions as regards conducting same-sex marriage ceremonies.[22] This means that a person's sex/gender is not entirely irrelevant in this context and that the state's interest in knowing may still be pertinent. I would therefore frame the issue differently and encourage any reform process to establish why it is the publicly available birth register that the state should look to for this information.

III. Framing a Birth-Registration Law-Reform Project

What I wish to say here has, in part, been pre-empted by the preceding section, that is, that in devising a law-reform project, I would prioritise and expand the authors' recommendation for a first-instance consideration of the needs and legitimate interests that the birth-registration system should serve. In this section, I offer some further musings on approaching this task.

As a (self-confessed) birth-registration nerd, it is always tempting for me to agree with asking lots of questions about birth registration. As a researcher, I found myself nodding approvingly at the two lists suggested by the authors as the types of questions a future Law Commission consultation could ask participants. Even so, I then started to feel overwhelmed at the sheer range of responses that such questions might elicit, and wondered how useful the responses would be in determining the priorities for reform of the birth-registration system. It felt a bit like the 'feedback' question on student-teaching evaluation surveys, whereby, even when there is extensive marking guidance and feedback, students still seek more. Yet providing more guidance and feedback elicits precisely the same response the following year (along with the complaint that there is too much guidance and feedback to read). In an epoch of information, our instinct is often that more information = good (open, transparent, empowering); less information = bad (closed, opaque, disempowering).[23] Birth registration, and in particular the information that should be recorded, is an issue about which everyone can have instinctive views.

[20] In the context of assisted reproduction, see esp J McCandless and S Sheldon, 'The Human Fertilisation and Embryology Act (2008) and the Tenacity of the Sexual Family Form' (2010) 73(2) *Modern Law Review* 175.

[21] Matrimonial Causes Act 1973, s 12.

[22] Marriage (Same Sex) Couples Act 2013, s 2.

[23] For critical commentary on this issue see: Z Smith, *Feel Free: Essays* (London, Penguin Books, 2019), esp 'Generation Why?'.

Emotions can also run very high, with people's personal experience, pain and sometimes grief informing their views. Often, personal experience is incredibly important for informing policy and legal change. However, we also need a way to filter this likely vast array of personal views and experiences into useful policy goals for reforming a birth-registration system that needs to serve the mutual interests of the state and the populace.

The authors' proposal certainly recognises this and makes clear that, just because people are curious about information, this does not mean there is a legitimate interest in the state's access to and storage of that information, whether for public or private purposes (ie, the core and supplementary registers). Yet, at the same time, they suggest asking questions about whether information that has never been recorded on UK birth certificates should be (eg, 'race',[24] disabilities, weight, length or eye colour). They also suggest a series of questions about what parental and procreation information, other than parental legal status, should be recorded. The tendency to 'cover all bases' in these questions distracts from what I took to be the more probing impetus behind the questions, such as teasing out *who* respondents thought the legal parents were in particular circumstances or *why* some information was more suited to the birth register rather than a child's medical record. Either way, it seems preferable that, if a law-reform consultation was going to involve a series of questions to which respondents submit written answers, these questions should be focused on the first-instance exercise of ascertaining the collective needs and legitimate interests that a contemporary birth system should serve, rather than on the nitty-gritty of the information recorded. Focusing on the latter before the former has been established seems to be putting the proverbial cart before the horse.

The authors' proposal also assumes, not unreasonably, that a future Law Commission project would take the form of an open, written consultation, whereby the Law Commission would ask questions, participants would respond, and the Law Commission would analyse responses, integrate this analysis with their wider research, then make recommendations.[25] However, is this the best way to proceed for such a singularly universal issue like birth registration? Lengthy, paper-based consultations can be stifling. The last Law Commission consultation that I engaged with – on surrogacy law[26] – asked over 100 questions and proposed a Draft Bill with a similar number of provisions; yet no commentator seems particularly happy with the result, despite widespread support for surrogacy law reform. I give this example not just to grumble about having too many

[24] 'Race' and other markers of difference have of course been recorded in birth and civil registers elsewhere, including in British-administered colonial registries. The inclusion of 'race' and other markers of difference were typically for exclusionary purposes. See, eg, SJ Pearson, 'Birth Registration and the Administration of White Supremacy' (2022) 5(2) *Modern American History* 117.

[25] C Jones, 'Exploring the Routes from Consultation to (In)forming Public Policy' in M Freeman (ed), *Law and Bioethics: Current Legal Issues* (Oxford, Oxford University Press, 2008) 257.

[26] Law Commission, 'Surrogacy: Current project status' (2023) at www.lawcom.gov.uk/project/surrogacy/.

consultation questions to answer and new legislative provisions to read, but to raise the more serious point about how law-reform projects are conducted by the Law Commission. Question-focused, online consultations can certainly be useful, as can private- and public-focused meetings and discussions. However, are detailed questions the best way to test people's intuitions or knowledge about what the birth-registration system does, or should do, in society? Might other methods encourage participants to work through the reasoning and logic of their intuitions, and to perhaps reflect on those initial responses, or why they think X or Y? What about wider academic analyses of registration, as well as comparative experiences? Do we need to understand the life course or biography of a birth certificate to fully appreciate how birth records are being used in contemporary society? Do we know who – other than family historians – accesses the public register and why? Importantly, given the role of birth registration in constructing wider identities and facilitating access to legal and administrative entitlements, who is excluded from birth registration and why? Foregrounding these types of questions may ultimately be more useful and revealing than asking about the specifics of what should be recorded, whether in the proposed core register or the supplementary register. Ultimately, might we need to imagine what things would be like *without* a birth-registration system, to fully figure out what is important about it?[27]

IV. The Supplementary Register – Recording Information and the Legal Imaginary

In this section, I return to my point about the relationship between law and registration. The authors' recommendation for a core register and a supplementary register is interesting. While the former register would be publicly available, the latter would be held by the state in a stewardship role, and accessible only by those with a legal interest in the information, namely the person whose birth is registered. The keeping and accessing of the supplementary register are meant to protect the legal interests of individual citizens – rights relating to privacy and legal rights to know information about their birth. During the parliamentary passage of what would become the Human Fertilisation and Embryology Act 2008, the issue of the annotation of birth certificates to record donor conception was heavily debated.[28] A few years prior to these debates, regulations had created a registry of gamete donors, administered by the Human Fertilisation and Embryology Authority.[29]

[27] On such a prefigurative law reform methodology, see esp D Cooper, 'Crafting Prefigurative Law in Turbulent Times: Decertification, DIY Law Reform, and the Dilemmas of Feminist Prototyping' (2023) 31(1) *Feminist Legal Studies* 17.

[28] See further C Jones et al, 'The Role of Birth Certificates in Relation to Access to Biographical and Genetic History in Donor Conception' (2009) 17(2) *The International Journal of Children's Rights* 207.

[29] Disclosure of Donor Information Regulations 2004 (SI 2004/1511).

For donor-conceived births from April 2005 onwards, once a donor-conceived person reached the age of 18, they could now request identifying information about their gamete donor(s). The problem, as some saw it, was that this legal right of the donor-conceived person was contingent on the knowledge of the person that they were donor-conceived, which, in heterosexual families, was not always the case.[30] Annotating birth certificates was effectively discussed as a way of mandating disclosure of donor conception. While, ultimately, the consensus reached amongst parliamentarians was that annotating birth certificates would be too great an interference with privacy rights, academics have continued to argue for some form of annotation.[31]

The authors' recommendation may seem to emerge from these debates, but their proffered rationale is different. They point to the legal right to know information about your genetic progenitors, as well as a likely legal right to identifying information about the person who gave birth to you.[32] They then argue that the birth-registration system, rather than separate registries maintained by specialised regulatory bodies, is the most administratively efficient and easily accessible place for this information to be stored by the state, on behalf of citizens. On the surface this seems very persuasive, but I would like to respond with three provocations.

First, there is the question of whether state registries are the best place for this information. The growth of direct-to-consumer genetic testing, combined with informal and peer-instigated donor registries, has led to transformations in the ability of those involved in donor conception to make connections.[33] There is also emerging evidence that donor-conceived persons – or, indeed, their parents when they are still young children – are as interested in, for example, connecting with donor siblings as they are with gamete donors themselves.[34] These developments raise questions about the extent of information that is recorded in a state registry and how quickly that would be deemed either irrelevant or inadequate. These complaints could also be levied at current official registers, but they can perhaps be changed with greater ease than state-administered civil registration procedures.

Second, and I have written about this previously, when we record information in the birth-registration system, it can give that information an official, or potentially legal, gravitas that may not have been intended.[35] For example, recording

[30] P Nordqvist and C Smart, *Relative Strangers: Family Life, Genes and Donor Conception* (Basingstoke, Palgrave Macmillan, 2014).

[31] See the proposals in Jones et al (n 28). See also: M Crawshaw et al, 'Can the UK's birth registration system better serve the interests of those born following collaborative assisted reproduction?' (2017) 4 *Reproductive Biomedicine & Society Online* 1.

[32] Referring to *R (McConnell and YY) v Registrar General and Secretary Of State For Health And Social Care And Others* [2019] EWHC 2384 (Fam); *R (on application of McConnell) v Registrar General* [2020] EWCA Civ 559 and adoption law. See ch 2, n 52.

[33] L Gilman et al, 'Direct-to-consumer genetic testing and the changing landscape of gamete donor conception: key issues for practitioners and stakeholders' (2024) 48(1) *Reproductive BioMedicine Online*.

[34] ibid.

[35] See McCandless (n 14).

whether a child was a 'boy' or a 'girl' has now come to be understood as meaning that people have a legal gender. This 'legalising' process is likely because the very origin of the birth-registration system was as a record of information and relations for legal purposes. It would be culturally quite a shift to record information about people intimately involved in a child's conception and birth, and for that not to eventuate as part of the legal imaginary. The authors have been careful to draw distinctions between their two registers. However, I think it is a suggestion that we would need to carefully prototype.[36] This would be to see how the wider populace understands the distinctions between the two registers and the potential coalescing of legal status with registration, even if that is restricted to the supplementary register. I also wonder if the recording of other suggested information, such as the parent's gender, or the child's sex/gender at birth, will simply serve to enact a legal right to this information. This would then re-entrench the coercive insistence on registering sex/gender in the current birth register, against which the authors have argued.

Third – and this is perhaps the most crucial provocation – the authors refer to the 'rights of citizens'. Not everybody whose birth is registered in the UK will be a British citizen. Similarly, not all of those who access donor conception through licensed fertility clinics in the UK will be British citizens, meaning that the state birth register is not necessarily the most obvious or administratively efficient place to store that information. Like the idea about imagining society without birth registration to figure out why we need it, looking at who is excluded and why could help us figure out the reach of legal rights and the entitlements that it can protect.

V. Conclusion

It is easy to see the birth-registration system as static and undynamic.[37] Records today do not look that different from the civil registration records introduced by the Births, Deaths and Marriage Act 1836. Some might say that means the system has simply stood the test of time and that vital events are not that different today from those of hundreds, or indeed thousands, of years ago. Yet the system is coming under increasing pressure, with individuals prepared to take legal challenges against what they regard as unfair rules. This is a problem, as the success of civil birth registration rests on the voluntary uptake and support of the population.

[36] See Cooper (n 27).

[37] I am guilty of this view, see J McCandless, 'The Changing Form of Birth Registration' in Ebtehaj et al (eds) (n 2) 187. I am grateful to Jess Smith and her generative work on registration, which has helped me rethink things. See Smith (n 11) and the collection of articles co-edited with Sara Keenan: J Smith and S Keenan, 'Registering the Everyday: Documents, Bureaucracy, and the Socio-Legal' (2023) 32(5) *Social & Legal Studies* 659. Sara Keenan's work on land registration and belonging has also been highly generative: S Keenan, 'From historical chains to derivative futures: Title registries as Time Machines' (2018) 20(3) *Social & Cultural Geography* 283.

In other words, a mutuality of recognition between the state and the population. The authors' proposal responds directly to the family-diversity and identity-based concerns and conflicts that have underpinned these legal challenges.[38] In my response, I hope that I have built on their adept reasoning and carefully constructed suggestions, in part by enlarging their first-instance consideration about why we have the birth-registration system and offering some wider questions to ask. I have also cautioned against the split between the core and supplementary registers, by arguing that the public/private delineation between the two registers may be difficult to maintain.

This argument is not completely without foundation, given that short birth certificates, introduced in 1947 to help ensure privacy for the increasing number of illegitimate births after the Second World War, have been rendered moot since shortly after my birth in the early 1980s.[39] A long birth certificate is typically now required for official administrative purposes, forcing people to share the full information on their birth certificate. Maybe it is the case that legal and bureaucratic processes other than birth registration are what need to be reformed.[40] Conversely, despite the abolition of the concept of illegitimacy in English law,[41] we still have the socially obsolete legal possibility to re-register a birth – as legitimate! – when parents get married after the birth of their child.[42] That this legal possibility has still not been revoked indicates that reform of birth-registration law is long overdue. However, what these examples tell us is that the problem was as much with the law – that is the concept of legitimacy – as with the birth-registration system. Reforming the birth-registration system will also necessitate a wider review of stigmatising, unequal and exclusionary law not just in the context of family law, but also in the contexts of social security, property and immigration. Moreover, that is before we get to hereditary titles, their strange inheritance rules and their power to evoke exemptions to progressive legal changes.[43] Reforming the birth-registration system will not be an easy task, but it is certainly a task worth thinking about in as imaginative a way as possible.

[38] See case references in n 10.

[39] See further McCandless (n 37).

[40] See also L Davis, 'The Evolution of Birth Registration in England and Wales and its Place in Contemporary Law & Society (2023) 87(2) *Modern Law Review* 245.

[41] Legitimacy Act 1976; Law Commission, *Family Law, Review of Child Law, Guardianship and Custody* (Law Com No 172, 1988); CA 1989.

[42] Births and Deaths Registration Act 1953, s 14.

[43] Black and Agnew (n 7).

3

Reform of the Legal Framework for Origin Information in Assisted Reproduction

ALAN BROWN AND KATHERINE WADE

I. Introduction

As Ludlow has commented, 'Reproductive technologies disrupt our understanding of identity, kinship, and familial connections, concepts underpinning most known cultures and societies.'[1] This potential for disruption has been evident throughout the law's attempts to regulate reproductive technologies in the United Kingdom (UK) over the past 35 years. This chapter focuses on one aspect of that regulation – the approach to information relating to the origins of individuals born through assisted reproduction. This chapter's central argument is that the legal framework for the collection, retention and disclosure of such information is inconsistent and, thus, in need of reform. We argue that it is crucial that the law provides a coherent system. Importantly, these practical justifications for reform are combined with principled, normative justifications, focusing upon protecting children's right to identity and respecting their developing autonomy.

The chapter begins by briefly setting out the authors' understanding of 'origin information in assisted reproduction'. It then considers the importance of taking a children's rights-based approach, and the implications of such an approach for both the legal framework and for law reform. Thereafter, the chapter details the current law in relation to origin information in cases involving gamete donation, surrogacy arrangements and mitochondrial donation, and these sections will highlight the inconsistencies between the approach adopted in each context. The chapter will then set out our proposals for law reform. These proposals are focused upon two distinct (but related) issues: (i) the collection and retention of origin information; and (ii) the disclosure of origin information. First, we

[1] K Ludlow, 'Genetic Identity Concerns in the Regulation of Novel Reproductive Technologies' (2020) 7(1) *Journal of Law and the Biosciences* 1, 8.

will propose that there should be a consistent approach for origin information in assisted reproduction across different reproductive contexts. Second, we will propose that such origin information should be collected and retained in a wider range of factual and reproductive circumstances than under the current law. Third, we will propose that a system of mandatory disclosure of origin information be adopted. These proposals are underpinned by our children's rights-based approach to origin information. Finally, the chapter will briefly consider the potential complexities that may arise due to novel reproductive practices and technologies in the future.

Ultimately, we argue that law reform relating to collection, retention and disclosure of origin information in assisted reproduction is necessary to develop a comprehensive and consistent legal framework that will allow for both the identity and autonomy of those born through assisted reproduction to be better protected than is the case under the current legal regime.

II. Origin Information in Assisted Reproduction

Assisted reproduction refers to medical treatment that aids pregnancy without sexual intercourse,[2] including intrauterine insemination, in vitro fertilisation (IVF) and IVF with intracytoplasmic sperm injection.[3] These procedures involve significant intervention in the 'natural' reproductive process, and mean that donor gametes, donor embryos and/or surrogacy can be used to assist reproduction. More recently, mitochondrial donation has become possible, whereby healthy mitochondria from a donor replace unhealthy mitochondria to avoid mitochondrial disease in children.[4] New technologies are also emerging as scientific progress rapidly continues to advance. Given these varied reproductive technologies and practices, the question that arises is 'What makes information "origin information"'? For the purposes of this chapter, we define this as information relating to an individual's conception that has the potential to be important to that individual's sense of self. Within this, we include the following categories: (i) information about genetic origins – the people who provided gametes for the reproductive process, if different from the legal parents; (ii) information about gestational origins – the person who gestated the pregnancy, if not a legal parent; and (iii) information about 'intention-based' origins – the people who initiated the

[2] National Institute for Health and Care Excellence, *Fertility Problems Assessment and Treatment,* (Clinical Guideline CG156, National Institute for Health and Care Excellence, 2023).

[3] ibid. Further treatments are described, eg gamete intrafallopian transfer (gametes are delivered directly into the fallopian tube) and zygote intrafallopian transfer (fertilised eggs are delivered into the fallopian tube).

[4] See A Claiborne, R English and J Kahn (eds), *Mitochondrial Replacement Techniques* (Washington, DC, National Academies Press, 2016).

reproductive process.[5] With that established, we will now consider the significance of children's rights to such 'origin information in assisted reproduction'.

III. Children's Rights and Origin Information

We argue for a children's rights-based approach to origin information, based on the United Nations Convention on the Rights of the Child (UNCRC). The UK is obliged under international law to implement the Convention.[6] This approach recognises children as independent rights holders[7] and agents.[8] Because this area has traditionally been underpinned by the interests of adults involved in reproductive decision-making,[9] we argue that a children's rights-based approach is necessary to protect children's rights in relation to their identity and developing autonomy.

First, concerning the child's identity, while information relating to genetic, gestational and intention-based origins might be important for parents, we argue that it holds more importance for children, as it has the potential to be relevant to the child's and future adult's sense of self in a way that it does not for parents. By 'sense of self', we refer to a person's 'narrative identity', whereby a person constructs an integrated life story by 'reconstruct[ing] the autobiographical past and imagin[ing] the future in such a way as to provide a person's life with some degree of unity, purpose and meaning'.[10] Under this approach, it is recognised that a person's identity is not fixed but rather evolves over their life.[11] A child's right to identity is recognised in the UNCRC, which provides that 'States Parties undertake to respect the right of the child to preserve his or her identity, including nationality, name and family relations as recognized by law without unlawful

[5] Such information is particularly important in surrogacy arrangements, but may be relevant in other circumstances involving donated gametes.

[6] Art 26, Vienna Convention on the Law of Treaties, opened for signature 23 May 1969, 1155 UNTS 331 (entered into force 27 January 1980). Art 4 UNCRC provides 'States Parties shall undertake all appropriate legislative, administrative, and other measures for the implementation of the rights recognized in the present Convention.' On 16 March 2021, the Scottish Parliament passed the UNCRC (Incorporation) (Scotland) Bill to incorporate the UNCRC into Scots law. The UNCRC Incorporation (Scotland) Act 2024 came into force on July 16th.

[7] See Committee on the Rights of the Child, *General Comment No 7 (2005) on Implementing Child Rights in Early Childhood* (CRC/C/GC/7), para 3.

[8] See generally UN Committee on the Rights of the Child, *General Comment No 12 (2009) The Right of the Child to be Heard* (CRC/C/GC/12).

[9] See K Wade, 'Reconceptualising the Interest in Knowing One's Origins: A Case for Mandatory Disclosure' (2020) 28(4) *Medical Law Review* 731, 738–42.

[10] D McAdams and K McLean, 'Narrative Identity' (2013) 22(3) *Current Directions in Psychological Science* 233, 233. See A Brown and K Wade, 'The Incoherent Role of the Child's Identity in the Construction and Allocation of Legal Parenthood' (2022) 43(1) *Legal Studies* 29.

[11] J Leech-Scully, 'A Mitochondrial Story: Mitochondrial Replacement, Identity and Narrative' (2017) 31(1) *Bioethics* 37, 42.

interference.'[12] While this right is undefined, the Committee on the Rights of the Child Working Group referred to 'true and genuine personal, legal and family identity'.[13] Concluding Observations by the Committee have suggested that it is important that children have access to information about their 'biological'[14] parents,[15] and that it is in a child's best interests to know who their 'biological parents' are.[16] However, we acknowledge that interpreting the Committee's guidance is not straightforward in assisted reproduction. While there is some guidance on genetic origins, it is not clear to what extent gestational links or intention-based links would be captured by the idea of 'true and genuine personal, legal and family identity'.

Second, a children's rights-based approach recognises children as agents who have developing autonomy. Freeman argues that a plausible theory of rights must take into account the normative value of autonomy, which recognises that 'persons … have a set of capacities that enables them to make independent decisions regarding appropriate life choices'.[17] Respecting autonomy protects the integrity of individuals in leading their own life, thereby recognising people as equal and as having capacity to live as separate and independent beings.[18] Article 5 UNCRC recognises the concept of the 'evolving capacities of the child'. This requires States Parties to respect the 'responsibilities, rights and duties' of parents and other caregivers to provide appropriate direction and guidance to children in the exercise of their rights. Article 12 UNCRC requires that States Parties ensure that children have the right to have their views taken into account in decision-making in line with their age and maturity. These articles both relate to the concept of narrative identity, which recognises that identity formation takes place over a person's life. Childhood is a fundamental time in the formation of a person's sense of self, and

[12] Art 8 UNCRC.

[13] Report of the Working Group on a Draft Convention on the Rights of the Child (1985) E/CN.4/1985/6 4, Annex 11 (1), para 35, cited in D Hodgson, 'The International Legal Protection of the Child's Rights to a Legal Identity and the Problem of Statelessness' (1993) 7(2) *International Journal of Law, Policy and the Family* 255, 265.

[14] While the Committee uses the term 'biological' parents, which is often used synonymously with 'genetic parents', we will use the term 'genetic', since gestation can give rise to biological connections. See A Mulligan, 'Protecting Identity in Collaborative Assisted Reproduction: The Right to Know One's Gestational Surrogate' (2020) 34(1) *International Journal of Law, Policy and the Family* 20, 23–25.

[15] D Lyons, 'Domestic Implementation of the Donor-Conceived Child's Right to Identity in Light of the Requirements of the UN Convention on the Rights of the Child' (2018) 32(1) *International Journal of Law, Policy and the Family* 1. She notes that the Committee has repeatedly expressed concerns regarding adoption regimes that protect the anonymity of genetic parents. See Committee on the Rights of the Child` (2005) Concluding Observations: Russian Federation CRC/C/RUS/CO/3 and Committee on the Rights of the Child (2012a) Concluding Observations: Azerbaijan, CRC/C/AZE/CO/3-4.

[16] Lyons (n 15), citing Committee on the Rights of the Child (2009) Concluding Observations: France CRC/C/FRA/CO/4, 10 and Committee on the Rights of the Child (2002a) Concluding Observations: Switzerland, CRC/C/15/Add 182, paras 28–29.

[17] M Freeman, 'The Value and Values of Children's Rights' in A Invernizzi and J Williams (eds), *The Human Rights of Children: From Visions to Implementation* (Farnham, Ashgate, 2011) 21, 29–30.

[18] ibid.

there should be recognition of the potential importance[19] of origin information in childhood, not just in adulthood.[20]

This recognition of children's developing autonomy means that a participatory approach to the regulation of origin information should be taken. The Committee has stated that 'participation' involves 'ongoing processes, which include information-sharing and dialogue between children and adults based on mutual respect, and in which children can learn how their views and those of adults are taken into account and shape the outcome of such processes'.[21] This would mean that children's views about the importance of, and access to, origin information should be taken into account as part of an ongoing dialogue between adults and children.[22] That is not to say that children's views are determinative. Article 12 UNCRC provides that decision-makers should give due weight to children's views in accordance with their age and maturity, and that their views can be overridden if there are justifications based on their best interests.[23] However, the Committee has established that Articles 3 and 12 of the Convention are complementary, stating that 'there can be no correct application of Article 3 if the components of Article 12 are not respected'.[24] Involving children's views about disclosure of origin information necessarily implies a legal framework based on openness about the nature of their conception and the availability of origin information.[25] Finally, a children's rights-based approach requires respect for children's rights without discrimination of any kind, including discrimination based on 'birth or other status',[26] particularly if the child is born in circumstances that 'deviate from traditional values'.[27] This requires consistency in the legal framework protecting the identity and developing autonomy of children born through different methods of assisted reproduction.

[19] We refer to the *potential* importance of origin information to stress that we do not argue that such information *is* important for a person's narrative identity but that it has the potential to be, based on a person's own views: see Wade (n 9) 737.

[20] See E Reese et al, 'Emerging Identities: Narrative and Self from Early Childhood to Early Adolescence' in KC McLean and M Pasupathi (eds), *Narrative Development in Adolescence: Creating the Storied Self* (New York, Springer, 2010) 23.

[21] UN Committee on the Rights of the Child (n 8) para 3.

[22] ibid para 12. The Committee recognised the importance of including children's views in 'policy-making and preparation laws and/or measures as well as their evaluation'. For a project that explores the children's views regarding the law on origin information, see 'What is Children's Voices in Surrogacy Law?' (Children's Voices in Surrogacy Law, 2023) at https://childrensvoices.bristol.ac.uk/.

[23] Art 3 UNCRC states that the best interests of the child 'shall be a primary consideration' in 'all actions concerning children'.

[24] General Comment No 12 (2009) (n 8), para 74. See also M Freeman, 'Taking Children's Rights More Seriously' (1992) 6(1) *International Journal of Law, Policy and the Family* 52; J Eekelaar, 'The Interests of the Child and the Child's Wishes: The Role of Dynamic Self-Determinism' (1994) 8(1) *International Journal of Law, Policy and the Family* 42.

[25] The implications of this are outlined below in section V.B.

[26] Art 2 UNCRC.

[27] Committee on the Rights of the Child (n 7), para 12. See P Gerber and K O'Byrne, 'Souls in the House of Tomorrow: The Rights of Children Born via Surrogacy' in P Gerber and K O'Byrne (eds), *Surrogacy, Law and Human Rights* (Farnham, Ashgate, 2016) 81, 97.

This chapter will now set out the current law in the UK relating to origin information in cases involving assisted reproduction.

IV. The Current Law

Currently, the law in the UK[28] provides different rules relating to origin information for different reproductive contexts. Identifying information is now collected and retained for gamete donation.[29] Such information is collected and retained for some surrogacy arrangements.[30] However, mitochondrial donation is undertaken anonymously.[31] The inconsistency occurs due to the law's pragmatic and piecemeal development in response to reproductive technologies.[32] Since the 1990 Act, there has not been any overarching (re)consideration of the normative basis for regulation. This disjointed legislative framework is further complicated by the use of informal arrangements outside of licensed clinics,[33] and by the growth of cross-border reproductive services,[34] which situate the reproductive processes outside of (domestic) legal regulation.[35]

Given that context, this section will set out the current legal rules regarding origin information in assisted reproduction and examine the extent to which these rules reflect the children's rights-based approach set out in section III.

A. Gamete Donation

For children conceived from 1 April 2005,[36] under the 2004 Regulations, identifying information regarding gamete donors is collected by licensed clinics. This is

[28] The Human Fertilisation and Embryology Act 1990 ('the 1990 Act') applies to England and Wales, Scotland and (subject to limited exceptions) Northern Ireland, and 'the subject matter of the Human Fertilisation and Embryology Act 1990' is a 'reserved matter' under the Scotland Act 1998, sch 5, pt 2, para J3.

[29] The 1990 Act, s 31ZA.

[30] The extent to which origin information is retained in surrogacy arrangements results from the operation of rules concerning gamete donation, birth registration and legal parenthood.

[31] Human Fertilisation and Embryology (Mitochondrial Donation) Regulations 2015 ('the 2015 Regulations'), reg 11 (SI 2015/572).

[32] eg the shift from anonymous gamete donation to identity release donation made by the Human Fertilisation and Embryology Authority (Disclosure of Donor Information) Regulations 2004 ('the 2004 Regulations') (SI 2004/1511).

[33] Where there will be no records beyond the birth certificate.

[34] See A Mulligan, 'Anonymous Gamete Donation and Article 8 of the European Convention on Human Rights: The Case for Incompatibility' (2022) 22(2) *Medical Law International* 119.

[35] We recognise that there will remain inconsistencies in origin information for those born through assisted reproduction. However, it is beyond this chapter's scope to address potential harmonisation of laws relating to cross-border reproductive practices.

[36] These provisions are not retrospective (the 1990 Act, s 31ZA(5)). For people conceived prior to the change in the law, only non-identifying information is available.

retained by the Human Fertilisation and Embryology Authority (HFEA),[37] and can be accessed upon request by the donor-conceived person at age 18.[38] This information includes the full name, date and town of birth, and most recent addresses of the donor.[39] The legislation also provides that certain 'non-identifying information' is accessible at age 16,[40] including: physical description; year and country of birth; ethnicity; children; marital status; relevant medical history; any additional information; personal description; and any goodwill message (if provided by the donor).[41] The current position is that while identifying and non-identifying information regarding gamete donors is collected and retained, identifying information is not available until adulthood, and so it can be argued that this system is not underpinned by children's rights.

Notably, due to the law regarding legal parenthood[42] and birth registration,[43] an individual will only know about donated gametes used in their conception if they are told about them.[44] Longitudinal research involving families with donor-conceived children suggests that openness is not the norm, with Golombok commenting that '[u]ntil recently, the majority of parents who gave birth to donor-conceived children did not tell their children about their genetic origins'.[45] Research published in 2002 found only 8.6 per cent of families involved had told their 11- and 12-year old children about their origins.[46] While more recent research shows increased openness, a lack of openness remains in many families.[47] A 2011 study found that 72.2 per cent of 7-year-old children conceived through donor insemination had not been told by their parents,[48] and a 2016 study found that 26.7 per cent of two-parent families did not intend to inform their children of their origins at any point.[49] This current framework prompted Bainham to describe the right to access information as 'largely illusory',[50] and a Parliamentary

[37] The 1990 Act, s 31.

[38] The 1990 Act, s 31ZA(4).

[39] The 2004 Regulations (n 32), reg 2(3).

[40] The 1990 Act, s 31ZA(1).

[41] The 2004 Regulations (n 32), reg 2(2).

[42] The Human Fertilisation and Embryology Act 2008 ('the 2008 Act'), under ss 41 (sperm donation) and 47 (egg donation), makes clear that gamete donation does not lead to legal parenthood under the 2008 Act.

[43] Birth certificates do not record gamete donation.

[44] Or if they find out through home-based genetic tests or medical processes.

[45] S Golombok, *Modern Families: Parents and Children in New Family Forms* (Cambridge, Cambridge University Press, 2015) 98.

[46] S Golombok et al, 'The European Study of Assisted Reproduction Families: The Transition to Adolescence' (2002)) 17(3) *Human Reproduction* 830, 836.

[47] For a summary, see S Golombok, 'The Psychological Wellbeing of ART Children: What Have We Learned from 40 Years of Research?' (2020) 41(4) *Reproductive BioMedicine Online* 743.

[48] J Readings et al, 'Secrecy, Disclosure and Everything in-between: Decisions of Parents of Children Conceived by Donor Insemination, Egg Donation and Surrogacy' (2011) 22(5) *Reproductive BioMedicine Online* 485, 487.

[49] T Freeman et al, 'Disclosure of Sperm Donation: A Comparison Between Solo Mother and Two-Parent Families with Identifiable Donors' (2016) 33(5) *Reproductive BioMedicine Online* 592, 595.

[50] A Bainham, 'Arguments about Parentage' (2008) 67(2) *Cambridge Law Journal* 322, 335.

Committee to observe that 'assisted conception by its nature involves the authorities and we are deeply concerned about the idea that the authorities may be colluding in a deception'.[51] The current regime locates power regarding knowledge of origin information with parents, rather than the state, arguably suggesting a lack of appropriate acknowledgement for the child's developing autonomy. It remains unclear whether the removal of donor anonymity will shift parental attitudes towards greater openness.[52] Nonetheless, simply providing a statutory right to access origin information does not create a substantive right to knowledge about one's origins. The issue of how the law should disclose such origin information will be returned to subsequently.[53]

B. Surrogacy Arrangements

There is no separate regime concerning origin information for surrogacy arrangements, and there is no systematic collection or retention of such information.[54] However, the rules described in section IV.A would apply if gamete donation were used within the surrogacy arrangement. The identifying and non-identifying information regarding donors, required under the 1990 Act, would be collected and retained. If the gametes of one (or both) of the intended parents are used, this would be recorded and the prefix 'IP' would be marked on the HFEA's register for children born since 2013.[55] However, as the Law Commission of England and Wales and the Scottish Law Commission's Report *Building Families Through Surrogacy: A New Law* noted, 'Because the intended parents were not treated as donors, information about them will not be disclosable via the disclosure provisions.'[56] Thus, the information is collected but is not discoverable. If the intended parents' gametes are not used then (self-evidently) no information will be recorded.[57] Currently,[58] the surrogate will be registered on the birth certificate as the legal mother,[59] providing a record of gestational origins. If the intended

[51] House of Commons and House of Lords Joint Committee on the Human Tissue and Embryos (Draft) Bill, *Human Tissue and Embryos (Draft) Bill* (Volume I: Report) (2007, HL Paper 169-I, HC Paper 630-I, August 2007), para (276), 73, available at publications.parliament.uk/pa/jt200607/jtselect/jtembryos/169/169.pdf.

[52] Golombok (n 45) 101–02, notes 'anecdotal evidence' of increased openness in countries where donor anonymity has been removed, 'but it remains the case that a substantial proportion of parents still choose not to tell'.

[53] See section V.B.

[54] *Building Families Through Surrogacy: A New Law* (Law Com No 411 and Scot Law Com No 262, vol 2, 2023) paras 13.9–13.36, states that those born through surrogacy can access limited information through birth certificates, court records and information held by the HFEA.

[55] ibid para (13.32).

[56] ibid.

[57] ibid.

[58] ibid, ch 2, proposes a 'new pathway' to parenthood, allowing the intended parents to become legal parents from birth in some circumstances.

[59] The 2008 Act, s 33(1), reflecting the presumption *mater est quam gestatio demonstrat.*

parents subsequently acquire legal parenthood through a parental order,[60] access to the original birth certificate is not possible in England and Wales.[61] A traditional surrogate (who uses her own egg) appears to meet the definition of donor under the 2004 Regulations.[62] However, the Law Commissions' Consultation Paper suggested, 'in practice, such identification would be unlikely to be possible, as the clinic would not have treated the surrogate as a donor, and she would not have given the necessary consent to disclosure of information'.[63] The potential absence of origin information for some children born through surrogacy arrangements is problematic in terms of the protection of identity rights and developing autonomy of those children. This is particularly problematic in light of obligations under Article 2 UNCRC to ensure children's equal enjoyment of their rights without discrimination.

In contrast to gamete donation, the nature of surrogacy arrangements (the visibility of the surrogate's role) means that it is far more likely for someone born through surrogacy to be informed of the circumstances of their conception and birth. As Golombok has written, 'Surrogacy parents are much more open with their children about the circumstances of their birth than are parents of children conceived by egg, sperm or embryo donation.'[64] The UK's major surrogacy organisations encourage openness about children's origins and contact between the surrogate, the intended parents and the child.[65] However, a 2012 study found that where the surrogate's gametes had been used, children were much less likely to be informed of this than the fact of the surrogacy.[66] At age 10, all children involved in the research who were born through traditional surrogacy had been told about the surrogacy arrangement, but only 58 per cent had been told about the use of the surrogate's egg,[67] illustrating the issue around the lack of information about genetic origins for those born through surrogacy.

As the Law Commissions have commented:

> To ensure surrogate-born people have access to information about their genetic and gestational origins, we recommend wholesale reform in this area. None of the current

[60] The 2008 Act, ss 54 and 54A, which allow for the post-birth transfer of legal parenthood to the intended parent(s).

[61] *Building Families Through Surrogacy* (n 54) paras 13.18–13.19. The position is different in Scotland (para 13.18), where original birth certificates can be accessed by surrogate-born children.

[62] Under reg 1(2), 'the person who has provided the sperm, eggs or embryos that have been used for treatment services in consequence of which the applicant was, or may have been, born'. See further *Building Families Through Surrogacy* (n 54) para 13.33.

[63] *Building Families Through Surrogacy: A New Law* (Law Com Consultation Paper No 244, Scot Law Com Discussion Paper No 167, 2019) para 10.60. The Final Report does not indicate that the Consultation Paper is incorrect regarding these practical implications.

[64] Golombok (n 45) 132. See further F MacCallum et al, 'Surrogacy: The Experience of Commissioning Couples' (2003) 18(6) *Human Reproduction* 1334.

[65] See, eg, Surrogacy UK's 'ethos of 'friendship first' (Surrogacy UK, 2023) at www.surrogacyuk.org/surrogacyuk/.

[66] V Jadva et al, 'Surrogacy Families 10 Years On: Relationship with the Surrogate, Decisions over Disclosure and Children's Understanding of their Surrogacy Origins' (2012) 27(10) *Human Reproduction* 3008.

[67] ibid 3011.

> methods for accessing information about one's origins were originally designed for use by people born as a result of surrogacy.[68]

We entirely agree, and a framework for origin information in surrogacy arrangements will be considered later in this chapter.[69] The consequence of the current framework is that, for children born through gamete donation, information is accessible but in practice many children are unaware of the circumstances of their conception; whereas those born through surrogacy are more likely to be aware of the circumstances of their conception, but there is no specific framework for the collection and retention of information about that conception. This highlights the inconsistency that results from the application of the piecemeal legal framework in different reproductive circumstances. We argue that utilising a children's rights-based approach would address such inconsistency, as the framework would be based on equal enjoyment by all children of their rights relating to their identity (Article 8 UNCRC) and autonomy (Articles 5 and 12 UNCRC) under the Convention, as required by Article 2.

C. Mitochondrial Replacement Therapy

In contrast with gamete donation and surrogacy arrangements, mitochondrial donation is anonymous,[70] and no identifying information regarding donors is collected and retained. This represented an explicit policy choice[71] when mitochondrial donation was regulated by the 2015 Regulations.[72] This policy choice was based upon a distinction drawn by the Government between mitochondrial donation and gamete donation, with a Department of Health consultation response stating that 'the difference between mitochondrial donation and gamete donation is so significant that providing identifiable information is not warranted'.[73] Notably, the distinction between mitochondrial and gamete donation is not universally supported within the literature,[74] and we will return to the viability

[68] *Building Families Through Surrogacy* (n 54) para 13.5.

[69] See section V.A.i.

[70] The 2015 Regulations (n 31), reg 11.

[71] 'Explanatory Memorandum to The Human Fertilisation and Embryology (Mitochondrial Donation) Regulations 2015', paras 7.9–7.11.

[72] The operation of reg 11 of the 2015 Regulations is that in cases involving mitochondrial donation, the 1990 Act, s 31ZA is to be read 'as if' subs (2A) is inserted. This includes, in s 31ZA(2A), the provision that no 'information which may identify the mitochondrial donor' can be made available to an applicant.

[73] Department of Health, 'Mitochondrial Donation: Government Response to the Consultation on Draft Regulations to Permit the Use of New Treatment Techniques to Prevent the Transmission of a Serious Mitochondrial Disease from Mother to Child' (Public Health Directorate, Health Science and Bioethics Division 10250, July 2014) 36 at www.assets.publishing.service.gov.uk/government/uploads/system/uploads/attachment_data/file/332881/Consultation_response.pdf.

[74] See, eg, R Brandt, 'Mitochondrial Donation and "The Right to Know"' (2016) 42(10) *Journal of Medical Ethics* 678; J Appleby, 'Should Mitochondrial Donation Be Anonymous?' (2018) 43(2) *Journal of Medicine and Philosophy* 261; C Mills, 'Nuclear Families: Mitochondrial Replacement Techniques and the Regulation of Parenthood' (2021) 46(3) *Science, Technology and Human Values* 507.

of the Government's justification for this distinction later.[75] The current position is that only non-identifying information can be made available to someone born through mitochondrial replacement therapy (MRT) upon request. This includes: the screening tests carried out on the donor; the donor's personal and family medical history; and any personal description or additional information provided by the donor.[76] Interestingly, the non-identifying information available for mitochondrial donation is significantly more limited than that available in gamete donation.[77] The reproductive technology used in MRT remains novel. There are no empirical data regarding whether families consider accessibility of information about mitochondrial donors as being important, how important children consider this information or whether parents are informing their children of the fact of donation. Moreover, because mitochondrial donation is anonymous, openness about it does not currently have the same implications as openness about donor conception, as identifying information cannot be accessed.

Overall, the current legal framework for origin information in assisted reproduction is fragmented, involving three different approaches in these three different reproductive contexts. In light of that fragmented approach, the chapter will now set out our proposals for reform of the legal framework.

V. Proposals for Reform

We argue that the law should adopt one overarching approach to origin information in all reproductive contexts. First, our argument is underpinned by normative justifications concerning the child's 'right to identity' and the need for a participatory approach based on children's developing autonomy. Second, our proposed approach would be more coherent and has the potential to respond dynamically and effectively to future developments in reproductive technology. Therefore, we will set out our proposals for reform to the law governing origin information, focusing on two (related but distinct) areas: (i) collection and retention of information; and (ii) disclosure of information.

A. Collection and Retention of Information

Our starting point is that the collection of information regarding genetic, gestational and 'intention-based' origins is fundamental to protecting the 'right to identity' of those born through assisted reproduction, and to providing a participatory approach. The legal framework described in section IV shows a piecemeal

[75] See section V.A.ii.

[76] The 1990 Act, s 31ZA(2A)(a)–(c).

[77] Only three categories of non-identifying information are replicated in the 2015 Regulations from the eight categories in the 2004 Regulations (n 32), reg 2(2).

response to the collection and retention of genetic, gestational and 'intention-based' origins.[78] Under our proposed regime, identifying information would be collected and retained about gamete donors, surrogates, intended parents and mitochondrial donors in one expanded central register maintained by the HFEA, in order to develop a consistent system for the retention of origin information.

i. Surrogacy Arrangements

We propose that information about surrogates be recorded in the central register. It is not our argument that the contributions of gamete donors and surrogates to the reproductive process are identical in either biological or normative terms. However, it can be argued that the rules that apply for gamete donors should apply in relation to children born through traditional surrogacy, since both groups have a genetic link to the donor/surrogate through the contribution of gametes.[79] Self-evidently, a child born through gestational surrogacy (where the surrogate's gametes are not used) does not have a genetic link with the surrogate, which raises questions about whether similar rules should apply. Mulligan argues that since it appears that the behaviour and lifestyle of the surrogate can affect foetal health, gestation would 'appear to have some significance' for identity formation.[80] This is because gestation has at least 'some bearing on a person's physical or psychological characteristics and therefore on their identity'.[81] We propose that the same information about the surrogate should be collected and retained as currently is the case for gamete donors under the 1990 Act and the 2004 Regulations. This proposal is premised upon the recognition that such information may be important for the child's right to 'identity'.[82] Relatedly, and for similar reasons, we propose that if the surrogate's gamete/s were used, this should be recorded.[83] First, this would align the legal positions of donor-conceived children and children born through traditional surrogacy in terms of the information about their origins that is collected and retained. Second, this would involve the collection and retention of information about gestational surrogacy to recognise the potential importance of this relationship for the child's identity. Third, this would mean that information for children born through traditional surrogacy is recorded in the same way as gestational surrogacy.[84]

[78] This is due to the application of the 2004 and 2015 Regulations, and the rules on birth registration and legal parenthood.

[79] Wade (n 9) 749.

[80] Mulligan (n 14) 25.

[81] ibid. Mulligan cites J Eekelaar, 'Family Law and Identity' (2018) 38(4) *Oxford Journal of Legal Studies* 1 and argues that this may be relevant to a person's individual identity (personal characteristics and self-perception) and their communal identity (characteristics shared with others), since the surrogate-born person may see themselves as part of a community with the surrogate, her family and other children the surrogate gave birth to.

[82] Mulligan (n 14) 21.

[83] See Joint Consultation Paper (n 63) para 10.90.

[84] This is in contrast to the proposal in *Building Families Through Surrogacy* (n 54) para 13.71.

We propose that the same identifying information concerning intended parents should be recorded. This would mean that, if the surrogacy arrangement were to break down and the surrogate retained care of the child, information about the intended parents would have been collected and retained.[85] Our proposal for individuals born through surrogacy arrangements reflects the proposal of the Law Commissions:[86] '[W]e recommend the introduction of an SR [Surrogacy Register] that would include the identities of the surrogate, the intended parents and any gamete donors.'[87]

However, one key point where our proposals differ is that the Report proposes that this origin information would be retained in a 'Surrogacy Register' maintained by the HFEA,[88] whereas our proposal is that information regarding surrogacy arrangements should be recorded in the same central register as information for those born through gamete donation. This reflects our overarching argument that a comprehensive and consistent legal framework for origin information is required, rather than continuing with a version (however reformed) of the current piecemeal regulatory approach.

ii. Mitochondrial Replacement Therapy

We propose that the same identifying information about mitochondrial donors should be collected and retained as currently for gamete donors, and as would be retained under our proposals for surrogates and intended parents.[89] The current approach is that mitochondrial donation is anonymous under the 2015 Regulations. However, as Appleby has previously argued:

> If regulators wish to treat mitochondrial donors differently under the law and make them anonymous, then a convincing argument must be provided to overturn the initial presumption that both forms of donation should have the same open-identity status.[90]

We agree with this normative starting point that donors of different types of genetic material should be treated the same in terms of origin information. However, the current regulation of mitochondrial donation is premised upon a distinction between the two types of donation. This distinction appears to be based upon an assessment of both quantity and quality of genes. First, in terms of quantity, a donated mitochondrial genome contains only 37 genes, which is approximately

[85] This would include their genetic links (if any) with the child.
[86] *Building Families Through Surrogacy* (n 54) ch 13.
[87] ibid para 13.49.
[88] ibid paras 13.49–13.83.
[89] See TC de Campos and C Milo, 'Mitochondrial Donations and the Right to Know and Trace One's Genetic Origins: An Ethical and Legal Challenge' (2018) 32(2) *International Journal of Law, Policy and the Family* 170, who argue that the current system, which maintains anonymity for mitochondrial donors, is discriminatory when compared to the system for donor conception and should be amended.
[90] Appleby (n 74) 262.

0.1 per cent of genes in the nuclear genome.[91] Second, in terms of quality, mitochondrial DNA is responsible for mitochondrial energy production, as opposed to physical or personality traits, which are associated with donated gametes.[92] These scientific differences underpin the legal distinction between types of donation; the Department for Health has previously offered the following explanation for the anonymity of mitochondrial donors:

> [T]he Government's view remains that a child born following mitochondrial donation would have two biological parents, who provide 99.9 per cent of their genes and that any relationship between the child and the mitochondrial donor is remote.[93]

However, we argue that the collection and retention of origin information is not about determinations of legal (or genetic) parenthood. Instead, collection and retention is about ensuring that information that is potentially important to an individual's identity can be made available to that individual, thereby allowing them to exercise their autonomy when deciding whether or not to access it. As Appleby has observed, these apparent justifications for the distinction between mitochondrial and gamete donors are not persuasive, since they are built on a 'geneticised' version of the sense of self.[94] It is not unreasonable to suggest that some people may find information about their mitochondrial donor important to their identity, regardless of the number of genes contributed by the mitochondrial donor to the embryo that created them.[95] The use of mitochondrial donation in conception is likely to be relevant to those born through MRT (or a significant proportion of them) for a range of motivations. Appleby notes studies that show that some people contact gamete donors to find out their motivation and to thank them. He argues against the assumption that those born through mitochondrial donation might not have the same desires.[96] Therefore, we propose that identifying information about mitochondrial donors should be collected and retained in the same way as currently applies for gamete donors, and that this information should be retained in the same central register as the other identifying information proposed. Our argument is not that the two types of donation are entirely comparable. Rather, we argue that each form of donation has the potential to be important to the child's identity, which justifies similar treatment. Therefore, allowing access to identifying information in each context is important for respecting the autonomy of the child to make their own decision about the significance of the information.

[91] Nuffield Council on Bioethics, *Novel Techniques for the Prevention of Mitochondrial DNA Disorders: An Ethical Review* (London, Nuffield Council on Bioethics, 2012) 19 at www.nuffieldbioethics.org/assets/pdfs/Novel_techniques_for_the_prevention_of_mitochondrial_DNA_disorders.pdf.
[92] ibid 18–20.
[93] Department for Health (n 73) 35.
[94] Appleby (n 74) 269.
[95] ibid 270.
[96] ibid 272.

B. Disclosure of Information

One of the most contentious issues in the regulation of assisted reproduction is disclosure of origin information. The fundamental questions that arise are: (i) should children be told about the method of assisted reproduction used in their conception; and (ii) should origin information be made available to children? As noted, currently, it is up to parents to decide whether or not to tell their children. One of the authors has previously argued that children should be told about origin information in gamete donation and surrogacy.[97] This is based on the argument that the harm or wrong that is caused by non-disclosure is more significant than the potential harms of mandatory disclosure, or, at least, that the harms of the latter can be mitigated.[98] It may be argued that, if children never find out, they are wronged, because they are not told information that is potentially important for their identity.[99] Conversely, mandatory disclosure does not result in an equally significant intrusion on parental autonomy and identity, since parents are not deprived of information that may be important for their identity; rather, information that they know exists is released.[100] It is difficult to defend a position whereby parents' own apparent attachment to the importance of genetic links, evidenced through non-disclosure (aimed at preserving the illusion of a genetic link), is used as a justification to deny children access to information about their own genetic links.[101] Such arguments underpin a legal framework based on mandatory disclosure, whereby individuals are told of the manner of their birth and the availability of information by birth certificate annotations[102] and/or through a notification system, for example by letter to the family's last-known address.[103]

The authors are aware that this is not an uncontroversial proposal. It can be argued that mandatory disclosure is an unjustifiable interference with parental autonomy, by not allowing parents to decide whether disclosure is in the

[97] Wade (n 9).

[98] ibid 12.

[99] ibid 13. See further M Warnock, 'The Good of the Child' (1987) 1(2) *Bioethics* 141, 151; and M Cowden, '"No Harm, No Foul": A Child's Right to Know Their Genetic Parents' (2012) 26(1) *International Journal of Law, Policy and the Family* 102, 111.

[100] ibid 13.

[101] ibid 14.

[102] On birth-certificate annotation, see E Blyth et al, 'The Role of Birth Certificates in Relation to Access to Biographical and Genetic History in Donor Conception' (2009) 17 *International Journal of Children's Rights* 207. See *Building Families Through Surrogacy* (n 54) para 13.232, which recommends making the surrogacy arrangement clear on the full form of the birth certificate. Such a system would not mean that children would necessarily find out during childhood, as this would require access to their birth certificate. However, the annotation may encourage early disclosure based on parental knowledge that children will likely find out the information.

[103] Such a system also does not guarantee disclosure during childhood since notifications could be intercepted or a change of address could occur, meaning that birth-certificate annotations may be more effective or, at the very least, should be used in conjunction with notification.

best interests of their children. However, we argue that a children's rights-based approach would support mandatory disclosure.[104] Article 5 UNCRC provides that States Parties should respect the exercise of parental responsibilities, rights and duties to provide appropriate direction and guidance in the exercise by the child of his or her rights in a manner consistent with the evolving capacities of the child. As Tobin and Varadan note, 'Article 5 mandates that the power of parents must be exercised not for their own benefit, but for the benefit of their child and the enjoyment of his or her rights'.[105] They note that this means that parents should refrain from actions that would threaten the enjoyment of rights by their children but also take positive steps to enhance the capacity of their children to enjoy their rights.[106] This approach is taken to parental decision-making under Article 18 UNCRC, which states that children's best interests 'will be their basic concern'.[107] Tobin and Seow argue:

> This phrase casts a new dimension over the responsibilities of parents with respect to their children under international law. Any notion that children were subject to the unfettered mandate of their parents is displaced with the requirement that the best interests of a child will be a parent's basic concern.[108]

If it is accepted that origin information has the potential to be important to a child's identity, and that children should be able to make decisions about access to such information, then openness about the availability of information is in their best interests.

Nonetheless, a recent HFEA Discussion Paper stated that 'nobody, including parents, should be legally required to inform donor-conceived children/adults of their donor-conceived status or of their genetic parentage, since this is not routinely legally mandated for children born in other circumstances'.[109] The reason for retaining this principle could be countered by the argument that the fact that individuals in other contexts face difficulties in accessing origin information should not per se be used as a justification for non-disclosure in a circumstance where that access is possible.[110] The justification for the current prioritisation of parental autonomy should be based on an equal consideration of the competing

[104] See *Building Families Through Surrogacy* (n 54) para 13.228, which states 'we are not persuaded by the concerns of those who consider that the intended parents should be left to decide whether to tell their child of the surrogacy; this is a matter that the child has a right to know'.

[105] J Tobin and S Varadan, 'Article 5: The Right to Parental Direction and Guidance Consistent with a Child's Evolving Capacities' in J Tobin (ed), *The UN Convention on the Rights of the Child: A Commentary* (Oxford, Oxford University Press, 2019) 159, 161.

[106] ibid 172.

[107] ibid.

[108] J Tobin and F Seow, 'Article 18: Parental Responsibilities and State Assistance' in Tobin (ed) (n 105) 646, 664.

[109] Human Fertilisation and Embryology Authority, *Donor Anonymity and Information Provision: Discussion Paper* (Legislative Reform Advisory Group, HFEA, 2022) para 27.

[110] Wade (n 9) 748, citing S Allan, *Donor Conception and the Search for Information: From Secrecy and Anonymity to Openness* (Abingdon, Routledge, 2017) 193.

interests of both children and adults involved. The Discussion Paper does not appear to be prompted by children's rights concerns but rather by an acceptance that donor anonymity is now threatened by the widespread availability of DNA testing.[111] Therefore, the underlying presumption that parental discretion should guide the question of disclosure has not been questioned.

Notwithstanding this, while moral and legal obligations to disclose have not been suggested by the HFEA, there appears to be support for openness during childhood. The Discussion Paper includes the following underlying principle: 'It is important for children to know, at an early age, of their donor conceived origins. Patients should continue to be encouraged and prepared to be open with their children about how they were conceived.'[112] Thus, four options for a new model are provided: (i) status quo plus; (ii) early identification by consent; (iii) complete removal of anonymity; and (iv) a double-track system.[113] First, 'status quo plus' would involve maintaining the current system, whereby individuals can find out identifying information about their donor at age 18, but the 1990 Act would be amended to require clinics to inform donors and recipients about the risk that children may find out the donor's identity before they are 18.[114] Second, 'early identification by consent' would involve a voluntary system allowing donors to opt to become identifiable, either at the outset or at any time before the child turns 18 with the consent of the parents, or with the consent of the child after a certain age.[115] Third, 'complete removal of anonymity' would mean that donors' details would be made identifiable to parents from birth or before.[116] Finally, a 'double-track system' would mean that donors could choose between the 'status quo plus' (being identifiable at 18) and a model involving identification of donors from the outset.[117]

As noted above, a model that allows access to information only at age 18 is not based on respect for children's autonomy or their right to identity, since such a system is concerned with the rights of donor-conceived adults. Instead, a children's

[111] See the comments of the HFEA's Chief Executive, Peter Thompson, in H Devlin, 'UK Fertility Watchdog Could Recommend Scrapping Donor Anonymity Law' *The Guardian* (20 May 2022) a www.theguardian.com/society/2022/may/20/uk-fertility-watchdog-could-recommend-scrapping-donor-anonymity-law: 'You can see a position in the future where confidentiality just becomes impossible, whatever the attitude of families, the honest truth is that people will just find out.'; and 'We feel that the technology of cheap DNA test throws into questions the underlying assumption [of anonymity] …'.

[112] HFEA Discussion Paper (n 109) para 27.

[113] *Building Families Through Surrogacy* (n 54) para 13.156, recommends access to the Surrogacy Register at 16 for non-identifying information and 18 for identifying information (16 in Scotland), with access permitted before this in the case of *Gillick* competency/capacity. See *Gillick v West Norfolk and Wisbech Area Health Authority* [1986] AC 112.

[114] HFEA Discussion Paper (n 109) para 30 (a).

[115] ibid para 30 (b). The Paper states that information could be accessible with the consent of the parent or 'consent varied by the child after a certain age'.

[116] ibid para 30 (c).

[117] ibid para 30 (d). The term 'outset' would be defined in legislation. Possible meanings given in para 30 (c) include: from the time of considering donors; after selecting a specific donor; when treatment commences; upon pregnancy; or birth.

rights-based approach to disclosure would require a system where it is possible to access information during childhood. Such a system would enable children 'to incorporate donor conception into their sense of identity, rather than requiring adjustments to their sense of self at a later time'.[118] This is supported by studies that have shown that disclosure at a young age is beneficial.[119] This would be possible with both the 'early identification by consent' and the 'complete removal of anonymity' models. These suggested options come closer to a children's rights-based model, as they both recognise that children may attach importance to this information during childhood. However, in the 'early identification by consent' model, it appears that information can be released solely based on parental consent; and in the 'complete removal of anonymity' model, parents would have access to the information when the child is born or beforehand. A distinct approach would be needed to ensure a participatory model. Participation under Article 12 UNCRC involves 'information-sharing' and 'dialogue' between children and adults, where their views are taken into account and shape the outcome of decision-making.[120] This would require a process allowing for origin information to be released on the basis of both parental and child consent or assent. For example, parents could have conversations with their children about the manner of their conception, as well as the fact that information is available from a young age. If the child feels ready to access this information, it could be applied for.[121] The child, with the support of their parents, could also decide the nature of the information received, such as identifying or non-identifying information.[122] Another issue is whether a child could access information without parental consent: one of the authors has argued that this could be permissible for a *Gillick*-competent child after application to a committee, given that children with such competency can consent to serious medical treatment.[123]

[118] Wade (n 9) 746, citing J Benward, 'Identity Development in the Donor-Conceived' in J Guichon, I Mitchell and M Giroux (eds), *The Right to Know One's Origins: Assisted Reproduction and the Best Interests of Children* (Brussels, Academic and Scientific Publishers, 2012) 175. See HFEA recommendations: 'Talk to your child about their origins' (Human Fertilisation and Embryology Authority, 2023) at www.hfea.gov.uk/donation/donor-conceived-people-and-their-parents/talk-to-your-child-about-their-origins/.

[119] See T Freeman and S Golombok, 'Donor Insemination: A Follow-up Study of Disclosure Decisions, Family Relationships and Child Adjustment at Adolescence' (2012) 25(2) *Reproductive BioMedicine Online* 193; V Jadva et al, 'The Experiences of Adolescents and Adults Conceived by Sperm Donation: Comparisons by Age of Disclosure and Family Type' (2009) 24(8) *Human Reproduction* 1909.

[120] General Comment No 12 (n 8) para 3.

[121] The Discussion Paper noted the administrative burdens this would place on clinics and the HFEA, and questioned whether the HFEA is the right body to undertake such tasks, see: HFEA Discussion Paper (n 109), Appendix, 11. This is not to argue that known donation is not a children's rights complaint. Where information is held by the state, the above participatory approach is preferable, but where the donor information is known by parents, children should also guide the introduction of donor information.

[122] Access rights for children of donors and surrogates to find out about other children born as a result of their parents' donation or surrogacy arrangement would also have to be considered: see ibid, Appendix, 10. Full consideration of these issues is outside the scope of this chapter.

[123] See Wade (n 9) 750.

We support a system whereby origin information is accessible to parents and children during childhood and can be accessed with the consent/assent of both. This system should be in place for gamete donation, mitochondrial donation and surrogacy.[124] We do not support a system that restricts access to information until the person is 18, nor do we support a 'double-track system' by which some children have access to information during their childhood and some when they are 18.[125] This is due to the overarching argument that there should be consistency in the protection of children's autonomy and their right to identity, in line with the principle of non-discrimination under Article 2 UNCRC.

Before concluding the chapter, we will briefly consider the potential implications of some novel reproductive technologies.

VI. Novel Reproductive Technologies

Novel assisted reproductive technologies will inevitably raise new legal challenges. This section will briefly consider two such technologies: uterine transplantation (UtX); and in vitro-derived gametes (IVG).[126] UtX involves the transplantation of a healthy uterus into a recipient to achieve pregnancy,[127] that is through the donation of an organ to aid reproduction, which raises a new question: should the identity of the person who donated the organ be identifiable? IVG involves the creation of gametes in vitro from various sources, including embryonic stem cells, germline stem cells, haploidisation and pluripotent stem cells.[128] It could be used to produce gametes for egg and sperm banks, to allow individuals to create gametes from their own cells (single parenthood), and to allow same-sex couples to have a genetically related child without a donor, because a female could produce a sperm and a man could produce an egg.[129] These potential uses of the technology

[124] We acknowledge that in most domestic arrangements organised by surrogacy organisations, the surrogate's identity is known to the family. Nonetheless, such children may also be interested in information regarding her genetic contribution, if relevant, or information about intended parents, if a parental order was not made.

[125] Human Fertilisation and Embryology Authority Legislative Reform Advisory Group, *Meeting Notes* (LRAG, 27 May 2022) reported consensus among members for the 'double-track' model.

[126] Ectogenesis is not considered in this section because that technology alters the process of gestation (with some of the process potentially taking place outside the human body) and therefore would not necessarily have an impact upon origin information.

[127] See, eg, L O'Donovan, N Williams and S Wilkinson, 'Ethical and Policy Issues Raised by Uterus Transplants' (2019) 131(1) *British Medical Bulletin* 19; L Johannesson and S Jarvholm, 'Uterus Transplantation: Current Progress and Future Prospects' (2016) 8(1) *International Journal of Women's Health* 43.

[128] See S Hendricks et al, 'Artificial Gametes: A Systematic Review of Biological Progress Towards Clinical Application' (2015) 21(3) *Human Reproduction Update* 285, as cited in A Smajdor, 'Article Gametes: Background Paper' (London, Nuffield Council of Bioethics, 2015) for the different ways in which gametes can be created.

[129] Smajdor (n 128) 8–11.

raise different questions; if IVGs were used for same-sex reproduction without a donor, Newson and Smajdor have asked whether being genetically related to two parents of the same sex would alter the experience of childhood. and whether the man whose genetic material is contained in the egg should be legally recognised as a 'biological mother'.[130] If IVGs were used to allow for single parenthood, the resulting child would be born with no second genetic parent, which, as Cutas and Smajdor note, creates a unique situation for the child, having no second 'genetic family thread to which they can relate'.[131] Such IVGs could also allow for 'multiplex parenting', through a process by which an embryo is created that has four or more genetic contributors.[132] This is described as follows:

> [T]wo embryos would be generated from either couple through IVF with either naturally or in vitro generated gametes. [Human embryonic stem cell] lines would be then established from both embryos and differentiated into IVG to be used in a second round of IVF. The resulting embryo would be genetically related to all four prospective parents, who would technically be the child's genetic grandparents.[133]

This would clearly challenge the current legal and societal understandings of parenthood and, as Smajdor has noted, some might argue that that could cause confusion for children who are born through this process.[134] Finally, if embryonic stem cell-derived gametes were used, some scholars have questioned whether the 'parent' of the gametes would be the cloned embryo that was used to produce them.[135] Smajdor has noted the potential psychological impacts for children of knowing that their 'parent' was destroyed in the process of their creation.[136]

This brief discussion illustrates that the ethical questions raised by novel technologies are complex.[137] Therefore, for the purposes of this chapter, our proposals for reform focus only upon the currently regulated reproductive technologies, though we note that emerging technologies are likely to present future challenges for the law relating to origin information. Ultimately, it would be beneficial for any reformed regime to be able to respond dynamically to novel reproductive technologies.

[130] A Newson and A Smajdor, 'Artificial Gametes: New Paths to Parenthood?' (2005) 31(3) *Journal of Medical Ethics* 184, 186.

[131] D Cutas and A Smajdor, '"I am Your Mother and Your Father!" In Vitro Derived Gametes and the Ethics of Solo Reproduction' (2017) 25(4) *Health Care Analysis* 354, 364.

[132] C Palacios-González, J Harris and G Testa, 'Multiplex Parenting: IVG and the Generations to Come' (2014) 40(11) *Journal of Medical Ethics* 752.

[133] ibid 756.

[134] Smajdor (n 128) 13.

[135] See H Mertes and G Pennings, 'Embryonic Stem Cell-Derived Gametes and Genetic Parenthood: A Problematic Relationship' (2008) 17(1) *Cambridge Quarterly of Healthcare Ethics* 7, who argue that this technique does not lead to genetic parenthood.

[136] Smajdor (n 128) 13.

[137] ibid 12. These include concerns regarding the potential for genetic abnormalities.

VII. Conclusion

In this chapter, we have proposed reforms to the legal framework for origin information in assisted reproduction. To underpin this, we have adopted a children's rights-based approach, emphasising the importance of protecting and promoting children's rights in relation to their identity and their developing autonomy. We have shown that the current law adopts an inconsistent approach to such origin information across different reproductive contexts, including: gamete donation; surrogacy arrangements; and mitochondrial donation. We have highlighted how the legal framework is not premised upon a children's rights-based approach but instead generally reflects the interests of the adults involved in the reproductive processes. We have argued that the inconsistencies in the current law should be remedied through the creation of an overarching system for origin information across these reproductive contexts. To that end, we have proposed a national registry for the collection and retention of origin information in assisted reproduction, to be maintained by the HFEA. This proposal would result in the collection of information in a wider range of circumstances than is currently the case, including information about genetic, gestational and 'intention-based' origins, as well as information about gamete donors, surrogates, intended parents and mitochondrial donors. Relatedly, we have proposed that the law concerning the disclosure of origin information should be reformed to better protect the developing autonomy and identity rights of children born through assisted reproduction. On balance, mandatory disclosure of information that has the potential to be important for a child's identity is more appropriate in protecting the autonomy and identity of children than a system governed by parental discretion. Finally, a model of disclosure should be introduced that allows access to information during childhood, with the consent of parents and the consent/assent of children based on a process of open dialogue during childhood.

Overall, we argue that our suggested reforms will provide a comprehensive system for the collection, retention and disclosure of origin information in cases involving assisted reproduction, and that this reformed system will better respect the rights of those children born through assisted reproduction than the current legal framework.

Response to Chapter 3

Reform of the Legal Framework for Origin Information in Assisted Reproduction

KIRSTY HORSEY

I. Introduction

Alan Brown and Katherine Wade contend that the UK's existing legal framework regarding origin information (including the collection, retention and disclosure of such information) for those conceived through reproductive technologies should be reformed. Their position is that the current provisions are inconsistent and incoherent, lacking 'principled, normative justifications, focusing upon protecting children's right to identity and respecting their developing autonomy'.

In accordance with their children's rights-based analysis,[1] Brown and Wade propose that a consistent approach should be adopted for the collection, retention and disclosure of origin information across different forms of assisted reproduction; that origin information be collected and held in a wider range of circumstances than is the case now; and mandatory disclosure of such information. They apply this to children conceived via gamete donation or surrogacy, as well as – more controversially – to those born following mitochondrial donation. This response considers and reflects on three things that may cause us to question aspects of Brown and Wade's proposal, as well as some other broader points. Specifically, it is arguable that the proposal raises potential issues related to privacy and practicalities, and risks (over-) geneticisation of familial relationships. First, some comment generally on state interference in families in the context of origin information.

[1] And presumably supported by others who favour an approach under the 1989 United Nations Convention on the Rights of the Child (UNCRC), with a particular interpretation of Art 7, which provides that '[e]very child has the right to be registered at birth … and, as far as possible, to know and be cared for by their parents' and Art 8, which requires States Parties to 'respect the right of the child to preserve his or her identity, including nationality, name and family relations as recognised by law without unlawful interference'. See also similar considerations regarding a child's interest in discovering the identity of their genetic parent under Art 8(1) of the European Convention on Human Rights (the right to respect for private and family life), as in *Mikulic v Croatia* App no 53176/99 [2002] FCR 720.

II. State Interference in Families and Origin Information

It is broadly acceptable that the kinds of origin information that Brown and Wade discuss should be *available* to the people who want it. It is undeniable that some people might want/would be curious about it – or even place great importance on it – not only in a medical context, but also in terms of their self-identity. It is also a fact that there is no consistency about the type, amount and quality of origin information held about children born from the various assisted reproductive techniques we are concerned with here.[2]

In their 2019 consultation on surrogacy, the Law Commission of England and Wales and the Scottish Law Commission identified that it is somewhat anomalous that access to information about a surrogate who has used her own egg is not covered by the current rules on disclosure of donor information.[3] Neither is the law sufficiently clear about who can have access to exactly what information and in what situation in the context of different types of surrogacy arrangements. Consequently, there are certainly reforms that ought to occur. However, we must also note that the background reality is that many private or 'do-it-yourself' sperm donation and traditional[4] surrogacy arrangements occur, where no information is required to be collected and stored at all (other than the name of the birth parent required to register the birth).[5] Additionally, there will be overseas surrogacy arrangements or other procedures using donated gametes, where some origin information is unlikely to be available. Indeed, some people purposely travel to overseas destinations specifically to use anonymously donated gametes.

What is less clear than the idea of the *availability* of origin information (if obtained) is that the *disclosure* of such information as is collected and stored should be the mandate of the state. We must decide what value we place on identity/origin information (as compared with other information, such as medical histories), with full consideration of what identity 'means' (and whether it means different things to different people, depending on their circumstances). As the Law Commission of England and Wales explained when not taking forward a project on the reform of birth registration in its last programme of reform, if such a project *were* to be undertaken, a key consideration would be the 'fundamental questions of for what reason and for whose benefit the record is kept'.[6]

[2] As identified by, eg, N Tohme et al, 'A comparative study of sperm and egg donors' personal descriptions and goodwill messages' (2024) 48(1) *Reproductive Biomedicine Online* 1.

[3] *Building Families Through Surrogacy: A New Law* (Law Com No 244 and Scot Law Com No 167, 2019) para 10.60.

[4] In which the surrogate uses her own egg, usually involving home insemination.

[5] Births and Deaths Registrations Act 1953, s 10.

[6] Law Commission of England and Wales, *Thirteenth Programme of Law Reform* (Law Com Consultation Paper No 377) para 4.5.

Years ago, Carol Smart questioned the 'assumption that [a child] has a need to know her origin' and the 'certainty that scientifically based knowledge/truth is best', especially since 'earlier generations were just as certain that a child's welfare would be best protected if she was raised in ignorance'.[7] We must be mindful of proceeding on the basis of such changed assumptions, without first really and deeply investigating what it is that people want – or think that they want – and why they want it, or substituting views of adults for the supposed views of children.[8] There is a potential danger that the narrative underpinning such a proposal is driven by particular voices, with particular stories and (negative) experiences of finding out about their origins, often at an extreme and unusual end of the scale.[9] We also know that sometimes it can be in a child's best interests *not to know* of their (genetic) origins. For example, various cases have found, with reference to the UNCRC, that all children have the 'right to know the truth', unless this is outweighed by any considerations for their welfare.[10]

We must take care that access to origin information is not posed as a utopian ideal, where everyone having children via assisted reproduction is (or should be) comfortable with it and ready for all that it brings, puts the correct information on the correct forms, etc. We know from the consent form issues that resulted in dozens of cases a few years ago, where consent was at issue and had affected the legal parenthood situation, that this is not always the case.[11] For one thing, access to all origin information is not the case in 'normal' reproduction. Furthermore, people, relationships and families are complicated – particularly in this area, where there may already be a lot of hurt and sensitivity (including cultural sensitivity) about how people have arrived at requiring help to have a child. People and families are also very *different*: if an interviewer asked people (even children) 'Who is part of your family?', or 'Who do you feel a connection with?', or even 'Who would you like to know more about?', it can be presumed that those questions would generate enormously varying answers.[12] As one example, Children's Voices in Surrogacy Law shows that different children – even those with some

[7] C Smart, *Personal Life* (Cambridge, Polity Press, 2007) 125.

[8] As identified by Jane Fortin in 'Children's right to know their origins – too far, too fast?' (2009) 21(3) *Child and Family Law Quarterly* 336, questioning her own previous position on knowledge of one's (genetic) origins as stated in J Fortin, 'Re F: "The Gooseberry Bush Approach"' (1994) 57(2) *Modern Law Review* 296.

[9] eg, *Rose v Secretary of State for Health and Human Fertilisation and Embryology Authority* [2002] EWHC 1593 (Admin).

[10] Such as *Re H (Paternity: Blood Tests)* [2001] 2 FLR 65. See also *Re D (Paternity)* [2007] 2 FLR 26; and *Re J (Paternity: Welfare of Child)* [2007] 1 FLR 1064.

[11] See, eg, *In the matter of the Human Fertilisation and Embryology Act 2008 (Case K)* [2017] EWHC 50 (Fam), the twenty-fourth case of many to arise – appropriate consent forms in each of the cases had either been lost or were not the consent forms mandated for use by the Human Fertilisation and Embryology Authority under the 2008 Act.

[12] See, for a recent example of a situation generating very complicated familial relationships, *A v B & Ors* [2023] EWHC 1680 (Fam).

shared experiences – appear to attach different weights to genetic and origin information, and disclosure thereof.[13]

III. Privacy

Privacy-based responses to contributions such as Brown and Wade's are well-rehearsed. Therefore, much of what is here is about playing devil's advocate and questioning some assumptions. Brown and Wade's argument is based on children's rights, as derived from the UNCRC (or interpretations of it) – and there is obviously something in this. We also know that adults have rights, including the right to respect for private and family life as guaranteed under Article 8 of the European Convention on Human Rights. Is it the case that children's rights *necessarily* trump adults' rights? It is not just information about the children's origins that is being given, but also what is often very personal information about their parents.

Talking about privacy usually means engaging in some kind of balancing exercise. Children have the right to private and family life, too – is there not at least a question that providing information could disrupt what is otherwise a perfectly happy and stable family? And for what? Individual family circumstances can generate competing rights, not only between different parties but also as regards the interests of a single child.[14] On this basis, it is evidently arguable that there should be no mandatory origins information disclosure, or automatic disclosure by the state, even if there is agreement that all of the information that Brown and Wade propose should be recorded is available. Within this may be what could be called cultural arguments – for example, it is still the case that for some cultures or religions the use of donor gametes is sacrosanct, or that to have a child when unmarried has social consequences.[15]

IV. Three Practicalities

A. Telling

As is currently the case, unless automatic disclosure (either of the fact that information is held, or of the information itself) is mandated, the argument rests on parents telling their children about the way in which they were conceived. This

[13] See K Wade, K Horsey and Z Mahmoud, 'Children's Voices in Surrogacy Law: Phase One Preliminary Report' (Leicester, University of Leicester, January 2023); and K Wade, K Horsey and Z Mahmoud, 'Children's Voices in Surrogacy Law: Phase Two Preliminary Report' (Leicester, University of Leicester, April 2023).

[14] See discussion in Fortin (n 8) 345–46.

[15] R Lamont, *Family Law*, 2nd edn (Oxford, Oxford University Press, 2022) 329.

means – as now – that children born outside the heteronormative nuclear family form are at an advantage, as it will be self-evident that a third party (at least) will have been involved in their conception.

We probably all agree that telling the truth about how someone was born – and being open from a young age, as research in adoption, donor conception and surrogacy shows – is a good thing in most circumstances.[16] Research on surrogacy shows a slightly higher level of telling and intending to tell – and at a younger age – among those who had undertaken surrogacy domestically, compared to those who went overseas. There was also a difference (especially in the 'intending to tell' category where telling had not yet taken place) between married heterosexual couples (who were less likely to have told) and other parents.[17] The Law Commissions' consultation on surrogacy highlighted research showing that even where there is telling about the surrogacy and/or the surrogate, children may still not be told if an egg donor is also used. What this, and broader research on disclosure more generally, evidences is the need for more work on telling and supporting people to tell, but not that mandatory disclosure – or even 'nudge disclosure' – would be a good idea.

B. Private/ DIY Arrangements

As well as the issues raised by DIY arrangements noted in section II, children conceived in heterosexual relationships using donated sperm (including for surrogacy) *outside of a clinical context* are not captured by this proposal, and nor can they be. Therefore, this proposal results in a two-tier system (at least), with one group disadvantaged in informational terms compared to the other, almost a mirror image of the problem the proposal is trying to solve. What, if anything, can be done about this?

C. Comparisons

By extension, what about 'normal' conception families where there has been, for example, an extramarital affair, deception or children born to a single mother who 'just got pregnant'? Do we not risk a Jeremy Kyle-type situation where, if everyone *should* know their origins, then direct-to-consumer genetic testing (DTCGT) is

[16] Which is why these norms have found their way into policy and law: see Adoption and Children Act 2002, ss 56–65; Human Fertilisation and Embryology Authority (Disclosure of Donor Information) Regulations (SI 2004/1511), reg 2(2) and (3); Law Commission and Scottish Law Commission, *Building Families Through Surrogacy: A New Law*, vol II: *Full Report* (Law Com No 411, Scot Law Com No 262, 2023) ch 13.

[17] K Horsey et al, 'Surrogacy in the UK: Myth busting and reform', Report of the Surrogacy UK Working Group on Surrogacy Law Reform (Surrogacy UK, November 2015) at kar.kent.ac.uk/59740/.

going to drive this (and is indeed already having an effect in the donor-conceived world)? This could potentially *harm* children and families (while making vast amounts of profit for testing companies).

V. Over-Geneticising

The rise of DTCGT and ancestry tracing services arguably drove the understanding that genetic testing could/should be used to, for example, establish paternity where that is contested – including in the context of the Government's earlier drive to make sure that men, especially unmarried fathers, paid child maintenance. The availability of these services marked a cultural shift in terms of potential knowledge about origins, which filtered into discussions about children conceived by assisted reproduction.[18] As Freeman and Richards noted, commonly held beliefs that 'biological origins are a significant determinant of identity and kin relationships' were given new credence by our 'entrance into the new genetic era, marked by the Human Genome Project'.[19] This does not make it fact, and the idea that genetic relatedness is so important should be robustly questioned before such heightened assumptions drive us to change law and practice.[20] This is particularly the case in a context where the law has deliberately and rightly recognised the social aspects of parenthood in contexts such as gamete donation and, to an extent, surrogacy.[21]

Of course, well-established research indicates that it can be psychologically damaging for adopted children to learn late in life that they are adopted – and similarly in relation to donor conception.[22] It is perhaps inevitable that we reason by analogy that everyone should learn the 'truth' about who our parents are (or our genetic origins), whether or not we were adopted, donor conceived or born through surrogacy. However, questioning what this 'truth' means and its assumed importance significantly overlaps with the 'telling' issue. Where telling and knowledge of the manner of conception is the norm from a young age, such psychological issues are likely to be far less prevalent as the situation is normalised. This does not automatically translate to the right to know *who* (all) the people involved in one's conception were. It does translate to educating and counselling fertility patients,

[18] Fortin (n 8) 342–43.

[19] T Freeman and M Richards, 'DNA Testing and Kinship; Paternity, Genealogy and the Search for the "Truth" of our Genetic Origins' in F Ebtehaj, B Lindley and M Richards (eds), *Kinship Matters* (Oxford, Hart Publishing, 2006) 67, 79.

[20] Though see F Darroch and I Smith, 'Establishing Identity: How Direct-to-Consumer Genetic Testing Challenges the Assumption of Donor Anonymity' (2021) 59(1) *Family Court Review* 103.

[21] With the potential for such relationships to be increasingly recognised in surrogacy, should the Law Commissions' proposal for a new 'pathway to parenthood' ever become law. As Brown and Wade note, this would be accompanied by a new surrogacy register (akin to the current donation register) though, as noted, not all surrogacy arrangements will be (able to be) captured.

[22] Rose (n 9).

parents and even children at school, in the context of relationships and sex education, that telling and openness is best.[23]

In particular, over-geneticising origin information is relevant to mitochondrial donation. Even the terminology is somewhat controversial here – by including this technique with other reproductive technologies, Brown and Wade adopt a particular position. There is considerable irony in Brown and Wade's argument about recording mitochondrial donors because of the over-geneticisation we already see as regards *nuclear* DNA. Others view mitochondrial donation (where there is no inheritance of nuclear DNA) more as a medical treatment that relies on IVF for its performance than a reproductive technology per se, and more like other tissue donation (including blood, bone marrow or even stem cells) or organ donation. That is, as the solution to a medical problem, geared not towards creating a child for someone who could not otherwise have one, but rather to allow for the birth of a *healthy* (or unaffected) child. Recording the mitochondrial donor, other than as a medical record, would double down on (over-) geneticisation[24] and play into the hands of the tabloid-style 'three-parent children' headlines prevalent during parliamentary debates.[25]

VI. Conclusion

This response is not to dismiss Brown and Wade's calls for better collection, retention and availability of origin information, or the need to encourage telling. Indeed, it may be that origin information is potentially important in developing a sense of narrative identity throughout a child's life and as they develop into adulthood. However, there is much to be worked out first. The fact that – as the authors concede – this information is *potentially* important to some does not indicate mandatory or automatic disclosure to all, particularly as it may be *unimportant* to some and create conflicts of rights for, and with, others. Beyond privacy issues,

[23] This would also be the position of support organisations like the Donor Conception Network (dcnetwork.org/) and, as the authors identify, the Human Fertilisation and Embryology Authority. One interesting and perceptive observation from a young person involved in Children's Voices in Surrogacy Law (n 13) was that 'in an ideal situation [children] should be told as soon as possible, like, there shouldn't be a kind of sit down "OK, here is how you came to be." It just should, kind of, always be a known thing.' Another put forward the idea of 'drip feeding' the information to 'normalise' it: see Phase 1 report, 23.

[24] This would be even more so in the context of future potential reproductive technologies, such as in vitro gametogenesis (IVG) and UTx (uterine transplant following donation), where what we are talking about is the donation of a body part or somatic cell.

[25] In its review of the techniques conducted prior to their being allowed in law, the Nuffield Council on Bioethics said 'mitochondrial donation does not indicate, either biologically or legally, any notion of the child having either a "third parent", or "second mother"' and that a 'donor of mitochondria should not have the same status in regulation as a reproductive egg or embryo donor in all aspects'. See Nuffield Council on Bioethics, *Novel Techniques for the Prevention of Mitochondrial DNA Disorders: An Ethical Review* (London, Nuffield Council on Bioethics, 2012) xvi.

there are practical problems raising issues of equity when the children discussed here are compared with others. Finally, over-geneticisation must be considered. In working through all this, I agree with the authors that a participatory approach to any new regulatory scheme would be best. We cannot assume what children's views on what information should be available to them will be – so we should ask them.

4

Grandparents and Kinship Carers Act or Granny 'Annex'? Waiting for the Government

SAMANTHA DAVEY*

I. Introduction

Millions of children form significant, beneficial, emotional attachments to a range of individuals within the family, in addition to (or instead of) their parents. Aunts and uncles, brothers and sisters, cousins, step-parents, grandparents and others have differing roles to play, depending on the specific family circumstances. Relatives, such as grandparents, may become kinship carers (a last port of call before children are removed into the care of state) or have subsidiary (but still significant) responsibilities in children's lives via regular contact. This chapter seeks to explore the limiting, and outdated, aspects of the Children Act 1989, such as the provisions on the welfare checklist,[1] parental responsibility[2] and the need for most grandparents to obtain leave[3] before commencing legal proceedings. Sections 1, 3 and 10, in their current form, are non-inclusive, outdated and do not fit in well with subsequent child law statutes, such as the Adoption and Children Act 2002.[4] This chapter explores whether comprehensive legal reform is needed of both the private and public law aspects of the 1989 Act, or whether legislative reform is best focused on a few discrete elements, such as an amendment or 'annex' to the presumption of parental involvement to extend to other important relationships and/or the need for non-parental figures typically to seek 'leave' from the court to apply for court orders.

* I am grateful for the assistance of Charlotte Bendall, Rehana Parveen and Sharon Thompson from the Family Law Reform Now project. I would like to give thanks to colleagues who provided me with feedback on this chapter. I would also like to thank Audrey Guinchard, Felicity Kaganas, Sabine Michalowski, Nausica Palazzo, Matt Stone and Maurice Sunkin.

[1] Children Act 1989, s 1(3).

[2] ibid s 3.

[3] ibid s 10.

[4] The core Act of Parliament in England and Wales that pertains to adoption proceedings.

The focus of this chapter is on grandparents, since research demonstrates that it is largely grandparents who take on the responsibility as kinship carers.[5] Disputes between parental and non-parental figures, due to breakdown in contact, often occur between grandparents and parents. Moreover, most academic and political discussion in this sphere has focused on grandparents, rather than relationships between children and other attachment figures. While this chapter will focus on the challenges faced by grandparents, these challenges can be seen as representative of the hurdles faced by other attachment figures in a child's life, in the face of a framework that does not comfortably reflect the complexity of the twenty-first-century family. Many of the points made within this chapter will focus on increasing legal protection for all family forms, via considering the example of grandparent/grandchild relationships. It is important to realise that there are positive and empowering relationships between children and attachment figures, within a familial setting, which may warrant increased recognition and protection via suitable legal frameworks.

Although grandparents have long had importance to children and parents, changes such as increased rates of divorce mean that it is common for relationships between grandparents and grandchildren to become fractured. It is also not uncommon for parents to remarry, and children may become part of reconstituted family units. This means that children may lose out on vitally important support links, despite developing and maintaining new relationships with step-parents and step-siblings. The fact is that many children are experiencing greater diversity in family forms in the twenty-first century. Yet, despite the importance grandparents have, they often lack the 'tools' to protect the welfare of their grandchildren, including the continued enjoyment of mutually supportive relationships. It is argued that legal reform to protect relationships such as those between the grandparent and grandchild is needed to reflect social changes that have already occurred. This chapter is distinct from other work exploring the relationship between grandparents and grandchildren, since it ultimately suggests 'holistic' statutory reforms to aspects of private and public law, within the Children Act 1989, which may improve the protection of relationships that have a significant, positive impact on children's lives.

II. The Twenty-First-Century Shift in Family Patterns: The Increasing Role of Grandparents in Children's Lives

The Children Act 1989 is an important, comprehensive legal document that has, in many ways, stood the test of time. It is a broad piece of legislation that covers a

[5] I Zuchowski et al, 'Convenient Yet Neglected: The Role of Grandparent Kinship Carers' (2019) 49(3) *The British Journal of Social Work* 615.

myriad of issues pertaining to public and private law matters. It is, however, over 30 years of age at the time of writing, and has been amended several times including vis-à-vis the Adoption and Children Act 2002 and the Children and Families Act 2014. This chapter identifies specific aspects of the Children Act 1989 that could be reformed, which have not been identified within the existing academic literature. Further reform to the Children Act 1989 is required because of the distinct shifts in family patterns during the twenty-first century that have not been reflected in these amendments. Clarke and Roberts suggested back in 2002 that 'demographic, social and economic changes have affected the living arrangements and family experiences of both parents and children'.[6] Over 20 years later, there have been greater shifts in living arrangements and family forms. However, despite this increased diversity in family forms, successive governments' reform agendas have suffered from tunnel vision. According to Brown, most legal reform and changes in social 'norms' have centred around the 'nuclear' family,[7] rather than an extended family model of care provision. This is despite the fact that, arguably, '[the] nuclear family is only sustainable with the support of the wider family around it'.[8] In fact, grandparents have prominence in twenty-first-century western family life,[9] and provide a range of 'inter-generational transfers'.[10] These include money,[11] time[12] via childcare while both parents work,[13] and moral and practical support, especially in single-parent families.[14] Grandparents, in particular, perform important functions for many children living with their parents, as providers of care[15] and mentors.[16] Grandparents may also intervene where a child is at risk of significant harm and, in circumstances where children cannot remain with their parents, may step in as alternative carers.

[6] L Clarke and C Roberts, 'Policy and rhetoric: The growing interest in fathers and grandparents in Britain' in A Carling, S Duncan and R Edwards (eds), *Analysing Families: Morality and Rationality in Policy and Practice* (London, Routledge, 2002) 164.

[7] A Brown, *What is the Family of Law? The Influence of the Nuclear Family* (Oxford, Hart Publishing, 2020).

[8] Grandparents Plus, *Rethinking Family Life: exploring the role of grandparents and the wider family* (London, Grandparents Plus, 2009) 2.

[9] A Buchanan and A Rotkirch, 'Twenty-first century grandparents: global perspectives on changing roles and consequences' (2018) 13 *Contemporary Social Science* 131.

[10] DA Coall et al, 'Interdisciplinary perspectives on grandparental investment: a journal towards causality' (2018) 13 *Contemporary Social Science* 159, 162.

[11] Grandparents Plus (n 8) 4.

[12] Coall et al (n 10) 159.

[13] J Wheelock and K Jones, 'Grandparents Are the Next Best Thing: Informal Childcare for Working Parents in Urban Britain' (2002) 31 *Journal of Social Policy* 441.

[14] S Harper and I Ruicheva, 'Grandmothers as Replacement Parents and Partners: The Role of Grandmotherhood in Single Parent Families' (2010) 8 *Journal of Intergenerational Relationships* 219.

[15] G Di Gessa, K Glaser and P Zaninotto, 'Is grandparental childcare socio-economically patterned? Evidence from the English longitudinal study of ageing' (2022) 19 *European Journal of Ageing* 763.

[16] J Michalek-Kwiecieńn, 'The Mentoring Relationship with the Closest Grandparent and Identity Processes Among Emerging Adult Grandchildren in Poland: The Role of Perceived Grandparents' Perspective Taking' (2022) 30(3) *Journal of Adult Development* 279.

Herring and Choudhry noted that, despite the increased significance of grandparents, it is 'surprising'[17] that grandparents have no special status. They describe it as an 'uphill task'[18] for grandparents to argue their case in the context of private law proceedings. In contrast, Douglas argued that there is insufficient 'evidence' to support providing grandparents with 'special status'.[19] Regardless of one's perspective on whether grandparents ought to be afforded 'special status', the loss of grandparent relationships may detrimentally affect children's welfare. When grandparents are denied contact with their grandchildren, the effect on the children themselves can be harmful. Nigel Huddleston MP has observed:

> Large numbers of children in family breakdowns are left very sad and confused about the sudden loss of contact with their grandparents, which in many cases goes completely and utterly unexplained. The children are then left feeling that they have been unloved by their grandparents or believe that their grandparents simply did not want to see them anymore.[20]

Similarly, the loss of these relationships, in the wake of breakdown in grandparent/parent relationships, is harmful to grandparents themselves. The position has been summarised by Huddleston:

> [T]he family dynamic that is all too often overlooked is that between grandparents and their grandchildren. When access to grandchildren is blocked, some grandparents call it a kind of living bereavement. Unlike some other countries, grandparents in the UK have no automatic rights to see their grandchildren, and vice versa.[21]

Despite the importance of the grandparent/grandchild relationship to many children, especially as regards those grandparents who act as permanent carers for their grandchildren, English and Welsh law does not recognise or protect the status of grandparents, and aspects of the Children Act 1989, such as sections 1, 3 and 10, can be argued as non-inclusive in the twenty-first century. Unfortunately, this law has often been slow to recognise and protect the existence of certain family forms. Lesbian and gay couples, for instance, have in the past faced difficulty in having important aspects of identity[22] and relationships acknowledged and protected due to a lack of 'inclusivity' in the law. They have struggled to be recognised within legal frameworks, first as couples[23] and then as parents.[24] Hayward, in chapter 9

[17] S Choudhry and J Herring, *European Human Rights and Family Law* (Oxford, Hart Publishing, 2010) 271.

[18] ibid.

[19] G Douglas, 'Re J (Leave to Issue Application for Residence Order) – Recognising grandparents' concern or controlling their interference?' (2003) 15(1) *Child and Family Law Quarterly* 103, 103.

[20] HC Deb 2 May 2018, vol 640, col 171WH.

[21] ibid col 170WH.

[22] N Hudson-Sharp and H Metcalf, *Inequality among lesbian, gay, bisexual and transgender groups in the UK: a review of evidence* (London, NIESR, 2016).

[23] C Bendall, 'A "divorce blueprint"? The use of heteronormative strategies in addressing financial remedies on same sex partnership dissolution' (2016) 31(2) *Canadian Journal of Law and Society* 267.

[24] A Tryfonidou, 'The parenting rights of same-sex couples under European law' (2020) 25(2) *Marriages, Families and Spirituality* 176.

in this volume, has considered similar challenges faced by cohabiting couples due to differential treatment, following family breakdown, when compared to married couples. While gay and lesbian families struggled to be acknowledged due to prejudice, grandparents face a similar quandary. The lack of legal recognition that they face stems from poor social awareness of their importance and because the law has not 'kept up' with social norms. While the dilemmas suffered by gay and lesbian families are distinct, grandparents and other kinship carers likewise suffer from a lack of legal protection. The law fails to provide the 'recognition', or the 'tools' needed to protect the grandparent/grandchild relationship (while simultaneously acknowledging the need to protect children from the risk of significant harm).

III. Consensus on the Need to Protect Children's Relationships with their Grandparents

There are few empirical UK-based studies on the grandparent/grandchild relationship,[25] with most of the research having been undertaken in the USA.[26] Despite the relative paucity of UK-based empirical legal research, there has been valuable dialogue within the academic community,[27] and several reports from non-governmental organisations[28] and successive governments[29] on grandparents, suggesting that there are 'gaps' in the support provided to protect and promote the relationship between grandparents and grandchildren. Rather than simply providing a critique of the existing legal frameworks, this chapter evaluates the existing legal frameworks' ability to protect children's rights to relationships with important attachment figures, rather than solely to protect the 'rights' of grandparents. This current lack of protection of the grandparent/grandchild relationship can make it challenging for grandparents to safeguard relationships with their grandchildren and intervene, when required, to protect and promote children's welfare when they are at risk of significant harm. The consensus for reform is apparent from the work

[25] Such as N Ferguson et al, *Grandparenting in Divorced Families* (Bristol, Policy Press, 2004).

[26] Clarke and Roberts (n 6) 173. See, eg, M Harrington Meyer and A Kandic, 'Grandparenting in the United States' (2017) 1(2) *Innovation in Aging* 1; R Margolis and A Verdery, 'A Cohort Perspective on the Demography of Grandparenthood: Past, Present and Future Changes in Race and Sex Disparities in the United States' (2019) 56(4) *Demography* 1594.

[27] M Purnell and B Bagby, 'Grandparents' rights: Implications for family specialists' (1993) 42(2) *Family Relations* 173; L Spitz, 'Grandparents: their role in 21st century families' (2012) 42 *Fam Law* 1254.

[28] Grandparents Plus (n 8); Grandparents Plus, *Kinship Care State of the Nation Survey* (London, Grandparents Plus, 2020). Grandparents United for Children, *Grandparents United for Children Report* (Leeds, Grandparents United for Children, 2024). See also discussion in F Kaganas, 'Grandparents' Rights and Grandparents' Campaigns' (2007) 19(1) *Child and Family Law Quarterly* 17.

[29] Ministry of Justice, *Family Justice Review* (London, Ministry of Justice, 2011); House of Commons, *Children: Grandparents and others who require leave of the court to apply for access*, 2016 (HC Briefing Paper, Cm 07574, 2016) 8.

and high-profile campaigns of organisations such as Kinship,[30] Grandparents Apart UK[31] and the Bristol Grandparents Support Group.[32] This can also be seen via politicians' attempts to introduce legal reform via Private Members Bills within Parliament.[33] Where the disagreement lies, however, is whether it is desirable to address this lack of recognition at all and, assuming that such reform is desirable, the approach to take in reforming the law.

Specifically, assuming that grandparents ought to be more explicitly recognised within legal frameworks, should reform be modest and focus on procedural aspects of the law (such as the leave requirement and legal aid) or, alternatively, should a bespoke framework be created to protect those who have undertaken the full-time care of their grandchildren? The main suggested options for reform have included the following:

- A legal presumption in favour of contact.[34]
- Removal of the leave requirement before a court application can be made.[35]
- Easier access to legal aid for grandparents.[36]
- Statutory duties for local authorities to provide financial and practical support.[37]

The options above focus on distinct issues within 'private' law (grandparents versus parents) or 'public' law (grandparents versus the state), rather than opting for a holistic approach as advocated within this chapter. Organisations such as Grandparents Apart UK have argued for procedural changes, focusing more on disputes between parents and grandparents.[38] Organisations such as the Family Rights Group[39] and Kinship[40] have tended to focus on the needs of grandparents in the context of full-time caring roles. Reforms that focus on the law in such a

[30] Kinship, *Out of the Shadows: A vision for kinship care in England* (London, Kinship, 2022).

[31] Grandparents Apart UK, *Grandparents Speak Out for Vulnerable Children* (Glasgow, Grandparents Apart UK, 2016).

[32] The Bristol Grandparents Support Group at bristolgrandparentssupportgroup.co.uk.

[33] Kinship Care Bill (2022-23) at bills.parliament.uk/bills/3308.

[34] F Kaganas and C Piper, 'Grandparent contact: another presumption?' (2020) 42(2) *Journal of Social Welfare and Family Law* 176.

[35] R Taylor, 'Grandparents and grandchildren: Relatedness, relationships and responsibility' in B Clough and J Herring, *Ageing, Gender and Family Law* (Abingdon, Routledge, 2018) 230, 230.

[36] L Dickson, 'Grandparents and contact – What's the solution?' (2019) 49 *Fam Law* 1091.

[37] In addition to the expenses faced by grandparents in the provision of care for grandchildren, research demonstrates increases in financial transfers from grandparents to grandchildren: B Beach, *Grandparental Generosity: Financial transfers from grandparents to grandchildren* (London, International Longevity Centre, 2013). See also Tryfonidou (n 24) 11, eg via a 'Kinship Care' Act. Note that a provision providing for the extension of parental leave to grandparents is a measure of support that passed through the Houses of Parliament as the Kinship Care (Parental Leave) Bill. This Bill was unsuccessful and did not become an Act of Parliament.

[38] Grandparents Apart UK at www.grandparentsapart.co.uk.

[39] Family Rights Group, *First Thought Not Afterthought: Report of the Parliamentary Taskforce on Kinship Care* (London, Family Rights Group, 2020).

[40] Kinship, *The Cost of Loving: Annual survey of kinship carers 2022* (London, Kinship, 2022).

narrow way overlook that many cases in this context have a 'hybrid'[41] element. In public law proceedings (where a child is subject to a care order), for instance, a grandparent or kinship carer may use private law to apply for a child arrangements order.[42] In private law cases (where a grandparent seeks contact with a grandchild), public law issues may arise where there are concerns about the child's welfare while under the parent's care. Such issues could include, for instance, whether a care or supervision order is required.[43] It is argued within this chapter that a more comprehensive approach needs to be taken towards legislative reform, which will tackle issues in both private and public law contexts. The reform proposed, therefore, takes a more holistic approach towards the grandparent/grandchild relationship, as well as exploring the need for the Children Act 1989 to become more inclusive.

Moreover, while these proposals all provide grandparents with important tools, they fail to tackle a key criticism of existing child law previously identified by Bendall and Davey.[44] Principally, they are not grappling with the fact that legal frameworks, such as the Children Act 1989, are based on a largely 'nuclear', 'binary' model of care. An argument can be made that 'piecemeal' reform, tackling one of these issues, might be better than no reform at all. Yet such reform would be a lost opportunity to effect more significant changes that would benefit grandparent/grandchild relationships, in addition to other important familial relationships. It is argued, then, that substantial reform to legal frameworks is needed. Reform needs to attend to the 'bigger picture', and to maximise the benefits that grandparents (or other kin) may have concerning their grandchildren's welfare, regardless of their specific involvement in a child's life. Such reform is also needed to make the law more inclusive and in line with other Acts of Parliament, such as the Adoption and Children Act 2002.

IV. The Proposal: A Holistic Approach to Reform through Minor Changes to the Children Act 1989

A. Inclusivity within the Children Act 1989

In this chapter, it is argued that legislative reform to protect the grandparent/grandchild relationship ought to pave the way for considering other sorts of

[41] A Bainham, 'Private and public children law: an under-explored relationship' (2013) 25(2) *Child and Family Law Quarterly* 138.

[42] Children Act 1989, s 8.

[43] ibid s 31.

[44] C Bendall and S Davey, 'The "Grandparent Problem": Encouraging a More Relational Approach towards Child Arrangements via Mediation' in S Davey and J Lindsey (eds), *Grandparents and the Law: Rights and Relationships* (Oxford, Hart Publishing, 2023) 21.

beneficial relationships. The chapter seeks to argue that the Children Act 1989 should be amended so that it is more 'inclusive' and reflects the changing face of the 'family' in the twenty-first century. Moreover, such legal reform ought to address both private *and* public law matters, rather than provide piecemeal reform that would fail to address complex cases, involving diverse relationships that do not fit the 'binary' model referred to above, in full. Similarly, it is problematic to pigeonhole cases concerning children's lives within the 'public' law or 'private' law system, in stark contrast to family law disputes between adults over matters such as divorce and finance. Bainham has, in fact, observed that the family justice system faces difficulty with 'hybrid' cases that have both private and public law elements.[45] Such reform also ought to be mindful of increased familial diversity in the twenty-first century.

It is not suggested that it is time to 'reinvent the wheel' but that it is time for the wheel to be revisited, due to the diverse range of relationships that impact on children's lives (including their relationships with grandparents). Modern families are complex, inter-woven and often blended. As Bendall and Davey note, different family forms sit uneasily with existing legal provisions, and this is particularly true as regards acknowledging the importance of the grandparent/grandchild relationship.[46] The discussion in this section will therefore outline the main proposals for change and consider their potential effectiveness. In doing so, it will explore how 'holistic' legal reform, via minor changes to the Children Act 1989, could provide greater protection for diverse family forms and relationships, including the grandparent/grandchild relationship. This section will demonstrate that any proposed reforms to the current state of affairs ought to be 'inclusive' and reflect the diversity in family units, specifically the importance of grandparents and other extended kin in children's lives. It will also consider why existing legal frameworks, such as the Children Act 1989, need to be reviewed and potentially reformed, to afford better protection to children's meaningful relationships.

Protection of the grandparent/grandchild relationship is an area of inchoate policy that has quietly simmered on the backburner for many years. Several changes have been proposed to the existing law and policy pertaining to grandparents, which have been repeatedly ignored by successive governments. There have been several high-profile attempts to introduce reform.[47] We have seen organisations such as Kinship (formerly known as Grandparents Plus[48]) and the Family Rights Group, more recently, campaign for change. This will evaluate specific reforms suggested over the last decade and consider the following: the creation of a statutory presumption in favour of grandparental contact; removal of the leave

[45] Bainham (n 41).

[46] Bendall and Davey (n 44).

[47] Including via the Kinship Care Bill (n 33) that is currently passing through the Houses of Parliament.

[48] Grandparents Plus, *Kinship Care: State of the Nation* (London, Grandparents Plus, 2017).

requirement; reform to the provision of legal aid; and the creation of statutory duties of financial and practical support for grandparents. In doing so, the appropriateness of incorporating each of these proposals within a Grandparents and Kinship Carers Act, with the aim of achieving reform that is both holistic and inclusive, will be addressed.

B. Statutory Presumption in Favour of Grandparental Contact

One solution to the lack of legal recognition and protection of the grandparent/grandchild relationship has been perceived to be the development of a new 'grandparent' presumption. In fact, the creation of a statutory presumption of parental involvement,[49] under section 11 of the Children and Families Act 2014, has led to suggestions of a similar presumption in favour of grandparental contact.[50] The presumption of parental involvement has the effect that, in court proceedings, the court must give regard to the presumption of 'involvement' of both parents in a child's life. This presumption was the culmination of years of government discussion and academic debate about whether there ought to be a presumption in favour of shared residence in custody disputes between parents.[51] This approach was rejected in favour of a broad presumption in favour of parental involvement under section 11 of the Act, which provides:

> (2A) A court, in the circumstances mentioned in subsection (4)(a) or (7), is as respects each parent within subsection (6)(a) to presume, unless the contrary is shown, that involvement of that parent in the life of the child concerned will further the child's welfare.
>
> (2B) In subsection (2A) 'involvement' means involvement of some kind, either direct or indirect, but not any particular division of a child's time.

A similar presumption with respect to grandparents would undoubtedly strengthen their legal status and provide protection to those who face difficulty in maintaining contact with their grandchildren, particularly after parental separation and/or divorce.[52] As Huddleston observes:

> The estrangement of grandchildren from grandparents happens for a wide variety of reasons: divorce, bereavement, marital breakdown or just a falling out between family members. However the estrangement has come about, rarely is it anything to do with the grandchildren.[53]

[49] Children and Families Act 2014, s 11.

[50] J Stather, 'Enhancing the rights of grandchildren to see their grandparents' *1 Crown Office Row* (May 2018) at www.1cor.com/brighton/2018/06/19/enhancing-rights-grandchildren-see-grandparents/.

[51] A Newnham and M Harding, 'Sharing as caring? Contact and residence disputes between parents' (2016) 28(2) *Child and Family Law Quarterly* 175.

[52] Ferguson (n 25).

[53] HC Deb 2 May 2018, vol 640, col 170WH.

Huddleston has, moreover, suggested that conflict can be far-reaching and lead to consequences other than court:

> I have heard from a number of grandparents who have tried to send birthday cards or Christmas gifts to their grandchildren and found themselves being visited by the police and accused of harassment.[54]

Introducing a 'grandparent' presumption would provide legal protection to the grandparent/grandchild relationship. This could take the form of a new presumption entirely or, as suggested by Huddleston, be introduced as an amendment to the existing 'parental' presumption:

> I am calling for the Government to introduce an amendment to the Children Act 1989, to enshrine in law the child's right to have a relationship with their grandparents by adding the words 'and extended family' or 'and any grandparents' to the section on parental involvement in relation to the welfare of the child.[55]

The introduction of such a presumption would also be in line with the approach that has worked well, according to Sauvé, in some other jurisdictions.[56] France's Civil Code, for instance, provides that 'Any child has a right to maintain personal relations with his ancestors.'[57] There is a rebuttable presumption in favour of contact between grandparents and grandchildren, in circumstances where disputes arise. This approach would address the concerns raised about the powerlessness of grandparents in circumstances where contact with their grandchildren is brought to a halt. Sauvé's comparative research is the first attempt to analyse the efficacy of French law and compare it with the approach taken towards grandparents in England and Wales. Her research suggests that French law has worked well, and that since the presumption in favour of grandparent contact can be rebutted where it is not in the child's best interests, this serves to protect children from the maintenance of relationships that may be unhealthy at best and traumatic at worst. The approach taken in France shows that it is possible to recognise and protect relationships between grandparents and grandchildren while protecting the children's welfare.

At first glance, a presumption of this nature appears to provide greater protection to the grandparent/grandchild relationship. It can also be seen as a way of providing grandparents with rights to protect relationships with their grandchildren, without explicitly referring to them as such. It could be created via a very minor amendment to section 11 of the Children and Families Act 2014, which, as noted above, provides for a presumption in favour of parental involvement.

[54] ibid col 173WH.
[55] ibid.
[56] L Sauvé, 'A French Perspective on Grandparents and Private Law: The Right of the Child to Maintain Personal Relationships' in S Davey and J Lindsey (eds), *Grandparents and the Law: Rights and Relationships* (Oxford, Hart Publishing, 2023) 187.
[57] French Civil Code, Art 371-4, first para.

This section could be amended to encompass a presumption in favour of 'grandparental' involvement too. Despite the potential advantages that might lie within this type of amendment, though, there are reasons for caution. While it might appear to promote inclusivity and acknowledgement of diverse family forms, there are also reasons to suggest that this amendment would not produce the desired results. This author favours reform that is 'inclusive' in nature, rather than reform that merely serves to complicate a 'hierarchy' of rights. In fact, there is a danger of promoting 'grandparent' adult rights over the rights and best interests of children (and, potentially, adult parents with vulnerabilities, including those who have been victims of domestic abuse).

Kaganas and Piper have argued that the existing presumption of parental involvement could 'prejudice the interests of mothers and children'[58] because 'parental involvement' is presumed to be in the child's best interests, even in cases of domestic abuse. Moreover, according to Harwood, the parental involvement presumption may be harmful since it reinforces a 'dominant narrative that children "need" contact',[59] despite the detrimental impact of factors such as domestic abuse on resident parents and children. Although the presumption is 'rebuttable' if there is evidence that contact is harmful to the child, in practice it is unusual for contact to be denied by the courts. A narrative of 'contact at all costs' is damaging in the context of the parent/child relationship[60] and ought not be extended to the grandparent/grandchild relationship.

Harwood has made similar, commonsense arguments in relation to the danger of extending this presumption to favour grandparents.[61] Not all organisations representing grandparents support such a reform either. Grandparents Plus, now known as 'Kinship', have expressed concerns previously that a similar presumption in favour of grandparental contact may result in the maintenance of unhealthy and harmful relationships.[62] These relationships could be harmful due to concerns about the behaviour of the grandparents themselves. Alternatively, a presumption of grandparental involvement could be used to circumvent limitations, on or even outright prohibitions, on contact between a non-resident parent and child. As Kaganas and Piper observe, a presumption in favour of grandparent contact could create the risk of a 'backdoor', to provide contact between a child and a non-resident parent who is a risk to that child's welfare.[63] This could occur, for instance,

[58] Kaganas and Piper (n 34) 176.

[59] J Harwood, 'Presuming the status quo? The impact of the statutory presumption of parental involvement' (2021) 43(2) *Journal of Social Welfare and Family Law* 119.

[60] A Barnett, 'Contact at All Costs? Domestic Violence and Children's Welfare' (2014) 26(4) *Child and Family Law Quarterly* 439.

[61] J Harwood, 'Symbolic and Expedient "Solutions", Grandparents and the Private Family Justice System: The Risk of Unintended Consequences' in S Davey and J Lindsey (eds), *Grandparents and the Law: Rights and Relationships* (Oxford, Hart Publishing, 2023).

[62] Grandparents Plus (n 8) 34.

[63] Kaganas and Piper (n 34) 176.

in cases where children have suffered physical harm and/ or emotional harm due to witnessing domestic abuse perpetrated against the resident parent. Thus, it is suggested that a presumption in favour of grandparent contact may place a child at risk of significant harm and replicate the difficulties created by the presumption in favour of parental involvement. Reform to extend the 'lexis' of this presumption would be hasty, in any event, since the parental presumption is itself currently under review by the Ministry of Justice.[64] Although, at the time of writing, it is uncertain what the outcome of this report might be, it makes little sense to seek to create a statutory provision mirroring one that may, itself, either be repealed or amended in future.

Moreover, this author has suggested elsewhere, with Bendall, that many private law disputes between parents and grandparents could be addressed more effectively via increased promotion of, and engagement with, mediation.[65] While ensuring that language within legislation is up-to-date and reflective of diverse family forms, a presumption in favour of grandparental involvement is a narrow solution that fails to address the importance of other relationships in a child's life. It has the potential to tilt the balance in favour of adult rights, rather than the child's welfare and rights. Further, it does not promote an 'inclusive' approach and recognise the role of other family members who may also have importance in a child's life. This could include, for instance, step-parents, siblings, as well as aunts and uncles.

It is argued, therefore, that the creation of a 'grandparent' presumption must be addressed with caution. Such a presumption could replicate the challenges considered above and, in some circumstances, place a child at risk of significant harm. A 'grandparent' presumption could also, potentially, perpetuate a 'binary' inter-generational narrative, emphasising the role of 'biological' paternal and maternal grandmothers and grandfathers in turn, rather than the wide range of family members and their value in children's lives. This would assume the primacy of parents and then grandparents, rather than providing meaningful reform to reflect the diverse familial, social and cultural networks enjoyed by children. Consequently, whilst, at first glance, a 'grandparent' presumption might look like an effective solution, it is not the best way to afford protection to the grandparent/grandchild relationship, nor indeed to acknowledge wider kinship links. A presumption in favour of grandparental involvement, it is argued, has no place within a potential Grandparents and Kinship Carers Act. It is considered, in section IV.F, that other aspects of the legal language could be reformed. Language in and of itself, however, cannot tackle all the issues that exist for grandparents seeking to engage with the legal system. An important statutory provision that has caused some difficulty for grandparents is the leave requirement, considered in further detail in section IV.C.

[64] HC Deb 9 November 2020, vol 683, HCWS562.

[65] Bendall and Davey (n 44).

C. Removal of the Leave Requirement

The 'leave' requirement is an initial step that needs to be taken prior to applying for a court order. It may, in some circumstances, act as a barrier requiring an additional hearing, or prevent grandparents from applying for a court order (eg, for a child arrangements order under section 8 of the Children Act 1989) at all. Whether or not to remove the 'leave' requirement for grandparents has been debated for much longer than a presumption of grandparental involvement. Removal of the leave is, arguably, less controversial than a presumption in favour of grandparent involvement, since it removes a barrier to the court rather than being a method of bestowing grandparents with rights 'by the back door'. Prior to 1989, grandparents had the automatic right to make court applications in relation to children. The Children Act 1989 'reversed' the prior law, under which grandparents had the right to automatic leave. The existing approach is 'non-inclusive' and limits grandparents' ability to apply for court orders in relation to a child. Unless the grandparent comes within the scope of section 10(4) or (5), they must now seek leave to apply for a court order under section 10(9), which provides as follows:

> Where the person applying for leave to make an application for a section 8 order is not the child concerned, the court shall, in deciding whether or not to grant leave, have particular regard to—
>
> (a) the nature of the proposed application for the section 8 order;
> (b) the applicant's connection with the child;
> (c) any risk there might be of that proposed application disrupting the child's life to such an extent that he would be harmed by it; and
> (d) where the child is being looked after by a local authority—
>   (i) the authority's plans for the child's future; and
>   (ii) the wishes and feelings of the child's parents.

The reason for this reform was explained by Sir Oliver Heald: 'The leave requirement is designed not as an obstacle, but as a filter. The idea is to sift out applications that are not in the child's best interests.'[66] The Law Commission took the perspective that the leave requirement was justified on that basis that it would not pose a substantial hurdle for 'close relatives such as grandparents'.[67] While not overtly in favour of a leave requirement, Herring and Taylor both concur with this perspective,[68] suggesting that, in practice, leave will not serve as a bar (in most cases) for grandparents seeking relationships with their grandchildren. There are those, however, who note the challenges faced by grandparents in the context of

[66] HC Deb 25 April 2017, vol 624, col 500WH.

[67] *Family Law Review of Child Law: Guardianship and Custody* (Law Com No 172, 1988) para 4.41.

[68] J Herring, *Older People in Law and Society* (Oxford, Oxford University Press, 2009) 246; R Taylor, 'Grandparents and grandchildren: Relatedness, relationships and responsibility' in B Clough and J Herring (eds), *Ageing, Gender and Family Law* (Abingdon, Routledge, 2018) 230.

being entitled to engage in court proceedings.[69] There have been calls to remove the leave hurdle, in line with the approach adopted by the Scottish legal system.[70] In Scotland, there is no leave requirement for grandparents, and there is no evidence that this creates difficulties within the Scottish family justice system. Grandparents Plus (now known as Kinship) have argued that those favouring the retention of the leave requirement do so 'based on a fundamental misunderstanding of the motivations and actions'[71] of grandparents, and that the requirement ought to be removed. Leave has been viewed by some as an unnecessary 'hurdle'[72] for well-intentioned grandparents.[73]

There are several reasons why it is argued that it is time to review the leave requirement. First, family law frameworks have 'moved on' since the enactment of the Children Act 1989, affecting the plight of grandparents and others seeking to maintain relationships with children. Two features of particular importance are the withdrawal of legal aid in most family law matters[74] and the increase in litigants in person.[75] In the light of these developments, a further court application and a court hearing to consider leave impose practical and financial burdens upon grandparents, with additional hearings and further expense. Thus, while the leave requirement might not serve as an 'insurmountable' barrier to the court process, its impact, at a time of rising living costs, may act to deter grandparents from making applications to the court. Second, it is possible that a grandparent may have a valid arguable case but face a risk of being refused leave, due to appearing 'vexatious'[76] and 'frivolous'[77] in court statements written without the assistance of a solicitor or barrister.

Third, it has been argued by Bendall and Davey that the removal of the leave requirement could form an important 'symbolic'[78] step for grandparents, and it would ensure that grandparents, regardless of court literacy,[79] could make their case. Therefore, it is proposed that, despite some resistance to calls for changes,[80] a review of the current landscape is long overdue. Finally, it is argued that this amendment would bring the approach to leave in England and Wales in line with the process within the Scottish legal system.[81] In Scotland, grandparents are not

[69] HC Deb 25 April 2017, vol 624, col 497WH.
[70] Children (Scotland) Act 1995 and Children (Scotland) Act 2020.
[71] Grandparents Plus (n 8) 32.
[72] ibid.
[73] ibid.
[74] Legal Aid, Sentencing and Punishment of Offenders Act 2012.
[75] K Barnes and R Taha, 'Litigants in Person – Access to Justice via the Court Process?' (2020) 1 *LJMU Student Law Journal* 5.
[76] HC Briefing Paper (n 29) 8.
[77] *Re M (Care: Contact: Grandmother's application)* [1995] 2 FLR 86; *B (A Child)* [2012] EWCA Civ 737.
[78] Bendall and Davey (n 44).
[79] L Trinder, 'Taking Responsibility? Legal Aid Reform and Litigants in Person in England' in M Maclean, J Eekelaar and B Bastard (eds), 'Delivering Family Justice in the 21st Century' (Oxford, Bloomsbury, 2015) 236.
[80] Ministry of Justice (n 30) 31; HC Briefing Paper (n 29) 8.
[81] Children (Scotland) Act 1995, s 11.

required to apply for leave. There is no evidence, including empirical research, to suggest that the Scottish courts are flooded with a significant number of 'vexatious' claims from grandparents. It is thus argued that a Grandparents and Kinship Carers Act ought to encompass removal of the leave requirement, restoring the process to the pre-Children Act 1989 situation. This would also serve to create a more 'inclusive' approach to the entry point of litigation, eliminating one of the barriers that some grandparents face when opting for the legal route. Consequently, a simple amendment to the Children Act 1989 could have significant implications for grandparents.

Although the removal of the leave requirement would be an improvement, there are further challenges that grandparents face that would need to be addressed, which will be considered in detail in what follows.

D. Reform of Means-tested Legal Aid

The paucity of legal aid is a challenge for grandparents seeking to engage with the court process. Legal aid is no longer available in private law family disputes, unless one of the parties is a victim of domestic abuse or the child is at risk of significant harm.[82] This is despite the fact that there may be circumstances such as when grandparents seek to put themselves forwards as carers in the context of care or adoption proceedings, or to maintain a relationship with their grandchild. It is argued here that extending the scope of legal aid for grandparents, and others, promotes the best interests of the child.

In chapter 5 of this volume, Maclean has raised concerns about the limited scope of legal aid and has advocated reform to rectify a thorny and complex issue. This writer agrees with the perspective taken by Maclean and supports a thorough review of means-tested legal aid. The lack of access to legal aid has affected the protection of grandparents' relationships with their grandchildren. This has been shown through discussion within *Hansard* debates, with David Hinchcliffe MP sharing the following:

> I had fought for a woman who is the grandparent of a six-year-old child. She brought up the child, was the only figure in the child's life and loved and cared for him in the absence of a mother. Then he was adopted, and she had no rights. She could not get legal aid, because she had no right to be heard in court.[83]

Currently, unless they satisfy strict means-testing requirements, grandparents (or other family members who wish to obtain a court order to 'safeguard' a child) will not usually qualify for legal aid and will have to fund litigation themselves.[84]

[82] See Legal Aid, Sentencing and Punishment of Offenders Act 2012.
[83] HC Deb 27 October 1989, vol 158, col 1307.
[84] Grandparents Plus (n 8) 27.

While the financial status of grandparents varies, with some grandparents able to afford litigation, this will not be true for all. Research by Kinship suggests that the reduced access to legal aid will be especially harrowing for grandparents who may have a limited income due to retirement, or who are unable to work due to illness or disability.[85] In public law disputes, where a child is subject to care or adoption proceedings, parents will have automatic access to legal aid. Grandparents will not have access to legal aid in the same circumstances, unless they have parental responsibility for the child or have a child arrangements order (with residence)[86] or special guardianship order[87] in effect. Where children are 'looked after' by the state and local authorities support court applications by kinship carers, grandparents might receive a 'one-off' sum, which will usually be sufficient only to cover an initial consultation.[88] This is, however, entirely discretionary, without specific guidance from the Government on the circumstances in which local authorities ought to provide such financial assistance. Where local authorities do not support grandparents as carers, they will not typically provide such financial support. Where grandparents are parties or third parties to care or adoption proceedings, they may have limited access to legal aid, which is means-tested. This potential challenge in accessing public funding can directly affect grandparents' ability to be involved in children's lives on a long-term basis.

It is argued that grandparents ought not be subject to means-testing where they: (i) apply for a court order, such as a child arrangements order, because a child is at risk of significant harm; or (ii) oppose care or adoption orders so that they can be carers of a child. The difficulty in accessing legal aid is not the only challenge that grandparents face in the context of both private and public law proceedings. It is suggested, however, that reform to legal aid would need to be dealt with comprehensively as a separate reform entirely (potentially as envisaged in chapter 5). There is, however, a light at the end of the tunnel, since the All Party Parliamentary Group (APPG) on Kinship Care has recommended reform to the existing provision of legal aid for kinship carers.[89]

Section IV.E will explore further challenges that may be faced in obtaining financial and practical support, after legal proceedings have been concluded.

E. Statutory Duties of Financial and Practical Support

It has long been argued that grandparents (and others) who take on care of children who would otherwise be cared for by the state ought to be provided with financial

[85] Kinship (n 40).
[86] Children Act 1989, s 8.
[87] Children Act 1989, s 14A.
[88] All Party Parliamentary Group on Kinship Care, *Lost in the legal labyrinth: How a lack of legal aid and advice is undermining kinship care* (London, APPG, 2022) 25–26.
[89] APPG Legal Aid Inquiry at frg.org.uk/policy-and-campaigns/kinship-care/appg-on-kinship-care/legal-aid-inquiry/.

and practical assistance. Back in 2008, discussion in *Hansard*, for instance, considered that grandparents need financial help, including an immediate lump sum for essential items and ongoing maintenance.[90] The government 'financing structure', in this context, has been described as 'inappropriate'[91] and may be seen as unfit for purpose.

Grandparents and other relatives who provide kinship care often struggle financially, especially when they provide 'informal' care. Although they may be entitled to limited benefits, such as child benefit or child tax credit – depending on whether a child arrangements order or special guardianship order is in place – local authorities have no specific duties to provide financial assistance unless children are 'looked after' by the state.[92] If local authorities have facilitated a kinship placement, relatives are entitled to a kinship allowance, which is equivalent to the (higher) foster care allowance.[93] Unfortunately, grandparents still may need to challenge local authorities in court to receive this money in practice, since local authorities do not have to provide automatic funding for private non-statutory kinship care arrangements.[94]

Organisations such as Kinship[95] have argued strongly in favour of a requirement for financial support for such carers (who are not classed as foster carers), to be provided for via statute. Several Members of Parliament favour providing similar statutory protection for grandparents,[96] with Munira Wilson MP describing kinship care as a 'Cinderella service of our children's social care system'.[97] A Kinship Care Bill was introduced by Wilson on 5 July 2022, using the Ten Minute Rule, which passed through the House of Commons but was ultimately unsuccessful. If this proposed law had come into effect, this would have: created a statutory definition of kinship carers; provided automatic financial support for kinship carers that would equal the support allowance already provided to foster carers; provided kinship carers with paid leave when a child comes to live with them; and provided the children with educational benefits stemming from the Pupil Plus Premium.[98]

This Bill had laudable aims and would have made a significant impact. If it had become law, it would have been an important item in the 'toolkit' of grandparents and other kinship carers. Its disadvantage, however, was that it can be regarded as an example of 'piecemeal' reform addressing only 'public' law issues,

[90] HL Deb 17 March 2008, vol 700, col 58.

[91] Children and Young Persons Bill 2008 (HL) 17 March 2008.

[92] Grandparents Plus, *Growing up in Kinship Care* (London, Grandparents Plus, 2017) 24.

[93] *R (SA) v Kent County Council* [2011] EWCA Civ 1303.

[94] *R (CO) v Surrey County Council* [2014] EWHC 3932 (Admin); House of Commons, *Research briefing paper: Financial Support for family and friends carers (Kinship Carers)* (London, House of Commons, 2021) 9.

[95] P McGrath and L Ashley, *Kinship Care: Financial Allowances Survey 2022* (London, Kinship, 2022).

[96] Such as Jim Shannon and Matthew Offord.

[97] HC Deb 5 July 2022, vol 717, col 747.

[98] A type of funding to help disadvantaged children reach higher levels of attainment educationally.

largely providing regulation of the relationship between children, kinship carers and local authorities, rather than a more comprehensive reform of the legal landscape concerning grandparents and kinship carers. It is suggested, therefore, that while these provisions would have addressed important matters that are in need of reform, and which ought to have been included within the Grandparents and Kinship Carers Act, the legislation proposed within this chapter should be broader in its scope. There is an appendix at the end of this chapter, providing an amendment to the Children Act 1989.

F. Other Reforms to the 'Lexis' of the Law

Many social and legislative changes have taken place since the enactment of the Children Act 1989, and there are ways in which it could be modernised to provide greater protection to diverse family forms, including grandparents and kinship carers who arguably have increased importance in the context of the modern family. As considered earlier in this section, the 1989 Act could be amended to remove the leave requirement and provide additional practical and financial support for grandparents. It is suggested that a new Grandparents and Kinship Carers Act should provide grandparents (and others) with important symbolic and practical legal protection of valuable relationships. The reform suggested here is different from the types listed so far, since the emphasis on clarifying existing relationships and providing for greater 'inclusivity' in the language of the Children Act 1989, as well as substantive reform.

The Family Rights Group has campaigned for a statutory definition of 'kinship carer'. This author would agree that, to effect meaningful reform, it is important to clarify relationships between children and other adults who have significant involvement in those children's lives. It is time for an Act of Parliament to define the concept of 'kinship carer' or 'grandparent', and for this to be applied universally within the family law justice system. Ad hoc reference to 'kinship carers' can be found in statutes, such as section 36 of the Children and Young Persons Act 2008, which provides for the entitlement of relatives to apply for child arrangements orders.[99] Under section 17 of the Children Act 1989, local authorities have a duty to 'promote the upbringing of such children by their families'. Although the latter provision refers primarily to those with 'parental responsibility', it includes care provided by relatives and carers.[100] These brief mentions to extended kin fail to provide sufficient acknowledgement of the grandparent/grandchild relationship.

It is suggested that 'grandparent' and 'kinship carer' ought to be defined widely, to be as 'inclusive' as possible, considering the diverse family forms emerging

[99] After providing care for at least one year.
[100] Department for Education, *Family and Friends Care: Statutory Guidance for Local Authorities* (London, Department for Education, 2010) 14.

within the twenty-first century. A 'kinship carer' is typically regarded to be a blood relative, but could be construed more widely to include, for instance, close family friends, including a child's godparents. The definition of 'grandparent' gives rise to similar issues, since it raises questions of whether this should be limited to blood relatives only or extended more widely to include, for example, step-grandparents and great-grandparents. One option, for the purposes of simplicity, is that a definition of 'grandparent' can be drawn from the traditional definition implemented by France, which limits grandparents to those with blood ties only.[101] Another possibility would be to adopt a wider definition of 'grandparents', which may be drawn from the suggestion of Baroness Lane-Fox:

> Grandparent in relation to a child means a grandparent whether of the blood or by affinity and includes, where the child is illegitimate, any person who would be such a grandparent if the child were the legitimate child of his mother and father.[102]

A 'kinship carer' could be defined similarly as 'a member of extended family whether by blood or affinity'. The definition of these individuals, and the types of relationships that they signify, would enable them to have symbolic recognition and to protect the rights and welfare of children in their families. Although defining terms such as 'grandparent' and 'kinship carer' are important, the reform to the legal 'lexis' ought not end here. It is proposed that reform could shift away from the language of 'parental responsibility', which itself emphasises 'exclusivity',[103] towards more 'inclusive' language, such as 'welfare responsibility'. It is also argued that 'responsibility' itself could be defined more comprehensively, including some examples of the types of responsibilities falling under the provision (eg, responsibilities in relation to health, education, etc).[104] At present, there is no specific list or guidance provided on which responsibilities are encompassed by the scope of parental responsibility.

It is suggested that shifting the language from 'parental' responsibility to the non-binary language of 'welfare' responsibility would provide greater reflection of diverse family forms. This is because it is more 'neutral' language, focused on protecting the child rather than on narrowly defining the carer's relationship with the child. While necessitating an adjustment for legal professionals, this change in language would not only benefit grandparents, but would constitute more 'neutral' language, appropriate to recognising other caregivers who may or may not be blood relatives of the child. It is also argued that the shift from 'parents' to more child-orientated language is in line with the child-centred ethos of the UNCRC[105]

[101] Sauvé (n 56).

[102] HL Deb 18 June 1986, vol 476, col 953.

[103] P Marcus, 'Parental responsibilities: Reformulating the paradigm for parent-child relationships Part 2: Who has responsibilities to children and what are these responsibilities?' (2017) 14(2–3) *Journal of Child Custody* 106.

[104] N Lowe et al, Bromley's *Family Law*, 12th edn (Oxford, Oxford University Press, 2021) 436–70.

[105] This Convention is discussed in more detail, in the context of the voice of the child, in Barlow and Ewing, ch 1 in this volume.

and more recent legislation, such as the Adoption and Children Act 2002, which has emphasised the paramountcy of children's welfare.

Another way in which the 'lexis' of the Children Act 1989 could be improved, and made more inclusive, is through reform to the welfare checklist under section 1(3) of the Act. This checklist could be modified to provide consideration of children's 'relatives' and be aligned with the welfare checklist under section 1(4)(f) of the Adoption and Children Act 2002, which provides that the court must have regard to 'the relationship which the child has with relatives … and with any other person in relation to whom the court or agency considers the relationship to be relevant'. Although the courts have wide discretion under the welfare checklist in section 1(3) of the Children Act 1989, introducing alignment with section 1(4)(f) of the Adoption and Children Act 2002 would improve legislative consistency between the welfare frameworks, since the 1989 Act makes no direct reference to relatives in its welfare checklist. Moreover, it would promote the importance of relatives in matters extending beyond adoption, such as in disputes over contact and residence arrangements between grandparents and parents. This would, as with the removal of the leave requirement, introduce a symbolic change. While including section 1(4)(f) within the Children Act 1989 would provide no guarantee of its being considered in every case, it would be an important step in the right direction.

V. Conclusion

The issues highlighted by the 'grandparent debate' are significant and demonstrate the difficulty that lawmakers and policymakers face in grappling with diverse relationships. Lind, Bremner and Moscati have considered this difficulty in chapter 2 of this volume in the context of birth registration, but the failure to recognise and protect diverse family forms has been problematic in the context of legal proceedings too.

Overall, it has been argued in this chapter that legislative reform could be achieved via a Grandparents and Kinship Carers Act, or an amendment (a 'granny annex') to the Children Act 1989, designed to reflect greater 'inclusivity' of extended family members (namely, grandparents). It is suggested that holistic and 'inclusive' reform is best achieved by way of an Act of Parliament that removes the requirement for leave, provides for legal aid in specified circumstances, and improves the practical and financial support available for grandparents. A new Act could also amend specific sections of the Children Act 1989 (ie sections 1(3), 3 and 10) to improve the inclusivity of its language and its approach to diverse family forms. Such an Act would constitute an important practical and symbolic change to the law. This is of particular importance in circumstances where grandparents are long-term caregivers, making decisions for children daily.

The Act, it is argued, would need to be worded carefully to include principles that serve to promote inclusivity in both private and public law contexts. While the focus, outside of parental disputes, tends to be on the grandparent, parent and child, other extended kin – including aunts and uncles, great-grandparents and step-relatives (including step-grandparents) – may also have meaningful relationships with children that are deserving of protection.

As a society, we have moved from openly favouring a traditional, nuclear, heterosexual 'two-parent' model of parenting towards acknowledging the existence of a wide range of families. These families with children are created in various ways, and include those born from reproductive assistance via fertility treatment and/or surrogacy, same-sex parents, 'blended' families and single parents. In circumstances where parents are unable to care for their children, grandparents may even step in as full-time carers. Yet this chapter has identified a range of impediments that, it is argued, fail to facilitate the grandparent/grandchild relationship. While my focus has been on the status of this relationship, it has been asserted that there are circumstances in which other kinship carers ought similarly to have rights that are recognised and protected. These are relationships that serve, ultimately, to benefit children and need to be placed on a legal footing.

Whilst it is conceded that further research is required to assess the extent to which children *do* value their relationships with their grandparents, it is important that the law provides adequate protection for the relationships that *are* indeed valued by children. This would ensure that children's best interests, in maintaining positive, beneficial relationships, are protected.

Any changes to the law must strike the balance between protecting the relationships between children and parents, children and grandparents, parents and grandparents, and those between children and other key attachment figures, whilst simultaneously ensuring the protection of children from significant harm. It can by no means be asserted that all potential avenues for reform have been exhausted within this chapter. What can be said, however, is that it has addressed many challenges that grandparents (and kinship carers) face while attempting to protect their relationships with their grandchildren. The creation of a Grandparents and Kinship Carers Act, which incorporates the changes to the law suggested above, as well as modifications to the legal 'lexis' within the Children Act 1989, would be far-reaching. The existence of such an Act would clarify that the grandparent/grandchild relationship, and other de facto relationships, deserves greater recognition, commensurate with the level of involvement that these adults have in children's lives. An Act of this nature would be a significant step in modernising the legal 'lexis', acknowledging greater diversity in modern relationships, and would also provide greater protection to non-parental attachment figures via formal legal frameworks. In conclusion, then, this chapter proposes that reform should be holistic, via a comprehensive Act of Parliament dedicated to grandparents and extended kin, but which also amends the Children Act 1989, rather than simply a minor amendment or 'granny annex'.

Appendix

Grandparents and Kinship Carers Bill

A BILL TO

Make provision to define 'grandparents' and 'kinship carers'; to provide legal recognition of children's relationships with their grandparents and kinship carers; to provide financial support for grandparents and kinship carers; to provide an amendment to the Children Act 1989 to 'parental responsibilities' changing this to 'welfare responsibilities'; to provide a comprehensive definition of 'responsibilities' and provide kinship carers with statutory rights of financial support.

BE IT ENACTED by the King's most Excellent Majesty, by and with the advice and consent of the Lords Spiritual and Temporal, and Commons, in this present Parliament assembled, and by the authority of the same, as follows:—

Section 1

(1) Definitions

Defines 'grandparent' and 'kinship carer' in an amendment to the Children Act 1989:

> 'Grandparent' shall be defined as: 'a grandparent whether of the blood or by affinity and includes, where the child is illegitimate, any person who would be such a grandparent if the child were the legitimate child of his mother and father'.[106]

A 'kinship carer' shall be defined as 'a member of extended family whether of the blood or by affinity'.

Section 2

(2) An amendment to the section 1(3) welfare checklist of the Children Act 1989 via section 1(3)(h):

> 'the relationship which the child has with relatives, and with any other person in relation to whom the court considers the relationship to be relevant, including—
>
> (i) the value to the child of having, or continuing to have, a relationship with a relative or any such person;
> (ii) the ability and willingness of any of the child's relatives, or of any such person, to provide the child with a secure environment in which the child can develop, and otherwise to meet the child's needs;
> (iii) the wishes and feelings of any of the child's relatives, or of any such person, regarding the child.'

[106] Using the definition recommended by Baroness Lane-Fox. Children and Young Persons Amendment Bill 1986, HL Deb 18 June 1986, vol 476, col 953.

Section 3

(1) An amendment to 'parental responsibility' within sections 2–4 of the Children Act 1989:

> All references in the Children Act 1989 to 'parental responsibility' will be replaced with 'welfare responsibility'.

(2) Amends the Children Act 1989, section 3 definition of parental responsibility to state that

> 'welfare responsibilities include, but are not limited to safeguarding the protection of the child's:
>
> (i) Health and well-being
> (ii) Education
> (iii) Physical, emotional and moral development
> (iv) Safety
> (v) Child support
> (vi) Property
> (vii) Rights.'

Section 4

(1) Amends the Children Act 1989, section 10(4) to provide the following definition of persons able to apply for a section 8 order in relation to a child, to include: 'parent, grandparent, guardian or special guardian of the child'.

Section 5

(1) Provides:

> 'local authorities shall provide financial support for kinship carers equal to the support allowance already provided to foster carers'.

(2) Provides:

> 'kinship carers shall be provided with paid leave when a child comes to live with them'.

(3) Provides:

> 'children cared for by kinship carers shall be entitled to claim the Pupil Plus Premium'.

Response to Chapter 4

Grandparents and Kinship Carers Act or Granny 'Annex'? Waiting for the Government

FELICITY KAGANAS

I. Introduction

Samantha Davey is proposing legislation that 'should provide grandparents (and others) with important symbolic and practical legal protection of valuable relationships'. She suggests that

> legislative reform could be achieved via a Grandparents and Kinship Carers Act, or an amendment (a 'granny annex') to the Children Act 1989, designed to reflect greater 'inclusivity' of extended family members (namely, grandparents).

In particular, she argues that the leave requirement should be abolished and that the welfare checklist in section 1(3) of the Children Act 1989 'could be modified to provide consideration of children's "relatives" and be aligned with the welfare checklist under section 1(4)(f) of the Adoption and Children Act 2002'.

There is much in Davey's proposal that I endorse. For example, she argues that there is a need to review the support available to kinship carers, and that legal aid should be reformed.[1] There is little to contest in these arguments. The same applies to her warnings of potential negative consequences that could flow from extending the presumption in favour of parental involvement in children's lives to grandparents. This response will focus on her proposals for alternative ways of strengthening grandparents' legal position and status in cases of disputes about arrangements concerning the child's spending time with, or living with, grandparents.

[1] In contrast to Davey, it is my view that any reforms to legal aid should be embodied in a Legal Aid Act, rather than in an Act dealing with grandparents and kinship carers.

II. Identifying the Problem

In order to argue for a change in law, a case usually has to be made that the current situation constitutes a social problem: '[s]ocial problems represent conditions that should not be allowed to continue because they are perceived to be problems for society, requiring society to react to them and find remedies'.[2]

To make a case for removing the leave requirement and strengthening the legal position of grandparents, it is necessary to show that there are significant numbers[3] of grandparents who are being denied access to the courts to apply for child arrangements orders, or that numerous applications are being refused. It also needs to be shown that grandchildren are being detrimentally affected because the grandparent/grandchild relationship is important for children's well-being. This is not self-evident. King explains that 'except for the basic physical requirements for healthy development', children's needs are socially constructed.[4] To change law or policy, it is important to be able to persuade powerful groups that change is needed.[5]

A. The Numbers

The numbers of grandparents seeking child arrangements orders are arguably not significant: the Parliamentary Under-Secretary of State for Justice said in 2018 that 'some 2,000 grandparents go down that route every year'.[6] Cusworth's figures are potentially higher, at around 10 per cent of 46,572 applications in 2019/20.[7] However, this figure includes both grandparents and other family members.

B. The Grandparent/Grandchild Relationship

The case for constructing the issue of grandparent contact as a social problem is weakened by the fact that there is little empirical evidence that the relationship

[2] J Clarke and A Cochrane, 'The Social Construction of Social Problems' in E Saraga (ed), *Embodying the Social: Constructions of Difference* (Oxford, Routledge, 1998) 3, 8.

[3] ibid 5.

[4] M King, 'Welfare and Justice' in M King (ed), *Childhood, Welfare and Justice* (London, Batsford Academic and Educational, 1981) 110.

[5] ibid 112–13.

[6] The Parliamentary Under-Secretary of State for Justice, *Access Rights to Grandparents*; HC Deb 2 May 2018, vol 640, col 183WH.

[7] L Cusworth et al, *Uncovering Private Family Law: Who's Coming to Court in England?* (London, Nuffield Family Justice Observatory, 2021) 19.

with grandparents is important for children in general. Much depends on the nature and closeness of the relationship between the individuals concerned. In addition, Douglas and Ferguson's research showed that '[g]randchildren were usually more important to their grandparents than their grandparents were to the grandchildren'.[8]

There are also differences between maternal and paternal grandparents. Douglas and Ferguson found that maternal grandparents were generally more involved in grandchildren's lives than paternal grandparents, both before and after parental separation.[9] Moreover, grandmothers were more involved than grandfathers. Kaspiew et al reported the same patterns in their Australian study.[10] So while maternal grandparent involvement is more likely to be beneficial for grandchildren, it is paternal grandparents who are most likely to need to resort to the law.[11]

C. Court-ordered Contact

Studies that point to the benefits of grandparent involvement do not examine cases where there is serious conflict between grandparents and parents. Nor do they examine cases of court-ordered contact.[12]

Goldberg, writing in Canada, argues that it is not clear that the benefits of grandparent/grandchild relationships can be secured by court-ordered visitation, nor even that such benefits are generally present. He points out that generalised presumptions about such benefits appear, from the available research, to have little or no basis in fact.[13]

Newman, in turn, is critical of court-ordered grandparent–child interactions. He argues that, among other things, children see that they are at the heart of family strife; they experience loyalty conflicts; they have to deal with pressure to take sides; and they suffer anxiety as a result of having to have contact that the parents oppose.[14]

[8] G Douglas and N Ferguson, 'The Role of Grandparents in Divorced Families' (2003) 17(1) *International Journal of Law, Policy and the Family* 41, 45.

[9] ibid 45. See also R Kaspiew et al, *Evaluation of the 2006 family law reforms* (Melbourne, Australian Institute of Family Studies, 2009) paras 12.2.2–12.3.3.

[10] Kaspiew et al (n 9) paras 12.2.2–12.3.3.

[11] ibid paras 12.6.2–12.7.2.

[12] F Kaganas and C Piper, 'Grandparent contact: another presumption?' (2020) 42(2) *Journal of Social Welfare & Family Law* 176, 191.

[13] D Goldberg, *Grandparent-Grandchild Access: A Legal Analysis* (Department of Justice, Canada, 2003) 16.

[14] SA Newman, 'Grandparent Visitation Claims: Assessing the Multiple Harms of Litigation to Families and Children' (2003) 13 *Boston University Public Interest Law Journal* 21, 28–29. See also L Cowan, 'There's No Places Like Home: Why the Harm Standard in Grandparent Visitation Disputes is in the Child's Best Interests' (2007) 75(6) *Fordham Law Review* 3137, 3178–80.

III. Children Act 1989

Notwithstanding these possible negative consequences, the litigation route is available to anyone with a sufficiently important relationship with a child. Any section 8 order, including a child arrangements order, can be granted to anyone. However, if the person seeking an order does not fall within the categories of entitled persons, the applicant must first get the leave of the court and the factors embodied in section 10(9) come into play. These include the applicant's connection to the child and any risk of disruption resulting from an application. When deciding a substantive application for a section 8 order, the court must apply the paramountcy test and the section 1(3) checklist.

A. Removing the Requirement for Leave

While the number of cases of grandparents applying for child arrangements orders appears to be relatively small, there is no evidence that this is because grandparents are not easily able to seek leave or are having applications for it denied. Indeed, some grandparent support groups warn against going to court because of financial and emotional cost, as well as problems of enforcement of orders.[15]

In 2011, the Family Justice Review recommended that the leave requirement should remain to protect families from vexatious and unmeritorious applications.[16] It was not, said the chair of the Review, unduly burdensome or costly. Leave can be a 'quick paper exercise'.[17] In most cases, there is no objection in response to the letter asking parents whether they object to the granting of leave; any objections tend to be in relation to contact itself.[18] It has also been suggested that there is, in practice, a presumption that grandparents are to be given leave.[19] Furthermore, it was pointed out by the Parliamentary Under-Secretary of State for Justice, during a Westminster Hall debate in 2018, that the paperwork can be submitted by ticking a box on the relevant form along with the substantive application. There is no extra expense:

> [E]xperience shows that grandparents do not usually experience any difficulty in obtaining permission when their application is motivated by a genuine concern for the interests of the child. …

[15] See Bristol Grandparents Support Group, 'Your Rights', *Bristol Grandparents Support Group* (nd) at bristolgrandparentssupportgroup.co.uk/help-and-support/your-rights/.

[16] D Norgrove, *Family Justice Review: Final Report* (London, Ministry of Justice, Department for Education and the Welsh Government, 2011) paras 4.45–4.48.

[17] R Nugee (ed), *Relative Values … Missing out on Contact* (Harlow, Grandparents' Association, 2003) 5 (cited in F Kaganas, 'Grandparents' Rights and Grandparents' Campaigns' (2007) 19(1) *Child and Family Law Quarterly* 17, 21).

[18] Nugee (ed) (n 17).

[19] C Talbot and P Kidd, 'Special Guardianship Orders – Issues in Respect of Family Assessment' [2004] *Family Law* 273, 274.

> The leave requirement is not designed to be an obstacle to grandparents or other family members; it is meant to be a filter to sift out applications that are clearly not in a child's best interests.[20]

The leave requirement, then, does not present a significant impediment to well-intentioned grandparents. Further, it seems that it can protect families from the stress, disruption and expense of vexatious litigation. Nevertheless, Davey argues that the leave requirement should be removed as this would be an 'important "symbolic" step for grandparents'.

B. Amending the Children Act

Davey also suggests that section 1(3) be amended to align with section 1(4) of the Adoption and Children Act 2002. However, whether such alignment is warranted may be open to question. The adoption legislation deals with the complete legal severance of the child from the birth family, rather than the protection of a relationship against the wishes of the parents. It is arguable that the purpose of section 1(4)(f) is to ensure that this severance, with its implications for the child's sense of identity, should not be effected without ascertaining whether less drastic measures, such as kinship care, would suffice:

> The possibility that a grandparent might step into the shoes of a parent and take over the full-time care of a grandchild, to avoid the need to place a child outside the family, is likely to require a different approach to that taken in response to a situation where a grandparent is seeking contact after estrangement with the parent.[21]

In any event, while neither grandparents nor other relatives are specifically mentioned in the welfare checklist, they, along with any other important figure in the child's life, can potentially apply for (if granted leave) a child arrangements order. They would be successful if factors such as the child's wishes and needs, as well as the ability of the grandparent to meet those needs, pointed in favour of an order. Nevertheless, for Davey, the change is needed for consistency, to promote the importance of relatives and for its symbolic value.

In Australia, the law was changed[22] to make specific reference to children's right to spend time with grandparents and other relatives. This change, according to Kaspiew et al, was to recognise 'the important role that grandparents (and other relatives) can play in children's lives following the separation of their parents'.[23] The goal was to 'facilitate greater involvement of extended family members in the lives of children'.[24]

[20] HC Deb (n 6) col 185WH.
[21] G Douglas, 'Re J (Leave to Issue Application for Residence Order) Recognising grandparents' concern or controlling their interference?' (2003) 15(1) *Child and Family Law Quarterly* 103, 111.
[22] Shared Parental Responsibility Act 2006 (Cth), s 60B(1)(2)(b).
[23] Kaspiew et al (n 9) para 12.1.
[24] ibid, quoting from Explanatory Memorandum, para 39, Family Law Amendment (Shared Parental Responsibility) Bill 2006 (Cth).

The change meant that more parents than previously were giving consideration to grandparent contact, particularly in discussions with each other. Such contact arrangements were presumably consensual.[25] That said, the change additionally seems to have led more grandparents to consider the legal route. Half of the lawyers surveyed by Kaspiew et al thought that, after the law changed, more grandparents were seeking their advice about contact, and the majority of those lawyers were more inclined to advise grandparents that they were in a stronger position as a result of the change.[26] The researchers reported that about two-fifths of paternal grandparents and one-fifth of maternal grandparents made use either of a service, usually lawyers and legal services, or of the courts.[27] The researchers were told of grandparents who demanded their rights to contact to the point where '[t]hey're actually wanting a parenting plan for their grandkids'.[28]

A number of practitioners mentioned the practical difficulties in terms of division of time; both mothers and children were under pressure to fit in the time for visits.[29] Some professionals 'were concerned that … grandparents can be more focused on their own rights than on the wellbeing of their grandchildren and the children's parents'.[30]

The Australian experience, then, suggests that an explicit reference to grandparents in the legislation would indeed heighten awareness of the role of grandparents. However, from the point of view of primary carers, it would also be likely to have negative effects; it may affect informal negotiations and legal advice, as well as increase the likelihood of litigation or the deployment of other forms of pressure on mothers and children.[31]

IV. Promoting the Importance of Grandparents

Legal recognition of the importance of grandparents to the well-being of grandchildren has already been achieved, to some extent, in England and Wales without legislative change; grandparent contact seems to have become an approved norm.[32] Government ministers, policymakers and welfare professionals appear to have accepted that contact with grandparents is generally good for children. For example, grandparent contact is specifically mentioned in the Parenting Plan pro formas on the CAFCASS and CAFCASS Cymru websites.[33]

[25] Kaspiew et al (n 9) para 12.4.
[26] ibid para 12.5.
[27] ibid para 12.6.2.
[28] ibid para 12.6.1.
[29] ibid para 12.7.2.
[30] ibid para 12.7.2.
[31] See, for a therapeutic approach, J Jackson, 'Court is not the answer' (Bristol, Bristol Grandparents Support Group, 14 July 2022) at bristolgrandparentssupportgroup.co.uk/blog/court-is-not-the-answer/.
[32] See generally Kaganas (n 17).
[33] CAFCASS, Parenting Plan (CAFCASS, 2023), www.cafcass.gov.uk/grown-ups/parents-and-carers/divorce-and-separation/parenting-together/planning-together-for-children/; CAFCASS Cymru,

Kaganas argues that the state (and, it should be said, also CAFCASS professionals) is 'seeking, through non-legislative means, to "radiate" messages about how to reorder family relationships, especially after separation or divorce'.[34] The apparent emergence of a norm in favour of grandparent contact has implications for informal negotiation, as well as mediation.[35] It also has the potential to influence the advice that lawyers give to clients.[36]

The norm is appearing in the courts too. In *B (A Child)*,[37] the mother opposed contact and made serious allegations of domestic violence and abuse against the father and grandmother. The Court transferred residence to the paternal grandmother, saying:

> [7] If the child remains with the mother she will never have a relationship with the grandmother or any member of the paternal family. This will have a profoundly adverse impact on the child's emotional development.

On appeal, the Court ordered a retrial, and the leave requirement was crucial to the decision:

> [13] … [T]he transfer of contact [*sic*] from the obdurate parent to the alternatively available parent is a weapon of last resort … I know of no case in which such a dire sanction has been exercised … to transfer the primary care to a grandmother. Manifestly grandparents are not on equal footing with parents. Statute requires an application for leave before a grandparent may make [an] application. Inevitably there are disbenefits for a child to be brought up by an adult of a different generation to either of her parents.

However, in contrast to this case, in *D (Children)*,[38] the Court was prepared to order a transfer of residence to grandparents. The father had sexually abused his stepdaughter and the mother said that he was a paedophile. She opposed contact with the paternal family. The Court rejected the mother's concerns and said that she was abusive because she held a 'false belief system' that the grandparents would be likely to facilitate abuse of the children by the father. The children's fears for their safety when with the grandparents were also dismissed.[39] Residence was transferred to the grandparents to enable the children to be 'normal children again enjoying a normal relationship with grandparents'.[40]

In *CW* v *NT*,[41] the Court authorised one session of supervised contact between the children and paternal grandparents, to be followed by a return to court. This was despite the grandparents' hostility to the mother and complete identification

The Parenting Plan, (CAFCASS Cymru, 2018) www.gov.wales/sites/default/files/inline-documents/2019-05/180212-parenting-plan-en.pdf. Both documents refer also to other relatives.

[34] Kaganas (n 17) 25.

[35] ibid 25–26.

[36] ibid 26.

[37] *B (A Child)* [2012] EWCA Civ 858.

[38] *D (Children)* [2010] EWCA Civ 496.

[39] ibid [15].

[40] ibid.

[41] *CW* v *NT* [2011] EWHC 76.

with, and support for, their son, who was banned by the court from having any contact with the children. The judge said:

> 27. … On the one hand there is a powerful case for saying that the children should be in touch with the paternal side of their family. On the other is the fact that … the grandparents are entirely in the father's camp.
>
> 31. … Grandparents usually have the capacity to deliver the vital quality of normality. … They can provide a haven for children whilst … keeping them in touch with the absent side of their family. But can these grandparents do this?
>
> 32. I have, in the end, come to the conclusion that they can … I believe Mrs BAW … recognises that – were contact to take place freely at or near her home – she would find it impossible to keep the father away. Secondly, I think that Mrs BAW recognises the harm that the children may suffer if she seeks to proselytise the father's case to the children. I may be wrong about that. I hope I am not.

The Court in this case appears to be concerned about the risk of facilitation of paternal contact by grandparent contact. That grandparent contact can be used in this way is documented by Neilson in Canada.[42] She cites a report[43] recording cases where grandparents apply for contact to circumvent a ban on contact with their son who has perpetrated domestic violence. The Court in *CW* was prepared to take that risk in the light of the perceived importance of grandparent/grandchild relationships.

V. Symbolic Law-making

Davey advocates for the removal of the leave requirement and for the change to the welfare checklist, at least partly because of the symbolic impact these changes would have. This raises the question of what impact is intended.

Law can be used to send 'messages' with the aim of altering behaviour. However, these messages may not be 'read' or heeded by the target audience. Public education does not necessarily have an effect on individual behaviour.[44]

If the intention is to get parents to change their behaviour and accede to grandparent contact despite conflict or relationship breakdown, this is unlikely to be achieved except in a relatively small proportion of cases. Kaspiew et al report in the Australian context that 'there appears to be a little more willingness among post-reform separated parents to include grandparents in post-separation parenting arrangements'.[45]

[42] L Neilson, *Responding to Domestic Violence in Family Law, Civil Protection and Child Protection Cases*, Canadian Legal Information Institute, 2nd edn (2020), 2017 CanLIIDocs 2, para 7.4.24.

[43] L Bancroft and J Silverman, *The Batterer as Parent* (Thousand Oaks, CA, Sage, 2002) 126.

[44] F Kaganas, 'A Presumption that 'Involvement' of both parents is best: Deciphering law's messages' (2013) 25(3) *Child and Family Law Quarterly* 270, 288.

[45] Kaspiew et al (n 9) para 12.4.

In England and Wales, the Children Act 1989 was amended to encourage agreement between parents that both should be involved in their children's lives. A presumption that parental involvement is best for children was embodied in section 1(2A). It is clear that, where there is conflict between parents, changes in the law have not had much effect. While most parents internalise the norm that a relationship with both parents is good for children in general, mothers may take the view that the contact they are opposing is not good for their children. Fathers, in turn, may see the fight for contact as important for their children's welfare and to show that they care.[46] Similar psychological processes could well be at play in disputes between grandparents and parents.

If the proposed changes are meant to acknowledge the importance of grandparents, and so mollify disgruntled grandparents, it is doubtful whether they will have this effect. The real-world problem for grandparents lies in the fact that they rank in the legal and social hierarchy below parents, and that the welfare principle tends to favour the child's relationships with the parents. Grandparents' chances of obtaining a child arrangements order may not change with a change in the welfare checklist. There will still be unsuccessful outcomes for some grandparents and they will be disappointed. Some will blame the family justice system, just as disappointed fathers have done.[47]

Symbolic legislation could also be used in an attempt to bring about a 'societal shift' towards greater recognition of the value of grandparents.[48] Such legislation can be used in an attempt to change, or at least to reinforce, a norm. The use of what Sunstein refers to as the 'expressive function' of law in this way aims to 'reconstruct existing norms through a legal expression or statement about appropriate behaviour'.[49] This can have the effect of inducing shame in those who internalise, but do not obey, the norm.[50] It can also have the effect of designating those who do not obey the norm as 'deviant'.[51]

To seek to strengthen the norm in favour of grandparent/grandchild relationships by legislative change could place increased pressure on mothers to agree to contact. Vulnerable mothers may internalise the norm that contact is beneficial and accept that they must agree to it to remain good mothers. This may mean that they feel compelled to accept contact not only with fathers, but with grandparents too. Agreed or court-ordered contact would increase pressure on children's time and may not even be in their best interests. Court-ordered contact could also lead to enforcement proceedings. Mothers who resist contact are already constructed as

[46] See F Kaganas and S Day Sclater, 'Contact Disputes: Narrative Constructions of Good Parents' (2004) 12 *Feminist Legal Studies* 1.

[47] Bancroft and Silverman (n 43) 282–86.

[48] ibid 288.

[49] C Sunstein, 'On the Expressive Function of Law' (1996) 144 *University of Pennsylvania Law Review* 2021, 2031; cf C Schneider, 'The Channelling Function in Family Law' (1992) 20(3) *Hofstra Law Review* 495, 498.

[50] Sunstein (n 49) 2032.

[51] Bancroft and Silverman (n 43) 290.

deviant by courts and professionals when it comes to contact with fathers. They are increasingly being constructed as alienators and child abusers who must change their behaviour or lose their children. Grandparent pressure groups have adopted the terminology of alienation[52] and could deploy it, as fathers have done, to the detriment of mothers and children.

VI. Conclusion

There is no evidence that large numbers of grandparents are being denied the relationship with grandchildren that they want because of the law. In addition, there is no evidence that the grandparent/grandchild relationship is important for the well-being of children in general, as opposed to specific children. While symbolic legislation might strengthen grandparents' position in disputes with parents, this effect can have adverse real-life consequences, especially for mothers and children.

[52] See Kaganas and Piper (n 12) 193–94. See also J Jackson, 'Should we stop using the words parental alienation?' (Bristol, Bristol Grandparents Support Group, 12 July 2022) at bristolgrandparentssupportgroup.co.uk/blog/should-we-stop-using-the-words-parental-alienation/.

5

The Case for a Legal Support for Children Bill, to Swiftly Reinstate Legal Aid for those at Risk of Harm or Neglect

MAVIS MACLEAN

I. Introduction

The Legal Aid, Sentencing and Punishment of Offenders Act (LASPO) 2012 removed private family law matters, with a few exceptions, from the scope of publicly funded legal help and representation. Cases relating to children are no longer to be supported by publicly funded legal help where the matter consists of, for example, a private dispute about arrangements for children between separating parents, that is, individual adults. Legal aid was, however, retained for public law matters, where the state has a responsibility to protect a child at risk of neglect or harm, for example in a family matter involving possible abuse. The aims of the new legislation had been stated as: to discourage unnecessary adversarial litigation; to target legal aid at those most in need; to make substantial savings in legal aid expenditure; and to bring about better value for money for the taxpayer.[1] However, in January 2015, the Ministry of Justice was criticised in the Thirty Sixth Report of the House of Commons Public Accounts Committee in the first stage of Post-Implementation Review of the Act.[2] This stated that a reduction in spending had indeed been achieved, but at the cost of failing to meet the other three objectives, and that access to justice had been harmed for some litigants. The terms of reference of the Evidence Gathering Exercise for the Review included taking the time necessary to consult and engage with interested

[1] Ministry of Justice, *Legal Aid Sentencing and Punishment of Offenders Act 2012: Post legislative memorandum* submitted to the Justice Select Committee (Cm 9486, 2017).

[2] House of Commons Committee of Public Accounts, *Implementing Reforms to Legal Aid* (London, 4 February 2015) at www.parliament.uk/globalassets/documents/commons-committees/public-accounts/HC-808-civil-aid-final-web-version-v2.pdf.

parties, and to provide an opportunity for government to consider what the future should look like. It is the purpose of this chapter, first, to note the impact of some of the LASPO changes in children cases.[3] Second, the chapter identifies emerging evidence that suggests ways in which reform of the law might alleviate some of the problems currently arising for children involved in matters related to post-separation parenting. In particular, we are interested in the question of whether the boundaries between a private dispute between adults and a case where there is a public interest in children at risk of harm or neglect, which determine access to legal aid, are always clearly defined. For example, might a mother be resisting a child's contact with the father because she has concerns about possible abuse but is afraid to express these? Might a father be afraid that a mother is influencing her children against spending time with him, that is, alienating the children's affections? These kinds of very difficult cases have come to be known as the 'cross-over cases', presenting initially as private law adult issues not eligible for publicly funded legal support, but where public law issues about the safety of the child, which would place the case within scope, may also be present but hidden from view.

The matters removed from the scope of legal aid under LASPO in 2012 were those where the state was not thought to have an interest. These included financial arrangements after a divorce. It could also be argued that such arrangements might well affect public expenditure through their impact on the budgets of government departments, such as education, health or the Department for Work and Pensions (DWP), if, for example, a family was not helped to make best use of the available family resources, or state help was required to ensure suitable housing for a single parent and her children. Yet legal aid was only to remain in scope where there was direct evidence of public interest, such as the protection of a child from the effects of domestic abuse.[4]

Protecting the state from spending 'public money for private quarrels' has long been a government concern ever since legal aid for family matters ceased to be seen as a way of helping troubled families, and thus benefiting society as a whole, following the difficulties that arose after the Second World War. Instead, it became categorised as an unwelcome and increasing drain on scarce public resources. By 1996/7, the net cost of civil legal aid had reached £807.3 million, of which 48.5 per cent was being spent on family and matrimonial cases.[5] The phrase

[3] See also M Maclean and J Eekelaar, *After the Act: Access to Family Justice after LASPO* (Oxford, Hart Publishing, 2019).

[4] See Ministry of Justice and Legal Aid Agency, *Legal Aid Data: Civil Representation* (London, Ministry of Justice and Legal Aid Agency, 17 July 2023) at www.data.justice.gov.uk/legalaid/legal-aid-civil-representation#table-tab-legal-aid-civilrepresentation-dvca-applicationsreceived: 'LASPO removed legal aid for most private law including issues such as contact or divorce. However legal aid remains available for such cases where there is a risk of domestic violence or child abuse. … Applicants are granted legal aid funding for these cases if they can prove the incidence or risk of domestic violence or child abuse through a range of prescribed forms of evidence.'

[5] See Legal Aid Board annual reports 1996/97.

'supplier-induced demand' had come into use, suggesting that family practitioners, who were being paid for legal aid work by the hour, could be incentivised to escalate conflict in order to increase their income.[6] The reality was, however, very different: the divorce rate was rising rapidly,[7] and the growing demands on the legal aid budget were the result of increased case volume, not increased cost per case. In addition, little was known about the impact on the legal aid budget of resolving disputes arising from the work of other government departments, such as poor decision-making in benefit claims by the DWP.

Consequently, by 2013, when LASPO came into effect, we found ourselves in a position where child arrangement matters in private law, such as contact with a non-resident parent after divorce or separation, would be excluded from the scope of legal aid. This was to be the case unless there were not only concerns about, but also *evidence* of, risk of neglect or abuse. Parents in public law child protection cases could still be supported through legal aid. Even in this context, though, there were (and still are) concerns about cases where a local authority, anxious to avoid the cost of a care case, might encourage parents to agree to a voluntary placement under section 20 of the Children Act 1989, without any certainty that the parents had received necessary information, and with there being none of the safeguards and protections that would accompany proceedings for compulsory care.[8]

II. The Issue: Eligibility for Legal Aid and the Complex Relationship between Public and Private Children Cases

Family matters, particularly those concerning parenting after separation, are frequently not clearly or easily divisible into private or public law cases. There may be a connection, sometimes called a 'crossover', from private to public law issues. A difficult contact dispute may include not only a private argument between two adults, but also elements of potential concern to public authorities of possible harm to a child if there are elements of abusive parental behaviour, such as physical violence, coercive control or parental alienation. Such elements may be apparent in the early stages of trying to make arrangements for children, but may also not develop until later, as a problem becomes a dispute. Yet they may fail

[6] G Bevan, 'Has there been Supplier-induced Demand for Legal Aid?' (1996) 5 *Civil Justice Quarterly* 98.

[7] The divorce rate (number of divorces per 1,000 of the ongoing married population) increased from 2.4 (1951–60) to 13 (1997). See M Maclean and J Eekelaar, *Lawyers and Mediators: The Brave New World of Services for Separating Families* (Oxford, Hart Publishing, 2016) 5.

[8] See Lady Hale's judgment in *Williams v London Borough of Hackney* [2018] UHSC 37 [34]. See also *Herts CC v AB* EWFC 10; and M Parr 'Pre-proceedings and s 20 of the Children Act 1989' (2020) *Family Law* (31 January 2020) at www.familylaw.co.uk/news_and_comment/pre-proceedings-and-s-20-of-the-children-act-1989.

to be recognised or appropriately considered, particularly in cases involving litigants in person, as they are difficult for a non-lawyer to identify and define in order to present the situation in the terms required for accessing support under LASPO. It is becoming increasingly possible that parents and children may be in urgent need of free access to legal help in such circumstances in order to be safe. Despite our excellent legal framework for promoting the best interests of children in the Children Act England and Wales 1989 (where the principle of welfare paramountcy requires that the welfare of any child involved in litigation must be the paramount consideration of the court in decision-making), since LASPO we have found ourselves in difficulty. Hence, this chapter argues for increasing the scope of statutory provision of legal support for children. This would clearly be desirable in all cases relating to children, but urgent priority must be given to ensuring the provision of the free legal help that is essential in the 'cross-over' cases, where a private matter may have a public child protection dimension.

III. The Background

We might best begin by considering carefully what government has been aiming to achieve through the family justice system over time, by looking to the straplines that have been published, and used, by the Ministry of Justice for many years.

At the time of the Children Act 1989, the strapline stated the aim of the family justice system as being 'to protect the vulnerable'. This indicated a comprehensive and needs-based proactive approach to include all vulnerable groups and to offer protection to all, with implications of a generous preventive approach, as well as care for those already in need. Nevertheless, by 2010, when David Norgrove began his review of the family justice system (at a time of acute pressure on public funds, following the financial problems of 2008–09), this aim had been modified to 'seeking fair and informed settlement'. This subtly acknowledged the current pressure on resources, and gave greater attention to seeking ways of potentially reducing the cost of rapidly increasing recourse to the courts. The question of 'cross-over' cases, where a private dispute between parents about contact might include child protection issues, was indeed raised in the Norgrove Report in 2010.[9] However, these concerns were not addressed in the forthcoming legislation, LASPO, two years later. Since then, growing concerns about the way in which the family justice system responds to issues of domestic abuse has led the Ministry of Justice to commission a review from a Harm Panel of experts,[10] whose

[9] Ministry of Justice, *Family Justice Review Final Report November 2011* (London, Ministry of Justice, Department for Education and the Welsh Government, 2011) at www.gov.uk/government/publications/family-justice-review-final-report.

[10] See Ministry of Justice, *Assessing Risk of Harm to Children and Parents in Private Law Children Cases: Final Report* (London, Ministry of Justice, June 2020) at www.gov.uk/government/consultations/assessing-risk-of-harm-to-children-and-parents-in-private-law-children-cases. This questioned the

report stressed a number of problems in private law children cases, including the difficulty of evidencing domestic abuse. The President of the Family Division, in his judgment in *Re H-N and Others*, stated that in the preceding year

> [t]he Family Court received 55,252 applications by parents for a child arrangement order seeking to resolve a dispute with the other parent relating to future care arrangements for the child. Although the figure is by no means firm, it is thought that at least 40% of private law children cases now involve allegations of domestic abuse, that is 22,000 cases each year (ie, over 5,000 per quarter).[11]

The number of cases involving children receiving legal aid after LASPO appears to fall far short of this total. Moreover, legal aid statistics released in September 2020 showed a 37 per cent decline in applications since the same period April–June in the preceding year for legal aid in domestic violence or child abuse cases, with the volume of applications granted falling by 39 per cent.[12] The number of new family law cases in the period January–March 2022 was 68,134, with 4,248 starts in public law children cases and 13,197 in private law, which included 41 per cent with no legal representation at all and 29 per cent with one legal representative.[13] Furthermore, the expectation that LASPO would lead to increasing use of mediation as an alternative to court had not been met, with mediation starts standing at one third of pre-LASPO levels in 2020.[14]

The Harm Panel has recommended that a more investigative, less adversarial approach should be taken by the courts in domestic abuse cases, supported by the Domestic Abuse Act 2021 (which ended cross-examination of victims by perpetrators and aims to make return to court more difficult).[15] Following this recommendation, two pilot schemes are now underway in Dorset and in North Wales, known as the Pathfinder Pilot, which are being evaluated over a two-year period. Agencies will begin by gathering information and assessing whether there are concerns for any child or person involved in a case about substance abuse,

limitations on raising domestic abuse issues as a result of the pro-contact culture of the courts, difficulties in evidencing abuse, lack of communication between the courts and other agencies, and the use of adversarial court process in cases where there is often not a level playing field for the parents and little involvement of the child.

[11] *Re H-N and Others* [2021] EWCA Civ 448 [3].

[12] All-Party Parliamentary Group on Legal Aid, *October Bulletin from the APPG on Legal Aid* (London, APPG, October 2020) at www.apg-legalaid.org/sites/default/files/October%20Bulletin%20 2020.pdf.

[13] APPG, *APPG on Legal Aid Bulletin – Legal Aid Statistics and Analysis January–March 2022* (London, APPG, 30 June 2022) at www.apg-legalaid.org/sites/default/files/APPG%20on%20Legal%20 Aid%20Bulletin%20-%20Special%20Bulletin%20-%201st%20Quarter%202022%20Legal%20Aid%20 Stats%20-%20June%202022.pdf.

[14] See Ministry of Justice, *Legal Aid Statistics Quarterly, England and Wales* (London, Ministry of Justice, Legal Aid Agency, 25 March 2021) at assets.publishing.service.gov.uk/media/605b2c2c8fa8 f545d5c33a21/legal-aid-statistics-bulletin-oct-dec-2020.pdf.

[15] Ministry of Justice, *Pioneering Approach in Family Courts to Support Domestic Abuse Victims Better* (Press Release, Ministry of Justice, HM Courts & Tribunals Service and Lord (David) Wolfson of Tredegar KC, 8 March 2022) at www.gov.uk/government/news/pioneering-approach-in-family-courts-to-support-domestic-abuse-victims-better.

domestic abuse or other welfare issues. There will then be a hearing to decide what interventions or decisions are required, and whether the case could be suitable for mediation or a separated-parent programme. The process aims to take the confrontational element out of the court system, and focuses more on investigating and solving problems to reduce potential harm to those involved. It remains to be seen whether this process might also prove to be more supportive to parties acting as litigants in person, if legal aid continues to be restricted to public law children matters.

IV. The Way Ahead from Desirability to Feasibility: The Potential Impact of Emerging Evidence

Even if mediation were to become more widely used and reduce court use, and even if court process becomes more inquisitorial, requiring less advocacy, the case for restoring legal support in children matters remains strong. A lawyer provides information, advice and support to families where a problem is becoming a dispute. Legal help is not restricted to court activity but has a major part to play in helping people to avoid court by enabling them to negotiate to reach agreement. If, as suggested, there is now widely accepted interest in looking carefully at the post-LASPO situation and making the case for change by extending eligibility for free legal help in private law children matters, the next step must be to explore the feasibility of any proposal for change. This will require further information on how potentially eligible cases might be defined, and how a firm estimate of potential numbers of cases might be made. Fortunately, we now have new evidence, both local and national, about what kind of cases might be covered and how they might approach the courts.

At the local level, we are fortunate to have detailed information from Jane Krishnadas from the University of Keele on the kinds of cases being referred locally to the pro bono service provided by CLOCK (Community Legal Outreach Companions Keele) for help in the absence of legal aid post-LASPO.[16] At the national level, we have evidence and analysis on the relationship between public and private children cases in England from Matthew Jay and colleagues at the Great Ormond Street Legal Epidemiology Group, University College London. This team looked at the numbers of public and private law children cases reaching court, showing how many children in private law cases have problems that continue after an initial hearing, as indicated by rates of return to court on either public or private law matters.[17] It is therefore rapidly becoming feasible to begin to

[16] J Krishnadas, 'Falling through the public divide in family law: Access to Far Proceedings and Risk of Harm to Children and Society' (Cardiff, Socio-legal Studies Association Conference, 20 March–1 April 2021).

[17] See Jay et al, *Using administrative data to quantify overlaps between public and private children law in England: Report for the Ministry of Justice on the Children in Family Justice Data Share Pilot* (London, UCL, April 2019) at www.ucl.ac.uk/child-health/sites/child-health/files/moj_report_-_final.pdf.

move forward from establishing the desirability of change to examining its feasibility. It is becoming possible to make estimates of the potential cost of widening the scope of legal aid to include these private cases, and thereby to ensure compliance with the welfare paramountcy principle set out in the Children Act 1989, requiring a court in any matter concerning a child whose future is being determined by that court to give paramount consideration to the welfare of that child. The matter has become more urgent since the COVID crisis, as levels of family stress have increased and children during periods of lockdown were less visible to doctors, social workers and even teachers. Furthermore, as the availability of legal help has been reduced, many family legal aid firms have found it difficult to continue their work. The majority of family cases currently involve litigants in person. One practitioner described how, in 2020, if she employed a legal aid solicitor at £30,000 a year plus overheads, at current rates, 25 hours' work would be paid as a fee of £608, that is, £24.32 per hour.[18] It is consequently not surprising that, since LASPO, it has become increasingly difficult to retain legal staff. Without early legal help, parties are in fact more likely to go to court, as they cannot access help to negotiate towards agreement. In a firm with a workload of which 80 per cent is legally aided work and 20 per cent private work, the private work would be providing half of the total income.

Before examining the new evidence further, it may be helpful to list here, for reference, the relevant court actions under consideration. A section 8 order is used to determine disputes between private individuals about the upbringing of children, including child arrangement orders, specific issue orders and prohibited steps orders. A section 7 report may be ordered by the court from CAFCASS or the local authority on such matters relating to the child's welfare as the court requires. A Rule 16.4 appointment covers the appointment of a guardian to advocate for a child in private law proceedings. A section 37 report can be ordered by the court from a local authority with a view to considering applying for a care or supervision order.

V. How are the Cross-over Cases Becoming More Visible to Practitioners and Researchers?

A. The Emergence of Local Detailed Evidence on Cases Supported by CLOCK

When legally aided help became difficult to find, the voluntary sector responded in various ways. These included the development of clinical legal education services by universities, whereby legal information and support could be provided

[18] Interview with M Maclean (2020).

by students, supported and supervised by academic or 'pracademic' advisers (who are qualified to teach and also to practise, and may hold current practising certificates).[19] The story of the Community Legal Outreach Companions Keele (CLOCK), in particular, was to give a clear and worrying account of the kinds of cases that were being excluded from legal aid in children cases in one local community.[20] During research for the study reported in 'After the Act', we had been invited by a local district judge to meet this university-based group who were helping his court to deal with the post-LASPO increase in the numbers of litigants in person.[21] CLOCK is a student group, trained in the traditions of community outreach by Jane Krishnadas to help those in need of legal help: this benefits not only the clients, but also the lawyers and the court. The activity forms a part of the Law undergraduate course at Keele University. The costs of administration are met by the University, which benefits from the higher attainment of the students and from being able to support research using data from the project. Students run a helpdesk on court days – including during university vacations – sitting in pairs at the entrance to the court with a laptop and the court list, and are able to go into court with an anxious unrepresented party, or to help to sort out papers, and even to help to draft a position statement. The students have extensive training with local practitioners and are able to guide a client through court procedure, and they have a file with guidance on ethics, conflict of interests, forms and more. When the judge is confronted by an anxious client, he is able to ask the CLC (Community Legal Companion) to speak, otherwise they act as *McKenzie* friends, supporting (but not representing) a party in a hearing.

Following the COVID emergency, CLOCK gave evidence to the Means Test Review in January 2021. CLOCK described how, during the COVID lockdowns, they had received 162 requests for support for child-arrangement cases, including 51 from the local authority Children's Service. CLOCK identified and signposted 43 of these cases for legal aid. Yet, only five received legal aid, as a result of the narrow merit test, despite the inability of parents experiencing domestic abuse to access equity in property or having limited income and being unable to afford private representation. CLOCK was, at the time, assisting in five cases where a mother had not been able to see the child for up to 12 months as, once a case is in private law, it is not considered a priority, compared to public law cases.[22] For a case currently in proceedings, there is also no access to supervised contact

[19] A full account of student advice work can be found in M Maclean and J Eekelaar, *After the Act: Access to Justice after LASPO* (Oxford, Hart Publishing, 2019) ch 8, 'After the Act'.

[20] See J Krishnadas, 'Legal needs across the family justice system: Who needs what, where and when?' in M Maclean, B Dijksterhuis and R Treloar (eds), *What is a Family Justice System For?* (Oxford, Hart Publishing, 2022) 171.

[21] L Trinder et al, *Litigants in Person in Private Family Law Cases: Ministry of Justice Analytical Series 2014* (London, Ministry of Justice Analytical Series, 2014) at assets.publishing.service.gov.uk/government/uploads/system/uploads/attachment_data/file/380479/litigants-in-person-in-private-family-law-cases.pdf.

[22] Krishnadas (n 16).

or the necessary psychiatric reports. These issues have been raised by CLOCK at their local Family Justice Board Private Family Law Committee. Court staff, judges, CAFCASS and solicitors all shared their concern that – compared to children being protected in public law proceedings through legal representation of all parties and social work involvement – once a case is moved to private law proceedings, the parents and child are outside the scope of legal representation and public support, and hence at significant risk that a judge will be unable to make a clear and informed decision. CLOCK recommended that any case that evidences significant risk to a child needs to have legal aid to cover representation, and access to supervision and expert reports, to protect the rights of the parents to family life and (critically) the rights of the child to safe living conditions. Their key concern is regarding the artificial distinction between providing legal aid to parents in public law cases but not private law cases where, in CLOCK's experience, the risk of harm to children through court proceedings for children of parents who are litigants in person is currently higher (due to the fact that they are unable to collate adequate evidence for the judge to make a fully informed and fair decision). One service user said:

> I could not afford a solicitor, and there were massive safeguarding issues regarding my ex-partner, who was fighting in court, with full legal representation, for unsupervised contact! CLOCK was really helpful … [they] helped me to feel calm and got me in touch with a solicitor who did her best to get me legal aid, but unfortunately legal aid was denied. CLOCK never gave up and persisted in getting me the help I needed … and along came a Community Legal Companion … without CLOCK I would have drowned in all the jargon of massive legal words and the overwhelming time I spent in court rooms.

CLOCK has assisted 5,000 litigants in person in the last eight years without external funding, and celebrated their 10th Anniversary in September 2022.[23] In 2019, they assisted nearly 50 per cent of the C100 applications for dealing with child arrangements made in Stoke on Trent Family Court.[24] Moreover, in the first year of COVID (March 2020 to 2021), 212 cases were brought to CLOCK's attention, 35 per cent by the local authorities, 18 per cent by family doctors and domestic violence services, and others by CAFCASS and other sources.[25] Local authority referrals to CLOCK included matters currently outside the scope of legal aid, such as the non-return of a child after contact, possible domestic violence, substance abuse and mental-health issues. Sometimes there had been welfare concerns, and the local authority had been involved but the case had been moved to private proceedings. However, there is now clearly a well-trodden pathway to the door of CLOCK, which tries to secure legal aid if at all possible and, if not, seeks other forms of support. Krishnadas nevertheless still stresses

[23] ibid.
[24] ibid.
[25] ibid.

the need for public funding wherever there is a risk to a child, and for the judge to make informed decisions on the welfare of the child.[26] She also argues that legal aid should be provided to respond to the changing needs of the litigant in person, and to prioritise their agency capacity and transition through a multi-agency pathway for transformative justice across the public and private sectors.[27]

This local detailed information about the nature of the overlap that can occur between public and private law in children cases makes a strong argument for the desirability of extending legal aid to these cases. However, to estimate the possible cost of changing the eligibility rules, we also need information on the number of such cases that may be occurring nationally.

B. National Data on the Prevalence of Children Involved in Both Public and Private Cases

How many cases can be documented nationally as having crossed over the boundary in the content of their case as it has developed between public and private law? For example, a disagreement about access days for a child may have developed to include accusations of domestic abuse. We have noted in section III the President's recent estimate of private law cases with a possible child protection issue. We now also have the work of Matthew Jay and his team, who began their report to the Ministry of Justice in 2019 by saying:

> A conceptual distinction is often drawn between public and private children law under the Children Act 1989. Yet it has been suggested, in practice, that there is considerable movement of cases and individuals between public and private systems.[28]

They took advantage of the Children in Justice Data Share led by the Ministry of Justice (which uses data from the family courts, CAFCASS, the National Pupil database and children's social care) to identify children involved in private children cases. Each case would be described when it entered the justice system as an index case, and then the proportion of these children who later also became involved in public law proceedings, or returned to the private family court, was quantified. They observed 32,000–40,000 private law cases per year from 2011 to 2016, involving 48,000 to 66,000 children. Overall, 18 per cent of the children in section 8 private law proceedings in 2011 went on to experience further private law proceedings by the end of March 2016, and 3.45 per cent had been involved in public family cases during this period, mainly becoming the subjects of care orders.[29] At least 1.9 per cent had become looked-after children.[30] The authors

[26] ibid.
[27] ibid.
[28] See also Jay et al (n 17).
[29] ibid 3.
[30] ibid.

point out that private cases may be driven by the local authorities' encouragement of extended family members (eg, grandparents, siblings) to apply for care arrangement orders under section 20. In other cases, the local authority may already be involved in the life of the child incidentally to any private law proceedings, while public cases can result in a private law order or a combination (including, for example, an order for guardianship with a care arrangement order or supervision order).

When the sample was divided into children with welfare concerns at the time of the index case and those without, there was a clear difference between the later experience of those whose cases would, or would not, have been in scope for legal aid. The analysis was based on information from the Children in Family Justice Data Share, which provided linked data from the family courts, CAFCASS and social care services between 2011 and March 2015, that is, 4.25 years. The number of children involved was over 50,000 per year. Table 5 of Jay et al's report states that, of children with an index case in private family law in 2011 who returned to court by the end of March 2015, 31,290 had welfare concerns at the initial hearing and 23,718 did not.[31] Of those who did have welfare concerns in 2015, 18.4 per cent returned to court; and of those who did not have welfare concerns, 22.44 per cent returned.[32] This means that children identified with welfare concerns at the first private law hearing were less likely to return to court than those without. It is a small difference, possibly related to the statistical analysis. However, it could be related to the effect on those with concerns of having received help earlier. There was little difference in the reasons for return. That said, while one in four or five children are known to have experienced repeated involvement in both private and public family law, the study found that 3.4 per cent of children subject to private law proceedings become involved in public law proceedings within 4.25 years (which is a far higher incidence than the 1–2 per cent expected per child lifetime rate of involvement in public family law for all children).[33] The authors of the report conclude that strategies to reduce the large number of children experiencing repeated family law involvement need to be informed by further research into parents and family characteristics associated with recurrent proceedings and violence, abuse or neglect of children or partners.

VI. What Might We Expect in the Future?

COVID-related distortions in behaviour and practice may remain. Data sharing could develop further. There are also increasing concerns arising from the present situation about the need to restore legal aid to families in cases where a child is

[31] ibid 24.
[32] ibid.
[33] ibid 3.

involved. The question remains whether this should happen urgently for private law matters where a possibility of underlying protection issues can be evidenced, or, quite simply, whether this change could include all children cases as soon as resources can be found? Is this 'AQWA' – a question worth asking? There was encouragement to think this could be the case on reading the then-Lord Chancellor's words in *Family Matters*, the Family Law Bar Association journal, in summer 2021, where Rhys Taylor asked in an interview:

> Given the almost universal condemnation among lawyers and judges of the effect of the withdrawal of legal aid in most private family law matters, is there any possibility that further consideration might be given to this most vexed topic?[34]

In his reply, Sir Robert Buckland, who served as Lord Chancellor from 24 July 2019 to 15 September 2021, began by making clear that there would be no going back to the position pre-2012. However, he then referred to the post-LASPO review of 2019 as an important staging post, and said:

> We are looking to make sure that in the spirit of that review that we are testing different interventions that really focus on the most needy and vulnerable … The interesting point for me is what I'll call the cross over cases, where what starts as a private case develops elements of what we call public law cases: what about these particular cases and how to deal with them?[35]

Given the level of political uncertainty in the following year, it is perhaps not surprising that the matter has received less attention than might have been expected following the publication of the LASPO Post-Implementation Review. It is hoped that the Law Commission may now be able to develop and support further interest in the issue under the following administration. Given the now well-established key policy aim for the Ministry of Justice of reducing demand on the family courts, the reintroduction of eligibility for legal aid in children cases where there may be a welfare issue could be helpful by leading to a higher rate of settlement for some private matters outside the courts through negotiation. It may also lead to more focused presentation of the matters in court for cases involving suggestions of abuse or neglect, which could enable a judge to make a decision that would avoid the need for a later return to court. The recent renewal of interest in the way that family courts are able to work with cases of abuse or harm, following the work of the Harm Panel set up by the Ministry of Justice, has already led to interest in new procedures based on a firmer knowledge base. It is time to consolidate these developments, and to continue to move forward.

[34] (Summer 2021) *Family Matters* 2.
[35] ibid.

VII. Conclusion: An Example

This account closes with the story of a young woman, known to the author, who recently separated from her husband. They are the parents of two lively boys who, like many lively boys, do not go to bed quietly. The father has an alcohol problem, which, in the past, on occasions, has led him to hit his younger son during a bedtime row. The mother very much wants the boys to spend time with their father, but is nervous about overnight stays where the boys are likely to be disobedient and the father, after several drinks, may again lose his temper and hurt them. This is a case where legal support could help the mother to explain this concern to the court, and it is hoped that an arrangement might be devised involving some form of support or supervision for the father. Without such help, the mother can only refuse the father's request; but when facing the father's applications in court without support, she may well fail to explain the problem clearly or find a solution to propose, and a judge might quite possibly make an order for overnight stays. Legal support could offer her a chance to put her case more clearly and persuasively, and create a better opportunity for the court to reach a more nuanced and positive resolution of the problem, while giving paramount consideration to the best interests of the children. Legal help in supporting negotiation to settlement may not only promote the best interests of the children involved but, at the same time, reduce the duration, stress and cost of a contested hearing, and the possibility of a return to court. In this way, legal aid in children cases would not only be helpful to the parties in the case and give effect to the welfare paramountcy principle, but would also offer value for money in terms of the public purse.

Response to Chapter 5

The Case for a Legal Support for Children Bill, to Swiftly Reinstate Legal Aid for those at Risk of Harm or Neglect

MANDEEP DYAL

I. Introduction

The Law Society's *LASPO four years on: a Law Society review* was, overall, not positive, and concluded that the Government needs to consider the impact of the legislation on access to justice and the wider justice system, and knock-on costs for the public purse.[1] Professor Maclean's proposal summarises the need to address the adverse impact on justice, and on parties to proceedings, to which LASPO inadvertently gave rise. The potential solution suggested is to extend legal aid to 'cross-over' cases.

This response will argue that there are likely financial benefits to reinstating legal aid in 'cross-over' cases and, further, to all private law children cases. More specifically, these benefits relate, first, to a reduction in the number of litigants in person in the family court and, second, to the prevention of the descending of some 'cross-over' cases into public law care proceedings. Reducing the prevalence of these two factors could help courts to deal with cases more expeditiously and utilise fewer resources. As such, Professor Maclean's proposal may be too modest, and there may be scope for it to be expanded further.

II. Reduction of Number of Litigants in Person

The 2012 provisions resulted in a significant increase in numbers of litigants in person. The proportion of cases where both parties had legal representation fell

[1] The Law Society, *LASPO four years on: a Law Society review* (The Law Society, 29 June 2017) at www.lawsociety.org.uk/topics/research/laspo-4-years-on, 2.

from 41 per cent in January–March 2013 to 18 per cent in July–September 2022. Moreover, whereas the proportion of cases where neither party had any legal representation was 13 per cent in January–March 2013, this had risen to 39 per cent by July–September 2022.[2] The Ministry of Justice (MOJ) has acknowledged that '[t]he removal of legal aid for many private law cases in April 2013 resulted in a change in the pattern of legal representation over time'.[3]

The time that it takes to resolve private law proceedings has been increasing year on year since 2016. In July–September 2016, it was taking on average 21 weeks from a case's start date to final order. By July–September 2022, it was taking more than double that time – on average, 45 weeks – to reach final order.[4] Whilst these statistics are not broken down so as to confirm the cause of the increased time taken to resolve these private law proceedings, there is evidence that litigants in person are problematic from a cost perspective. The Law Society's 2017 Review found that litigants in person are

> [l]ess likely to settle cases outside of court hearings; likely to have more court orders and interventions in their cases; likely to lack the knowledge and skills required to conduct their case efficiently; [and] create additional work for judges and court staff, which can make court listing processes less efficient.[5]

In practice, litigants in person require significantly more court time than two represented parties. They are less likely to be able to enter into meaningful pre-hearing discussions to narrow down and refine the issues to be tried by the court, and are more likely to need the judge to assist them in understanding the proceedings and the applicable law and procedure. The judge will also need to complete additional time-consuming paperwork, such as drafting court orders following each hearing, which would ordinarily be completed by the applicant's legal representative. The more complex a case, the more pronounced these difficulties become. 'Cross-over' cases, by their very nature, involve a greater degree of complexity. The Review concluded:

> The dramatic increase of litigants in person … following LASPO has created a severe strain on the court system. Often forced to represent themselves due to a lack of legal aid, litigants in person can struggle to understand court procedures and their legal entitlements, and cases involving them take longer to resolve. This doesn't just create bad outcomes for the litigant, but it can be a huge burden on court finances and resources – and ultimately the public purse.[6]

Alongside the increased number of litigants in person, there has been a shortfall in the number of district judges available to hear cases, which has been raised by

[2] National Statistics, 'Family Court Statistics Quarterly: July to September 2022' (London, Ministry of Justice, 15 December 2022) at www.gov.uk/government/statistics/family-court-statistics-quarterly-july-to-september-2022/family-court-statistics-quarterly-july-to-september-2022#children-act---private-law.

[3] ibid.

[4] ibid.

[5] Law Society (n 1) 25.

[6] ibid 2.

the Lord Chief Justice, Lord Burnett, on a number of occasions (and confirmed again most recently on 11 June 2021 in his Annual Seminar at the conference of the Association of District Judges).[7] The shortfall has led to a sustained recruitment drive for district judges and deputy district judges, all of which costs money. This further compounds the strain on court time, and makes resolution of the litigant-in-person issue even more pressing.

Whilst the MOJ has recognised the need to address the issues created by the significant increase in the numbers of litigants in person, its proposed support may not actually resolve these issues. In its 2019 publication, *Legal Support: The Way Ahead. An action plan to deliver better support to people experiencing legal problems*, the MOJ proposed to 'conduct a review into the thresholds for legal aid entitlement, and their interaction with the wider criteria', and further to 'enhance the support we offer to litigants in person'.[8] There was no plan to specifically address private law children cases and the unique difficulties that litigants in person face in such proceedings (such as the often immense emotional strain of dealing with matters relating to their own children and personal lives in a court arena, without legal representation). The focus of this action plan appeared to be on providing legal 'support' to potential litigants prior to the issue of proceedings, in an attempt to encourage early resolution and avoid court proceedings, as opposed to extending legal aid to fund legal representation once applications are made to court:

> We believe that high quality early legal support may help people understand their options and empower them to resolve their problems earlier. This may avoid unnecessary financial and non-financial costs to the individual and those around them (through inactivity or pursuing an ineffective course of action), society (through wider societal costs from unresolved legal problems – eg negative mental and physical health outcomes) and government (through preventable demand for services) … [M]any of our discussions with stakeholders have focused on the wider benefits of supporting early resolution. We are keen to explore this further, especially the most effective ways for central government to help enable this.[9]

The suggestion is made for a Civil Legal Aid telephone service to provide legal support to litigants,[10] and the report focuses on how '[b]etter information and signposting at early stages could enable people to resolve their legal problems earlier and through other means outside of the formal justice system where appropriate'.[11]

However, this suggested pre-proceedings legal 'support' is not a substitute for legal representation for a number of reasons. First, the telephone service would

[7] National Statistics (n 2).

[8] Ministry of Justice, *Legal Support: The Way Ahead. An action plan to deliver better support to people experiencing legal problems* (London, Ministry of Justice, 2019) 19 at www.gov.uk/government/publications/legal-support-action-plan.

[9] ibid 19 and 21.

[10] ibid 22.

[11] ibid 26.

not resolve the additional court time required when dealing with litigants in person and problematic interactions in court, with the corresponding cost to the public purse.

Second, there is already a requirement for parties to have attended a Mediation Information and Assessment Meeting (MIAM) prior to issuing a section 8 Children Act application, which encompasses the vast majority of private law proceedings. Notwithstanding this, the time taken to reach the stage of final order in these proceedings has continued to increase year on year.

Third, the provision of 'better information and signposting at early stages' will not necessarily discourage litigants from issuing court proceedings in private law matters, as the source of the dispute in such proceedings is often not that the parties are ill-informed and require information but, rather, much more complex. The source of the dispute may relate to welfare issues, safeguarding concerns, significantly different parenting styles and/or a host of other issues; the provision of 'information' is unlikely to resolve issues such as these.

Fourth, the role played by legal representatives is wider than merely providing legal advice and drafting paperwork. Family law proceedings are generally emotionally difficult for parties. They frequently involve disputes about very personal and emotive parts of parties' lives – their children, their close relationships, their homes and their private lives. The proceedings can be upsetting, and going to court can be intimidating. In some cases, there are elements of abuse and control perpetrated by one party, which may not be immediately apparent, as the person suffering the abuse has inadvertently or intentionally kept it hidden. The role of legal representatives has to be seen within this context. For parties to proceedings, a legal representative often provides the reassurance of having someone who is consistently present and 'on their side', ensuring that their voice is heard. They act as a filter for litigants – the courtroom is not set up for airing the sorts of frustrations that are often vented in the privacy of legally privileged discussions with a representative. They provide a means of assisting the parties to narrow the issues via fair and balanced negotiation, which two litigants in person would find difficult and a mediator would be unable to achieve (as mediators are ordinarily involved long before full evidential disclosure has taken place). There is insufficient judicial time and capacity to deal with these sorts of discussions and negotiations. In the absence of legal representation of the parties, judges are forced to engage in the time-consuming exercise of dealing with lay parties directly, resulting in reduced judicial productivity.

III. Preventing Cases from Escalating

A further argument in support of extending legal aid is that it will prevent private law cases from escalating into care proceedings. Care proceedings are generally much more costly than private law proceedings, as they typically involve at least four parties (the local authority; the children via their guardian and their solicitor;

the mother of the children; and the father of the children), as opposed to the two parties involved in private law proceedings (the mother and father). As a general rule, the legal representation of all four of the parties in care proceedings is funded via the public purse, with the parents entitled to legal aid. Legal representation of the parties in 'cross-over' cases may help to prevent these 'cross-over' cases from descending into costly care proceedings. This is because legal representatives are in a position to identify, and help to address, any concerns at an early stage, and they offer clients strong and consistent advice on the consequences of *not* addressing the concerns. In addition, they are able to assist clients to make the necessary referrals to mental-health services, counselling and/or other support services, to help to deal with the issues that, if left unaddressed, could lead to an escalation of local-authority involvement and, ultimately, to care proceedings.

There may also be a wider cost-saving were legal representation in 'cross-over' cases to reduce the number of cases becoming care proceedings. Legal costs aside, local authorities incur significant financial costs when they become involved with a family. There is a statutory duty on every local authority to

> [s]afeguard and promote the welfare of children within their area who are in need; and so far as is consistent with that duty, to promote the upbringing of such children by their families, by providing a range and level of services appropriate to those children's needs.[12]

Where a referral is made to a local authority in respect of a child, and it appears that the child's needs are not being met and/or that the child may be at risk, the local authority will usually complete an assessment.[13] If the need for local authority intervention and support is subsequently identified, the subject child may be placed on a Child in Need Plan.[14] Where concerns continue to escalate, the child may be placed on a Child Protection Plan.[15] With each stage, the local authority is required to hold statutory meetings and reviews (either Child in Need meetings or Child Protection Conferences) at regular intervals. Child Protection Conferences require input from multiple professionals, including the 'lead' or allocated social worker, other local authority staff, representatives from the child's school and often medical professionals, such as the health visitor, school nurse, family doctor or Child and Adolescent Mental Health Services. There is also a requirement for the child to be visited on a regular basis. Where the concerns continue, or escalate, and the subject child continues to be at risk of significant harm, the local authority will initiate the pre-proceedings protocol and ultimately consider issuing care proceedings. All of this is time-consuming and costly. If legal representation could assist, in the ways set out above, to prevent 'cross-over' cases from deteriorating in this manner into care proceedings, there would likely be benefits to the public purse.

[12] Children Act 1989, s 17(1).
[13] See ibid, ss 17, 37 and 47.
[14] ibid s 17.
[15] ibid s 47.

Consideration should be given to opening legal aid up more widely to all private law proceedings as, indeed, it may well prevent certain cases from becoming 'cross-over' cases in the first place. This is particularly so in cases involving a significant risk of emotional harm and parental alienation, where early, consistent legal advice and guidance can assist parties in reducing parental conflict (which is very often at the centre of the emotional harm and/or parental alienation).

IV. How Such Cases may be Defined and Identified

Professor Maclean's proposal raises the issue of 'how potentially eligible cases might be defined'. A definition of 'cross-over' cases, and guidance on how to identify them, will be necessary to enable practitioners and parties to make legal-aid applications.

Certain criteria are likely to be relatively uncontentious, for instance where there is evidence of current local authority involvement with a family and the local authority's concerns are such that the children have been placed on Child in Need or Child Protection Plan. Other 'cross-over' cases, however, may be more difficult to identify. In certain cases, there may be a number of factors that, taken individually, do not place a child at risk of significant harm, but the aggregate effect of which may make the child extremely vulnerable. There will also be cases that have not come to the attention of the local authority, but where it appears to the court that the subject child is at risk of significant harm. These cases are likely to prove more challenging to pinpoint. Any definition would need to take care to include these sorts of cases.

A potentially valuable tool in identifying these cases in practice is CAFCASS.[16] In every application for a Child Arrangements Order, after the issue of the application but prior to the First Hearing Dispute Resolution Appointment, CAFCASS will interview each party to the proceedings and complete a safeguarding letter.[17] This letter will set out issues relating to the safety of the child, including: the outcome of police checks on each party; whether the family is known to the local authority; a precis of the issues, welfare concerns and any safeguarding concerns; and preliminary recommendations. This letter could play an important role in identifying 'cross-over' cases at an early stage in proceedings. It is acknowledged that this may not be ideal, as the letter is produced after, not before, an application has been issued. Further, some cases will evolve into 'cross-over' cases after completion of the safeguarding letter as the family environment deteriorates during the course of proceedings. However, the safeguarding letter is a significant document that is routinely prepared by CAFCASS in all private law proceedings, and it could be used to form the basis of a legal aid application where it may not

[16] The Children and Family Court Advisory and Support Service.
[17] Family Procedure Rules 2010, Practice Direction 12B, para 13.

be immediately apparent, prior to issuing the application, that the case meets the 'cross-over' criteria.

There are possible drawbacks to the approach that is proposed here, including the potential cost to the public purse and the lack of financial incentive to settle at an early (or any) stage. Therefore, consideration would need to be given to building in safeguards, such as: (i) the preservation of means-testing; and (ii) compulsory reviews of the legal-aid certificate based on the merits of pursuing the application at certain stages of proceedings, to ensure that legal aid is not being misused. For example, in cases where the court has identified welfare issues, it will often direct CAFCASS to complete a welfare assessment under section 7 of the Children Act 1989 (a 'section 7' report). This report will contain recommendations for resolution of the issues in the case. If a party does not agree to follow the professional recommendations contained in that report, they are entitled to challenge the author of the report, but it requires listing a costly final hearing, at which the author of the report can be cross-examined. This is an ideal stage at which to review the legal-aid certificate, as the merits of pursuing particular issues to final hearing stage are usually much clearer upon receipt of the recommendations in the section 7 report.

V. Conclusion

Following the Law Society and MOJ's consideration of how best to tackle the consequences of LASPO, COVID struck. Prior to the COVID pandemic, the family courts were trying to tackle significant delays within the system caused by the sheer volume of applications being made and moving through the system, with court lists being very full and courts frequently being over-listed. The pandemic has added further strain to an already buckling system, the family courts having ground to a halt for several months whilst Her Majesty's Courts and Tribunal Service struggled to create, at very short notice, a system of remote hearings. This adds a new urgency to ease the pressure on courts – a pressure that is increased by a lack of legal aid for parties to private law children proceedings.

The function of the family court is to ensure that such cases are dealt with fairly, within the overriding objective, and in accordance with the child's welfare – either party not having legal representation tends to make that more difficult and, as argued, potentially more costly. The cuts to legal aid may well have resulted in a reduction in spending in certain areas, but have arguably also led to an increased need to spend in others. Opening up legal aid to 'cross-over' cases and, beyond that, to all private law children cases, may well be a case of 'speculating to accumulate'.

6

A New Law of Family Property

SHARON THOMPSON*

I. Introduction

Niamh has left her job. She has two young children and, with escalating childcare costs, she cannot afford to return to the labour market. Her husband works in finance. She has no control over the family finances and no knowledge of her partner's assets or earnings. They are not a particularly wealthy couple. Now they have recently separated; he is claiming to have no assets and to be in debt. She, on the other hand, is convinced he has the ability to provide her with support as the primary carer of their children – but she cannot prove it.

Though divorce is now more straightforward, thanks to removal of fault from the process by the Divorce, Dissolution and Separation Act 2020,[1] Niamh's concerns are about property. She is worried about divorcing, because she is in the dark about the household finances and fears her husband has the upper hand in negotiations. She is used to the idea that the money her husband earns is 'his' money and not hers, even though she has provided almost all of the domestic labour and childcare throughout their relationship.

While the substantive law provides the court with discretionary power to make Niamh financial provision that is fair,[2] recognises her non-financial contributions and facilitates an 'equal start on the road to independent living',[3] these outcomes do not reflect the practical realities for many on divorce. Most cases are never adjudicated before a judge.[4] Sometimes, cases are not even settled at all.[5] There is also a gendered disparity between spouses on divorce.[6]

* I am grateful to all *Family Law Reform Now* participants for their engagement with the paper on which this chapter is based. I am particularly indebted to Alison Diduck, Andy Hayward, Anna Heenan and Russell Sandberg for reading and commenting on earlier drafts, and to Charlotte Bendall and Rehana Parveen for the opportunity to be involved in this project.

[1] Amending s 1 of the Matrimonial Causes Act 1973.

[2] *White v White* [2000] UKHL 54.

[3] *Miller v Miller; McFarlane v McFarlane* [2006] UKHL 24 [144].

[4] E Hitchings, 'Official, operative and outsider justice: the ties that (may not) bind in family financial disputes' (2017) 29(4) *Child and Family Law Quarterly* 359.

[5] See, eg, A Barlow et al, *Mapping Paths to Family Justice: Resolving Family Disputes in Neoliberal Times* (Basingstoke, Palgrave Macmillan, 2017).

[6] H Fisher and H Low, 'Recovery from Divorce: Comparing High and Low-Income Couples' (2016) 30 *International Journal of Law, Policy and the Family* 338.

Thus, Niamh's story represents three fundamental problems with the law of financial remedies: economic inequality; lack of transparency regarding available finances; and spouses' misconceptions over entitlement on divorce. Put simply, the need for reform of the financial consequences of divorce is made more acute by the pervasive gendered power imbalance in marriage.

Niamh's individual story is fictional, but the data that it represents is not. Research and statistics reveal this type of scenario to be relatively common.[7] Yet while bringing these issues to light is one struggle, thinking about how to address them is quite another. There is consensus as to the *need* for reform, but an impasse as to the question of *how*. Such stalemate is not helped by the fact that extensive reform of the law is probably needed – something that cannot be achieved overnight. There needs to be an achievable stepping stone to build momentum for broader change.

To be clear, this chapter does *not* seek to provide a solution for economic inequality on divorce. However, it does consider a potential path *towards* reform. One option is to deal with the rules during the relationship first, by introducing a new law of family property. This would facilitate joint ownership of certain assets during the marriage only, and would not introduce any form of community of property (which automatically triggers pooling of assets and affects distribution on divorce). Such a scheme could help clarify questions of property ownership before separation. Rights to property during a marriage or civil partnership can be important, because there is a link between power, money and inequality in the relationship. Currently, in England and Wales, there is no set of rules determining who owns what during marriage. Instead, the default is separate property. Questions of property ownership are not normally addressed until the relationship breaks down. There are instances when property ownership matters during marriage, such as on bankruptcy or death. Knowing who owns what during marriage might be very important indeed for those who earn much less than their partner. And even if a new law of family property would not *directly* affect the property consequences of divorce, it could give couples a starting point to work from when negotiating the redistribution of property. There are clear benefits to this as, in the context of legal aid cuts and out-of-court settlements, couples need to be able to bargain effectively in the shadow of the law, and should not have to wait until relationship breakdown to understand questions of property entitlement. Such reform could also provide a better picture of how the financial consequences of divorce could be reformed in future without compromising notions of fairness and equality. In other words, as the language

[7] See, eg, OECD, *Net Childcare Costs* (OECD, 2022) at data.oecd.org/benwage/net-childcare-costs.htm; Office for National Statistics, *Working and workless households in the UK: January to March 2022* (Statistical Bulletin, ONS, 1 June 2022) at www.ons.gov.uk/employmentandlabourmarket/peopleinwork/employmentandemployeetypes/bulletins/workingandworklesshouseholds/januarytomarch2022; M Costa Dias, R Joyce and F Parodi, 'The gender pay gap in the UK: children and experience in work' (Institute of Fiscal Studies, 5 February 2018) at www.ifs.org.uk/publications/10356.

of sharing assets is an important feature of relationship breakdown, it could be beneficial to embed this language of sharing during the marriage too.

In section II, the broader context of financial remedies is explored further. It asserts that marital property agreements should not be made binding under legislation without broader reform of the financial consequences of marriage and divorce. Though it is widely considered that the financial consequences of divorce need to be changed, there is significantly less focus on the financial consequences of marriage. Subsequent sections make a case for a new law of family property, which includes reforming the rules that determine property ownership *during* marriage and civil partnership. Section III will argue that looking at these rules could provide an important and necessary precursor to reform of the financial consequences of divorce. Then, in section IV, the Law Commission's 1988 draft Bill is outlined, which, if enacted, would have set out new rules regarding the beneficial ownership of matrimonial property. Finally, section V argues that this Bill should be revisited and redrafted for the 2020s, as well as considering whether its provisions should extend to interests in land (and potentially pensions) and to unmarried cohabitants. For although the context in which the 1988 Bill was first drafted has changed, this does not mean its provisions are now redundant. Far from it: this chapter asserts that these proposals should be resurrected as an important stepping stone to much-needed comprehensive reform.

II. The Need for Reform

The current law that determines financial remedies is based upon a statute drafted in 1969 and given effect in 1971, when the landscape of marriage and divorce was very different.[8] Marital property agreements were virtually unheard of, while there is now evidence to indicate that agreements such as 'prenups' are relatively widespread. Today, property issues on divorce are much less likely to be resolved inside a courtroom, if at all.[9] If couples are making arrangements in the shadow of the law, they need to know what the law is. Herein lies the problem: the system is complex and requires knowledge and understanding of case law, as well as statute.[10]

The current law of financial remedies was introduced because divorce reform threatened to leave spouses in an economically precarious position on divorce. For many married women of the 1960s, divorce meant financial disaster. The main concern – and a major threat to the passage of the Divorce Reform Bill – was the clause providing that a woman could be divorced by her husband without

[8] Matrimonial Proceedings and Property Act 1970.

[9] E Hitchings et al, 'Fair Shares? Sorting Out Money and Property on Divorce' (2023) 1 *Financial Remedies Journal* 47.

[10] E Hitchings, J Miles and H Woodward, *Assembling the Jigsaw Puzzle: Understanding Financial Settlement on Divorce* (Bristol, University of Bristol and the Nuffield Foundation, November 2013) 101.

her consent after a period of five years' separation.[11] With this new era of divorce on a no-fault basis, including divorce without consent, traditional notions of marriage as a lifelong commitment were challenged like never before. Although this would be potentially liberating for women stuck in unhappy marriages, it had as much potential to oppress women, given that equal economic status in marriage was still far from being a reality. As a result, the Divorce Reform Act 1969 was not brought into effect until 1971, so that the Law Commission could investigate fully the financial consequences of divorce. The recommendations in the Law Commission's report sought to ameliorate the concerns of those opposed to divorce because of the potential consequences for married women.[12] These were enshrined in the Matrimonial Proceedings and Property Act 1970, now consolidated in the Matrimonial Causes Act 1973 and still in force today (albeit with some slight amendments[13]).

It could be argued that the Divorce, Dissolution and Separation Act 2020 has opened up similar issues – this more logical divorce law is not compatible with an impenetrable law of financial remedies. The divorce process has been streamlined, with parties able to apply solely or jointly simply by submitting a notification that the relationship has broken down irretrievably. Divorces can be defended only on exceptional, technical grounds, thus the consent of both parties is not needed. Fault has also been removed from the process entirely. In light of this new context, the property consequences of marriage and divorce need to be revisited, as they stand in stark contrast to this new, simplified regime. Since the Act was brought into effect in 2022, there have been renewed calls for reform. In response, Lord Parkinson, on behalf of the Government, responded:

> In April, the Government commenced the Divorce, Dissolution and Separation Act, the biggest change to divorce law and practice for nearly half a century. Now that we have implemented the Act, we have turned our minds to consideration of the legislation surrounding financial provision on divorce. We deliberately kept that as a separate issue, and we will be announcing our intentions for the work in due course.[14]

Nevertheless, determining *how* this area should be reformed is not straightforward. In 2014, the Law Commission concluded its project on matrimonial property,

[11] Which is one of the routes to establishing irretrievable breakdown pursuant to the Divorce Reform Act 1969 and s 1(2)(e) of the consolidating Matrimonial Causes Act 1973. S Thompson, 'Behind Casanova's Charter: Edith Summerskill, Divorce and the Deserted Wife' in J Miles, D Monk and R Probert (eds), *Fifty Years of the Divorce Reform Act 1969* (Oxford, Hart Publishing, 2022) 117.

[12] *Financial Provision in Matrimonial Proceedings* (Law Com No 25, 1969).

[13] For example, the removal of the minimal loss principle and introduction of the clean break pursuant to the Matrimonial and Family Proceedings Act 1984, as well as reform to pensions pursuant to the Welfare Reform and Pensions Act 1999.

[14] HL Deb 12 May 2022, vol 822, col 216. Lord Bellamy later confirmed this in HL Deb 8 March 2023, vol 828, col 790: 'These matters will be considered fully in a forthcoming review, hopefully by the Law Commission.'

needs and marital-property agreements.[15] It recommended a route to reform for marital-property agreements, producing a draft Bill that, if introduced, would make them binding.[16] However, it did not make recommendations regarding the law of matrimonial property. Introducing the Law Commission's draft Nuptial Agreements Bill without broader reform would be a missed opportunity to take a more streamlined look at dealing with the need to reform the law of financial remedies – a problem that is not going away and is only growing as time goes on.

Marital property agreements are not currently binding under legislation. They should not be made binding without reform of financial remedies, because this would send a message that the wealthy can buy certainty and reassurance over what will happen to their assets in the event of divorce, while the rest of the population cannot. Standalone reform of such agreements is not the answer.[17] Thanks, in part, to the work of numerous notable academics, the aforementioned issues of economic inequality, transparency regarding available finances, and spouses' misconceptions over entitlement on divorce are identified and supported by a broad base of evidence.[18]

A. Economic Inequality and Lack of Transparency

Understanding why and how the law of financial remedies is fraught with economic inequality requires considering the gendered aspects of family living, and how partners' choices are constrained by the state's support and valuation of care.[19] Recent statistics paint a worrying picture. The number of women not working in order to look after family increased by 5 per cent in 2021.[20] As reported in *The Times*, this was the first sustained increase in women leaving the workforce for at least 30 years.[21] Approximately 28.5 per cent of economically inactive women were not working in order to look after home or the family, compared with 6.9 per cent of men. The number of women not working also rose by

[15] *Matrimonial Property, Needs and Agreements* (Law Com No 343, 2014).

[16] Under the Law Commission's Nuptial Agreements Bill, in order for an agreement to be a 'qualifying' nuptial agreement, certain procedural safeguards would have to be met. Qualifying agreements could not be used by parties to contract out of meeting the financial needs of one another and of any children.

[17] See S Thompson, *Prenuptial Agreements and the Presumption of Free Choice* (Oxford, Hart Publishing, 2015).

[18] See, eg, A Diduck, 'Autonomy and Family Justice' (2016) 28 *Child and Family Law Quarterly* 133; J Miles and E Hitchings, 'Financial remedy outcomes on divorce in England and Wales: Not a "meal ticket for life"' (2018) 31(2) *Australian Journal of Family Law* 43; Barlow et al (n 5).

[19] See A Heenan, 'Neoliberalism, family law, and the devaluation of care' (2021) 48(3) *Journal of Law and Society* 386.

[20] Office for National Statistics (n 7).

[21] T Calver, 'Held back: the mothers who can't afford to return to work' *Sunday Times* (5 June 2022) at www.thetimes.co.uk/article/held-back-the-mothers-who-cant-afford-to-return-to-work-r5r3k9bxl#.

13 per cent in the age group 25–34.[22] Other surveys indicate that, with childcare costs strikingly higher than almost everywhere else in Europe,[23] mothers cannot afford to return to work.[24] This is unsurprising, given that the cost of a full-time nursery place for children under the age of 2 rose from £236 a week in 2018 to £274 in 2022 – a jump of 16 per cent.[25]

Structural inequalities that contribute towards one spouse's development of their career prospects, income and pension to the detriment of the other spouse can be exacerbated by other factors too, such as lack of transparency. On divorce, parties are obliged to provide full and frank disclosure of assets.[26] Even so, there are concerns in some cases that assets are being concealed, yet there is insufficient evidence to challenge this in court.[27] If one party controls most of the finances, they may also have information about the family's assets that the other party does not. There is no legal right to information about one's spouse or civil partner's income and finances. It is perfectly lawful to keep one's partner in the dark about this. Even in cases where proper disclosure has been made, outcomes can still be affected by gendered power imbalance. In their court file survey of 399 financial remedy cases in 2011–12, Emma Hitchings et al found evidence of domestic abuse in 25 per cent of consent order cases and 38 per cent of contested cases.[28] Furthermore, Liz Trinder et al found that 35 per cent of financial remedy cases included evidence of domestic abuse (and, in this study, all cases were inflicted against wives).[29] As these data were based on divorce paperwork, they do not necessarily reflect a history of domestic abuse during the relationship. However, Judith Crisp et al have suggested that these figures 'are likely to be an underestimate'.[30] From this perspective, it is perhaps unsurprising that research shows a gender gap in recovery rates on divorce, with women impacted more than men by the financial consequences of relationship breakdown across all age groups and wealth brackets.[31]

[22] Office for National Statistics (n 7).

[23] OECD (n 7).

[24] See also '1 In 4 Parents Have Had To Cut Down On Heat, Food and Clothing To Pay For Childcare' *Pregnant Then Screwed* (25 March 2022) at pregnantthenscrewed.com/one-in-four-parents-say-that-they-have-had-to-cut-down-on-heat-food-clothing-to-pay-for-childcare/.

[25] Calver (n 21).

[26] Family Procedure Rules 2010, Practice Direction 9A.

[27] See, eg, anxieties expressed by practitioners after the case of *Tchenguiz v Imerman; Imerman v Imerman* [2010] EWCA Civ 908; Anon, 'Grant Thornton's matrimonial survey shows the effects of the recession on financial settlements' *Family Law Week* at www.familylawweek.co.uk/grant-thorntons-matrimonial-survey-shows-the-effects-of-the-recession-on-financial-settlements/.

[28] Hitchings et al (n 10) 101–02.

[29] L Trinder et al, *Litigants in Person in Private Family Law Cases* (London, Ministry of Justice, 2014).

[30] J Crisp, R Hunter and E Hitchings, 'Domestic Abuse in Financial Remedy Cases' (2022) 2 *Financial Remedies Journal* 123, 126.

[31] Fisher and Low (n 6); D Price, 'Pension Accumulation and Gendered Household Structures: What are the Implications of Changes in Family Formation for Future Financial Inequality?' in J Miles and R Probert (eds), *Sharing Lives, Dividing Assets: An Inter-Disciplinary Study* (Oxford, Hart Publishing, 2009) 279.

B. Misconceptions about Entitlement

During marriage or civil partnership, the doctrine of separate property means that the person who earns the property legally owns that property too. On divorce, these assets suddenly become susceptible to division, and the lesser-moneyed spouse has access to that property. Yet there is sometimes a perception that property earned by the moneyed spouse is his alone, rather than property generated directly and indirectly by both spouses working outside and inside the home.[32]

Misconceptions about entitlement could exacerbate gendered disparities post-divorce, and may also explain why there is a concerning lack of pension sharing. Though pension sharing has been possible since the Welfare Reform and Pensions Act 1999 was brought into effect in 2000, some studies suggest that as many as seven in 10 couples are not including pensions in the pot of assets being redistributed on divorce.[33] Buckley and Price's analysis indicates that 'very widespread disparities persist' between men and women's pension wealth within couples at all ages, all income levels and all pension wealth distributions.[34] Furthermore, failure to pension share is directly connected to women's poverty. The economic gulf created by caregiving sacrifices is, in part, because putting one's career on hold also means compromising one's pension in retirement. Priorities on divorce are gendered too, with women's most urgent concern often being to 'keep a roof over the family's head'.[35]

Stacking these inequalities on top of one another underscores the urgency of reform of financial remedies law. Reform making marital property agreements binding under legislation is unlikely to help address these imbalances of economic power in relationships. Despite the increasing privatisation of family justice and the shift towards valorising autonomy on divorce, this crisis of inequality is not being faced head-on. Private agreements are not the answer. However, the route to reform is not clear-cut. These issues sprout from a deeply embedded framework of structural inequality, made more acute by the cost-of-living crisis, childcare costs, inflexible working conditions (even post-pandemic) and lack of state support. It is unrealistic to suppose that the law can address these issues without broader, sweeping structural reform. But this does not mean the law is impotent, and even small, incremental steps to ameliorate economic inequalities within marriage on divorce are steps worth taking. A new law of family property could be one of those steps, as the next section explores.

[32] For misperceptions about this area of law, see S Thompson, 'A millstone around the neck? Stereotypes about wives and myths about divorce' (2019) 70(2) *Northern Ireland Legal Quarterly* 181.

[33] Note, this is not an academic study: C Gifford, 'Seven in 10 divorcing couples don't share pensions' *Which* (25 July 2022) at www.which.co.uk/news/article/seven-in-10-divorcing-couples-dont-share-pensions-aDHbd4A9tStW.

[34] J Buckley and D Price, 'Pensions on divorce: where now, what next?' (2021) 33(1) *Child and Family Law Quarterly* 5, 5.

[35] ibid 24.

III. A New Law of Family Property

At present, determining who owns what within marriage requires placing significant emphasis on who paid for that property. The message in law during marriage, therefore, is that the owner of the asset is most likely the person who directly paid for it. This not only conflicts with the discretionary redistribution of property on divorce – which takes a much broader view of property ownership based on a range of factors – but also does not reflect the reality of how many couples jointly manage property. Taking another look at the rules determining property ownership during marriage and civil partnership could, therefore, provide a potential route forwards when considering how to address uncertainties and hostilities on divorce, while reflecting the actuality of property ownership during marriage. This section explores why a new law of family property could be an incremental step towards addressing some of the problems explored in section II.

A. Why Reform Property Ownership During Marriage?

Unlike neighbouring jurisdictions,[36] there is no marital property regime in place in England and Wales. A system of immediate community of property, which automatically pools and equally divides communal assets from the beginning of the relationship, has been rejected numerous times as an option for England and Wales.[37] Sharing half of all property and debt might still leave some parties in a financially precarious position. For instance, if the sole asset was the family home, half of the proceeds of its sale might not leave the lesser-earning spouse with enough capital to rehouse themselves in the event of divorce.

As a result of these concerns, reforming the financial consequences of marriage and civil partnership may appear for some to be too radical a proposal. It could be argued, for instance, that recent proposals for rules of automatic equal sharing of matrimonial property – mirroring the Scottish system – should be treated with caution.[38] However, it is important to distinguish a new law of family property from a system of community of property. The reform proposed in this chapter, as section IV explores in more detail, builds upon the Law Commission's previous recommendations that new rules regarding the ownership of matrimonial property would not apply to separating spouses. Separate property rights would be maintained, and co-ownership would apply only in certain situations. Furthermore, ownership would not be determined by a formula triggering the automatic pooling of assets.

[36] eg, France, the Netherlands, and Germany.

[37] E Cooke, A Barlow and T Callus, *Community of Property: A Regime for England and Wales?* (London, Nuffield Foundation, 2006).

[38] S Thompson, *Submission of Written Evidence on Divorce (Financial Provision) Bill 2017–2019* (unpublished 2018).

An additional potential criticism is that it is not immediately apparent how the proposed reform would have any bearing on the financial consequences of divorce. After all, why consider reform of property ownership during the relationship if it does not determine financial remedies on divorce? There are a number of reasons why this is important. For instance, there could be occasions during the marriage or civil partnership when knowledge of who owns what could be important, such as on bankruptcy and death.[39] Indeed, if inequalities continue to exist within marriage, why should questions of property ownership matter only when the relationship has broken down? As the Commission put it:

> It is a false dichotomy to split marriages into the happy and the unhappy, and to say that while the couple are happy, property ownership does not matter and that, if they are not, they will get divorced and that the court will reallocate the property. Most marriages do not end in divorce.[40]

In other words, it is not right to consider ownership of marital property only at the end of the relationship. Questions of entitlement to property could be important for spouses or partners who earn significantly less than their partner, or who do not have property in their name.[41] Sociological research also demonstrates that property ownership during the relationship can have a profound effect on the construction of conjugal power. In his longitudinal study of 6,070 couples in the UK, Yang Hu found that 'managing household finances may indirectly enable individuals to derive relative or autonomous power from the money they manage to negotiate their housework participation'.[42] Further, he found that the literal transfer or sharing of property between partners during the relationship has a direct correlation with marital power and household performance. When men had more financial power and controlled financial decisions in the household, this reduced the time they spent on housework because they could 'bargain out' of the domestic labour.[43] Yet this was not the case for women, for Hu's findings implied 'a tale of two genders':[44]

> [M]y findings clearly show that individual earnings obtained from paid work are only the starting point for women's development of individual autonomy. I have demonstrated that to 'opt out' or 'buy out' of housework, it is insufficient for women to merely participate in paid work. Rather, they also need to be able to access their earnings (through financial management) and control these earnings (by influencing financial decisions).[45]

[39] *Family Law: Matrimonial Property* (Law Com No 175, 1988) para 1.4.

[40] ibid.

[41] The family home is not always owned jointly, and spouses must register their matrimonial home rights on the deeds of the property pursuant to the Family Law Act 1996.

[42] Y Hu, 'What about money? Earnings, household financial organization, and housework' (2019) 81(5) *Journal of Marriage and Family* 1091, 1105.

[43] ibid 1106.

[44] ibid 1105i.

[45] ibid 1106.

This bolsters the case for the reform proposed in this chapter. By providing parties with additional beneficial ownership interests – and therefore control over finances – a new law of family property applicable during the marriage or civil partnership could, in theory, level the playing field where one party wields financial power over the other.[46] For example, if one party were suffering relationship-generated disadvantage as a result of caring responsibilities, they could be empowered to learn they have joint rights of ownership with their partner. Instead of placing emphasis on who pays for property in the relationship – which could disadvantage the lesser-earning spouse or civil partner – these proposals would instead focus on how such property is used.[47]

This distinguishes a new law of family property from proposals in recent years for automatic equal division of matrimonial assets, which could have the unintended consequence of limiting provision for the lesser-earning spouse.[48] Instead, by *enhancing* the property rights of the lesser-earning spouse during marriage in a way that balances the financial and non-financial contributions of the parties, the value of care is recognised and normalised under law throughout the course of the marriage, instead of being raised suddenly when the relationship breaks down.

Nevertheless, as section III.B considers, it is likely that some will view reform of property ownership during marriage as an unnecessary and unwelcome interference in the autonomy of married couples, who can currently manage their own property as they see fit and arrange their own rules for sharing through private agreement.

B. Autonomy

While autonomy is important, the way in which it is exercised must be properly understood. The concept of neo-liberal autonomy[49] has been a powerful influence on policies surrounding family breakdown in recent years. Its supremacy has been widely criticised as promoting an individualised form of justice that does not engage with disparity of power between the parties. As Alison Diduck has put it, '[a]utonomy has become more than one aspect of justice in the new, "modernised" family justice system, it is becoming almost its very essence'.[50]

[46] See J Pahl, 'Household Spending, Personal Spending and the Control of Money in Marriage' (1990) 24(1) *Sociology* 119; C Burgoyne, 'Money in marriage: How patterns of allocation both reflect and conceal power' (1990) 38(4) *The Sociological Review* 634.

[47] A full explication of the meaning and scope of family property is outside the scope of this chapter; however, the Law Commission has already considered in detail how this could operate – *Family Law: Matrimonial Property* (Law Com No 175, 1988).

[48] See, eg, the provisions outlined in the Divorce (Financial Provision) Bill (2019–21).

[49] J Mant, 'Neoliberalism, family law and the cost of access to justice' (2017) 39(2) *Journal of Social Welfare and Family Law* 246; A Heenan, 'Neoliberalism, family law, and the devaluation of care' (2021) 48(3) *Journal of Law and Society* 386.

[50] A Diduck, 'Autonomy and Family Justice' (2016) 28(2) *Child and Family Law Quarterly* 133, 134.

This version of autonomy focuses on the individual, who is expected to seek the best deal for themselves. If the reality of how individuals make decisions is to be appreciated then it is important to challenge the idea that, in contracts, autonomy simply means a rational and voluntary choice. Particularly in the complex realm of intimate family law agreements, it would be fair to ask whether individuals ever make completely voluntary, rational choices. While neo-liberal notions of autonomy are built on assumptions that decision makers are independent, self-interested and rational actors, relational autonomy asserts that '[t]o be autonomous is not to be isolated and free of responsibility, but to be in a network of relationships, with their dependent responsibilities'.[51] Our autonomy when making these decisions is inherently impacted by relationships with others, and the relationships with those we are entering into agreements with.[52]

The approach adopted previously by the Law Commission appears to have been sensitive to balancing autonomy against parties' behaviour, distinguishing between property that parties would (if they thought about it) want to own jointly with their partner and property they would want to own independently of their partner.[53] This could be a timely project for the Law Commission to revisit now.[54]

IV. Family Property and the Law Commission

In the 1970s and 1980s, the Law Commission carried out a great deal of work on the ownership of property during marriage. However, the matter has not been an area of focus since, and appears to have been shelved. This section revisits the Law Commission's work, with particular focus on its 1988 report and the draft Matrimonial Property Bill 1988.

In 1973, the Law Commission recommended automatic joint ownership of the matrimonial home and of household goods.[55] In Lady Hale's words, this was a period 'when enthusiasm for the equality of the sexes was at its height'.[56]

[51] J Herring, *Relational Autonomy and Family Law*, 4th edn (London, Springer, 2014) 68.

[52] S Thompson, 'Feminist relational contract theory: a new model for family property agreements' (2018) 45(4) *Journal of Law and Society* 617.

[53] Law Commission (n 39) para 3.7.

[54] *Reform of the Grounds of Divorce: The Field of Choice* (Cmnd 3123, 1966); *Matrimonial and Related Proceedings- Financial Relief* (Law Com WP No 9, 1967); Law Commission (n 12); *Family Property Law* (Law Com WP No 42, 1971); *First Report on Family Property: A New Approach* (Law Com No 52, 1973); *Second Report on Family Property – Family Provision on Death* (Law Com No 61, 1974); *Third Report on Family Property: The Matrimonial Home* (Law Com No 86, 1978); *The Financial Consequences of Divorce: The Basic Policy, A Discussion Paper* (Law Com No 103, 1980); *The Financial Consequences of Divorce* (Law Com No 112, 1981); *Property Law: The Implications of Williams & Glyn's Bank Ltd v Boland* (Law Com No 115, 1982); *Transfer of Money Between Spouses – the Married Women's Property Act 1964* (Law Com WP No 90, 1985); Law Commission (n 39).

[55] *First Report on Family Property: A New Approach* (Law Com No 52, 1973).

[56] B Hale, *Spider Woman: A Life – by the former President of the Supreme Court* (London, Penguin, 2021) 108.

However, when these proposals were translated into the Matrimonial Homes (Co-Ownership) Bill five years later, this enthusiasm had waned.[57] Later in the 1980s, the Commission once again considered the rights of spouses in the matrimonial home and noted two consistent themes to their work: that the rules for determining property ownership during marriage were 'arbitrary, uncertain and unfair';[58] and that property ownership during marriage is important. Nevertheless, as we shall see, the recommendation of joint ownership of the family home was abandoned.

One of the areas that the Law Commission identified as being in need of reform was the Married Women's Property Act (MWPA) 1964, which provides – for it is still in force today – that where a husband makes a housekeeping allowance to his wife, money derived from the allowance and property bought with it belong to husband and wife in equal shares. The 1964 Act originated as a Private Member's Bill, introduced by the feminist MP, Edith Summerskill.[59] Though it was scrapped in Scotland in 1985,[60] is narrow in scope and has been criticised as piecemeal,[61] Summerskill never viewed the MWPA 1964 as the final word on the issue. Rather, she saw the Act as a stepping stone towards broader reform of property ownership during marriage. Yet it was, and still is, the only Act that overrides the doctrine of separate property created by the MWPA 1882.

In 1985, the Law Commission decided it 'would be timely'[62] to look again at the MWPA 1964, to go beyond ownership of housekeeping savings, and even beyond the 'land, bricks and mortar'[63] of the co-ownership proposals in the Matrimonial Homes (Co-Ownership) Bill. It published a report in 1988 that considered ownership of 'all the material possessions which enable a married couple to enjoy life together in their home'[64] and included a draft Matrimonial Property Bill, which was never introduced. It was to be an 'Act to make new provision with respect to the beneficial ownership of matrimonial property'.[65] It set out rules for determining beneficial ownership of property when property was transferred between spouses or used for the benefit of both spouses under clause 1. Beneficial ownership would vest jointly in both parties to the marriage,[66] provided that the parties lived together in the same household and the property fell into one of the following four classes:

[57] ibid.

[58] Law Commission (n 39) para 1.4.

[59] The history of this Act and its shortcomings are documented in S Thompson, *Quiet Revolutionaries: The Married Women's Association and Family Law* (Oxford, Hart Publishing, 2022) 161–82.

[60] Pursuant to the Family Law (Scotland) Act 1985 following recommendations in *Family Law: Report on Matrimonial Property* (Scot Law Com No 86, 1984).

[61] Also overturned by s 199 of the Equality Act 2010 in England and Wales, though this provision has not been implemented.

[62] Law Commission (n 39) para 1.1.

[63] ibid para 1.3.

[64] ibid.

[65] ibid app A.

[66] Including valid polygamous marriages and voidable marriages.

(a) property transferred from one spouse to the other that is wholly or mainly for the benefit of both spouses;[67]
(b) property transferred by one spouse to into the joint names of both spouses;
(c) property purchased by one spouse that is wholly or mainly for the use or benefit of both spouses;
(d) property purchased jointly by both parties.

In short, the purchase or transfer of property by one or both spouses for their joint use or benefit would give rise to joint ownership of that property (subject to express contrary intention).[68] All property would be included, except for interests in land, life insurance policies, contracts for deferred annuities, and transfers or purchases made wholly or mainly for the purposes of a business. These rules would not apply to separating spouses but could clarify ownership interests and streamline the distribution of property on divorce.[69] The proposals would also make the presumption of advancement – where transfers between spouses are presumed to be gifts – apply equally as between husband and wife.[70]

As noted above, the Bill excluded interests in land, meaning that the Law Commission decided not to recommend joint ownership of the matrimonial home. The Commission said 'most of us would support the extensions of the principle of this Bill to land',[71] but that doing so would 'be seen to be controversial' and 'may attract inappropriate opposition', even though it 'would not have a major practical impact' since the case of *Williams & Glyn's Bank Ltd v Boland*.[72] In the context of England and Wales today, the Law Commission's proposals could still have merit, but their scope and reasoning – particularly in relation to land – should be reappraised. More than three decades have passed since this report was published, and the background against which these proposals were first made has changed too.

[67] This would include housekeeping money and would have made the MWPA 1964 redundant.

[68] Law Commission (n 39) paras 5.1–5.2. These ideas also resonate with Lord Denning's development of the family assets doctrine in cases such as *Fribance v Fribance (No 2)* [1952] 1 WLR 384.

[69] A system of co-ownership of matrimonial property was proposed in Northern Ireland too: Law Reform Advisory Committee for Northern Ireland, *Matrimonial Property* (2000), LRAC no 8. See also L Fox, 'Co-Ownership of Matrimonial Property: Radical Proposals for Reform' (2001) 52 *Northern Ireland Law Quarterly* 20; A Barlow and C Lind, 'A matter of trust: the allocation of property rights in the family home' (1999) 19(4) *Legal Studies* 468; I McDonald, 'Sharing homes: a law commission discussion paper with a difference' (2003) 25(1) *Journal of Social Welfare and Family Law* 83; J Pearce and G Douglas, 'Money, Property, Cohabitation and Separation: Patterns and Intentions' in Miles and Probert (eds) (n 31) 139; C Burgoyne and S Sonnenberg, 'Financial practices in cohabiting heterosexual couples: A perspective from economic psychology Intentions' in Miles and Probert (eds) (n 31) 89.

[70] The presumption of advancement has since been abolished by s 199 of the Equality Act 2010, though this legislative provision has still not been brought into effect. In any case, the effect of the Law Commission's proposal would be different from the presumption of advancement because it creates a rule rather than a presumption, and the rule can only be displaced if the contrary intention is not known to the other spouse.

[71] Law Commission (n 39) para 4.4.

[72] *Williams & Glyn's Bank Ltd v Boland* [1981] AC 487. Following this case, if a spouse has an interest in the home that is registered land (eg, the house is registered in joint names, as most matrimonial homes are), she does not have to register her interest to gain protection, provided she is in actual occupation.

V. Bringing the Bill into the Twenty-First Century

When revisiting the Law Commission's 1988 proposals, one must account for how trends in property ownership during marriage have since changed. This section considers how such changes could influence the Law Commission's Bill, as well as whether the Bill goes far enough to provide property rights in return for domestic and/or reproductive labour in the home. This requires considering whether reform could encapsulate the sharing of other assets not included in the Law Commission's initial proposals, such as the spouses'/civil partners' pension and the family home. It also means asking difficult questions, such as whether these reforms can justifiably be limited to married couples. After all, it is increasingly difficult to justify prioritising the economic vulnerabilities and inequalities of married parties over unmarried parties when, through a gendered lens, the issues are much the same.[73]

A. Which Property?

In effect, the Law Commission's proposals for automatic joint ownership (unless the parties have opted out) would cover two types of property: property acquired for the use or benefit of both spouses (whether in sole or joint names); and property transferred from one spouse to the other. The beneficial elements of separate property are preserved, co-ownership would apply only in certain situations and the proposals would not apply to spouses/civil partners undergoing divorce/dissolution. One of the strengths of this Bill is that, if introduced today, it is clear in scope yet still maintains some flexibility. Such clarity is important, for Andy Hayward has noted issues with defining 'family property'[74] and, in the 1970s, the Law Commission said that it did not exist:

> There is really no such thing in English law as 'family property'. We have a very elaborate law of property, but the family, though a social unit of great importance and recognised as such by the law, is not an entity that is given rights or even defined: it has failed to attract rights and duties comparable with those of an individual human being, a company, or a partnership … [I]t is not surprising that English 'family property law' is hardly more than a label given to the hesitant moves made by Parliament during the last hundred years to eliminate the grosser injustices influenced by the common law upon married women in property matters.[75]

[73] See K Griffiths, 'From "form" to function and back again: a new conceptual basis for developing frameworks for the legal recognition of adult relationships' (2019) 31(3) *Child and Family Law Quarterly* 277.

[74] A Hayward, '"Family property" and the process of "familialisation" of property law' (2012) 24(3) *Child and Family Law Quarterly* 284. For further comment on the concept of 'family assets', see T Haggie and F Stewart, 'Sharing and the Family Home' (2022) 2 *Financial Remedies Journal* 104.

[75] Law Commission, *Family Property Law* (WP No 42, 1971) para 0.1.

In other words, individuals have property rights but families do not. Property is separate during marriage; and on divorce, when the marriage is long and assets are noteworthy, the court may consider whether assets are matrimonial or non-matrimonial. Even the boundaries between matrimonial and non-matrimonial property are not neatly drawn, such that it was one of the matters focused upon by the Law Commission in its 2014 report.[76] From this perspective, the limited scope of the Matrimonial Property Bill in the Law Commission's 1988 report makes sense. For instance, property acquired for the 'use and enjoyment' of both parties is intended to have a broad meaning and so, in cases where one party buys a car for the couple to share, joint beneficial ownership will be automatic. However, the Bill could be interpreted restrictively. What about assets that are not initially *acquired* for the parties' joint enjoyment but are ultimately used as such?[77]

There are also clear arguments in favour of extending these proposals to the family home. In 1988, the Commission conceded that extending its Bill to cover land could have some value, for instance in cases where parties may regard the family home as joint, though it is registered in the name of one spouse only. These cases still exist today, even if they are statistically less significant.[78] The Commission noted further:

> Excluding the home from its recommendations may create a new and potentially serious anomaly, in that where one spouse pays for the matrimonial home and the other buys the furniture, the furniture will become jointly owned but the house will not. We recognise that this is more likely to prejudice women than men.[79]

The spirit of the reform proposed in this chapter is to carve out a new law of family property that enhances fairness and equality, and so extending joint beneficial ownership to include the home makes sense. The Law Commission's 1988 report was published in the aftermath of a men's rights backlash, which had quashed proposals in the early 1980s for co-ownership of the home.[80] It therefore seemingly limited the scope of its proposals to avoid such controversy. More than 30 years later, it is possible that attitudes have changed.

The Law Commission is clear that its Bill does not give rise to joint ownership *simply because the parties are married*; it is not providing for any form of community of property. Rather, where parties transfer assets, or acquire them for their joint use, the Bill gives rise to legal joint beneficial ownership – an intention that is already being expressed implicitly by the parties' conduct. This makes joint

[76] Law Commission (n 15).

[77] The changing purpose and use of assets was recognised in the context of financial remedies on divorce in *K v L* [2011] EWCA Civ 550, where the Court of Appeal noted that over time, non-matrimonial property can become matrimonial property.

[78] The prevalence of joint ownership is noted in R Auchmuty, The limits of marriage protection: In defence of property law' (2016) 6(6) *Oñati Socio-Legal Series* 303.

[79] Law Commission, *Family Law: Matrimonial Property* (Law Com No 175, 1988) para 4.4.

[80] The Campaign for Justice in Divorce opposed the Matrimonial Homes (Co-Ownership) Bill. For more information, see Thompson (n 59) 215.

beneficial ownership of other assets, which *are* susceptible to division on divorce, impossible. The most notable of these assets (aside from the family home) is the parties' pension wealth, which, for many couples, exceeds their property wealth.[81] As outlined earlier in this chapter, though pension sharing has been possible for more than 20 years, pensions are not always divided on divorce.[82] As Sir Andrew McFarlane put it, '[t]ales of divergent approaches to pension sharing in different court centres have brought the integrity of the system into question'.[83] This confusion, compounded with the gulf between men and women's pensions, makes economic inequality substantially more acute on divorce.[84] Therefore, effectively addressing such inequality would seemingly require addressing this gap in pension wealth. The corollary of this is that, by excluding assets such as pensions from its scope, the Bill can only go so far in supporting principles of equal sharing during marriage and on divorce.

One option might be to explore whether automatic pension sharing could be incorporated into the Bill. Yet this would change the underlying purpose of the Bill, which is to give legal force to the reality of how parties manage money during the relationship. If property for the parties' joint use is acquired with pension money, this will be jointly owned. Or if one party transfers their pension money to the other, this will also fall within the remit of the Bill. There will not, though, be joint beneficial ownership of pensions. This would need to be reformed by a different Act.[85]

By making new provision with regard to the ownership of relationship property, the division of beneficial interests would depend upon how the parties acquire and manage assets. Thus, when revisiting this Bill in the twenty-first century, it is important to consider how spouses and civil partners own and acquire property, and the extent to which this has changed since the 1980s.[86] Some studies suggest that same-sex civil partners are less likely to merge their finances (there is, as yet, no study on how mixed-sex civil partners manage finances).[87] There are also data indicating that some married couples manage their finances

[81] Buckley and Price (n 34).

[82] H Woodward, *A Guide to the Treatment of Pensions on Divorce* (Pension Advisory Group, Nuffield Foundation, 2019) at www.nuffieldfoundation.org/sites/default/files/files/Guide_To_The_Treatment_of_Pensions_on_Divorce-Digital(1).pdf.

[83] ibid i.

[84] Buckley and Price (n 34).

[85] eg, Buckley and Price have noted that the Insuring Women's Futures group of the Chartered Institute of Insurers has suggested automatic pension sharing on divorce: ibid 24.

[86] Hu (n 42); N Sharp-Jeffs, 'A review of research and policy on financial abuse within intimate partner relationships' (Child and Woman Abuse Studies Unit, London Metropolitan University, December 2015) at repository.londonmet.ac.uk/1482/1/Review-of-Research-and-Policy-on-Financial-Abuse.pdf; Y Hu, 'Divergent Gender Revolutions: Cohort Changes in Household Financial Management across Income Gradients' (2021) 35(5) *Gender & Society* 746.

[87] R Auchmuty, 'The experience of civil partnership dissolution: Not "just like divorce"' (2016) 38(2) *Journal of Social Welfare and Family Law* 152; C Bendall, 'A Divorce Blueprint: The Use of Heteronormative Strategies in Addressing Economic Inequalities on Civil Partnership Dissolution' (2016) 31(2) *Canadian Journal of Law and Society* 267; B Heaphy, 'Reflexive convention: civil partnership, marriage and family' (2018) 69(3) *The British Journal of Sociology* 626.

independently.[88] These patterns could dilute the power of the Bill to enable sharing on legal terms during the relationship. For instance, in relationships of economic abuse, where property is segregated from one of the parties, it is unlikely that there will be much property transferred between the parties giving rise to joint ownership. Much less property will be shared.[89] Yet even in these situations, it still is likely that there will be property that will be jointly beneficially owned, which in turn could bolster the value of domestic contributions.[90] By applying the presumption of joint beneficial ownership to almost all property, this means that in situations of coercive control and economic abuse, where one party may prevent the other from accessing money on a daily basis, there is still a safety net for joint beneficial ownership of other assets, such as the home.[91] Reform along these lines would also provide stronger justification for marital property agreements, such as 'prenups'. This is because these agreements would be used to contract out of a default system of property ownership during marriage, which spouses could opt out of through contract.

B. Application to Cohabitants

Many of the structural inequalities affecting married women affect unmarried women too. The cost of childcare, career sacrifices and relationship-generated disadvantage are gendered power imbalances characteristic of intimate relationships both inside and outside marriage. Often, cohabiting women are even more vulnerable because they are 'disproportionately disadvantaged'[92] by the lack of legal recourse on relationship breakdown, compounded by intersecting factors such as class, race and religion.[93] They have no recourse to the Matrimonial Causes Act 1973, which provides married couples with discretionary redistribution based upon their circumstances. Instead, beneficial ownership of property depends upon complicated trust law principles. For instance, when determining beneficial interests in the family home, the extent to which parties' non-financial contributions can be taken into account depends, in part, upon whether the home is in sole or joint names.[94] This sort of inconsistency creates a minefield for

[88] C Vogler, 'Money in the Household: Some Underlying Issues of Power (2008) 46(4) *Sociological Review* 687.

[89] These power imbalances could also harm the potential value of the Bill in tackling inequality if the parties express a 'contrary intention'.

[90] A Barlow, 'Valorisation of household labour through relationship and property law: Challenging perspectives from England, Wales & Scotland' in C Declerck and L Verstappen (eds), *Valorisation of Household Labour in Family Property Law a Comparative Perspective* (The Hague, Eleven International, 2018) 43.

[91] This also depends upon the parties not opting out of this scheme.

[92] Women and Equalities Committee, *The Rights of Cohabiting Partners* (2022–23, HC 92) 12.

[93] ibid 12–13.

[94] *Stack v Dowden* [2007] UKHL 17; *Jones v Kernott* [2011] UKSC 53; *Dobson v Griffey* [2018] EWHC 1117 (Ch).

cohabitants,[95] and the need for reform is well documented by both Andy Hayward and Russell Sandberg in chapters 9 and 8 of this volume, respectively.[96]

But could a few tweaks to the Law Commission's Matrimonial Property Bill – expanding it to be a 'Relationship Property Bill' – improve the situation for cohabitants too?[97] Such expansion would further strengthen arguments in favour of a Bill covering beneficial ownership of interests in land, such as the family home. The Law Commission concluded in 1988 that its provisions should exclude land, because this would make little practical difference to those married couples who tend to register the home in joint names. This may be so in joint-names cases, but in cases where the home is registered in only one party's name, including land could make an important difference.[98]

The amendments would be straightforward – the first line of clause 1 of the Bill could be easily amended by removing the words 'to a marriage': 'Where the parties to a marriage ("A" and "B") are living together in the same household …' This would mean taking the radical step of introducing an equitable presumption of joint ownership applicable to property intended for the joint use of both parties. It would avoid the need to navigate a series of complex trust law principles and case law, and would provide much-needed safety for economically vulnerable cohabiting families. It would not constrain cohabitants who do not intend such ownership; as noted previously, the Law Commission's Bill also includes a clause permitting parties to opt out of this scheme.[99] Moreover, while divorce would override this equitable presumption of joint ownership for married couples, on the breakdown of cohabiting relationships, the presumption could stand. As there is no legislation regulating the economic consequences of relationship breakdown for cohabitants, there is nothing to extinguish the presumption.

Even in the 1980s, before the slew of data and research showing the urgent need to extend the property rights of unmarried cohabitants, the Law Commission was considering the viability of extending its proposals:

> These proposals do not create co-ownership as a result of marriage, but as a result of spending money for joint use or benefit and where it seems appropriate to assume

[95] Women and Equalities Committee (n 92).

[96] See also A Barlow et al, *Cohabitation, marriage and the law: Social change and legal reform in the 21st century* (Oxford, Hart Publishing, 2005); J Pearce, H Woodward and G Douglas, 'Dealing with property issues on cohabitation breakdown' (2007) 37 *Family Law* 36.

[97] Relationship property can take different forms, eg the system in New Zealand is quite different from the scheme proposed here: M Henaghan and R Ballantyne, 'Recent Changes to the Division of Relationship Property in New Zealand: A New Way Forward' (2015) *International Survey of Family Law* 229.

[98] *Dobson v Griffey* [2018] EWHC 1117 (Ch).

[99] Opt-out agreements could be modelled on those in New Zealand under the Property (Relationships) Act 1976, whereby certain procedural formalities must be complied with to ensure, as Margaret Briggs has put it, 'that both parties are fully informed and independently advised as to what they stand to gain or lose by waiving their statutory entitlements'. M Briggs, *Supplementary evidence on the status of de facto relationships in New Zealand* [HAB00383] at www.committees.parliament.uk/writtenevidence/43558/html/; Women and Equalities Committee (n 92).

> that joint ownership is likely to be an acceptable result to those spending the money. We did not consult on the position of cohabitants in our working paper, but some of those who responded suggested they should have been considered. We make no recommendation on this point now but mention it as a suitable topic for further consideration.[100]

More than 30 years later, these proposals should be resurrected and reconsidered as reforming the property interests of both married and unmarried parties. Statistically, the number of cohabiting families has grown considerably since the 1980s.[101] Reform recognising joint ownership of property used and enjoyed by both parties, or transferred from one to another, is also in line with couples' expectations. There is now a wealth of data suggesting that unmarried cohabitants believe they acquire interests in their partner's property over the course of the relationship. As Anne Barlow and others have shown, this common law marriage myth is both pervasive and persistent.[102]

VI. Conclusion

The financial consequences of divorce is an area in urgent need of reform. However, reforming this area is complex, and providing a clear basis for reform must not mean compromising the concepts of equality and fairness that are important when determining financial remedies. As a result, it could be useful to explore alternatives by shifting attention away from the point of separation. One potential route to reform could be to review the rules for determining property ownership during marriage and civil partnership. The central aim of this proposed reform would be to support notions of equality and sharing during the relationship, for, as this chapter has explored, economic inequalities on gender lines are getting progressively worse. The Law Commission's 1988 proposals could provide a launchpad for further research into the matter, obviously bearing in mind that the socio, legal, economic and political context of family life is different today. As the Law Commission made clear previously, the intention of such reform would not be to undermine party autonomy but to *facilitate* it by reflecting the reality of how parties manage property during the relationship.

This would neither cure all of the current problems with this area of law, nor negate the need for reform of the financial consequences of divorce. Indeed, the

[100] *Family Law: Matrimonial Property* (n 39) para. 4.21.

[101] In the past decade, the number of cohabiting couple families saw an increase of 22.9% to 3.6 million: Office for National Statistics, *Families and Households in the UK: 2021* (Census 2021, ONS, 9 March 2022) at www.ons.gov.uk/peoplepopulationandcommunity/birthsdeathsandmarriages/families/bulletins/familiesandhouseholds/2021. In 1980, only 8% of dissolutions were among cohabiting couples with a child under 18, but this surged to 30% in 2009: SY Chao et al, *How partnerships have changed in the UK over the last 30 years* (Southampton, Centre for Population Change, 2020).

[102] Barlow et al (n 96); A Barlow, 'Almost half of us mistakenly believe that common law marriage exists' (London, NatCen Social Research, 22 January 2019).

road to comprehensive reform of this area is likely to be lengthy and sinuous. Still, a new law of family property, which provides clearly defined rights during the marriage or civil partnership, could be beneficial. It could potentially resolve (or at least alleviate) some disputes over property that might otherwise become intractable on relationship breakdown. It could encourage transparency, plainly delineate property ownership during the relationship, reflect parties' expectations and reduce uncertainty on divorce. In other words, a clear understanding of who owns what during marriage or civil partnership could be useful when redistributing assets on divorce. The certainty that such reform could offer could also provide justification for legislative reform of marital-property agreements, whereby parties wishing to depart from rules of co-ownership could do so by private agreement. However, reform of such agreements without consideration of these broader reform proposals would be a missed opportunity to clarify questions of property ownership throughout the relationship; questions the answers to which couples entering marital-property agreements will need to know in order to make informed decisions over how to distribute their assets.

Another option is to expand the Law Commission's Bill to unmarried cohabitants, changing its title from 'Matrimonial Property Bill' to 'Relationship Property Bill'. As this chapter has outlined, issues with property ownership between unmarried couples are well documented, and defining beneficial interests with regard to certain types of property again could be a positive step towards reforming this complex and messy area of law. The Law Commission foresaw the potential of its Bill to be extended in this way in the 1980s. As the Bill would clarify beneficial ownership, rather than creating automatic co-ownership by virtue of the relationship alone, such proposals might even be palatable for those resisting more expansive reform of the cohabitants' property rights. This could be a strategic gain on an issue in urgent need of reform.

Taking a step towards a new law of family property is ostensibly piecemeal. It would not reform financial remedies law, which needs to be addressed if economic disparities on divorce are to be handled effectively. It would not necessarily provide appropriate relief to unmarried cohabitants either. Therefore, it is tempting to conclude that a Relationship Property Bill is a waste of time. Yet, in the context of family property law, history suggests that a piecemeal approach is the most effective route to reform when there is little political appetite for more radical change.[103] Historically, feminist campaigners have taken the view that compromising on their ultimate aims could lead to the worst of both worlds: reform that does not get to the root of the problem, while simultaneously killing momentum for comprehensive change. However, piecemeal reform has sometimes been a successful strategy, and the Law Commission's 1988 project is an example of this. As this chapter has explained, the project

[103] As I have found when exploring the strategies of feminists campaigning to reform family property law (n 59).

came about because the Commission wanted to consider the viability of the MWPA 1964, which, at the time, was only ever seen as a strategic stepping stone on the path to equal partnership in marriage by the feminist agitators who introduced it. Thus, a step-by-step approach has the potential to expose the need for further reform and could increase, rather than snuff out, pressure for change, just as the relatively arcane MWPA 1964 did. There is a consensus that *something* needs to be done to address worsening inequalities relating to the family and property, and incremental reform is the way to achieve this. A Relationship Property Bill could be the beginning of a new phase of legal rules based upon equality and sharing. As this chapter has argued, this is only becoming more urgent as time goes on.

Appendix

Relationship Property Bill*

A BILL TO

Make new provision with respect to the beneficial ownership of relationship property.

BE IT ENACTED by the King's most Excellent Majesty, by and with the advice and consent of the Lords Spiritual and Temporal, and Commons, in this present Parliament assembled, and by the authority of the same, as follows:—

1. Beneficial Ownership of Relationship Property

(1) Where a married, civilly partnered, or unmarried couple ('A' and 'B') are living together in the same household and—

  (a) A transfers to B property which is wholly or mainly for the use or benefit of both A and B;
  (b) A transfers property to A and B jointly;
  (c) A purchases property which is wholly or mainly for the use or benefit of both A and B; or
  (d) A and B jointly purchase property;

beneficial ownership of the property shall vest in A and B jointly.

(2) Where the parties to a marriage ('A' and 'B') are living together in the same household and A transfers to B property which is not wholly or mainly for the use or benefit of both A and B, beneficial ownership of the property shall vest in B alone.

(3) Subsections (1)(a) to (c) and (2) above do not apply where A has a contrary intention and that intention is known to B.

(4) Subsection (1)(d) above does not apply where either A or B has a contrary intention and that intention is known to the other.

(5) Subsection (1)(c) above does not apply in relation to any policy or life insurance or contract for a deferred annuity.

(6) Subsections (1) and (2) above do not apply in relation to a transfer or purchase made wholly or mainly for the purposes of a business.

(7) In this section—

'transfer' includes—

  (a) in relation to any property, the doing by one person in relation to another of any act which, but for this Act, would vest the property in the other; and
  (b) in relation to a sum of money, the handing over of that sum in cash;

'use' includes enjoyment or consumption.

* Amended version of the Matrimonial Property Bill 1988.

2. Extent, commencement and short title

(1) This Act may be cited as the Relationship Property Act 2023.
(2) The Married Women's Property Act 1964 is hereby repealed.
(3) Nothing in this Act applies in relation to a transfer or purchase made before the commencement of this Act.
(4) This Act extends to England and Wales only.

Response to Chapter 6

A New Law of Family Property

ALISON DIDUCK

I. Introduction

Ideas about property, or at least home ownership, during marriage were once a live issue in England and Wales. The Law Commission's 1988 proposals about co-ownership of the family home, for example, drew attention to the inequality of wealth in many families. These concerns have not abated in the 35 years since their publication. Sharon Thompson's proposal, like the Law Commission's in 1988, would have many benefits. As she says, legislating for a presumption of co-beneficial ownership of property during marriage and civil partnership would embed the language of sharing, which would also embed more clearly the idea of entitlement to property on divorce or dissolution, as, despite Lord Nicholls' words in *Miller/McFarlane*,[1] we do not always see this idea of entitlement in the cases. Thompson's proposal would also recognise non-financial contributions during marriage and civil partnership in a way that the Matrimonial Causes Act (MCA) 1973, section 25(2)(f) does not always do on divorce or dissolution. Finally, this proposal would allow us to keep our focus on gender inequality, and on gender power in accumulating and managing family wealth. We cannot abstract partners from those conditions of structural, and often personal, inequality and treat them as degendered autonomous individuals who are able simply to make free choices about how they live their family lives and acquire property. These are all very good reasons to think about reforming the law of family property. Indeed, the Law Commission is, at the time of writing, doing just that, albeit in the context of the MCA 1973. The difference here, of course, is that Thompson envisions a reform to ownership *before* separation or divorce, and which will also extend to unmarried cohabitants. The reform is about property, but it is about more than that. It seems to me also implicitly to reform ideas of what family relationships mean. Thompson is creating a new relationship to property, but it is one that is mediated through newly understood relationships to another person.

[1] *Miller v Miller*; *McFarlane v McFarlane* [2006] UKHL 24 [9]: 'The financial provision made on divorce by one party for the other, still typically the wife, is not in the nature of largesse. It is not a case of "taking away" from one party and "giving" to the other property which "belongs" to the former. The claimant is not a supplicant. Each party to a marriage is *entitled* to a *fair* share of the available property.'

II. Marriage and Civil Partnership

Thompson's proposal is almost a hybrid of community and separate property regimes. This, in itself, is not a problem; neither community property nor separate property regimes have any inherent integrity or 'rightness' about them. They are simply the results of the histories and contexts in which they have developed. If society sees the family as a single social unit, and the law is concerned to protect partners' rights and equality within that unit, then community property makes sense. If the family is understood as a collection of separate individuals and the law is concerned to protect the property rights of those individuals, then separate property makes sense. Moreover, this hybrid that would merge these two understandings and policies may not be as radical as it seems at first. Ideas of spousal interdependence and independence have coexisted as a part of English family law and policy for some time.[2] Partnership solidarity and autonomy both feature in the MCA 1973 and its case law.

We see evidence, for example, of law's blurring of these ideas in the way that it valorises both individual autonomy and 'the value of care, support and personal commitment undertaken within the family to the collective benefit of both family and wider society'.[3] The marital relationship has been called both 'a partnership of equals'[4] and the family 'its own little social security system'.[5] There have been for some time, in other words, 'mixed messages'[6] in law about the nature of the marital relationship, and the value of the roles that family members undertake for each other, and for society. These mixed messages need not collide but, while ideas about family property ownership and post-divorce distribution remain firmly within the common law's property rhetoric, they can only go so far. This 'property rhetoric'[7] includes the understanding of autonomy as independence from others, limiting obligations to those that can be characterised as voluntarily assumed and seeing property as a reward for economically productive labour.[8] It comprehends even marital relationships through what Cotterrell calls 'law's supporting ideologies of property, liberty, the minimal state, and the rule of law'.[9] Therefore, while Thompson's proposal remains within this rhetoric – sharing the *legal* ownership of property is not proposed, indeed would be difficult within this rhetorical frame in which individuals and their property

[2] A Barlow, 'Solidarity, autonomy and equality: mixed messages for the family?' (2015) 27 *Child and Family Law Quarterly* 215.
[3] ibid 235.
[4] See *Miller/McFarlane* (n 1) [16] per Lord Nicholls.
[5] B Hale, 'What is a 21st Century Family?' (Watford, International Centre for Family Law, Policy and Practice, 2019) at www.supremecourt.uk/docs/speech-190701.pdf.
[6] Barlow (n 2).
[7] MC Regan Jr, *Alone Together: Law and the Meanings of Marriage* (Oxford, Oxford University Press, 1999) 162.
[8] ibid.
[9] R Cotterrell, 'Feasible Regulation for Democracy and Social Justice' (1988) 15 *Journal of Law and Society* 5.

rights are protected – it does bring within the frame some small element of a solidarity, or community, idea of relationship. Yet that it does so, in part, by ascribing even notional economic value to 'contributions' to the family means that it remains within the property rhetoric. Further, like other incursions into the property rhetoric made historically, Thompson's comes through equity and direct statutory intervention.[10] While this proposal is about property, then, it also shifts slightly what the marital or civil partnership relationship means in 2023. It is not ready to take them out of the 'formal equality, property rights, economic rationality and autonomy' frame, but would be another example of the mixed messages law projects about family.

Thompson's idea is that this incremental reform is likely to receive a better reception than a more far-reaching reform that might, for example, draw more closely from community property ideas of co-ownership. This may be true, and the proposal resonates with modern socially and legally blurred understandings of relationships, as we have seen. I worry, though, that implementing the proposal relies upon what is *assumed* to be the twenty-first-century idea of marriage or civil partnership, which is then presumed to be the parties' understanding of their relationship. This presumption would, by default, bring them within the proposed legislation, while any personal understanding otherwise would require the property owner to opt out if it. Indeed, it seems to be only their understanding and intention that is relevant. Both the presumption and its opt-out seem, additionally, to have all of the evidentiary difficulties associated with ascertaining intention (how would A need to demonstrate his intention not to share with B?) and of quantifying shares (are they assumed to be equal? Can they be unequal?). They also do not account for gendered understandings of the relationship, or for the inequalities of bargaining power in any choice to remain within the statutory presumption or opt out of it. As Thompson explains, coercive control is too often a feature in relationships, bargaining power is often linked to wealth and economic abuse in relationships is not uncommon. And of course, while the idea of co-beneficial ownership during the relationship may be empowering for some women in some relationships, it really only matters when the relationship ends. Again, not only are issues of unequal bargaining power, and then also potential litigation power, relevant at that point, but disputes about whether, for example, A's intention was known to B could arise. All of these issues could undermine the certainty that Thompson claims the reforms would achieve. Arguments to keep a larger share, or all, of a particular co-owned property may arise just as frequently as arguments now arise in trust law, or under the MCA 1973, to share (equally or unequally) a solely owned property, especially as these disputes would centre around intention. While judicial discretion remains a feature of the MCA 1973,

[10] See, eg, Thorpe LJ's comments in *Dart v Dart* [1997] 1 FCR 286, 294: 'The scheme of [MCA 1973] must also be set in the wider perspective of history and general civil law. In this jurisdiction rights of property are not invaded or reduced by statutory powers save for specific and confined purposes.' See also family home trust cases such as *Stack v Dowden* [2007] UKHL 17; *Jones v Kernott* [2011] UKSC 53.

and even though fairness remains its object, it is difficult to see how either the failure to opt out of the statutory presumption at the beginning of (or during the course of – there is no temporal direction) the relationship, or indeed the opt-out itself, would not offer the opportunity for dispute and further litigation.

The proposal offers some security for non-owning partners and, in this way, also aims to reduce the gendered wealth distribution in relationships. This is an important and worthy goal. The statistics that Thompson provides about the gender gap in home/housework and childcare, earnings, and the consequent acquisition of all forms of wealth (from pensions to property) offer a compelling argument to suggest that, if the law is truly concerned about gender fairness, it must think about wealth distribution, both during and at the end of relationships. This reform does indeed offer some sense of property security to those women who are in a relationship with men who own and purchase property. It means, however, that their economic security is dependent upon their men and, in this way, allows the state to abdicate any responsibility for the feminisation of poverty. It also allows private employers, for example, to continue gendered hiring, promotion and leave policies and practices, and does little to acknowledge the cost of childcare, which, as Thompson explains clearly, has such a profound effect upon men's and women's ability to accrue wealth.[11]

Finally, it does little to alleviate the economic conditions of parties who have little or no property. Home ownership and property wealth are largely classed concerns, and this focus on them is part of family law's traditional preoccupation with the middle and wealthy classes. This proposal would not do much for a couple living in rented accommodation and/or employed on minimum wage or zero hours contracts. Of course, I do not mean simply to say that, because a reform does not help all, it should not be permitted to help some. However, a bolder idea, even though one which definitely contradicts the law's 'property rhetoric' and would further blur the idea of family, would be for wages or salary to be included in the presumed sharing. Despite the Court of Appeal's declaring[12] that earning capacity is not an 'asset' that can be shared on divorce, we could think about A's ability to have increased his earnings as being as much a result of the support he received in the relationship as is any increase in value of his capital assets, which is considered as shareable in the marital pot.[13]

We might also think further about pensions. Pensions are sometimes the highest-value asset people have.[14] We know the research on pensions, which shows

[11] See also A Topping, 'Nursery for under-twos cost parents in England 65% of wage' *The Guardian* (7 October 2022) at www.theguardian.com/money/2022/oct/07/nursery-under-twos-costs-parents-england-65-percent-wage; C Aguilar García, 'One in three parents of under-fives struggling to afford child-care in England' *The Guardian* (27 July 2023) at www.theguardian.com/money/2023/jul/27/one-in-three-parents-of-under-fives-struggling-to-afford-childcare-in-england.

[12] *Waggott v Waggott* [2018] EWCA Civ 727.

[13] I am grateful to Rob George for this point, made in email correspondence.

[14] H Woodward Pensions Advisory Group, *A Guide to the Treatment of Pensions on Divorce* (Pensions Advisory Group, Nuffield Foundation, 2019).

that gender disparity in ownership still exists.[15] Thompson's proposal does not include pensions – she explains that to do so would change the purpose of the reform, which is to give legal effect to the reality of how parties manage money during the relationship. Yet if the purpose of the proposal is also to provide economic security to spouses, and to promote, or at least support, a more community- or solidarity-based understanding of the relationship, beneficial sharing of the pension during the relationship may offer that sense of security and further that understanding. It will make clear that the pension is family property. The non-pensioned spouse will know that, in the event of divorce, she already has a beneficial share in the pension. Even though all of the difficulties with intention, quantification and opt-outs discussed above are also relevant for pensions, this knowledge is important, as we know that too few financial provision orders or agreements include pension-sharing orders.[16] The reasons why pension sharing is so rare are manifold. Buckley and Price remind us that men tend to have emotional attachments to their pensions and women to their houses, and so women often give up pension entitlement in exchange for the house.[17] Many women simply do not feel that the fight over it is worth it.[18] Consequently, while I agree that proposals for reform must be based upon evidence, including the evidence of twenty-first-century couples' expectations around, and use of, their property, we need to keep our gender lenses acute here too. Women have a different relationship to 'home' than do men.[19] Men make different use of their income than do women. Women, for example, tend to prioritise spending on the household, and to benefit children before their own individual needs for leisure,[20] and tend to characterise spending on their own leisure as 'wants', whereas men tend to characterise leisure spending as 'needs'.[21] Couples' expectations and attitudes around property ownership and money management are important, therefore, but cannot be the sole focus for reform. As George et al said in the context of prenuptial agreements, permitting the 'owner' to opt out of sharing, based upon gendered attitudes and gendered living, should not provide the basis for opting out of measures designed to promote equality.[22]

[15] J Buckley and D Price, *Pensions and Divorce: Exploratory Analysis of Quantitative Data* (Manchester, Manchester Institute for Collaborative Research on Ageing, 2021).

[16] See n 10.

[17] Buckley and Price (n 15) 7–8.

[18] Pensions Advisory Group (n 14).

[19] L Fox O'Mahoney, *Conceptualising Home: Theories, Laws and Policies* (Oxford, Hart Publishing, 2006). See also A Diduck, '*Royal Bank of Scotland Plc v Etridge (No 2)*: Commentary' in R Hunter, C McGlynn and E Rackley (eds), *Feminist Judgments: From Theory to Practice* (Oxford, Hart Publishing, 2010) 149.

[20] R Lister, J Goode and C Callender, 'Income Distribution within Families and the Reform of Social Security' (1999) 21 *Journal of Social Welfare and Family Law* 203.

[21] C Burgoyne, 'Hear-strings and Purse-strings: Money in Heterosexual Marriage' (2004) 14(1) *Feminism and Psychology* 165.

[22] R George, P Harris and J Herring, 'Pre-nuptial Agreements, For Better or For Worse?' (2009) 39 *Family Law* 934.

Thompson's proposals would also need to be considered in the light of the Law Commission's current work on the MCA 1973. Its terms of reference that are relevant to her proposal include: whether there is scope for reform of the discretionary basis of the current law; whether 'conduct' might be a factor to which the court must have particular regard when deciding to make financial remedies orders; and the treatment of pensions on the division of parties' assets on divorce.[23] We cannot predict what, if anything, the Law Commission will recommend about family property, nor whether any recommendations will be taken forward by Government. It is clear, though, that there is some appetite to rethink the law and ideas about the changing nature of marital relationships, and relationships to marital property may be a part of that rethinking.

III. Unmarried Cohabitants

All of the arguments that Thompson makes for beneficial co-ownership of property during marriage also make sense for co-ownership during unmarried cohabitation. Indeed, the arguments might be stronger for cohabitants than they are for spouses or civil partners. Because there is no statutory entitlement on separation for cohabitants to claim a share in what is, in effect, family property, defining beneficial interests before separation may, as Thompson says, provide a much-needed safety net for the more economically vulnerable party. I also agree that the demographics since the Law Commission last looked at reforming the law for cohabitants have continued to change, as have public attitudes to cohabitation. Further, the common law marriage myth is still pervasive, despite attempts to counter it through public education.[24] While some policy-makers remain reluctant to assimilate cohabitation with marriage and civil partnership, most legal commentators agree that some change is needed.[25] So, as Thompson argues, 'clarify[ing] beneficial ownership, rather than creating automatic co-ownership by virtue of the relationship alone' might make this proposal 'palatable [even] for those resisting more expansive reform of the cohabitants' property rights'. These are all good reasons for bringing cohabitants into this reform.

But while there may be 'mixed messages' about the nature of the marital relationship that would soften the reception of beneficial co-ownership of property during marriage and civil partnership, it is not clear that these mixed messages exist about cohabiting relationships, despite claims about their functional similarity. Cohabitants are still perceived as autonomous individuals *choosing* not

[23] 'Financial remedies on divorce: Assessing the reform options for the laws governing finances on divorce and the ending of a civil partnership' (Law Commission, 2023) at www.lawcom.gov.uk/project/financial-remedies-on-divorce.

[24] A Barlow et al, 'Cohabitation and the Law: Myths, Money and the Media' in A Park et al (eds), *British Social Attitudes – The 24th Report* (British Social Attitudes Survey, Sage Publications, 2008) 29.

[25] See Hayward, ch 9 of this volume.

to formalise their relationships[26] and so, for them, the property rhetoric will outweigh any of the solidarity or community values that may have become a part of formal relationships. Further, all of the difficulties around power imbalances highlighted with respect to spouses and civil partners also apply to cohabitants, perhaps with even greater intensity, especially because one of them can stop the other from entering into a marriage and so getting the protections of the divorce regime in the first place. At least fairness and equality lie at the heart of the MCA 1973, however imperfectly these principles may or may not be applied from case to case. Fairness is not the goal for separating cohabitants, though.

IV. Conclusion

There is something to be said for a scheme that would provide increased economic security to financially weaker parties in relationships. The fact that this weakness is usually gender-based only increases its urgency and strengthens its justification. One way to proceed would be to introduce a community-property approach that would encourage family 'solidarity' (as Barlow calls it[27]) and, in doing so, protect the equality of the parties. Such a dramatic reform is clearly not on the cards, however. The common law system is too firmly entrenched in its separate property rhetoric. It is nevertheless possible for reforms to make tweaks within that system, and so the Law Commission's review of the MCA 1973 is welcome. Whether it will succeed in bringing equality and gender fairness on divorce more to the forefront we have yet to see, but I hope, and I think that Thompson does too, that it does not continue further along the autonomy road and become even more mired within the property rhetoric. Thompson's proposal is another example of a possible tweak; it relies upon accepted and acceptable ideas of equity and statutory intervention that do not violate too blatantly the rhetoric of the common law.

The legal and social frames within which we perceive family and property relationships can and do change. Family law shifted from paternalism to an autonomy-based partnership of equals frame, for example, as social conditions changed over the years.[28] While neither of us is advocating the seismic change a community property scheme would bring for England and Wales, Thompson and I do agree, I think, that some softening of the separate property rhetoric in the light of those still changing conditions is necessary.

[26] Even though this may not be true for a great many cohabitants. See George, 'Response to Chapter 9' in this volume.

[27] Barlow (n 2).

[28] Not always to the advantage of women.

7

Reform of Financial Provision on Divorce

BARONESS RUTH DEECH

I. Introduction

The problem that requires reform was addressed, but not completely resolved, in the Law Commission report *Matrimonial Property, Needs and Agreements*.[1] It concerns the difficulties, stress, uncertainty and expense of the English/Welsh (hereafter 'English', for brevity) law relating to the division of assets and ongoing maintenance awards on divorce. The current law is section 25 of the Matrimonial Causes Act 1973, which has not been reviewed by Parliament for nearly 50 years despite radical changes in society and families. It spells out in no particular hierarchy the factors to be taken into account when the court is deciding on financial provision after divorce. It does place the welfare of the minor child as the first consideration, as it is placed in most areas of family law. As will be seen, this prominence has not in fact achieved very much for the children of divorce, whose needs have merged into the general disposition of the family assets, and that is one of the situations deserving of remedy. The other factors listed in section 25 are, in brief: the income, earning capacity, property and other resources of the couple (adding that the court should take account of earning capacity that might be acquired – another somewhat overlooked requirement); the needs and obligations of the couple; their standard of living, age and the duration of the marriage; any disability of the parties; the contributions made to the welfare of the family; the loss of benefits on divorce; and conduct, if it would be inequitable to disregard it.

This law has been the subject of calls for reform from the Law Commission, Resolution[2] and the Centre for Social Justice.[3] Reform is urgent because the law

[1] *Matrimonial Property, Needs and Agreements* (Law Com No 343, 2014); D Hodson, 'The Law Commission proposals: a wasted opportunity' *Family Law* (28 February 2014) at www.familylaw.co.uk/articles/the-law-commission-proposals-a-wasted-opportunity-passing-the-reform-buck-and-continued-unpredictability-for-future-settlements.

[2] 'Call for early legal advice to soften blow of divorce' *Resolution* (30 November 2020) at www.resolution.org.uk/news/call-for-early-legal-advice-to-soften-blow-of-divorce/.

[3] D Hodson, *Every Family Matters: An in-depth review of family law in Britain*, 2nd edn (London, Centre for Social Justice, 2010); S Cretney, 'The Maintenance Quagmire' (1970) 33 *MLR* 662.

is uncertain. It has become largely judge-made law, which bears little resemblance to the statute. Judicial discretion has led to unpredictability and conflicting decisions, which make it hard for parties to negotiate and lead to disproportionate costs. Legal aid has been removed and parties of modest means are left unrepresented, with little guidance as to the right outcome. Baroness Shackleton (solicitor) and I have introduced in the House of Lords in successive years the Divorce (Financial Provision) Bill,[4] which would implement provisions very similar to those pertaining in Scots law, and in the laws of most European and North American states. It would introduce as a fair starting point the equal division of all the property and pensions acquired by the couple *after* marriage; provision for short-term maintenance for an ex-spouse[5] and longer maintenance for children; flexibility to allow the home to be retained for the carer and children; and binding prenuptial agreements. This is intended to facilitate mediation, reduce litigation and costs, and recognise equal partnership in marriage.

The present chapter proceeds to expand on the reasons why change is necessary in this area, and the form which it should adopt.

II. Why Reform?

There are three fundamental unresolved principles at stake in the law of financial provision. England has resolved none of them, while other countries have faced up to them and determined them. Those principles are, first, the value of certainty in the law; second, finding any basis at all on which to require one spouse to support the other after no-fault divorce; and, third, determining a balance between women's autonomy and the need of some for financial assistance when they are on their own after dissolution.

A. Certainty

There is a balance to be struck in several areas of the law between absolute certainty and unpredictable judicial discretion; here it is posited that the stance taken by current English law is too close to unpredictability, with its knock-on effects on affordability of litigation, negotiation out of court and speed of decision.[6] Despite the relevant Act's being in force for 50 years, many unresolved issues remain, many new precedents emerge, and the family law reports are replete with ground-breaking new judgments and those that unsettle previously apparently settled issues. Some of these are referred to here.

[4] Divorce (Financial Provision) Bill 2021 at www.bills.parliament.uk/bills/2564/publications.

[5] Experience has shown that it is politically impossible to abolish ongoing support entirely.

[6] E Hitchings and J Miles, 'Rules Versus Discretion in Financial Remedies on Divorce' (2019) 33(1) *International Journal of Law, Policy and the Family* 24.

An example is the ongoing judicial discussion about equality in the division of assets, a concept not mentioned in section 25. Recent cases illustrate this, for example *JM v KK*,[7] in which it was held that the aim of financial provision should be a fair outcome, not necessarily equality, and that circumstances demanded a departure from equality in this case. If that judgment is followed, it would remove the faint hope that once existed that one could rely on equality of division as a lodestar. On the other hand, in *L v L*,[8] the court decided that the parties should emerge as equals, even though the business that generated the husband's fortune was acquired by him from his father before he met his ex-wife. In *AD v BD*,[9] after a discussion of equality the original award of 80:20 was changed to 61:39. Finally, just one year later, the opinion was given that in dividing assets, fairness and equality usually ride hand in hand.[10] Plenty of room for argument, then.[11]

Another issue currently in flux is the judicial attitude to sharing post-separation earning capacity. *Waggott v Waggott*[12] was taken to mean that it could not be shared, but in *Rossi v Rossi*,[13] Nicholas Mostyn QC, as he was then, had decided that an asset could be non-matrimonial if it related to a working period 12 months post-separation. Unsurprisingly, as Mostyn J, he reaffirmed this cut-off point in *E v L*,[14] despite *Waggott*.

The extent to which conduct should affect an award is still in contention. Section 25 refers to conduct that it would be 'inequitable to disregard'. According to *Miller v Miller; McFarlane v McFarlane*,[15] this was only to be raised in exceptional cases. In the intervening years it has been raised,[16] and in *OG v AG*[17] 'financially measurable' was added as a determinant. However, in *VV v VV*,[18] there was a return to the older catch-all definition of 'gross and obvious'. It will be tempting to use these differences in disputes after the introduction of no-fault divorce in 2022, because misconduct that has seemed extreme to one spouse, but which cannot be mentioned in the divorce proceedings, may find an outlet for airing in the financial litigation.

[7] *JM v KK* [2021] EWFC 54.

[8] *L v L* [2021] EWFC B83.

[9] *AD v BD* [2021] EWFC B48.

[10] *P v Q* [2022] EWFC B9.

[11] On exorbitant costs, equality and the 'unedifying contradictory mess' of financial provision law, see Mostyn J, 'Family Law – Not the Poor Relation' *Financial Remedies Journal* (25 August 2022), paper delivered to the 19th National Family Law Conference, Adelaide, 16 August 2022 at financialremediesjournal.com/content/family-law-not-the-poor-relation.a306bc0f3bdd49bd9768d905451a6290.htm?mc_cid=d906c4f6ed&mc_eid=712ea1f6da.

[12] *Waggott v Waggott* [2018] EWCA Civ 727.

[13] *Rossi v Rossi* [2007] 1 FLR 790.

[14] *E v L* [2021] EWFC 60.

[15] *Miller v Miller;McFarlane v McFarlane* [2006] UKHL 24.

[16] eg*S v S* [2007] 1 FLR 1496.

[17] *OG v AG* [2020] EWFC 52.

[18] *VV v VV* [2022] EWFC 41.

Another old issue still returning for definition is whether premarital cohabitation should be taken into account in the division of assets, with the effect, if so, that the marriage is of longer duration than might at first have appeared. In *VV v VV*,[19] the test was said to be whether the parties themselves thought they were in a quasi-marital arrangement, a test that would be of less value as a determinant where they differed on this; the judge searched for 'solidity of cohabitation', a concept that could provide fruitful grounds for more such inquiries in future.

i. Prenuptial Agreements and Certainty

Prenuptial agreements are a current concern. The 2014 Report *Matrimonial Property, Needs and Agreements* by the Law Commission contained a draft bill on prenuptial agreements.[20] The Law Commission recommended that qualifying nuptial agreements, as it called them, should have statutory footing and should be made by deed not less than 28 days before the marriage, after legal advice to each party and with material disclosure of the parties' assets. The important and potentially destructive discretionary element in this proposal was that these agreements could not be used to contract out of meeting 'financial needs', not defined. While one could suggest that the bill therefore contained too many discretionary provisions that might thwart certainty, nevertheless it would have been an improvement had it been brought into law. Prenuptial agreements have become more acceptable and common since then,[21] especially in international marriages, but the uncertainty as to whether they are enforceable has given rise to very costly litigation to determine whether or not they are valid.[22] This defeats the purpose, even though more than 10 years have passed since the groundbreaking *Radmacher* judgment.[23]

If prenuptial agreements were enforceable with defined criteria, it might mean less costly litigation over them and would recognise their widespread use in foreign jurisdictions, and hence in international marriages being litigated in England. Enforceability would persuade some couples, especially older couples where one or other has been married before and has children, that they will not risk losing their assets to a second spouse on divorce or death but will be able to preserve them for their children. Inheritances from the family of one side could be protected. In the case of international marriages, couples expect those agreements to be enforceable. They became enforceable in Australia in 2000 by the Family Law Amendment Act of that year. Prenuptial agreements are enforceable

[19] *McFarlane* (n 15).

[20] *Matrimonial Property, Needs and Agreements* (n 1).

[21] H Benson, 'One in five weddings now start with a prenup' (Romford, Marriage Foundation, 2021) at marriagefoundation.org.uk/wp-content/uploads/2021/08/MF-briefing-note-on-prenups-FINAL.pdf.

[22] *S v H* [2020] EWFC B16; *Ipekci v McConnell* [2019] EWFC 19; *Brack v Brack* [2018] EWCA Civ 2862 and many more.

[23] *Radmacher v Granatino* [2020] UKSC 42.

in Canada, for example through the Ontario Family Law Reform Act of 1978. The French Civil Code makes provision for them.[24] Many countries are party to the Hague Convention on the Law Applicable to Matrimonial Property Regimes, which specifically authorises prenuptial agreements. They have also been given statutory basis in New Zealand by the Property (Relationships) Act 1976, part 6. In these and many other countries, the old common law presumption against prenuptial agreements has been set aside and the fear that they would somehow militate against lasting marriage overcome. Unfortunately, the UK Government has said no more than that it is considering the Law Commission's recommendations on qualifying nuptial agreements as part of a wider consideration of private family law reforms, and would respond in due course. One can only conclude that various governments do not have the will to take on private law reform in the financial field because they have not addressed themselves to the issues of principle outlined above. Nonetheless, a prenuptial agreement that was not signed by one party was held possible to be taken into account in considering the section 25 factors;[25] and in another recent case, the wife's distressed state at the time of signing the agreement was not held to affect it but its failure to meet her entire needs led to variation.[26] Such cases leave real doubt over the ability to predict any current prenuptial agreements.

This brief consideration of a few current issues may be enough to illustrate the uncertainties arising from constant interpretation, reinterpretation and ignoring of section 25 by judges.

B. The Lack of Principle

The Law Commission Report acknowledged the defects of financial provision but failed to come to a conclusion as to what to do. It famously stated:

> The situation facing family judges has therefore been likened to that of … a bus driver who is given a large number of instructions about how to drive the bus, and the authority to do various actions such as turning left or right. There is also the occasional advice or correction offered by three senior drivers. The one piece of information which he or she is not given is where to take the bus. All he or she is told is that the driver is required to drive to a reasonable destination.[27]

This remains the case, and the Family Justice Council guidance seemingly has been of no assistance to the drivers.[28] Statutory discretion may be a good thing where there is a situation involving uncertainty about what has occurred or who

[24] Civil Code, Arts 1387 et seq.
[25] *WC v HC* [2022] EWFC 22.
[26] *Traharne v Limb* [2022] EWFC 27.
[27] *Matrimonial Property, Needs and Agreements* (n 1) para 2.5.
[28] Family Justice Council, *Guidance on 'Financial Needs' on Divorce*, 2nd edn (London, Family Justice Council, April 2018) at www.judiciary.uk/wp-content/uploads/2018/04/guidance-on-financial-needs-divorce-2nd-edition-april-2018.pdf.

is responsible for damage or changes to people's lives, over which there could be reasonable disagreement. However, when there is discretion in a situation, such as financially supporting a former spouse long after the end of a marriage, for which there has been no rational basis for a century since the introduction of statutory equality and removal of fault in divorce, and where the governing legislation contains unranked and internally contradictory considerations, and where above all the cost of getting a judicial decision may be out of all proportion to the assets involved, to the detriment of children's support, then statutory discretion is not a good in itself. The lack of destination graphically outlined in the Law Commission Report was evident then and is even more evident today, when many other countries comparable to this one have set out destinations.

Scotland is satisfied with its destination.[29] Another example is New Zealand, which has a destination that would have benefited English litigants, and is now preparing to move to an even more certain and rational one. The New Zealand Law Commission[30] recommends an entitlement to share the fruits of the family joint venture, and a rules-based system, not relying on judicial discretion, with the aim of avoiding going to court. Property acquired before the marriage should be treated as separate property, even if it comprises the family home. Equal sharing should be the norm, save in cases of extraordinary misconduct. Commenting that 'the moral basis for why one partner should be liable to provide income support to the other partner through maintenance after the relationship has ended is unclear in contemporary New Zealand', the New Zealand Law Commission recommends sharing income for only a specified period, taking into account the length of the relationship. The principles adopted by, inter alia, Scotland and New Zealand are rules rather than judicial discretion, moving to self-sufficiency and avoidance of litigation. This direction of travel leaves the peculiarities of the English system even more exposed and isolated.

No-fault divorce was introduced in 2022.[31] Changing the ground of divorce to no-fault will not assist couples to reach an early amicable settlement because, as practitioners indicate, sudden and short notice of divorce makes couples less amenable to resolving issues than a more protracted and gradual period of coming to terms with it, as in, say, two years' separation.[32] It remains to be seen, but it is rational to suppose that no-fault divorce is as likely to make it harder to reach

[29] J Mair, E Mordaunt and F Wasoff, *Built to Last: the Family Law (Scotland) Act 1985–30 Years of Financial Provision on Divorce* (Glasgow, University of Glasgow, Nuffield Foundation, 2016) at eprints.gla.ac.uk/117617/.

[30] *Review of the Property (Relationships) Act 1976* (Report 143, 2019) para 49.

[31] The Divorce Dissolution and Separation Act 2020.

[32] Webb & Taylor, 'Could new divorce law mean even fewer couples share pensions? – new paper from former minister Steve Webb and specialist barrister Rhys Taylor' *LPC* (7 March 2022) at www.lcp.uk.com/media-centre/2022/03/could-new-divorce-law-mean-even-fewer-couples-share-pensions-new-paper-from-former-minister-steve-webb-and-specialist-barrister-rhys-taylor/; F Everett, 'Like Heston, I had a "slow divorce". It's the only sane way for a marriage to end' *The Telegraph* (26 April 2017) at www.telegraph.co.uk/family/relationships/like-heston-had-slow-divorce-sane-way-marriage-end/.

a settlement as it is easier. Harder, because the total blocking of any defence to the divorce and of any allegations of misconduct that led to it may be seen as an invitation to dwell on these in the financial negotiations, and because the quicker and more unexpected the divorce, the less likely it is that the claimant spouse will have come to terms with it or been able to make any plans for the future. On the other hand, it might be argued that the Government's encouragement to use mediation and the lawyers' disinclination to air fault may lead to smoother settlement. One might think that that is an overly optimistic view of human nature, and that it is unreasonable to expect that the temptations in financial provision law to battle on to the end will be more readily resisted. The Government's stress on using mediation may dampen allegations of misconduct, but it may also mean that there will be no publicly available information about whether conduct is resurgent.

There is no point in bringing in no-fault divorce law with the aim of removing the bitterness and deception alleged in fault-based divorce when the same elements, writ large, dominate financial provision law. Increasing numbers of divorcing couples are turning to arbitration and mediation in order to avoid the courts. Moreover, the Government has recently announced that it will pay couples to mediate.[33] If the Government has to help people avoid the law, there must be something very wrong with that law! The aim of no-fault divorce, according to the Government, is to end completely the need for separating couples to apportion blame for the breakdown of their marriage, helping them instead to focus on key practical decisions involving children or their finances, and to look to the future.[34]

As has been seen, the elements of apportionment and blame continue as strongly as ever in financial provision for now, and in the same press release on mediation the Ministry of Justice set out plans to review financial provision law. Although the substantive divorce and financial provision are separate procedures, they are of course inextricably linked, and there is a case for saying that no substantive divorce should be finalised until the finances are agreed. That would bring home to the spouses what the reality of the situation is, and might also serve to speed up the financial negotiations. According to a survey of 1,000 divorcees commissioned by the firm Irwin Mitchell, the most challenging part of divorce was general financial arrangements, costs and length of proceedings. Three in 10 respondents thought their divorce might have cost less if they had been friendlier. Two-thirds of respondents had lots of or some arguments during their divorce.[35]

[33] 'Mediation to help thousands more families avoid costly legal battles' (Press Release, Ministry of Justice, 3 June 2022) at www.gov.uk/government/news/mediation-to-help-thousands-more-families-avoid-costly-legal-battles.

[34] '"Blame game" ends as no-fault divorce comes into force' (Press Release, Ministry of Justice, HM Courts & Tribunals Service and The Rt Hon Dominic Raab MP, 6 April 2022) at www.gov.uk/government/news/blame-game-ends-as-no-fault-divorce-comes-into-force.

[35] I Mitchell, 'Doing Divorce Differently: New Report Reveals A Quarter Wished for Mediation or Arbitration As Answer to Divorce' *Irwin Mitchell* (21 July 2021) at www.irwinmitchell.com/

i. Increased Costs

There are many accounts of cases where nearly all the assets are wasted on the costs of litigation.[36] In *M v M*, each spouse emerged with £5,000 of liquid assets, having incurred nearly £600,000 of costs.[37] In *ND v GD*, costs of £483,000 exceeded the amount in dispute between the couple and represented 18 per cent of their wealth.[38] There are many more accounts of disproportionate costs and expressions of judicial disapproval of them. While some couples do litigate unreasonably, the uncertainty created judicially escalates costs. One judge at a Financial Dispute Resolution Hearing might estimate the award to a wife to be £Xm, and shortly thereafter another would estimate £2Xm, and the varying approaches of different judges are well known.[39] Recently, the legal costs in *E v L* attracted attention for their disproportionate nature.[40] An award of £2m to the wife generated £900,000 in costs. More significantly, in a lengthy judgment, Mostyn J attempted to clarify the principles of division of assets in a short, childless marriage, confining them to post-marital acquests. Despite the judge's welcome attempt to bring order into the law, an effort he makes frequently, doubt has been cast over whether his opInion about the relevance of childlessness and a short marriage will hold firm. There are comments in *Miller v Miller*[41] *and Sharp v Sharp*[42] that could well be resurrected to argue for the different treatment of childless marriages. One would have thought that, 16 years after the Supreme Court judgment in *Miller v Miller*,[43] the law in this area was settled, but it appeared to be far from the case. *E v L* could be a paradigm for reform of this law in the way that the harsh denial

news-and-insights/newsandmedia/2021/july/doing-divorce-differently-new-report-reveals-a-quarter-wished-for-mediation-or-arbitration.

[36] The litigation costs of £7m–8m were described as 'apocalyptic' in *Xanthopoulos v Rakshina* [2022] EWFC 30; in *ABX c SBX* [2018] EWFC 81, the assets were under £2m, costs £1.1m; in *HRH Prince Louis of Luxembourg v HRH Princess Tessy of Luxembourg* [2018] EWFC 77, the majority of the liquid assets were spent on costs of £500,000 and the child maintenance award was £4,000 pa; there was no money in *AJ v DM* [2019] EWHC 702 and an enormous amount of legal costs; *Piglowska v Piglowska* [1999] 2 FLR 7643, HL, where the assets were £127,400 and costs £128,000; *WG v HG* [2018] EWFC (Fam) 84, award to wife £4.05m, her costs £900,000; *MB v EB(No2)* [2019] EWHC 3676 (Fam), award to husband £485,000, his costs £650,000, wife's £600,000; *WC v HC* [2022] EWHC 40, costs were 13% of the total assets; *VV* (n 18), five-month marriage generated £1,235,000 costs.

[37] *M v M* [2020] EWFC 41.

[38] *ND v GD* [2021] EWFC 53.

[39] See, eg, Baroness Shackleton, HL Deb 27 June 2014, vol 754, col 1508.

[40] *E v L* [2021] EWFC 60. Mostyn J also indicated that 'financial remedy applications seem to be fast heading for Ritz hotel status – so expensive that it is only accessible by the very rich'. The comments came as part of a case where the parties had spent £1.7m in costs over a two-year period on what was thought to be a very straightforward matter, where less than two days were spent in court hearing the issues. He has previously urged the Lord Chancellor or the Family Procedure Rule Committee to take action to help prevent parties from incurring high level of costs, which he has described as 'such extraordinary, self-harming conduct'. 'Financial Remedies Update July 2022' *Family Law Week* (July 2022) at www.familylawweek.co.uk/articles/financial-remedy-update-july-2022/.

[41] *Miller* (n 15).

[42] *Sharp v Sharp* [2017] EWCA Civ 408.

[43] *Miller* (n 15).

(maybe deliberately so) of a divorce in *Owens v Owens*[44] was the catalyst for the introduction of no-fault divorce. In that case, the Supreme Court expressed its dissatisfaction with the existing divorce law; there has unfortunately been little or no criticism from the Supreme Court judges relating to financial provision law.

Certainty in the law would produce lower costs, or avoid litigation altogether, as seems to have occurred in Scots law, described in *Built to Last*. Despite judges' expression of disapproval of high costs, that disapproval comes too late, after the expenditure has been incurred. In some cases, the litigants are unreasonable, but it does seem to be the current legal framework that incentivises running up disproportionate costs. It is the lawyers involved who should be damping down the costs, but it is of course too much to expect of many professionals that they should be discouraging their clients from pursuing their cases all the way or lowering their rates: market forces and the desire for clarification keep them going. So the law, its administration and its uncertainty all work together to fail to discourage extensive litigation and consequent costs. For example, small cases can be infinitely more difficult than cases involving larger sums, where it is impossible to find a solution that can leave both parties happy.[45] In *Crowther v Crowther*,[46] there were 34 court hearings, costs amounted to £2.3 million and the couple's assets were £738,735, a loss of a significant sum to the detriment of the children. The judge imposed a clean break, that is, no further financial ties once the court order has been made and implemented, another concept that comes and goes. The judge commented:

> The only beneficiaries of this nihilistic litigation have been the specialist and high-quality lawyers. The main losers are probably the children who, quite apart from the emotional pain of seeing their parents involved in such bitter proceedings, will be deprived of monies which I am sure their parents would otherwise have wanted them to benefit from in due course.[47]

ii. Detriment to Children

The position of the children involved in divorce is not sufficiently considered in the law. The Divorce (Financial Provision) Bill provides that maintenance for children should continue to the age of 21, given that so many continue into higher education, and it shifts the emphasis of financial settlement towards the support

[44] *Owens v Owens* [2017] EWCA Civ 182.

[45] *JM* (n 7): assets £154,000, costs £150,000, exhausting the parties' savings and to the detriment of their child.

[46] *Crowther v Crowther* [2021] EWFC 88.

[47] ibid [87]. A particularly sad case is *Villiers v Villiers* [2022] EWCA Civ 772 (latest), which culminated in the husband's suicide, graphically described with comments from the public here: K Feehan and J Robinson, 'Tragedy as the Duchess of Cornwall's cousin – who was embroiled in one of Britain's longest divorce battles – "is found dead after taking his own life in a London hotel room"' *Daily Mail Online* (25 August 2022) at www.dailymail.co.uk/news/article-11143815/Camillas-cousin-Charles-Villiers-dead-taking-life-London-hotel-room.html.

and housing of children. The enormous legal costs attaching to disputed financial cases sometimes dissipate the very assets that should be preserved for the children. Recently, a monthly award of £177 for a child racked up £150,000 in costs.[48] Child maintenance has long been left behind in the consideration of children's welfare.[49] In divorce, it is arranged as part of the settlement or under the Children Act 1989. On reading judgments, it often seems to be an afterthought, and precisely calculated only when there are school fees or nannies whose costs are known. As distinct from the careful trawling through of the assets of a husband and the (excessive) needs of a wife, the provision for a child need only be 'adequate'.[50] It is hard to sympathise with the resistance by the father in *UD v DN*,[51] who successfully appealed against a settlement of property order under the Children Act 1989 in favour of his children, on the ground that the power to order financial provision in favour of an adult child who is not in full-time education is limited to exceptional circumstances, whatever they may be, leaving that door open for more such appeals. *Mesher* orders,[52] which enabled the caring parent to stay in the family home until the child reached 18 or completed secondary education, have fallen out of favour in recent years. A *Mesher* order might have contained the condition that the mother would have to leave the home if she cohabited with someone else; and now that half the young population go on to higher education, sale at age 18 is not at a good time. It would seem sensible in modern educational circumstances and the rental market to expect housing also to be needed by children at least until the age of 21.

Now that there is hardly any legal aid, and indeed even when it was available, costs associated with uncertainty are a deplorable waste of resources that ought to be preserved. The vested interests of barristers who act for the very few extremely wealthy couples, and who have opposed all reform, should not be permitted to block reform for the average and the many.[53] As Baroness Hale pointed out

[48] *JM* (n 7).

[49] House of Commons Committee of Public Accounts Committee, *Child Maintenance* (Ninth Report of Session 2022–23, 20 June 2022) at www.publications.parliament.uk/pa/cm5803/cmselect/cmpubacc/255/report.html.

[50] *Juffali v Juffali* [2016] EWHC 1684. This judgment is well worth reading for a description of the lifestyle that the law regards as relevant at the end of a 12-year marriage with one child.

[51] *UD v DN* [2021] EWCA Civ 1947.

[52] *Mesher v Mesher* [1980] 1 All ER 126.

[53] eg O Peirson, 'The Family Law Podcast: Baroness Deech's Bill on Financial Provision on Divorce' *Pump Court Chambers* (30 November 2021) at www.pumpcourtchambers.com/2021/11/30/baroness-deechs-bill-on-financial-provision-on-divorce/; J Bolch, 'Baroness Deech's Dangerous Divorce Bill' *Stowe Family Law* (19 November 2018) at www.stowefamilylaw.co.uk/blog/2018/11/19/baroness-deechs-dangerous-divorce-bill; 'Law Chiefs Seek to End 'Meal Ticket for Life' Divorce Deals' *IBB Law* (1 December 2017) at www.ibblaw.co.uk/insights/blog/law-chiefs-seek-end-meal-ticket-life-divorce-deals; opposition by James Turner QC with letter in *The Times*: R Deech, 'You must read "Built to Last" – Lord Hope's views strongly refuted. Why would a QC resist clearer law?' *X* (14 June 2017) at www.twitter.com/BaronessDeech/status/875116144671281152 and here J Bolch, 'Does our financial provision law even need reform?' *Stowe Family Law* (22 November 2018) at www.stowefamilylaw.co.uk/blog/2018/11/22/does-our-financial-provision-law-even-need-reform/; *Matrimonial Property, Needs and Agreements* (Law Com No 208, 2012), para 3.135, fn 63; an unusual attack on reform by

in her *Desert Island Discs* broadcast,[54] the preservation of the status quo is in itself an agenda, apparently meaning that not to reform is itself a statement. She made clear that her agenda was to promote equality and diversity, indicating that those who disagreed with her were trying to keep the status quo in relations between the sexes and between different groups. It is however an open question whether the judicial stance on financial provision does actually promote equality, or the reverse. It seems more like the preservation of the status of wife as a supplicant and dependant, not an entitled partner. In addition to the introduction of no-fault divorce, which ought to change working practices, COVID has accelerated another innovation, the move to remote and online handling of family disputes. The introduction of social-distancing measures during the COVID-19 pandemic resulted in family court hearings in England being conducted remotely by video or telephone, although not always with some drawbacks.[55] There is a strong case for a new law that is adapted to that, and to the situation of no-fault divorcing couples who have little legal advice and need ready guidelines.

III. What Happens in Practice?

A diminishing number of financial orders are being made.[56] Some practitioners say that joint lives orders are almost dead. The *Family Court Statistics Quarterly* has shown for a while that only about one-third of the divorce petitions are also financial provision petitions. Research has shown that almost nothing is achieved by way of ongoing provision for lower-income couples, either because no order is made or because the spousal award will be deducted from Universal Credit pound for pound (whereas this does not apply to awards for children). The availability of state benefits is taken into account by judges when assessing maintenance, and it is important to note the futility of an award when it is taken away by Universal Credit. Child maintenance is disregarded, which strengthens the case for loading payments towards children rather than the spouse. So, an elaborate, controversial

Baroness Hale in her lecture 'What is a 21st Century Family?' (Watford, International Centre for Family Law, Policy & Practice, 1 July 2019) at www.supremecourt.uk/docs/speech-190701.pdf; Lord Wilson, 'Changes over the Centuries in the financial consequences of divorce: Address to the University of Bristol Law Club' *Supreme Court* (20 March 2017) at www.supremecourt.uk/docs/speech-170320.pdf.

[54] 'Baroness Hale of Richmond, former judge' *BBC Radio 4* (24 September 2021) at www.bbc.co.uk/programmes/m000zt7b.

[55] L Harker and M Ryan, 'Remote Hearings in Family Courts in England and Wales during Covid-19: Insights and lessons' (2022) 60(2) *Family Court Review* 207; M Ryan, L Harker and S Rothera, 'Remote Hearings in the Family Justice System: A Rapid Consultation' (London, Nuffield Family Justice Observatory, 2020) at www.nuffieldfjo.org.uk/resource/remote-hearings-rapid-consultation; MacDonald J, 'The Remote Access Family Court' (London, Courts and Tribunals Judiciary, 2020) at www.judiciary.uk/wp-content/uploads/2020/03/The-Remote-Access-Family-Court-Version-2-Final-25.03.20.pdf.

[56] Resolution, *Family Law Handbook* (London, Resolution, 23 November 2020) at resolution.org.uk/publications-books/resolution-family-law-handbook/; see ibid ch 5, where it is also admitted that the English/Welsh law is out of step with every other western nation's law.

and costly financial provision law ends up benefiting only the well-off.[57] Theirs are the cases that reach the Supreme Court, resulting in new, unsettling precedents and making the news. The English jurisdiction is the one of choice for oligarchs' wives and other extremely wealthy claimants. Thus, in effect, financial provision law is catering for a very small number of couples and is otherwise almost entirely privatised, while children's needs come second.

Privatisation has arisen because it has been possible to choose arbitration in family cases since 2012, and demand has soared as the family courts were overloaded during lockdown.[58] Private family disputes are now common enough to be included as standard in practice.[59] Moreover, it is a requirement of the Children and Families Act 2014 for a person to attend a Mediation Information and Assessment Meeting before starting proceedings for a family remedy. In 2021, the Government introduced £500 vouchers for families to put towards mediation in divorce; the amount was increased, and the number of vouchers has been increased twice since then.[60] Despite that, the litigation reports continue to pour out. Practitioners point out, reasonably, that if the couple do not know what the law is, or what it is primarily meant to achieve, or are at loggerheads, it is unlikely that mediation will be successful, and the voucher finance will be exhausted long before a conclusion. Some studies indicate that women have the weaker hand in mediation.[61] Mediation will not add to transparency because some of the settlements, their amount and the costs, will be unpublicised.

IV. A Better Model

Scots law was reformed in 1985 to meet exactly the criticisms outlined here, largely due to the visionary and forward-looking Law Commissioner, Eric Clive, who has long defended his scepticism of the notion that wives must always be kept.[62]

[57] J Miles and E Hitchings, 'Financial remedy outcomes on divorce in England and Wales: not a "meal ticket for life"' (2018) 31(2) *Australian Journal of Family Law* 43. While attempting to disprove the 'meal ticket' description, at the same time this research shows how few spouses gain much from the financial provision law, while the Supreme Court precedents are almost always made in relation to wealthy cases.

[58] Data from the Institute of Family Law Arbitrators at ifla.org.uk/.

[59] N Mostyn et al, *Financial Remedies Practice Handbook*, 11th edn (London, Class Legal, 2022–23).

[60] 'Mediation to help thousands more families avoid costly legal battles' (Press Release, Ministry of Justice, 3 June 2022) at www.gov.uk/government/news/mediation-to-help-thousands-more-families-avoid-costly-legal-battles.

[61] M Stowe, 'Time for a Rethink on Helping Separated Couples' *Family Lore* (27 March 2021) at www.familylore.co.uk/2021/03/time-for-rethink-on-helping-separated.html; M Stowe and J Gilg, 'Family Mediation a Waste of Time' *Solicitors' Journal* (15 October 2012); M Brinig, 'Does Mediation Systematically Disadvantage Women' (1995) 1(2) *William & Mary Journal of Race, Gender, and Social Justice* 1; T Grillo, 'The Mediation Alternative: Process Dangers for Women' (1991) 100(6) *Yale Law Journal* 1545.

[62] E Clive, 'Financial Provision on Divorce (2006) 10(3) *Edinburgh Law Review* 413; E Clive, 'Marriage: An Unnecessary Legal Concept' in J Eekelaar and S Katz (eds), *Marriage and Cohabitation in Contemporary Societies* (London, Butterworths, 1980) 71.

He famously said 'there is something fundamentally repulsive about this whole idea of dependent women'. He was able to translate this into the Family Law (Scotland) Act 1985.[63] It was designed to address the problems that remain unaddressed, indeed resisted, in English law, as outlined here. The Scottish law reform project had explicit objectives, which were the then lack of clear guidance, too much judicial discretion and over-reliance on continuing periodical allowances. Scots law, on which the Divorce (Financial Provision) Bill is modelled, has received an excellent review from a recent inquiry, *Built to Last*.[64]

As a result of the Act, the legal process of divorce has moved in the direction of encouraging negotiation, reducing conflict and court involvement. Support for the couple from legal professionals is largely provided outside the courts. There was a determination to spell out principles for the financial settlements. They are set out in section 9 of the 1985 Act: first, the fair sharing of matrimonial property, deemed fair in the first instance if equally shared; matrimonial property is defined as the matrimonial home and property acquired after the marriage. The second principle is the balancing of economic advantage and disadvantage incurred by either spouse in the interests of the other or of the family. The third principle is a fair sharing of the burden of childcare, with financial provision for a period of adjustment of three years where one spouse has been financially dependent on the other, and provision for relief of serious financial hardship.[65] It is legislation of which to be proud, according to *Built to Last*.

Some specific findings from that Report:

- 'The legislation has been successful in achieving one of its aims which was to encourage parties to reach their own agreements about the financial and property consequences of divorce'.[66]
- There was also strong approval for the concept of 'matrimonial property', with many interviewees highlighting the clarity and certainty of the matrimonial property regime as being an aspect of the legislation that worked well.
- 'This is a well-designed statutory framework with no fundamental need for reform. It is regarded as combining certainty with flexibility in a way which facilitates the work of each group of legal actors who put the legislation into practice'.[67]
- '*English law is broken and needs mending: but ours doesn't. Ours doesn't. Ours can always be improved, of course it can always be improved; but generally speaking, it's a gem*' (quotation from an interviewee).[68]

[63] Based on Scottish Law Commission Report, *Family Law: Financial Consequences on Divorce* (Scot Law Com No 112, 1981).

[64] Mair, Mordaunt and Wasoff (n 29).

[65] J Fotheringham, 'Spousal Maintenance in Scots Family Law' (2019) 41 *Houston Journal of International Law* 601.

[66] Mair, Mordaunt and Wasoff (n 29) 170.

[67] ibid 179.

[68] ibid 155.

There is no European state with a law as discretionary and stereotyped as English law. Those jurisdictions often have community of property systems and no or short-term maintenance, as well as binding prenuptial agreements. The comparable laws of New Zealand, Australia and the USA resemble the Scottish model, not the English.[69] No reason has ever been shown why English law has to be so different from the law of its closest neighbour, both part of the United Kingdom.

V. The Solution: A New Basis

The drafting of the Divorce (Financial Provision) Bill is inadequate: members introducing their own Bills are given no drafting help. The aim of a Private Member's Bill is to persuade the Government to take up the proposed reform, at which stage counsel would undertake the detailed drafting. The principles that are set out in the Bill are: section 25(2) of the Matrimonial Causes Act 1973 should be replaced; only matrimonial property including pensions should be available for sharing at the end of a marriage; prenuptial and postnuptial agreements should be binding with certain conditions; as a starting point, property should be shared equally; limited-term periodical payments; and support for children up to the age of 21.

The aim is to give divorcing couples a firm formulaic basis on which to negotiate and estimate their settlement, and to minimise legal costs; to facilitate virtual negotiation and the use of online calculation. As in Scotland, departures from equality might be justified by, for example, particular childcare burdens or marked economic disadvantage suffered by one spouse that is attributable to the other and which cannot be compensated for in any other way.

[69] For comparative material, see J Scherpe, 'A comparative overview of the treatment of non-matrimonial assets, indexation and value increases' (2013) 25(1) *Child and Family Law Quarterly* 61; J Scherpe, *Marital Agreements and Marital Property* (Oxford, Hart Publishing, 2012) 42; J Scherpe, *Marital Agreements, Private Autonomy in Comparative Perspective* (Oxford, Hart Publishing, 2012); J Scherpe, 'Towards a Matrimonial Property Regime for England and Wales' in R Probert and C Barton (eds), *Fifty Years in Family Law: Essays for Stephen Cretney* (Cambridge, Intersentia, 2012). New Zealand's Property (Relationships) Act 1976 contains a presumption of equal division limited to the 'relationship property'. This has recently been reviewed by the New Zealand Law Commission in *Review of the Property (Relationships) Act 1976* (New Zealand Law Com No 143, 2016), whose recommendations if implemented would bring New Zealand law even closer to the provisions of the Divorce (Financial Provision) Bill 2021. Australia has modernised an online approach, as seen at www.familyproperty.com.au/, explained by P Parkinson, 'Family Property Division and the New Technologies' (Brisbane, University of Queensland, 2020) at www.osullivandavies.com.au/wp-content/uploads/2020/09/Family-Property-Division-and-the-New-Technologies-Prof.-Patrick-Parkinson.pdf; for a summary of the various laws of the EU states, see 'Divorce and Legal Separation' (Your Europe, 2020) at europa.eu/youreurope/citizens/family/couple/divorce-separation/index_en.htm. US States' laws are handily summarised at www.maritallaws.com/laws/alimony: some States have community of property; many have alimony calculators with less judicial discretion; only six allow for permanent alimony; and some are moving in the direction of the Divorce (Financial Provision) Bill. Florida is an interesting example, with the history of the reform movement set out at www.myfloridalaw.com/alimony/florida-alimony-reform/.

As a matter of principle, the Bill is also aimed at ending the status of the ex-wife (usually) as a supplicant asking for her needs to be met by her ex-husband, and instead of that to treat her as an equal partner in the venture of marriage. The default position of many judges and academics is that women should be regarded as permanently exempt from the job market once married, or at the very least somehow handicapped by marriage whether they are mothers or not.[70] The courts even allow ex-spouses to return to court to seek more money from former partners decades after the dissolution.[71] This is at odds with government calls for women to take up to half the positions on boards, in the judiciary, in universities and so on. It contrasts with the attitude of other western countries. It has been argued that maintenance has to be long-lasting and generous in England because social support for women is insufficient. Yet the EU Gender Equality Index has the UK at above the EU average, behind only five other countries, and nearly all the European states have financial provision laws resembling those recommended here.[72] The complex affairs of the very wealthy will no doubt always present difficulties and require the services of lawyers, but others should be assisted by this new approach. Judgments and recent academic writings[73] place great emphasis on the contribution made by a wife as the rationale for ongoing maintenance after the end of the marriage, styled 'compensation'. This takes one back to the arguments of more than 50 years ago when 'irretrievable breakdown' became the sole ground for dissolution, sweeping away with it in theory any reason for ongoing spousal support.[74]

This much was admitted by Leo Abse MP, a driver of reform, and incidentally a relative of the author.[75] The resistance to divorce reform in the late 1960s was on ideological grounds (the 'innocent' wife losing her status), but also, when it was clear that that position was not sufficiently convincing, the arguments switched to the inadequacy of support for the wife after divorce. That dichotomy is revived today: on the one hand, family law should reflect the independence and autonomy of spouses and the equality of women within marriage; on the other, the assumption that she has always to be protected financially through a man's resources. The economic position of women and the opportunities available to them have changed significantly over those 50 years, and it is alarming to see the neo-feminists of today chipping away unthinkingly at the grounds of women's equal standing.

[70] Family Justice Council (n 28) 14 ff; *Juffali* (n 50); *Miller* (n 15) fn 40.

[71] *Wyatt v Vince* [2015] UKSC 14. Reportedly 29,000 ex-spouses returned to court to seek more maintenance after this decision: see at www.familylawweek.co.uk/site.aspx?i=ed145425.

[72] O McEvoy, 'The EU Gender Equality Index in 2022, by country' *Statista* (28 February 2023) at www.statista.com/statistics/1209683/the-eu-gender-equality-index-by-country/. The cost of childcare in England is far too high, but financial provision law tends to apply similarly to women with or without children, caring for the children themselves or with help, in or out of work.

[73] Invariably by women who themselves are pursuing a career.

[74] HL Deb 30 June 1969, vol 303, cols 33 et seq; the history of the controversy is set out in Law Commission, *Matrimonial Property, Needs and Agreements* (Law Com No 208, 2012) paras 3.6 et seq.

[75] eg, HC Deb 24 January 1969, vol 776, col 819; HC Deb 12 June 1969, vol 784, col 2017.

A. Autonomy and Dependency

The contribution made by ex-wives as a rationale for maintenance is not only based on an untested model but is also associated both with the idea that a woman should expect to rely on providing womanly services as a *quid pro quo* and with the commodification of men's role in marriage. He is only good for financial support, it seems. The use of stereotypes in this debate reflects their use in court. Taken at face value, the typical wife's contribution through housework and childcare in marriage indeed attracts compensation, there and then, through the support provided by the typical husband throughout their joint lives, the housing, clothing, support, holidays, and every affordable need of the wife and children. She is paid, if that is how it is to be regarded, every day. On the other hand, no thought is given in this scenario to the very real burden which is borne, typically by men, in providing the family's financial support: the burden of always needing to be in employment, the cost of housing, taxes, the financial affairs, the insurance and pension. When it comes to the division of household work, insufficient weight is attributed to that which the typical man might well undertake, maintenance, the car, computing, electric devices, accounts, income tax. Yet in nearly every judgment cited here, the court looks to see whether the wife can support herself, whereas the husband is taken to be able to do so and continue to do so unless he proves otherwise.[76] Sadly, however, the message being given out by those who are too young to remember the many waves of feminism before the current one is that the best that a woman can do is attach herself to a man and count on him for support for all time. Moreover, the rewards are regressive. The better off the husband, the less burden the wife may have taken on and the more she will already have been compensated by way of being provided with necessaries and more. It is in the poorer families that the wife cannot afford the luxury of staying at home and has to have a job; but she is unlikely to receive any award of significance on dissolution because her ex-husband has no resources. Even the benefits system requires women to be available for work when the children are quite young. It is noteworthy that the departure from this stereotype is often marked in judgments where a better-off wife who is wealthier than her husband might find herself giving a great deal to a former husband, an outcome the judges seem reluctant to contemplate very often.[77] Unless radical reform is undertaken, the wife will remain a needy supplicant and not a partner in the financial dissolution.

It is puzzling and unexamined that by virtue of a sexual relationship (assumed), not a family or friend relationship, a woman becomes entitled to claim support from her husband (or, in some cases, cohabitant). Moreover, there is no provision

[76] Rupert Nightingale's case (unreported) is a good example, see P Dolan, 'Mr Nightingale gets the chance to sing' *Family Law LexisNexis* (12 February 2015) at www.familylaw.co.uk/news_and_comment/mr-nightingale-gets-the-chance-to-sing.

[77] eg*Stack v Dowden* [2007] UKHL 17; *Radmacher* (n 23); *Kianoosh Azarmi-Movafagh v SorourBassiri-Dezfouli* [2021] EWCA Civ 1184.

for help or support for the many women, and men, who truly deserve support because they have given lifelong care – the sisters, the daughter-carers of parents, who usually have no claim. It is hard to understand why a sexual relationship, even brief and childless, is taken as the passport to financial claims but not the family relationship. Importantly, all the emphasis laid by academic writers on the need to support ex-wives is blind to the needs of single women in jobs where they are paid less than men, or have lesser pensions, and single mothers where the father is not supporting the child.[78] Unpartnered women are disregarded, and worse, in and because of family law. They will never enjoy support and widow's benefits. Their claims in inheritance law by virtue of caring for a deceased parent are difficult to establish. This pressure for lifelong support for divorced women is hardly feminist at all in its focus only on women who attached themselves to a man.[79] The poorer situation of an ex-wife after the end of the marriage, if that is the case, is not necessarily attributable to the ex-husband. Moreover, in a time of easy and common divorce, it is foolhardy for a woman to set sail in life without a lifeboat.

B. The Benefits of Reform

If a more formulaic approach of the sort proposed were adopted, it would lend itself more readily to online use, as trialled in Australia;[80] and would be of assistance to couples who have no legal representation. They amount to about 38 per cent, a proportion that is rising.[81] It would save costs, leaving fewer issues over which to negotiate or litigate, and would provide a useful starting point for mediation. It would be fairer, being based on equal division and on equality of the sexes as former partners. It might dispel the widespread feeling of unfairness generated by existing law.[82]

[78] 'The cost of living alone' (Newport, Office for National Statistics, 2019) at www.ons.gov.uk/peoplepopulationandcommunity/birthsdeathsandmarriages/families/articles/thecostoflivingalone/2019-04-04; C Bollinger, C Nicoletti and S Pudney, 'Two can live as cheaply as one- but three's a crowd' (ISER Working Paper Series No 2012-10 (University of Essex and the Institute for Social and Economic Research, 2012) at www.econstor.eu/bitstream/10419/65924/1/717847640.pdf.

[79] As Baroness Hale said at the launch of Cambridge Women in Law on 27 September 2019, few women can make it on their own, and her most important advice was to pick the right partner: N Hellen, 'Lady Hale: Pick the right partner to be supreme at law' *The Times* (29 September 2019) at www.thetimes.co.uk/article/lady-hale-pick-the-right-partner-to-be-supreme-at-law-bg0nk699v.

[80] See Parkinson (n 69) fn 22.

[81] 'Family Courts Statistics Quarterly: Collection' (London, Ministry of Justice, 2014) at www.gov.uk/government/collections/family-court-statistics-quarterly.

[82] See the typical comments by *Guardian* and *Daily Mail* readers: K Gunn, 'Be honest, be kind: five lessons from an amicable divorce' *The Guardian* (16 March 2019) at www.theguardian.com/lifeandstyle/2019/mar/16/five-lessons-having-an-amicable-divorce; T McVeigh, 'The biggest financial risk for women today? Embarking on a relationship' *The Guardian* (19 March 2017) at www.theguardian.com/lifeandstyle/2017/mar/19/divorce-women-risk-poverty-children-relationship; O Bowcott, 'Woman wins right to seek money from ex-husband 30 years after breakup' *The Guardian* (11 March 2015) at www.theguardian.com/law/2015/mar/11/woman-wins-right-seek-money-ex-husband-30-years-after-break-up-dale-vince; B Quinn, 'Judge tells ex-wife of millionaire horse surgeon: "go out to work"'

i. Law would be Simplified

Some years ago, I ran an All Party Parliamentary Group on Divorce, to which members of the public were admitted. Their universal comment was the need for a booklet of information when they got married, or later, to explain what their liabilities were on dissolution. Most of them had no idea what they might be. I have also observed Financial Dispute Resolution Appointments in a Family Court. It is upsetting to see couples arrive before the judge, with no legal representation, and attempting to discuss financial remedies without even knowing, for example, that the welfare of children is important. It places an enormous burden on the judge, and takes up a great deal of time.

ii. The Rule of Law would be Restored

Lord Bingham explained that the law must be accessible and, so far as possible, intelligible, clear and predictable.[83] The English law of financial provision is none of these, and so the rule of law is currently being breached. The outcome varies from judge to judge and era to era. The result is unpredictable. The principles change every time the Supreme Court has the opportunity to give judgment in what tends to be a case concerning wealth. Even the most experienced of solicitors and barristers cannot predict the award. The uncertainty pushes couples to settle for fear of what a judge might unpredictably order, and that is not in accordance with the rule of law. The law is occasionally altered with retrospective effect, such as when many years after the divorce the claimant spouse returns to court for a fresh, or increased, order based on new situations. Valid contracts, that is prenuptial agreements, are set aside on grounds that may not seem fair or justifiable. Section 25 of the Matrimonial Causes Act 1973 has been interpreted out of all recognition by judges in the intervening years, one might say almost disregarded. Section 25A of the Act (clean break) is frequently ignored. It is also unsatisfactory that there should be such a difference between the law of England and Scotland, and between England and the rest of the western world, especially when there are so many international marriages.

The Guardian (24 February 2015) at www.theguardian.com/uk-news/2015/feb/24/judge-ex-wife-millionaire-work; A Matthews and S Cockroft, '"I'm paying for HER mistakes": Husband who was ordered to support his ex-wife for life 15 years AFTER they divorced calls for a time limit on maintenance after she blew her £230,000 payout on bad investment' Daily *Mail Online* (8 February 2017) at www.dailymail.co.uk/news/article-4204214/Court-order-makes-man-pay-ex-wife-s-mistakes.html#comments; E Dunkley, 'Men get a raw deal in divorce cases … according to the women they are splitting from' Daily *Mail Online* (20 February 2022) at www.dailymail.co.uk/news/article-10531601/Men-raw-deal-divorce-cases-according-women-splitting-from.html#comments; L McLoughlin and C Farmer, '"It's a draining situation": CBB's Jamie O'Hara reveals he's struggling to pay ex-wife Danielle Lloyd's £15,000-a-month maintenance as he confesses he's "not on that money no more" '*Daily Mail Online* (7 January 2017) at www.dailymail.co.uk/tvshowbiz/article-4097646/CBB-s-Jamie-O-Hara-reveals-s-struggling-pay-ex-wife-Danielle-Lloyd-s-15-000-month-maintenance.html#comments.

[83] T Bingham, *The Rule of Law* (London, Penguin Books, 2010).

iii. Access to Justice would be Improved

When couples are unrepresented and are drawn into financial disputes very rapidly after a no-fault divorce, they need to know what the law is, and to be able to negotiate free of complexity and preferably with little legal help. The Family Law Bar points to the Family Justice Council guidance for such couples.[84] That runs to 72 pages. It would make a great graduate thesis on the law, but I have never seen it cited in a judgment and it is far too complicated for a couple to use, setting out, as it does, all the twists and turns the law has taken recently.

VI. Conclusion

The marriage contract as we knew it 150 years ago has disappeared. No longer does the father have the right to his children; support of children or a spouse during marriage is unenforceable; no longer does the husband own his wife's property; it is not a crime or a ground of divorce to commit adultery, desert a spouse, or behave intolerably or unreasonably towards him or her; there is no assurance of indissoluble marriage provided one behaves; there is no need to find a breach of the contract in order to end the marriage, and only a few weeks' notice need be given. Many of those contractual or status obligations had some good sense behind them, but they have been removed in the pursuit of individual happiness and welfare. Only one obligation remains: the obligation to maintain after dissolution (and even after death), and it is perhaps the one with the least justification, the most unsuccessful and the most incomprehensible.

In relation to theoretical hardship resulting from reform, no answer from opponents has ever been given to the question why England is alone in the western, Antipodean and North American world in its treatment of spousal dependency and unequal division. Research shows that divorced women tend to recover their previous standard of living when they re-partner.[85] The ex-husband meanwhile is quicker to re-partner and will quite likely end up supporting another divorced woman, a zero-sum game. Lawyers benefit from the complexities and antagonistic nature of the current law. The proposed reforms would offer an off-the-peg solution. They would end the attitude of some barristers that, since we all look better in Savile Row suits, there must be no Marks & Spencer ready-made.

Financial independence of women is a major strand in feminist thinking.[86] Modern legislation on equality and employment has at its basis the freedom,

[84] Family Justice Council (n 28) fn 8.

[85] H Fisher and H Low, 'Recovery from Divorce: Comparing High and Low Income Couples' (2016) 30 *International Journal of Law Policy and the Family* 338.

[86] M McIntosh, 'The Dependency Culture: Welfare Women and Work' (1998) *Radical Philosophy* 091; M McIntosh, 'Engendering Economic Policy: The Women's Budget Group' (2001) 12(2) *Women a Cultural Review* 147; J Barrett, *Thinking like a Breadwinner: A Manifesto to Help Women Make the*

indeed the right, even the duty of women to go out and take advantage of the opportunities open to them now that were closed to them a few decades ago. Legislating for equal partnership would also bring an end to the demeaning situation that continues to be adopted in English law and society, namely, that the status of the woman is forever determined by the man she marries but not vice versa. Simone de Beauvoir captured this in 1949 when she wrote that 'man defines woman not in herself but as relative to him … she is defined and differentiated with reference to men … women live … attached through residence, housework, economic condition and social standing to certain men'.[87] Financial provision law should not remain rooted in this framework.

Most of their Money (London, Bluebird, 2012); V Woolf, *A Room of One's Own* (London, Hogarth Press, 1929); N Stoljar, 'Feminist Perspectives on Autonomy' *The Stanford Encyclopaedia of Philosophy* (11 December 2018) at plato.stanford.edu/archives/win2018/entries/feminism-autonomy/; K Gray, *Reallocation of Property on Divorce* (Abingdon, Professional Books, 1977); C Smart, *The Ties that Bind* (London, Routledge, 1984).

[87] S de Beauvoir, *The Second Sex: Introduction* (London, Penguin Books, 1949).

Response to Chapter 7

Reform of Financial Provision on Divorce

SIR NICHOLAS MOSTYN

In August 2023, I travelled to Edinburgh to watch the brilliant musical *IrrePressible*, written by my fellow *Mover & Shaker* Gillian Lacey-Solymar. It is about the life and loves of Emma, Lady Hamilton. In order to illustrate the deplorable plight of women, and most particularly married women, in Emma's time, Gillian asked me to pen a tongue-in-cheek piece for the programme, which I duly did. It is included at the end of this chapter.

I invited a distinguished member of the Inner House of the Court of Session to join me, Gillian and her husband Mike for lunch. There I attempted to explain to Gillian and Mike that, while we had come a long way since 1805, financial remedy law remained marooned in the past; was more or less unregulated; and was subject to the personal whims of individual judges.

With mounting disbelief, Gillian and Mike learned that the governing statute was passed in 1970, and merely listed a number of obvious things to be taken into account when deciding how to divide up the money. It had no particular objective, other than to eschew alimony unless the recipient would suffer 'undue hardship'. That objective was introduced in 1984, but had been astutely ignored by the judiciary from its inception.

I explained that such rules as there were, such as the equal sharing of the money accumulated during the marriage, had been invented by the judges, and had never acquired any solidity as they were constantly being modified and tweaked by other judges. In some remarks at a meeting in the House of Lords in June 2023, organised by Ruth Deech, I explained it this way:

> In my opinion the right to a fair trial in all civil litigation demands that justice is transparent, predictable, straight-forward, expeditiously administered, and economical. The substantive law of financial remedies fails every one of these criteria. This is why procedural reform after procedural reform designed to address the curse of excessive costs fails.
>
> In my opinion, in the sphere of financial remedies, the rule of law should be the law of rules (I acknowledge the mastery of Justice Scalia in coining this memorable phrase, even if I completely repudiate his politics). Following the seminal decisions of

> *White*[1] and *Miller*[2] I have tried to rationalise the principles handed down by the House of Lords into sets of simple rules.
>
> Thus, I have argued that an attempt should be made in every case to calculate, using simple arithmetical principles, the scale of the matrimonial property, which should be divided equally unless there is very good reason not to. And that there should only be an award of spousal maintenance to meet grave financial hardship. And that child maintenance should be determined by a simple formula.
>
> If those rules had been warmly endorsed by the Court of Appeal, I hazard that this Law Commission project would not be necessary.
>
> But no. Time after time, the law of rules is over-painted by the Court of Appeal applying the dogma of the 'bespoke solution crafted by the judge exercising his individual, unfettered, unbounded discretion'.
>
> …
>
> The reason reform is necessary now is this: for as long as the present system keeps overlaying simple rules with woolly discretion, it will never be predictable, transparent, economical or consistent. Any supposed advantage derived from a 'bespoke' solution will be entirely offset by the enormous costs, rancour and acrimony generated by lengthy trials, where both sides will spare no expense to try to get into the judge's head to manipulate his or her 'singular', 'unfettered', 'unbounded', 'individual' and 'personal' discretionary power.

With wry amusement, my friend from the Inner House watched the disbelief of Gillian and Mike that such a system had come into being with no democratic endorsement of any nature. Eventually, my friend simply stated that 'the English need legislation', and went on to explain that a rules-based system has to be passed by the legislature, and can only allow minimal wriggle room. A judge-made system of guidelines by definition is not written in marble and is easily by-passed. All of this is powerfully and persuasively expressed in Ruth Deech's essay in her customary, beautifully crafted, prose.

The lack of democratic input in our judge-made system is a major deficit. By its very nature, any legislation would have been preceded by specialist research. Further, surveys would have been done of wide sectors of society to see what the public's attitude is to the distribution of assets on divorce. Such steps would address the following major factors, which the present system has totally ignored.

First, it would address the phenomenon that, for unknown reasons, the majority of divorces (I include civil partnerships in the figures for marriages and divorces) do not give rise to a financial claim of any nature. In 2022, there were 80,443 divorces finalised in England and Wales. In the same 12-month period, there were just 31,277 financial remedy 'disposals' (ie final orders). Of these, about 7,000

[1] *White v White* [2001] 1 AC 596.
[2] *Miller v Miller; McFarlane v McFarlane* [2006] UKHL 24.

were contested cases; the balance of 24,000 were by consent.[3] Thus, in the calendar year 2022, nearly 100,000 people (ie 50,000 marriages) ended their marriage without going through a court process to sort out their finances. Astonishingly in 2022, only 39 per cent of divorces had a connected financial order made.

Those percentages have stayed broadly the same for at least the past four years (if not longer) and, looking at the most recently published figures from His Majesty's Courts and Tribunals Service (HMCTS) for the first six months of no-fault (and online) divorce, things are only getting worse. In the first quarter of 2023, there were 29,622 divorces dissolutions, but in only 32 per cent (9,505) of those divorces were financial orders made.

Put another way, 68 per cent of people who had finalised their divorce in England and Wales by that point last year did so without making use of the legal system (even by consent) to resolve their financial arrangements. Why? It is difficult to ascertain precisely why, but it is reasonable to assume that most of these people have property, savings, pension or earnings. In my opinion, the distributive system needs to be accessible by this very large non-participatory cohort.

The second reason is that we do not know what the principles were that governed those 31,000 cases where a final order was made. In *The Financial Remedies Court*: *A Year in Review*,[4] Peel J stated:

> As it happens, I suspect that the debate about transparency will only affect a handful of cases on the ground, probably at High Court level. In some ways, a better way to secure transparency is to obtain data about all financial remedies cases so that we can see prevailing trends. That would better enable the public, and the media, to understand the totality of the financial remedies system, rather than draw conclusions from a tiny minority of High Court cases which are invariably exceptional in terms of facts and finances. That in turn would better inform society, and our lawmakers. Currently, we know how many cases are issued (about 40,000–50,000 each year), and (approximately) how many are completed without proceeding to final hearing (85–90% thereof). We have some idea of how many parties are unrepresented. But we know next to nothing, beyond anecdotally, about: (1) the quantum of assets and income across the board; (2) the number of children and their ages; (3) whether parties have new partners; (4) the level of costs incurred; (5) whether a clean break is ordered, and so on. Armed with this information, I am confident that detailed analysis would confirm or explode preconceptions which we all have about the financial remedies system. To take one example: if we knew the costs incurred in every case, we would be better placed to evaluate whether the excessive and disproportionate costs seen in the High Court, and criticised by judges at that level, is as much an issue in the courts below. With this

[3] All figures are taken from Ministry of Justice, 'National Statistics: Family Court Statistics Quarterly: October to December 2022' (30 March 2023) at www.gov.uk/government/statistics/family-court-statistics-quarterly-october-to-december-2022/family-court-statistics-quarterly-october-to-december-2022.

[4] Hon Mr Justice Peel, 'The Financial Remedies Court: A Year in Review' *Financial Remedies Journal* (27 September 2023) at https://financialremediesjournal.com/content/the-financial-remedies-court-a-year-in-review.2b6d5c48715f4d45ab6c641dbae20da4.htm.

> sort of information, Parliament, rule makers, judges and HMCTS alike would be better placed to make informed decisions about policy, law and practice. Happily, there is a way for this to be done, if the will can be found. HMCTS has confirmed that it is able, from a technical perspective, to harvest the wealth of valuable information on the Form D81 (lodged for every consent order). What is needed is commitment and funding to make it happen. I am confident that data of this sort, properly analysed, would in the long run reap considerable savings, and I hope that this valuable project will receive the support it needs.

It is obvious to me that a statutory rules-based system, such as that proposed by Ruth Deech, needs to be preceded by statistical analysis of the shape, size and objectives of the cases that are dealt with at the coalface. Both Ruth and I have blithely implied that excessive costs are an almost universal and ineradicable bane, but without knowing whether this is actually true or not. I understand that pursuit of this data-collection project is presently opposed by the Ministry of Justice on the ground of 'insufficient resources'. I say no more. Perhaps this is something that academics may wish to pursue in gathering and analysing evidence.

Third, debate of the rules must take into account changes in social attitudes since the present system was enacted.

Take spousal maintenance, for example. In my speech of 12 June 2023 at the House of Lords, I stated:

> Consider spousal maintenance. I tried to set out in *SS v NS*[5] a historical analysis to demonstrate that there was no legal, and scarcely any moral, basis for alimony post-divorce. Before 1857 it was awarded because there could not be a divorce and there was a common law duty to maintain during a marriage. After 1857 those principles were adopted, provided that the wife was not guilty of adultery herself, but as Lord Atkin pointed out in *Hyman*[6] there was precious little moral basis for it, there being no common law duty to maintain an ex-wife after Decree Absolute – the only justification he offered was that it was a pragmatic award to prevent a wife from being thrown upon the public for support.
>
> Thus, in full agreement with Baroness Deech, I pronounced that alimony should only be awarded very sparingly to alleviate grave financial hardship, and that this principle was entirely consistent with the strangely ignored s25A Matrimonial Causes Act 1973 (inserted in 1984).
>
> But no: although we should be grateful for the small mercy that in *Waggott v Waggott*[7] the Court of Appeal decided that an earning capacity is not a shareable asset, the decision confirms that in the judge's individual discretion an alimony order can be made indefinitely to meet need, very broadly computed. No reference at all was made to the historical principles.

[5] *SS v NS* [2014] EWHC 4183.
[6] *Hyman v Hyman* [1929] AC 601.
[7] *Waggott v Waggott* [2018] EWCA Civ 727.

Many of the reported cases[8] have a judicial premise that a wife who has not worked during the marriage (with the agreement of her husband) has somehow earned the right not to work in the future, and is to be awarded life-long alimony. These views do not question at all the moral basis of such an award. More pertinently, they do not reflect the profound changes in the last few decades, not only in social attitudes, but in participation by women in the labour market. Sir John Curtice has pointed out that the economy now depends on the participation of married women with children.

On 21 September 2023, the National Centre for Social Research published its 40th annual British Social Attitudes survey,[9] exploring people's social, political and moral attitudes. Any legislator considering reform of the financial remedy system would do well to read this illuminating document. Among many other fascinating pieces of information, it shows:

- Agreement that a man's job is to earn money and a woman's is to look after the home and family has declined by 39 percentage points since 1987, from 48 per cent to 9 per cent in 2022.
- Only around 1 in 10 (12 per cent) people now agree that 'a job is all right but what most women really want is a home and children', compared to 1 in 3 (31 per cent) in 1989.
- Agreement with the view that a pre-school child is likely to suffer if his/her mother works has declined from 46 per cent in 1989 to 21 per cent now.

It is no exaggeration to say that many of the judicial attitudes underpinning the current system appear to be rooted firmly in the 1980s. The whole needs concept, as perhaps most vividly depicted in *Miller*, is stuck in the 1980s, where the governing attitude is paternalistic and patriarchal.

The Law Commission has a project, 'Financial remedies on divorce: Assessing the reform options for the laws governing finances on divorce'.[10] This ought to lead to sensible statutory reform, provided that all of the evidence I have outlined is obtained and carefully scrutinised.

I therefore fully support, in principle, Ruth Deech's lonely campaign, and salute her indefatigable energy in bringing her Bill before the House of Lords in parliamentary session after session. My support is subject always to the caveat that reform must be based on evidence and not on tropes gathered from a handful of unrepresentative big-money cases.

[8] See *Duxbury v Duxbury* [1991] 3 WLR 639, where the entire *Duxbury* theory was thus premised.

[9] J Curtice, *Secular or cyclical? 40 years of tracking public opinion* (London, National Centre for Social Research and British Social Attitudes, 2023) at https://natcen.ac.uk/publications/bsa-40-overview.

[10] 'Financial remedies on divorce: Assessing the reform options for the laws governing finances on divorce and the ending of a civil partnership' (Law Com Consultation, 2024) at https://lawcom.gov.uk/project/financial-remedies-on-divorce/.

Figure 7.1 Sir Nicholas Mostyn, 'Married Women: Know Your Place'

Married Women: Know Your Place

From our legal correspondent T. Ulking-Horn

Some of the more deluded of you unhappily married ladies may think that on the horizon is sexual, economic, parental and social equality.You might fantasise that a Custody of Infants Act will soon be passed allowing you, a married woman, to petition for custody of or access to your children[1]. You might fantasise that an Act will surely be passed in the near future allowing you to own your own property and to keep your own income and not to have to give it all to your husband[2]. You might think that you could refuse your husband sex and that if he forced himself on you, he would be guilty of rape[3]. You might fantasise that you could actually get a divorce when your husband has committed adultery and treated you with cruelty[4]. You might fantasise that you could vote[5]. You might imagine that you could not only get divorced but that all the assets of the marriage would be equally shared[6].

Ha Ha!

Dream on. In this enlightened year of Our Lord 1805 your husband can rape you with impunity. He has unassailable rights to the custody of your children. All your property and income belong to him. You cannot get a divorce. You cannot share the assets of the marriage. And you cannot vote. Nothing is going to change for decades,

Although your husband has a duty to support you, the only way you can enforce that is by trying to pledge his credit in West End shops, but the shopkeepers will shun you.

If you leave him, it had better be for a rich friend and protector; otherwise, destitution and prostitution await.

So Know Your Place.

[1] Not until 1839
[2] Not until 1882
[3] Not until 1991
[4] Not until 1857
[5] Not until 1918
[6] This did not happen until 2000!

* The cartoon is taken from W Hogarth (1758) *The Bench*.

8

The Adult Intimate Relationships Bill

RUSSELL SANDBERG

I. Introduction

Alan and Betty, both lukewarm members of the Church of England who attend church at Christmas and occasionally Easter, and who harbour a desire for their as yet unborn future off-spring to attend the acclaimed local Church of England School, want to get married in their local idyllic parish church. Christine and Derek, two committed Catholics, cannot countenance holding their wedding anywhere other than in the sight of God in their local Catholic church. Eric and Francis are focusing much more on their wedding reception and honeymoon, and are content for their wedding ceremony to take place in the local Register Office to tick the legal formalities. Gina and Harry have discovered the ideal hotel for their long-weekend wedding celebrations and, since it happens to be approved premises, they are thrilled that a registrar can marry them in the grounds of the hotel. Ian and Jane are ideologically opposed to marriage as a patriarchal institution and have resolved to enter into a civil partnership, just to make sure that the other will be protected should the worse happen. Katie and Lee, by contrast, are both perfectly content to continue to cohabit, not because of any objection to marriage as an institution but just because that level of formality and fuss is not for them. English law recognises and facilitates the choices and preferences of all of these people.

Mark and Nicola are both life-long committed humanists and want this reflected in their wedding ceremony. Ora and Pasha are Muslims, and it is important to them, and particularly their families, that their wedding takes place in the local community centre and complies with their religious and cultural traditions and customs. Quentin is a Methodist and Ruth is Jewish, and it is important to them both for elements of both of their faiths to be reflected in their wedding ceremony. Stanley wants his wedding ceremony to be conducted by the same independent celebrant who conducted the funeral of his late father so that he feels that his father is there, though he first needs to pluck the courage to propose to his long-term girlfriend. Taabah and Uday have had a Muslim marriage outdoors, and while Taabah has mentioned the need to book a Registry Office ceremony,

Uday is in no rush to do so, given that they are already married in the eyes of Allah and their community. Vincent and Wilma have found the venue of their dreams, a beach that means so much to them and to their families, and wish to tie the knot there. Xena and Yan are devoted followers of the local football team and have always dreamed of being married on the pitch. Zack is a self-confessed *Star Wars* addict and wants to be married by a Jedi Knight when he finds the woman of his dreams. English law does not recognise or facilitate the choices and preferences of all of these people.

There is no point of principle separating out the hypothetical couples in the first paragraph from those in the second paragraph. Yet in relation to the heterosexual[1] relationships sketched above, a line has been drawn between the couples in the first paragraph, whose weddings are legally recognised (provided certain conditions are met), and the couples in the second paragraph, whose weddings are not legally recognised in their own right and which only become binding if followed by a legally binding ceremony.[2] This is because the position under English law reflects historical compromises, rather than the sociological reality. It reflects the historical status of institutions, rather than the wishes of the parties.

II. The Current Law

The Marriage Act 1949 differentiates between marriages solemnised according to the rites of the Church of England[3] and marriages solemnised otherwise. This second category of marriages includes: (i) civil marriages in a register office or in approved premises; (ii) marriages 'according to the usages of the Society of Friends'; (iii) marriages 'between a man and a woman professing the Jewish religion according to the usages of the Jews'; and (iv) marriages in any place of worship registered under the Places of Worship Registration Act 1855 and section 41 of the Marriage Act 1949. All religions (other than the three specifically named in the Act: Church of England, Society of Friends and the Jewish religion) fall within

[1] In some cases, the situation would be slightly different if the relationships were homosexual rather than heterosexual, but this would be because of the choices and doctrine of the relevant religious body rather than the position of the state. See R Sandberg, *Religion and Marriage Law: The Need for Reform* (Bristol, Bristol University Press, 2021) ch 2.

[2] For a fuller discussion of the legal framework see ibid ch 1; and for an historical account, see R Probert, *Marriage Law and Practice in the Long Eighteenth Century* (Cambridge, Cambridge University Press, 2009) and R Probert, *Tying the Knot: The Formation of Marriage 1836–2020* (Cambridge, Cambridge University Press, 2021).

[3] For the purposes of marriage law, all references to the Church of England also include the Church in Wales: Welsh Church (Temporalities) Act 1919, s 6; Marriage Act 1949, s 78(2). See further N Doe, *The Law of the Church in Wales* (Cardiff, University of Wales Press, 2002); and N Doe (ed), *A New History of the Church in Wales: Governance and Ministry, Theology and Society* (Cambridge, Cambridge University Press, 2020).

this last category. They can therefore conduct lawful marriages, provided that their buildings are registered and there is a registrar or authorised person present.[4]

A. The Problem with the Current Law

The current law therefore excludes what have been called 'unregistered religious marriages' or 'religious only marriages'. These exist where the couple undergo a religious ceremony that does not comply with the Marriage Act 1949. Religious marriages are recognised under the Act but, in relation to religious weddings other than Church of England, Quaker and Jewish ceremonies, the ceremony must take place in a registered place of religious worship in order to be legally binding. Otherwise, though the couple are married in the eyes of their faith, they are not married in the eyes of the law. It is possible to identify several reasons why couples might have unregistered religious marriages: it may be the choice of the parties (in some communities, religious marriages effectively allow the couple to date, to be together without a chaperone); it may be because the parties are unsure of the law; or it might be because it is difficult or impossible for a religious ceremony reflecting their beliefs to be held in a way that is compatible with marriage law requirements. Marriage law discriminates against those religions that are without a building or that have a tradition of marriages taking place outside places of worship.

The current law also excludes what might be styled 'non-religious marriages', that is, those ceremonies that are conducted by belief organisations such as Humanists UK or by independent celebrants. Marriage law provides no means by which these can be legally binding in their own right. The only non-religious ceremonies recognised under the Marriage Act are those conducted by registrars either at the register office or in approved premises. This now includes weddings conducted in the grounds of approved premises, and it is intended to extend this to the grounds of registered places of worship.[5] However, despite the headlines that accompanied this change, this does not mean that outdoor weddings are now generally lawful. A marriage on a beach or anywhere other than in the grounds of approved premises is still not legally recognised. Any such weddings without registrars present would not be valid.

Couples who enter into either category of wedding – 'unregistered religious marriages' or 'non-religious marriages' – need to undergo an additional civil marriage ceremony in order to become legally married. This is discriminatory: it adds cost and inconvenience. And, more importantly, it does not reflect the wishes

[4] Under s 43 of the Marriage Act 1949, an authorised person (such as the minister) can be appointed by the governing body or trustees of the building, provided that their details are then certified to the Registrar General and to the superintendent registrar of the registration district in which the building is situated.

[5] Marriages and Civil Partnerships (Approved Premises) (Amendment) Regulations 2022 (SI 2022/295).

of those couples. Who, after all, describes their wedding as the happiest *days* of their life?

Moreover, many of these couples do not get around to the additional civil ceremony in the register office – and in some cases this is not a voluntary decision on the part of both of the parties[6] – with the effect that they lack the legal rights that they often think they will have in the event of separation or death. They are in the same legal position as cohabiting couples under English law.[7] This matter is made worse because, unlike many jurisdictions, there are limited rights afforded to them on relationship breakdown in England and Wales. There is no such thing as 'common law' marriage;[8] there are no legal remedies available to cohabiting couples on relationship breakdown that arise because of the relationship itself.[9] Other than where there are children as a result of the relationship, or where the couple have been renting, if a cohabiting relationship breaks down then any financial and property disputes are dealt with through the law of property, which focuses on the question of ownership rather than fairness.

B. The Reason for the Problem

History is the reason why the line is drawn where it is. The current legal position fails to reflect the sociological reality because it is the legacy of historical compromise and happenstance.[10] As we have seen, the current law found in the Marriage Act 1949 continues to distinguish between marriages conducted according to the rites of the Church of England and all other marriages. And that law, passed and enacted in the aftermath of the Second World War, largely reflects and replicates a legal framework that is much older still.

However, we need to be careful about blaming history. The problem is actually how the law and legal actors use history.[11] History is typically used in law to stabilise the present. Legal actors implicitly endorse and perpetuate a set of ideas that

[6] See, for instance, the facts that led to *Her Majesty's Attorney-General v Akhter* [2020] EWCA Civ 122.

[7] A point recognised and developed in RC Akhtar, P Nash and R Probert (eds), *Cohabitation and Religious Marriage* (Bristol, Bristol University Press, 2020).

[8] See A Barlow and J Smithson, 'Legal Assumptions, Cohabitants' Talk and the Rocky Road to Reform' (2010) 22(3) *Child and Family Law Quarterly* 328; and A Barlow, 'Modern Marriage Myths: The Dichotomy Between Expectations of Legal Rationality and Lived Lives' in Akhtar, Nash and Probert (eds) (n 7) 39, 43–44. The British Social Attitudes Survey conducted in 2018 showed that almost half those surveyed (46%) explicitly agreed with the erroneous statement that 'couples who live together for a period of time have a common law marriage which gives them the same rights as married couples'. Moreover, this figure rose to 55% in relation to households with children.

[9] See Sandberg (n 1) ch 9.

[10] For discussion, see R Sandberg, *Law and Religion* (Cambridge, Cambridge University Press, 2011) ch 2.

[11] See R Sandberg, *Subversive Legal History: A Manifesto for the Future of Legal Education* (London, Routledge, 2021).

Robert W Gordon described as 'evolutionary functionalism'.[12] Evolution refers to a basic Darwinian understanding that regards history as a constant, linear process of progress and improvement. Functionalism refers to a Durkheimian social theory that understands society as being comprised, like the human body, of various parts that perform different functions in order for society as a whole to operate as the result of order and consensus.

Evolutionary functionalism, the prevalent and dominant understanding that law improves itself over time as it adapts as part of a wider fundamentally harmonious and smooth-running social order, is a comfort blanket. It is also false and limiting. Legal actors look at our archaic law on marriage and point to the piecemeal changes that have been made as a sign of progress. Although many of these revisions are welcome, this does not negate the fact that the whole artifice is problematic and discriminatory. The tacit acceptance of evolutionary functionalist thought means that starting again with the equivalent of a blank sheet of paper is unthinkable. It means that the wider and often more profound irregularities and deficiencies are ignored. Legal change operates like a game of chess: technical, often tedious, and with no thought given to the lives, experiences, hopes and fears of the mere pawns affected by the game play.

As I have argued elsewhere, the wrong scientific framework to understand the historical development of law has been adopted: in place of evolutionary functionalism, I posit entropic complexity.[13] Rather than the dominant assumptions of evolution, the development of law is actually characterised by entropy. The concept of entropy denotes the gradual decline into disorder; the idea of increasing complexity and chaos. The current English law on marriage is a result of entropic complexity. The complexity of the law is the often unintended product of attempting to improve and adapt the law pragmatically in a piecemeal manner, in an effort to recognise changing social, political and religious contexts. This complexity breeds discrimination not only in its failure to truly adapt to the society in which we now live, but also because the sheer denseness and convolution of the law itself perpetrate misunderstandings. Piecemeal ad hoc reforms, though invariably justified and necessary on their own terms, are therefore part of the problem.

In short, there is a need to begin again; to be free of the shackles of history. However, this is not a rejection of history; rather, it is the rejuvenation of history. Rather than seeing history as stabilising the present, history should challenge the present; showing different ways and options that can be considered and taken now because they were considered and possibly even adopted in the past. This could prompt a truly radical approach. We could jettison the legal role and significance of marriage entirely. Alternatively, we could render marriage a truly secular phenomenon. Yet such radical strokes are politically unlikely. They would require taking away legal benefits that have existed for centuries. This raises the question

[12] RW Gordon, 'Critical Legal Histories' (1984) 36(1) *Stanford Law Review* 57.
[13] Sandberg (n 11) ch 5.

of what would be appropriate and whether non-radical approaches can be identified that are politically possible but also break out of the current entropic impasse. Further piecemeal reform, though desirable in itself, will lead to more complexity and crucially will fail to address the heart of the issue: removing the discrimination that currently exists between the fictitious couples in the first and second paragraphs of this chapter, and which is reflected in the lived experiences of couples up and down the country.

Reform needs to be comprehensive. It also needs to be principled, but this does not mean that it should go as far as removing the law or religion from marriage entirely or even moving towards one of those directions. However, it can mean getting rid of aspects of the law that have become part of the furniture. History shows us that the category of 'registered religious building' is a consequence of a piecemeal process of toleration that reflected the needs of a very different society. The distinctions made in the Marriage Act were historical constructions that were compromises that suited the eras in which they were made, and which have long passed their sell-by date. The category of approved premises is incredibly recent, a pragmatic adjunct to the established law that allowed some freedom of choice, led by Gyles Brandreth of all people. As entrenched as these aspects of marriage law seem, they are neither universal nor inevitable. They are rather the product of needs and compromises of a different society that can now be discarded as no longer of use and because they lead to discrimination.

III. A Way Ahead

In terms of principle, rather than embracing or recoiling from an ideological position for or against the role of religion or law, it is preferable to think about those fictitious couples introduced in section I and the millions of real-life couples they represent in an idealised form. The reform enacted needs to achieve the objective of legally recognising their personal wishes, convictions and beliefs about where and how their marriages should take place. This does not mean that every preference or belief about weddings should be legally recognised, nor even that all of the wishes of our fictitious couples should be legally recognised and facilitated. There is a debate as to where the line should be drawn, but it is clear that it should no longer be drawn between the couples in our first paragraph and those in the second.

Recent litigation challenging the absence of legal recognition of humanist wedding ceremonies in England and Wales has framed the issue in human-rights terms, citing the right to freedom of religion or belief under Article 9 of the European Convention on Human Rights (ECHR).[14] Put simply, the argument has been that to recognise religious marriages and not belief marriages constitutes

[14] R *(on Application of Harrison) v Secretary of State for Justice* [2020] EWHC 2096 (Admin).

discrimination, given that Article 9 ECHR is a 'precious asset for atheists, agnostics, sceptics and the unconcerned'.[15] This argument, however, can extend further than to recognised belief systems. The human right to manifest your belief in how you get married and for the state not to discriminate against you in relation to that undoubtedly applies to humanists. However, it surely also applies to interfaith couples who require a bespoke ceremony (often only available by an independent celebrant), or to a Muslim couple wanting a religious marriage that is legally recognised in their home or a community centre. The same human rights argument could also apply to those who want to get married in a place that is as important to them, or for whom a particular practice or officiant reflects their beliefs.

Indeed, this argument could also apply to weddings at a couple's beloved football stadium, or conducted by Jedi Knights, like the fictitious couples introduced in section I. As trivial or comical as such examples may be found by some people, the same is true of any religious or belief practice. Every religion was novel once: every religious tradition looks unfamiliar and strange to those who are not adherents and are not religiously literate enough to demonstrate basic levels of empathy. The seemingly idiosyncratic desire of those who hold non-religious beliefs could be as important to them, if not more so,as the legally recognised religious and civil weddings are to those couples. A couple marrying in the Church of England parish church may well have selected the location with more of an eye to how it would look on their Instagram posts, compared to those lifelong football fans whose family have a longer and much more intimate connection with their local football club than the first couple have to the picturesque parish church. It is possible that both venues could be the final resting places of loved ones, and so it is questionable why a legally recognised marriage should be permitted to occur in one place but not the other.

A principled dividing line could be drawn based on the strength of the belief. However, this would prove not only awkward to adjudicate but also inappropriate. As Lord Nicholls once put it, '[f]reedom of religion protects the subjective belief of an individual'.[16] This means that while courts may be concerned with whether the claim was made *in* good faith, they are not concerned whether it is *a* good faith in terms of judging the validity of that faith. This applies as much to beliefs as it does to religions. It is therefore preferable to adopt a hands-off approach to both defining 'religion or belief' and what constitutes a manifestation of a person's religion or belief.[17] The risk otherwise is that either a conservative approach will

[15] *Kokkinakis v Greece* (1994) 17 EHRR 397, para 31.

[16] *R v Secretary of State for Education and Employment and others, ex parte Williamson* [2005] UKHL 15 [22]–[23].

[17] For further discussion of the definition issue, see R Sandberg, 'Clarifying the Definition of Religion under English Law: The Need for a Universal Definition?' (2018) 20(2) *Ecclesiastical Law Journal* 132; and for discussion on the case law on the manifestation of religion or belief, see R Sandberg, 'Cross Words: *Eweida v UK* and the Reformulation of Religious Freedom' in R Barker, P Babie and N Foster (eds), *Law and Religion in the Commonwealth: The Evolution of Case Law* (Oxford, Hart Publishing, 2022) 49.

be taken, recognising by analogy, or that a confused and contradictory approach will follow.[18] It is preferable to focus on whether there is any justification for not permitting or recognising the manifestation to take place. This would involve looking to see if it was likely to cause any harm, whether it would interfere with or discriminate against the beliefs of others, for instance. Difficult decisions would still need to be taken but they would be fact-specific, focused on the social situation rather than on the legal construction of what makes a 'good' religion or belief.

Reform, therefore, should be predicated on legally recognising and protecting forms of marriage that are manifestations of the beliefs of the couple. There is a need for equal treatment. The law should not protect some beliefs more than others. This focus is undeniably individualistic. However, it is important not to assume a level playing field. A focus on individual autonomy often ignores the context and the power imbalances in play in the various relationships.[19] This includes the relationship between the couple and their communities (as well as the couple and the families). It also crucially includes the couple themselves. Particular attention needs to be paid to whether the choice of wedding has been wittingly and voluntarily made by both of the parties. Obviously, it is vital that both consent to getting married. That goes without saying and is not our focus here. Our concern is with situations where it is questionable whether the decision not to have a legally binding marriage was truly voluntary by one of the couple. Regardless of how the law is reformed, there will always be couples whose relationships are not legally recognised. They will miss out on the legal redress and consequences that can follow on the breakdown of a legally recognised relationship. It is unobjectionable where both parties have freely, wittingly and voluntarily decided on this. However, it is objectionable where one party did not know their relationship was not legally recognised, where they were duped into forgoing legal rights or where they are waiting for the other to fulfil their promise to pop to the register office to make the relationship official (often with financially adverse consequences for the reluctant partner, especially in the event of future relationship breakdown).

All this underscores that this is a delicate and difficult area. However, it also underlines that the crude, archaic and unprincipled dividing line currently drawn by the law needs to be recast. This recasting should not take the form of further piecemeal revisions, but equally a radical shift towards a new idealised system is politically unlikely. The following will argue and show that this can be achieved by means of a consolidating and modernising Act of Parliament, which we will call the Adult Intimate Relationships Bill.[20]

[18] The case law in the context of discrimination law provides an example of this. See R Sandberg, 'Is the National Health Service a Religion?' (2020) 22(3) *Ecclesiastical Law Journal* 343.

[19] See further R Sandberg and S Thompson, 'Relational Autonomy and Religious Tribunals' (2017) 6(1) *Oxford Journal of Law and Religion* 137.

[20] The following draws upon but develops and updates an argument previously published in Sandberg (n 1).

A. The Two Reforms Needed

The fictitious couples listed in the second paragraph of section I can be broadly grouped into three (overlapping) forms of relationship that are now commonplace and exist outside the legal framework: unregistered religious marriages; non-religious marriages; and cohabiting partnerships. These three forms of relationship underscore how the law on formalised relationships has failed to keep up with the changing social realities of adult intimate relationships in the twenty-first century. Couples in all three forms of relationships are treated in law as cohabiting partners and lack rights on separation.

As we have seen, there are two main defects with the law as it currently stands. First, the law currently provides an arbitrary threshold by regulating where marriages can take place, which discriminates against non-religious beliefs as well as those religions that either do not have places of religious worship or have a tradition of marriage outside those buildings. Second, there is a particular problem when cohabitation status has been an unwitting or involuntary decision by one or more of the parties. This might be because they are unaware of the legal requirements and think they are married, or it might result from delay to formalise the relationship by one or both of them. It is problematic where there has not been a witting and voluntary decision by both parties to enter into a 'non-religious marriage', an 'unregistered religious marriage' or any other cohabitation relationship, where both parties know that they will receive no legal rights and remedies on separation. Many couples entering into these relationship forms expect that they will have the same rights as those who are married or in civil partnerships, only to discover, if their relationships break down, that they cannot rely on the state and so are forced to either resolve any disputes themselves or use a form of dispute resolution. In relation to the breakdown of unregistered religious marriages, sharia councils and other forms of religious adjudication are no longer forms of *alternative* dispute resolution; they are the only option available in terms of public dispute resolution.

These two defects point towards two different solutions. The first problem points to the need to reform the law on getting married; the second highlights the need to explore cohabitation rights on separation. As desirable as each of these reforms would be on their own, there is a need to enact both reforms at once. These two reforms would complement each other. Reform of the law on getting married will inevitably not recognise all forms of relationship, and so without cohabitation rights on separation some couples will be denied protection, including some parties who did not wittingly and voluntarily assent to this. The introduction of cohabitation rights alone would recognise the relationship for those who have had weddings that do not comply with state law requirements, but crucially it would not recognise them as marriages. Reform of the law on getting married would rationalise and extend the types of wedding that are legally recognised, while cohabitation rights on separation would provide a back-stop protection for those whose marriages continue not to be recognised by the state. The two reforms would complement each other.

Furthermore, reforming both of these matters at the same time could not realistically be achieved by piecemeal legislation. Separately and collectively, they would require primary legislation. It would therefore make sense to tackle the two together as part of a consolidation project that could provide a much-needed opportunity to modernise the law on adult intimate relationships. Such a bill would be a once-in-a-generation opportunity to simplify and make more accessible the law on the matter. This in itself would be a powerful way to reduce the discrimination that results from the confusion as to the current complex legal framework. Similar consolidation opportunities have been taken recently by neighbouring jurisdictions, typically when they legislated to recognise same-sex relationships,[21] yet England and Wales did not consolidate the law when it recognised civil partnership and, later, same-sex marriages. As a result, the law in England and Wales has become more complex as a result of these welcome changes, and this has furthered the confusion about the law (epitomised by the continuing common law marriage myth) as well as the sense of unfairness and discrimination that many have about the current law. An Adult Intimate Relationships Bill would consolidate the law on opposite sex and same-sex marriage, opposite-sex and same-sex civil partnerships, and would introduce a limited opt-out system of cohabitation rights on separation. There may also be scope for consolidating the law on the termination of such relationships, including the law on financial remedies, into the same statute. The remainder of this chapter, however, will focus on how the bill could provide for reform of the law on getting married and on providing cohabitation rights on separation.

B. Reform of the Law on Getting Married

There is a need to move from a system that regulates buildings to one that regulates officiants. This is, in essence, what the Law Commission has concluded in relation to its wedding law project, which is now completed and awaiting a response by government.[22] This could solve the concerns around non-religious marriages and would lessen concerns about unregistered religious marriages, since the discriminatory requirements that prevent some religious weddings from complying with the law (the need for the ceremony to occur in a place of worship) would be removed. The Law Commission's suggestion that an officiant must be in attendance at all weddings is sound. However, unlike the Law Commission, my research proposes that the nominating organisation would not be limited to religion or belief organisations.[23]

[21] For a comparative analysis, see Sandberg (n 1) ch 7.

[22] *Getting Married: A Consultation Paper on Weddings Law* (Law Com No 247, 2020); *Celebrating Marriage: A New Weddings Law* (Law Com No 408, 2022).

[23] Sandberg (n 1).

Officiants, under the Law Commission's schema, would have 'specific legal obligations in relation to the wedding'.[24] Their responsibilities would be at the wedding itself rather than at the initial formalities stage. They may but do not have to be the person conducting the ceremony. They would need to be physically present at the ceremony.[25] Officiants would have three legal duties to discharge: (i) to ensure that the parties freely express consent to marry each other; (ii) ensure that the other requirements of the ceremony are met, including that the wedding is attended by two witnesses; and (iii) ensure that the schedule or marriage document is signed.[26] Officiants would not be 'required to explain the legal consequences of marriage to couples'.[27] However, 'all officiants will have a responsibility to uphold the dignity and significance of marriage in their role as officiants and in officiating at weddings'.[28] This is to be taken into account 'when agreeing to the form of ceremony', but will only extend to 'responsibility for the parts of the ceremony at which they are present'.

The Law Commission's scheme actually 'envisages little change to how registration officers and Anglican clergy are authorised'.[29] The focus is on the appointment and regulation of nominated officiants from religions and beliefs and independent celebrants. The Commission has interpreted its terms of reference as precluding it from deciding whether weddings by belief organisations and independent celebrants *should* be legally recognised, while ensuring that any new scheme it develops *could* include those two groups if the Government decides that the groups should be recognised. The report treats celebrants from belief organisations and independent celebrants differently. It distinguishes between civil marriages (which could include independent celebrants in addition to weddings at registry offices, and approved premises) and belief marriages (which could include belief organisations alongside the Anglican Churches and other religions). This distinction means that there are different and sometimes more onerous requirements upon independent celebrants than (say) humanist celebrants under the Law Commission's schema. Independent celebrants would be 'civil officials and under the same obligations to officiate at same-sex weddings as registration officers', for example.[30] The type of wedding (civil or belief) would be 'determined based on the identity of the officiant'.[31]

The basic distinction between the civil weddings conducted by independent celebrants and the belief weddings conducted by religious and belief organisations would be that while religious and belief organisations would be responsible for nominating and monitoring officiants to the General Register Office (GRO),

[24] *Celebrating Marriage* (n 22) para 2.4.
[25] ibid para 4.24.
[26] ibid para 2.37.
[27] ibid para 4.30.
[28] ibid para 2.38.
[29] ibid para 1.10.
[30] ibid para 4.287.
[31] ibid para 2.5.

independent celebrants would need to apply individually and be subject to GRO regulation directly. Further, 'civil ceremonies will be subject to specific rules about the content of the ceremony'. This would mean that independent celebrants but not humanist celebrants would 'additionally need to ensure that the couple express their consent using the required words of contract or words to similar effect' and would be required to ensure that the 'civil ceremony is identifiable as such'.[32] By contrast, in 'a belief ceremony – that is, a ceremony officiated by a member of the Anglican clergy or a nominated officiant – there will be no requirement as to how the couple expresses consent, as long as they do so clearly'.[33] It is difficult to see the justification for these slightly different requirements. If some religious 'wedding ceremonies involve the expression of consent by a series of rituals', then it is difficult to see why this should not suffice for ceremonies conducted by independent celebrants.

There would be no option for independent celebrants to be nominated by a professional association, as I argued for,[34] on the grounds that there is no jurisdiction in which this happens.[35] They would therefore be regulated directly by the GRO. This is the reason why they would be limited to officiating at civil weddings: 'This limitation would be consistent with them being appointed and regulated by the General Register Office. It would also ensure a clear distinction between independent officiants and belief officiants, as well as between civil and belief weddings.'[36] This would mean that while the same requirements that officiants be 'fit and proper' persons would apply to independent celebrants as to any officiant,[37] the difference for independent celebrants would be that *they* would need to demonstrate that they fulfil these requirements (rather than their organisation). Moreover, independent celebrants alone would be directly subject to GRO training, though that could be subcontracted out, possibly to professional associations. The Law Commission stresses how independent celebrants are different from other officiants:

> In our view, there are some fundamental differences between religious and non-religious belief organisations on the one hand, and celebrancy organisations on the other. The former reflects specific beliefs, while the latter do not. The fact that many celebrancy organisations are well placed to provide training does not seem

[32] ibid para 2.37.
[33] ibid para 2.59.
[34] ibid para 4.270.
[35] ibid para 4.264.
[36] ibid para 4.265.
[37] While Anglican clergy will be 'recognised automatically', the governing authority of other religions or belief organisations would nominate officiants to the GRO and would need be required to ensure that nominees are 'are "fit and proper" persons to be officiants, by being of good character; not having been convicted of any offence determined by the General Register Office as preventing a person from being "fit and proper" to be an officiant; being at least 18 years old (although in practice they are likely to be much older); having undertaken training on the legal aspects of being an officiant; and understanding the legal requirements for being an officiant and performing the role' (ibid para 2.40).

> to be sufficient reason in itself to allow such organisations to nominate independent officiants. We also note that celebrancy organisations welcomed our proposal that authorisation should be by means of individual application to the General Register Office and were not seeking the right to nominate officiants.[38]

I disagree. A bespoke wedding conducted by an independent celebrant could be a manifestation of belief, protected under Article 9 ECHR. If the existence of training is not sufficient for an organisation to be a nomination body, then it would be instructive to spell out what is and how all religion or belief organisations meet that requirement. It may be questioned, however, why the 'clear distinction between independent officiants and belief officiants, as well as between civil and belief weddings' matters: surely it could be achieved by treating independent celebrants as a separate category, as was the case in the Consultation Paper.

The distinction that the Law Commission is attempting to draw between independent celebrants conducting civil ceremonies and religion or belief organisations does not correspond to how such ceremonies are seen by the couple. Surely, the clear distinction is between marriages conducted by a state official and those that are not. A further problem with the Law Commission's approach is that it renders crucial the definition of religion or belief. It is unfortunate, therefore, that the Law Commission's final report on the matter remains wanting in this respect.

The definition of 'religion' for the purpose of establishing religious organisations who could nominate would follow that laid down by the Supreme Court in *Hodkin*,[39] in accordance with the Law Commission's terms of reference. Although that definition is not particularly helpful in terms of clear lines of demarcation, it appears that we are stuck with it and that the main bone of contention will be what a 'belief' is, rather than what a 'religion' is. Compared to its Consultation Paper,[40] the Law Commission's final report has changed its mind regarding the definition of 'belief'. While in the Consultation Paper it offered a definition parasitical to the *Hodkin* definition, the final report proposes that a non-religious belief organisation would be defined as 'one whose sole or principal purpose is the advancement of a system of non-religious beliefs which have a level of cogency, seriousness, cohesion and importance that brings them within the meaning of article 9 of the European Convention on Human Rights'.[41] This is a significant improvement, though it does mean that the line between the type of belief systems that the Commission has in mind and the bespoke beliefs of couples who use independent celebrants is not as clear-cut as the Commission seems to believe. The report states that 'this approach will help to convey that these are recognised belief systems

[38] ibid para 4.279.
[39] *R (on the application of Hodkin) v Registrar General of Births, Deaths and Marriages* [2013] UKSC 77.
[40] *Getting Married* (n 22).
[41] *Celebrating Marriage* (n 22) para 1.10.

that have been adjudged worthy of respect in a democratic society within the case law on protected beliefs under the Equality Act 2010'.[42] This, however, ignores the differences in definition between the case law under discrimination law and the human rights jurisprudence and the generally confused and contradictory state of the case law.

The Law Commission argues that it should be made 'explicit that the organisation should have the advancement of non-religious beliefs as its sole or principal object, reflecting the approach taken in both Scotland and Ireland'.[43] Also reflecting the position of other jurisdictions, the Commission maintains that it can 'see the value in explicitly excluding sports clubs, trade unions and chambers of commerce, together with political parties or organisations that have as their primary purpose the promotion of political parties, causes or candidates'.[44] However, there is no explanation of the principles underlying these exclusions. Indeed, they depart from the Irish position to agree with Humanists UK that 'it would be wrong to preclude non-religious belief organisations from championing political causes if no equivalent restriction applies to religious organisations'. Surely a preferable approach would be to allow any organisation to nominate an officiant, as I have argued?[45] This would also render redundant the likely ineffective requirements proposed by the Law Commission that religions or beliefs need to satisfy in order to nominate officiants. The final report proposes that in order to nominate, a religious or non-religious belief organisation will need to show that it

> has been established for a minimum period of time. During that period, it must have had members from at least 20 households who meet regularly in person for worship or in furtherance of or to practise their beliefs. It will also have to demonstrate that it has a policy in relation to nominating and monitoring officiants and that it would be a manifestation of an individual's religion or beliefs to have a wedding officiated at by an officiant nominated by that organisation.[46]

These requirements run the risk of excluding religions or belief organisations with a small number of members.[47] If the focus is on the officiant, then should it matter how well-established their organisation is? These requirements will place burdens on religious and non-religious belief organisations that will not be faced by independent celebrants. This underlines the question of why these requirements are needed.

[42] ibid para 4.14.
[43] ibid para 4.142.
[44] ibid para 4.144.
[45] Sandberg (n 1).
[46] *Celebrating Marriage* (n 22) para 2.43.
[47] The Law Commission also noted that these requirements may pose new difficulties for small religions. It acknowledged that there will 'be a small number of independent churches who will continue to rely on civil registration officers to officiate at their weddings and for whom our scheme will not work as well as the existing law' (ibid para 4.82).

The human rights arguments that necessitate the recognition of belief marriages do not stop with belief organisations. Moreover, in practice, there is little to distinguish marriages conducted by humanist celebrants from those conducted by independent celebrants. Different treatment therefore seems unsound. There is no reason to restrict the organisations who can conduct weddings to religious or belief organisations. Enabling all organisations to nominate officiants would also mean that umbrella organisations representing independent celebrants could do so. This would mean individual applications by independent celebrants would be exceptional and would apply only in the rare situation where the officiant was not a member of any organisation.

The move to an officiant system – whether it be the religion- or belief-nominated and independent celebrant individual application scheme envisaged by the Law Commission or the open-to-all organisations approach I favour – would deal with the problem of non-religious marriages. It would also lessen concerns about unregistered religious marriages, since the discriminatory requirements that prevent some religious weddings from complying with the law (the need for the ceremony to occur in a place of worship) would be removed. However, there would still be some unregistered religious marriages – and some of these would not result from a voluntary and witting choice by both of the parties. The introduction of limited cohabitation rights on separation would be required to deal with this. There is a need for what the Law Commission termed 'a statutory scheme for the adjustment of property rights or financial provision between cohabiting couples on separation'.[48]

C. Introduction of Opt-Out Cohabitation Rights

Cohabitation rights on relationship breakdown would provide a remedy to those who are in unregistered religious marriages and any still unrecognised non-religious marriages, where there has been no voluntary and free choice to remain as cohabitants. Cohabitation rights on separation would provide a lifeline where the decision not to enter into a legal marriage has not been entered into voluntarily, or where the relationship has changed over time so that one party has become reliant on the other or has suffered a detriment as a result of the relationship. This would apply, for instance, where one party has given up paid work, reduced their hours or forgone promotion in order to raise children, keep the home and/or to look after the other party. These detriments are likely to be gendered and can often be subtle.

However, it is also important not to take a too paternalistic approach. If the parties have made an autonomous choice not to marry, this should be respected.

[48] *Cohabitation: The Financial Consequences of Relationship Breakdown* (Law Com No 307, 2007) para 1.5.

The lead of other jurisdictions should be followed, to allow couples to opt out of such cohabitation-based protection while also ensuring that this is voluntary and fair. This opt-out rather than opt-in requirement would ensure that cohabitation rights are afforded to couples who are choosing to cohabit in the belief that they will accrue marriage-like legal rights, as well as those where there is an intention to marry but the couple do not get around to it.[49] It would also protect cohabiting couples while respecting a choice of those couples for their relationships not to be legally recognised with redress on relationship breakdown, where the couples have made an explicit and free decision to waive their legal rights.

There are four important precedents as to how a scheme providing opt-out cohabitation rights on relationship breakdown might operate: the system that applies in Scotland;[50] the Irish system;[51] the system suggested in Law Commission's proposed reform;[52] and the schema developed in two Private Members' Bills.[53] From these, three main characteristics of a scheme can be distilled.

The first characteristic is that the statutory scheme will apply to cohabitants on separation, provided they have not optedout. Most approaches provide for an opt-out either implicitly or explicitly. As the Law Commission argued, 'If we want to remove more couples from the scope of property and trust law and the unsatisfactory outcomes that it often produces on separation, and thereby provide better basic justice between cohabitants, then an opt-in approach is not the answer.'[54] The Law Commission and the Private Members' Bills explicitly provide for opt-out agreements and stipulate what they should contain – the agreement needs to follow legal advice, be in writing, and be signed and witnessed – and proformas would be made available to enable these requirements to be laid out and met. The Law Commission reasoned that a religious marriage agreement, such as a nikah contract, 'would only constitute an opt-out agreement if it indicated an intention to disapply the statute'.[55] Provision would also be made for the parties to vary or revoke the agreement, and for an agreement to be disapplied by the courts where it is manifestly unfair taking into account the circumstances at the time the agreement was made and at separation, and taking into account changes in circumstances between these dates.

The second characteristic is that the scheme would apply if the couple had been cohabitants, and this would be understood as having a child together or living together for a certain amount of time. Some of the approaches provide more details as to the definition of the term 'cohabitants' than others. The less detailed definitions, however, are often then supported by a list of criteria to be

[49] Such as the couple in *Akhter* (n 6).
[50] Family Law (Scotland) Act 2006.
[51] Civil Partnership and Certain Rights and Obligations of Cohabitants Act 2010.
[52] *Cohabitation* (n 48).
[53] Lord Lester's Cohabitation Bill in 2009 and Lord Marks' Cohabitation Rights Bill, which was first introduced in 2013 and mostly recently reintroduced in February 2020.
[54] *Cohabitation* (n 48) para 2.86.
[55] ibid para 5.67.

taken into account in determining cohabitant status. In the Scottish model, this includes the period during which the couple have lived together, the nature of their relationship during that period, and the nature and extent of any financial arrangements subsisting, or which subsisted, during that period. The Law Commission in England and Wales and the Private Members' Bills suggested that the test ought to be either that the couple had lived together for a specified number of years or that they had had a child together. This would seem to be the appropriate threshold. As the Law Commission noted, 'no jurisdiction which has legislated in this field has confined remedies to cohabitants with children' and there was 'evidence that cohabitants without children have the same potential to encounter unfairness on separation as cohabitants with children'.[56]

The third and final characteristic is that the scheme would allow a cohabitant to seek a financial order on separation if certain circumstances were met. The broadest approach to this can be found in Lord Lester's Cohabitation Bill, which simply said that an order can be made if 'having regard to all the circumstances, the court considers that it is just and equitable to make an order'. Most approaches, however, require evidence of an advantage or disadvantage. This is usually economic. Under the Law Commission's proposals, financial relief would be granted to the cohabitant 'based upon the economic impact of cohabitation' and only where 'the respondent has a retained benefit; or the applicant has an economic disadvantage as a result of qualifying contributions the applicant has made'.[57] It further stated that the welfare of any children of both parties will be 'the court's first consideration', but that a range of other factors should be taken into account, including the finances of both parties and their conduct.[58] It would be vital for the non-financial contributions of both parties to be considered, along with the changing circumstances of the relationship over time.

IV. Conclusion

The pragmatic piecemeal development of the law on adult intimate relationships has led to many welcome advances but has perpetuated a legal framework based on historic quirks that is not only antiquated but discriminatory. Consolidation of the law would itself be a major step forward. A clearer legal framework would reduce the prevalent myths, confusions and injustices that exist. This new law would also give an opportunity to enact two reforms that are both long overdue and would complement each other. We need a reformed law on getting married and we also need to introduce cohabitation rights on separation. Reform of either of these areas of law in isolation would not solve the concerns caused by the three

[56] ibid paras 2.81 and 2.77.
[57] ibid paras 4.32–4.33.
[58] ibid para 4.38.

forms of relationship that currently exist in the shadow of the law, with the effect that the couple are denied legal rights. This is particularly problematic where this is not the result of a voluntary choice by one or both of the parties.

Reform of the law on getting married can resolve the issue of non-religious marriages and can mitigate the problem of unregistered religious marriages, but it would do nothing for cohabiting couples. Reform of the law on cohabitation, on the other hand, could be expected to resolve the issue for cohabiting couples and would provide some redress for those in non-religious or unregistered religious marriages, but it would not recognise their relationships as such. Both reforms are therefore required, and there is a need for the Law Commission to build upon its previous work to develop these reforms into a new modernised, accessible and easily understandable legal framework that reflects the social reality of adult relationships in the twenty-first century. There is no reason why the relationship choices in our first paragraph in section I should be legally recognised and facilitated but those in the second paragraph should not. Where the line should be drawn remains an open question – and a matter on which I am not in complete agreement with the Law Commission – but it is clear that the current position is unsustainable. The discrimination suffered by Mark, Nicola, Ora, Pasha, Quentin, Ruth, Stanley, Taabah, Uday, Vincent, Wilma, Xena, Yan and Zack represents the experience of hundreds, if not thousands, of couples who deserve better. The current law has failed; there is a need for a new Adult Intimate Relationships Act.

Response to Chapter 8

The Adult Intimate Relationships Bill

SIMRAN KALRA

I. Introduction

Roshanyee and Imad met through family networks and desired to start a life together. They and their families had agreed to follow up the nikah with a civil marriage. Fifteen years later, with three children, stints of unemployment and the professional strides made by the couple, Roshanyee was asked by her Islamic-only husband to sign a cohabitation agreement, with the ultimatum that if she did not sign it, he would leave her, breaking up the family.

Midha and Mohan had met on a dating app. Midha, a devout Muslim, did not want to initiate sexual relations without a nikah. Midha avoided conversations about marriage because the relationship was in its early stages. However, hoping to build a steady relationship, Midha became more financially involved in Mohan's life. Although the couple did not live together because Mohan had care obligations towards his family in another city, they would meet several times a month, and he would stay with Midha over the weekends. After six months, Midha learnt that Mohan was in an Islamic and religious marriage with another woman. Her only access to rights claims was through civil law.

Russell Sandberg's proposal relates to rights of cohabitants. Cohabitation is a key means of family formation in England and Wales.[1] Yet not only are cohabitants' rights not protected under a statutory framework in family law, but aspects of the English marriage laws also introduce a risk that wedding ceremonies of those from minority religious backgrounds do not qualify as marriage. Thus, individuals who have minority religious ceremonies may find that their ceremonies do not constitute marriage in law, and that the only rights they can claim against each other are under trusts law. Their claims will be determined not by standards of fairness and equality, which form the basis of financial claims in divorce, but on the basis of factors such as contributions towards joint properties and the couples' common intention to share assets.

[1] J Eekelaar, 'Power' in J Eekelar, *Family Law and Personal Life*, 2nd edn (Oxford, Oxford University Press 2017) 23.

Thus, Sandberg's proposal deals with two aspects of family law. First, the proposal recommends amendments to the Marriage Act 1949. It is recommended that building-based compliances for conducting a religious marriage are replaced by officiant-related compliances. Presently, the Marriage Act 1949 only recognises religious marriage ceremonies held in buildings recognised as places of worship, and which additionally are authorised to conduct marriage ceremonies.[2] The proposal recommends prioritising the authority of the officiant over the authority of the building: akin to the Scottish marriage laws.[3] It thus reduces the risk that couples who intended to marry do not subsequently find that they do not have rights under the Matrimonial Clauses Act (MCA) 1973.

The second aspect of Sandberg's proposed reform focuses on the institution of a cohabitation rights regime. The proposal recommends recognition of non-financial contributions, and thus is more representative of couples' investments in their relationships. In order to avoid paternalism, Sandberg suggests that an opt-out mechanism is included within the rights framework.

While reforms in this area are urgently needed, Sandberg's proposal also allows us to contemplate the law's constitutive power in family relations. To this end, this response focuses on the second part of the proposal: rights of cohabitants. Two key concerns arise: (i) how the law conceives of individuals in intimate relations, and, relatedly, whether an opt-out mechanism would protect against power dynamics in marital relations; and (ii) how the law conceives of informal intimate relations, and whether the proposed changes could go further to address the needs of other informal adult unions.

To develop the arguments, I will rely on the scenarios set out at the beginning of this response. These scenarios emerge from narrative interviews I conducted with participants in my doctoral research on relationship progression within specific Muslim diaspora communities in England. Through my interviews, I sought to understand how law, religion and the social practices of doing relationships were used by the women to avoid marital obligations or secure religious and legal rights as wives. To be recruited, the participants were not required to be in adult unions, formal or otherwise. By removing a stipulation that participants be married or even in nikah unions, I was able to explore and identify relationship arrangements that were not envisaged in the law and how the participants understood these. In this note, I have changed names of all participants and excluded all information that may be used in identifying my participants.

While the scenarios I discuss here relate to religious minority communities, the pressures identified are just as likely to arise across all communities in England. As will be shown, in some cases, these pressures may be more acutely experienced where individuals lack access to alternative normative mechanisms such

[2] Also see R Sandberg, 'Marital Problem: The Law Commission's "Getting Married" Consultation Paper and Non-Qualifying Wedding Ceremonies' (2021) 23 *Ecclesiastical Law Journal* 140.

[3] Marriage (Scotland) Act, 1977; also see Law Commission, *Getting Married: A Consultation Paper on Weddings Law* (Law Com No 247, 2020) 15.

as religion, which emerged as a critical system of meaning-making and accessing rights in my case study.

II. The Opt-out Mechanism

The proposal for an opt-out is in line with legislation in other countries, as recognised by Sandberg. It ensures voluntariness and freedom for individuals to determine the form of commitments and property arrangements they desire. To protect individuals from unfair contracts, Sandberg also proposes that such agreements would require legal advice, thus providing a means to ensure informed voluntariness. In addition, he makes clear that opt out-agreements that are manifestly unfair at the time of their signing or at separation would not be enforceable.

Despite these protective measures, there is a risk regarding how such an opt-out mechanism might be operationalised. Within a context of prohibitive legal costs and individuals' lack of legal knowledge to represent themselves effectively in family courts, they may accept unfair settlements. In fact, in a recent study, Emma Hitchings et al confirmed that a majority of financial settlements at divorce were arrived at by the couples themselves.[4] It was only when couples were bargaining in the shadow of the law with the advice of lawyers that fairer decisions were reached.

While the proposal makes legal advice mandatory, this may be compared with cases of qualifying nuptial agreements (QNAs). Here, the availability of legal advice has been used as a blanket protection, overriding the relational context in which the advice was taken. For instance, as per English case law, factors such as obtaining independent legal advice, being aware of the implications of the QNA and having time to enter such agreements are likely to result in validation of such agreements. As noted by Sharon Thompson, the law does not account for power inequalities in a relationship that can impinge on individual autonomy.[5]

Thus, while the law and Sandberg's proposal include protective measures, these conceive of individuals as autonomous and equal agents. The messy and unequal relationships that people inhabit are ignored. It should be further recognised here that under English law, a contract can be set aside for duress when there is a threat to commit a crime or a tort.[6] However, the emotional pressures individuals experience in intimate relations may not meet this high barrier even though they impinge upon their autonomy. To elaborate on this,

[4] E Hitchings et al, 'Fair Shares? Sorting out money and property on divorce' (Nuffield Foundation, 2023) 14.

[5] *S Thompson, 'Thorne v Kennedy: Why Australia's Decision on Prenups Is Important for English Law' Family Law* (10 April 2018).

[6] E McKendrick, 'Duress' in *Contract Law: Text, Cases and Materials*, 10th edn (Oxford, Oxford University Press, 2022) 612.

I draw on the first scenario I describe in section I of this response: Roshanyee and Imad. The analysis here will show how decisions to enter cohabitation agreements can result from emotional manipulation and disparate interests for which the law does not account. This is particularly a concern for women's rights in cohabitation, as women may experience economic disadvantages more acutely,[7] which in turn can make them vulnerable to pressures in opting out of rights regimes.

At the time of the nikah between the couple, there was an agreement to have a civil ceremony, but that never occurred. Over the years, by reading newspapers and through friends, Roshanyee learnt that the nikah did not secure her rights under the MCA 1973. Imad also reiterated his promise and intention to marry. Whenever the couple spoke about a friend's upcoming nuptials, they discussed their own need to 'register' their marriage. The running joke turned sour when Roshanyee very seriously asked for a civil marriage and stressed that the couple needed to have their finances in order. In a few weeks, the conversation turned into an altercation. Imad presented Roshanyee with a cohabitation agreement excluding her rights in the property, despite the mortgage payments she made. Regarding financial contributions, Roshanyee had worked for most of her adult life, except for short childcare breaks. Despite these documented claims, Roshanyee's family suggested she sign the agreement. They explained that, in effect, she would continue with the relationship as it was: a cohabitating partnership, since no civil marriage had taken place. However, Roshanyee perceived the cohabitation agreement as distinct from the previously shared understanding that she, Imad and their families had developed at the time of the nikah, which they had cemented with every subsequent conversation and act of contribution and care.

Torn between her children's need for a stable family life and her desire to end an abusive relationship, Roshanyee turned to her religion for a solution. She signed the agreement, but, at the same time, refused to contribute to household expenses and maintained her bank accounts independently. Thus, she altered her subsequent behaviour. She explained, 'If this is not a marriage in (English) law, it is a nikah in Islam. In Islam, a woman does not have to contribute financially. She does not pay for expenses, rent, mortgage.' Accordingly, at first, she took leave from work; when she returned to work, she refused to pay towards expenses, spending that money on herself, her children or saving it. Consequently, the two legal orders offered conflicting solutions and required incompatible actions. Islam, in which Roshanyee found an immediate solution, protected her against pressures to contribute financially to the household, but did not protect her claims against her partner. On the other hand, trusts law required that she contribute financially in order to have claims. Though protective of her rights, this system imposed prohibitive costs.

[7] S Wong, 'Cohabitation Reform in England and Wales: Equality or Equity' (2015) 27 *Canadian Journal of Women and the Law* 112, 115.

Rights regimes that depend on voluntariness are embedded in principles of autonomy. As Roshanyee's case shows us, in intimate relations, when individuals are concerned about disparate interests and familial pressures, they may give in to power dynamics to their detriment. This may be further aggravated by an individual's fears on ending a relationship, such as fear of violence and the effect on their children. Such fears are particularly relevant for women, because their financial capacities are often affected by reproductive and care work, for which men are comparatively less responsible, despite changes in cultural trends.[8] Unequal care obligations increase women's dependency on their partners, making decisions on relationship progression, such as the choice between rights regimes, a male prerogative within heterosexual couples. As noted by Sassler and Miller, even in Western contexts, such as in the United States, although men and women are relatively equal in making relationship progression decisions such as dating and cohabiting, the decision to marry is dominated by male choice.[9] The difference between cohabitation and marriage is, among other things, a difference in the rights available to the parties. While a cohabitation rights regime would provide a framework to ensure some protections in these relations, the opt-out mechanism can reinforce socially produced inequality of men and women, while also creating opportunities for coercion and manipulation in intimate relationships.

III. Living Apart Together

Around the Western world, scholars have further noted the prevalence of a new form of family relations: living apart together (LAT).[10] Researchers have observed that a majority of individuals in such relationships chose these arrangements because it was felt too soon to move in together, or they simply preferred such arrangements.[11] These arrangements also emerged in circumstances where couples cannot live together because of financial constraints, or because they work in different parts of the country. Despite living separately, couples in such relationships may share intimacy and contribute to each other's lives, both financially and emotionally. This is evidenced in my second scenario, featuring Midha and Mohan.

[8] A Topping, 'Almost Half of Working-Age Women in UK Do 45 Hours of Unpaid Care a Week – Study' *The Guardian* (31 March 2022) at www.theguardian.com/world/2022/mar/31/almost-half-of-working-age-women-in-uk-do-45-hours-of-unpaid-care-a-week-study.

[9] S Sassler and AJ Miller, 'Waiting to Be Asked: Gender, Power, and Relationship Progression among Cohabiting Couples' (2011) 32 *Journal of Family Issues* 482.

[10] I Levin, 'Living Apart Together: A New Family Form' (2004) 52 *Current Sociology* 223; M Turcotte, 'Living Apart Together – Insights on Canadian Society' (March 2013) 75-006–X Statistics Canada; S Duncan and M Phillips, 'People Who Live Apart Together (LATs) – How Different Are They?' (2010) 58 *Sociological Review* 112.

[11] S Duncan et al, 'Living Apart Together: Uncoupling Intimacy and Co-Residence' (2013) 3 *The Sociology Teacher* 4.

Midha was duped into the relationship by Mohan, who was in several nikah unions and married to another woman simultaneously. Midha only realised this through a series of events that unfolded six months after the nikah ceremony. By this point, Midha had extended an interest-free loan of a few thousand pounds to Mohan, and allowed him to run a business from her house without charging him any rent. Midha chose not to pursue a claim through courts because she 'just wanted it to end'. She did not think there was much that the law could do since they were never married: a choice that she explained she had made deliberately because she was exploring the relationship and did not want him to marry her for her money. In fact, she had never revealed the extent of her assets to her Islamic husband.

To explain her actions, at the time of the nikah-proposal, Midha deliberately avoided talking about a civil ceremony. They both had desired religiously appropriate physical relations, yet Midha took steps to ensure that no mention of a civil ceremony was made and that any risk that the ceremony might result in a valid marriage was avoided. Since there has been an increase in compliance with marriage laws by mosques and Imams, who even ask the bride and groom to conduct civil marriages,[12] Midha successfully scouted for an Imam who agreed to conduct a nikah ceremony in his office: a venue that would not qualify as an authorised place for conducting a marriage. Furthermore, the Imam was asked to conduct only a blessing ceremony and no nikahnamma – the Islamic marriage certificate – was issued. While proposals for family-law reform have attempted to expand access to valid marriage ceremonies, Midha was actively trying to circumvent legal marriage.

Midha was aware that the couple would not be able to live together because Mohan's father was unwell, and Mohan would mostly be living with his parents, caring for his father in the initial period. Because of her work, Midha could not move closer to Mohan. Yet LAT introduces a degree of risk that individuals inhabiting different cities may live parallel lives, managing multiple marriage-like relationships that the distance makes it easier to hide. In the Islamic context, in which the religion is argued to permit polygamy, Muslim women may experience commitment to religious codes of fidelity when men are not only able to have multiple religiously sanctioned unions, but are also less monitored by similar cultural codes.[13] Given the absence of comprehensive official records of marriage and social monitoring (especially of men), there is a lack of certainty as to individuals' marital history. This is exacerbated by practices that Midha herself indulged in: initiating nikah ceremonies without any documentary record.

[12] A Bone, 'Islamic Marriage and Divorce in the United Kingdom: The Case for a New Paradigm' (2020) 40 *Journal of Muslim Minority Affairs* 162; I Uddin, 'Nikah-Only Marriages: Causes, Motivations, and Their Impact on Dispute Resolution and Islamic Divorce Proceedings in England and Wales' (2018) 7 *Oxford Journal of Law and Religion* 401.

[13] S Mohee, 'Young British South Asian Muslim Women: Identities and Marriage' (PhD thesis, Centre for Intercultural Studies, University College London, 2011).

Although Midha felt that she had managed to get the best out of the situation, by carefully avoiding a marriage, she was also worse off in several ways. Whilst Midha felt that her religion empowered her to leave Mohan because he had not provided for her financially, as Islam required, she also felt she owed him fidelity. This was aggravated by a desire to recover past financial and emotional investments. She had hoped that her commitment would lead him to choose her over other women. The only way for her to recover what she had invested was to give the relationship time.

In Midha's case, a small claims court might have offered an avenue for her to recover her loan. However, such an action would bring her personal experiences before a forum that might not protect her privacy or recognise her emotional involvement. If we prioritise function over form, Sandberg's proposal can be extended to account for interests of couples in other informal unions. Presently, the absence of legal recognition of these arrangements makes family-law-related claims unimaginable amongst the aggrieved. During early stages of adult relationships, English family law remains irrelevant. Protections available under the MCA 1973 are extensive and suitable for those in committed adult relations. On the other hand, English family law offers no rights with respect to these early stages, leaving couples to their own devices if love goes awry. Midha deliberately undertook a ceremony that did not result in a marriage. Accordingly, the couple were safe from claims of financial remedies in divorce. Yet this also meant that the couple had no claims under family law for contributions made during the course of their relationship. A law that recognises LATs would go further by protecting novel rights claims and reducing the risks that individuals in such relations may experience.

IV. Conclusion

Although there are many merits to Sandberg's proposal, this response argues that reform in this area might be taken even further. By identifying rightsholders as cohabitants, the law would create a new hierarchy in family arrangements. Where the present law prioritises legal bureaucracy, this new order would prioritise lived realities as a means of assessing rights claims. This could be further advanced by taking account of the financial and pragmatic arrangements individuals undertake when they opt to live apart together. A law on informal marital unions that addressed only cohabitants' rights would, by default, exclude couples in LATs, especially when they have not lived together for a significant period of time. Yet these relations are prevalent and require protection.

While I have argued that individuals in LATs should be included in the proposal, there is also a need to protect against onerous legal commitments early on in intimate relations. This is especially the case given that about 30 per cent of

LAT relations include instances of couples in the early stages of their relationship.[14] Legal obligations at such a stage may make stable relationships unviable. Such a challenge may be overcome by requiring that certain steps are met before the regime is applied to any couple. These steps could include the lapse of a certain time before the rights become available.

With reference to opting out, the proposal seeks to protect individuals from unfair cohabitation agreements. Yet its understanding of how unfair agreements may be avoided is embedded in a positivist framework centred around the concept of the autonomous individual. Such a framework would have deemed Roshanyee's cohabitation agreement valid, if she had received some legal advice.[15] Thus, the law must adopt a relational approach to autonomy instead of the objective, reasonable-person approach that has emerged in QNA cases. Accordingly, it would be helpful if the proposal were to disqualify agreements that were entered into with emotional manipulation.

English adult relationship laws will benefit from the reforms proposed by Sandberg. However, a question to be answered is how far the law can protect our needs within intimate relations when it refuses to accept the messiness of everyday lives, where relationship arrangements do not easily fit into the binaries of marriage and cohabitation, and consent and coercion.

[14] Duncan et al (n 11).
[15] *Radmacher v Granatino* [2010] UKSC 42.

9

Cohabitation Reform in England and Wales: Time for Action

ANDY HAYWARD

I. Introduction

In England and Wales, the cohabiting family has become a statistical reality. While the marital family remains the most common form, the cohabiting family is the fastest growing.[1] Despite the prevalence of cohabitation, the law has not kept pace with these changes. It is a simplification to say the law ignores cohabitants and instead just privileges and promotes marriage. Rather, while cohabitants do receive certain rights and entitlements, and at times at the same level as spouses and civil partners, there are other contexts where cohabitants receive inferior protections. The key problem is that the current framework, and the way that it is understood by cohabitants, can produce relationship-generated disadvantage. This disadvantage is felt most keenly by some couples upon separation, owing to the inability of the courts to redistribute assets as they do upon divorce or dissolution, but is also applicable following the death of one of the partners. Further issues arise owing to the widespread misunderstandings of cohabitants as to existing legal protections. While some cohabitants may self-regulate using contract and property law, many are unaware of the need to do so, instead believing they are 'common law' spouses. This dimension adds considerable complexity and demands a bespoke regime responsive to the needs of this jurisdiction.

This chapter presents the case for the introduction of financial remedies for qualifying cohabitants upon separation.[2] The chapter is divided into three further sections. Section II analyses the statistical data on cohabitation in England and Wales to underline why increased legal protections are needed today. It will also indicate that despite significant changes in family relationships and the options

[1] Office for National Statistics, *Families and households in the UK: 2021* (18 May 2023).

[2] Space precludes discussion of enhanced protections upon an intestate succession or by way of a claim for reasonable financial provision under the Inheritance (Provision for Family Dependants) Act 1975.

for formalisation, the current law applicable to cohabitants has the potential to generate relationship-generated disadvantage. Section III details the shape and ultimate parameters of the reform proposal. Unlike some countries, such as Australia and New Zealand, that treat qualifying cohabitants in an identical manner to spouses, the proposal advanced in this chapter is for the introduction of a more restricted, low-level financial claim upon separation. The rationale for that choice will be explained and arguments opposing reform challenged. Section IV confronts the potential opposition that this proposal might face and reflects on policy considerations and activism strategies that can be deployed so that reform has the greatest chance of being realised in England and Wales.

II. Making the Case for Cohabitation Reform in England and Wales

A. Demographics

It is indisputable that marriage no longer represents that definitive way of establishing a family. After the negative stigma associated with cohabitation began to evaporate in the mid-twentieth century, and once it became a 'statistically significant family form' in the early 1970s, we can chart an exponential rise in cohabitation.[3] We have now reached the position that while the marital family is the most common type of family, standing at around 12.7 million couples in 2022, cohabitation is the fastest growing.[4] The number of cohabiting couples jumped from 1.5 million in 1996 to around 3.6 million in 2021, which represents an increase of 144 per cent.[5] That figure amounts to one in five couples today, and it is predicted to rise to one in four couples by 2031. Of the 3.6 million couples cohabiting in 2022, around 1.3 million had dependent children, and for the first time since records began in 1845 more births (51.3 per cent) were registered to unmarried mothers than to married mothers.[6]

These figures should be read alongside the recent Census data, which reveal that more young people than ever are unmarried.[7] The proportion of adults who have never been married or in a civil partnership has increased for all ages under the age of 70 since the 2011 Census. Most striking here, and a point of key significance for this reform proposal, is the age bracket of 25- to 34-year-olds.

[3] R Probert, *The Changing Legal Regulation of Cohabitation: From Fornicators to Family, 1600–2010* (Cambridge, Cambridge University Press, 2012) 14. See also J Haskey, 'Cohabitational and Marital Histories of Adults in Great Britain' (1999) 96 *Population Trends* 13.

[4] Office for National Statistics, *Families and households in the UK: 2022* (18 May 2023).

[5] House of Commons Library, '"Common Law Marriage" and Cohabitation' (3 November 2022).

[6] Office for National Statistics, *Births in England and Wales: 2021* (9 August 2022).

[7] Office for National Statistics, *Marriage and Civil Partnership Status in England and Wales: Census 2021* (22 February 2023).

In 1991, 2.7 million individuals in that bracket were unmarried. Today that figure is more than double at 5.8 million. Within that age range, the largest increase is among individuals aged 25 to 29, with the number increasing from 73.9 per cent in 2011 to 84.2 per cent in 2021. For those aged 30 to 34 years of age, the increase is from 49.2 per cent to 58.9 per cent. While these statistics include single individuals within the calculation, when cross-referenced with earlier Office for National Statistics data, a clearly sizeable proportion of the population are cohabiting.

The age bracket of 25–34 is significant for several reasons. First, we know couples within that group of individuals are the ones most likely to have a child together. In 2021, the average mean age of mothers giving birth was 30.9 in contrast to 27.7 back in 1991.[8] For mothers this is the highest age since records began in 1938. As noted in section II.B, the arrival of a child often creates the context where relationship-generated disadvantage can materialise. Important decisions are made as to childcare, the division of labour and contributions to the home. At present those decisions, whether reached by the couple purposefully or conditioned by societal expectations of interpersonal relationships, assume important significance if the couple were to later separate. This recent Census statistic reveals that many couples within that age bracket are likely to face that decision-making process while cohabiting.

Second, we know this bracket encapsulates an important moment in time for couples deciding whether to marry or register a civil partnership. Statistics reveal consistently that couples are now either not marrying at all or marrying later in life. Indeed, research shows that pre-marital cohabitation has increased from around two years in the 1980s to four years in the early 2000s.[9] The average age for opposite-sex couples marrying is at the top end of that bracket – 35.3 for men and 33.2 for women.[10] Same-sex couples are marrying at an even later point in their lives – 38.1 for men and 34.6 for women. While some couples within that bracket will cohabit as a prelude to marriage, statistics reveal a general decrease in couples marrying, with the past 50 years seeing marriage change from 'near-universality to being merely one option for a relationship'.[11] Currently the marriage rate is at the lowest since records began in 1862, with one in a hundred couples marrying per year. It is therefore conceivable that many in the 25–34 age bracket will continue to cohabit, especially as research indicates that while couples under the age of 35 often say they wish to marry,[12] once they reach that age the number expressing that intention drops significantly.

[8] Office for National Statistics, *Birth characteristics in England and Wales: 2021* (19 January 2023).

[9] See Written Evidence submitted by John Haskey to the Women and Equalities Committee Inquiry, *The Rights of Cohabiting Partners* (2021).

[10] Office for National Statistics (n 4).

[11] R Probert, 'Cohabitation and marriage in England and Wales' (2015) 4(1) *Families, Relationships and Societies* 157, 157.

[12] See Written Evidence (n 9).

The related question of why fewer couples are marrying has been keenly debated. Financial resources are likely to play an important role here. Couples might not be marrying earlier because they are saving up for an expensive wedding. But equally they might not be marrying earlier, or even at all, because that money is being channelled towards house deposits and tackling ever-growing financial pressure prompted by increasing property prices, a real-time reduction in earnings, the absence of affordable childcare and flexible work arrangements, and the general cost-of-living crisis.[13] As marriages need not always be lavish and can be cheaper administrative ceremonies, money alone cannot be the sole explanation.[14]

Just as perceptions of marriage have evolved over time, so too have couples' perceptions of commitment and the public expression of their relationship.[15] Changing psychological, ideological, and emotional perceptions of marriage might explain why more couples are questioning whether it is the right fit for them. These conversations will likely continue, fuelled in part by the recent discourse surrounding civil partnerships for mixed-sex couples, which were advocated for, in part, on the premise that marriage is a patriarchal, heteronormative and sexist institution.[16] Similarly, socio-economic factors are also likely to determine whether couples marry or cohabit, as has been evidenced in other countries. Carbone and Cahn have revealed in the United States that statistically, cohabitants are more likely to come from lower socio-economic groups and less likely to be college- or university-educated.[17] Likewise in Canada, when compared to spouses, cohabitants find greater representation in lower-income groups with less college- or university-level education.[18]

In terms of demographics, it is not just younger cohabiting couples about whom we should be concerned. As Haskey points out, we see particularly significant increases in the rates of cohabitation among older couples, especially women.[19] Between 2002 and 2019, the number of women cohabiting aged 50–54 doubled, while the number of those aged 60–64 quadrupled. Although these statistics may look unusually striking because where the initial number is low any increase looks significant, it does tell us that a growing number of older couples are cohabiting today than previously. For older couples, we need to cross-reference

[13] Office for National Statistics, *How are financial pressures affecting people in Great Britain?* (22 February 2023).

[14] See J Eekelaar and M Maclean, 'Marriage and the moral bases of personal relationships' (2004) 31 *Journal of Law and Society* 510; and M Hibbs, C Barton and J Beswick, 'Why marry? Perceptions of the affianced' (2001) 31 *Family Law* 197.

[15] Explored in C Smart and P Stevens, *Cohabitation Breakdown* (Oxford, Family Policy Studies Centre, 2000).

[16] See, eg, A Hayward 'The Steinfeld Effect: Equal Civil Partnerships and the Construction of the Cohabitant' (2019) 31(4) *Child and Family Law Quarterly* 283.

[17] J Carbone and N Cahn, *Marriage Markets: How Inequality is Remaking the American Family* (New York, Oxford University Press, 2014) 8.

[18] R Leckey, 'Cohabitation, Law Reform, and the Litigants' (2017) 31(2) *International Journal of Law, Policy and the Family* 131.

[19] See Written Evidence (n 9).

that increase with whether the individual was previously married or in a civil partnership. It can be discerned, at a general level, that the older the age group, the larger the proportion of cohabitants who had had a previous divorce or dissolution of a civil partnership. More importantly, it is key to delineate what factors are driving couples to cohabit later in life. These may include a personal reluctance to remarry, perhaps owing to a difficult divorce or bereavement, or a practical resistance owing to the potential loss of existing pension or maintenance entitlements.[20] The cohort of older couples cohabiting is likely to increase further, as will the average age of cohabitants, considering the decrease in the marriage rate and the fact that more couples choose not to remarry.

What is clear is that a growing number of couples are cohabiting across all age groups for a variety of different reasons. Probert is correct to point out that the result is that the 'legal system has never before had to deal with cohabitation on such a scale as exists today'.[21] This is not particularly surprising, as comparative family law research shows similar trends across other European countries.[22] However, crucially for the argument presented in this chapter, prevalence of cohabitation alone is an insufficient basis for legal regulation; rather, it is the interaction of this large and diverse cohort of cohabiting couples with the law that necessitates reform.

B. The Legal Framework

Cohabitants are not ignored by the law. Context-specific entitlements and protections do exist in a range of areas with varying intensity, albeit often without consistency or a coherent rationale. At times, cohabitants will be treated equally with spouses and civil partners, while at others, they get lesser or, at times, no protection whatsoever. Navigating these protections can be tricky too – as there is no standard definition of cohabitant, an individual may be eligible under one statute but not under another.

If an automatic protection generated by the fact of the relationship does not exist, there is the potential of self-ordering for couples, notably through property law, contract law and trusts. Cohabitation contracts are no longer struck down for public policy reasons,[23] and for around £500 couples can draw up a personalised agreement regulating real and personal property, maintenance and child

[20] See Written Evidence submitted by Later Life Ambitions to the Women and Equalities Committee Inquiry, *The Rights of Cohabiting Partners* (2021). For evidence of this in the US, see SL Brown, *Families in America* (Oakland, CA, University of California Press, 2017) 50.

[21] R Probert, 'Cohabitation: Current Legal Solutions' (2009) 62(1) *Current Legal Problems* 316, 318.

[22] See, eg, Commission for European Family Law, *Principles of European Family Law Regarding Property, Maintenance and Succession Rights of Couples in de facto Unions* (Cambridge, Intersentia, 2019).

[23] See *Sutton v Mischon de Reya and Gawor & Co* [2004] 1 FLR 837, discussed in R Probert, 'Cohabitation Contracts and Swedish Sex Slaves' (2004) 16(4) *Child and Family Law Quarterly* 453.

arrangements. Without a contract, couples can use land law to facilitate joint purchases of property and create declarations of trust that would ensure legal entitlement upon separation.

So, certain protections do exist, and self-ordering is a possibility, but in practice we encounter many obstacles that underline the need for the introduction of basic protections. These obstacles may be classified in three ways: knowledge of the law; opportunity to self-regulate; and an appreciation of structural pressures imposed on interpersonal relationships.

i. *Knowledge of the Law*

Self-ordering using the general law is a recognised means of granting legal protections and has the clear benefit of respecting party autonomy. A bespoke arrangement mutually agreed by the parties is more likely to be followed because it is couple-led rather than court-imposed. But self-ordering is heavily reliant on several factors, such as a cooperative partner, financial resources and a basic knowledge of the law, or at the very least an awareness of the initial need to regulate. Evidence submitted to the recent Women and Equalities Committee Inquiry, however, exposed considerable misunderstandings. For example, Bendall noted that when couples make decisions as to finances, there is 'little to suggest that people are acting on the basis of a knowledge of the law, or even that they are aware of what the law is'.[24]

Empirical studies have revealed that a significant number of couples are unaware of the need to regulate, believing instead that they are already protected by the law. Barlow's research has analysed the extent of that lack of understanding and the prevalence of the so-called 'common law marriage myth'. In 2019, 47 per cent of the population were under the incorrect impression that cohabitants have a common law marriage, giving them the same legal rights as if they were married.[25] That figure has remained largely unchanged over the past 20 years – it stood at 51 per cent in 2006.[26] Among couples with children, this belief was held by over half of the population in 2019 (55 per cent). These misunderstandings are not necessarily that surprising, and it has been argued they are no different from those possessed by spouses who erroneously think they will get half of everything upon divorce.[27] However, it is arguable that the shock that a cohabiting partner might receive, as was the case in *Allan v Clibbery*,[28] when Miss Allan discovered

[24] See Written Evidence submitted by Charlotte Bendall to the Women and Equalities Committee Inquiry: *The Rights of Cohabiting Partners* (2021).

[25] See A Barlow et al, 'Cohabitation and the Law: Myths, Money and the Media' in A Park et al (eds), *British Social Attitudes: The 24th Report* (London, SAGE Publications, 2008) 29; and M Albakri et al, 'Relationships and gender identity' in J Curtice et al (eds), *British Social Attitudes 36* (The National Centre for Social Research, 11 July 2019).

[26] Barlow et al (n 25).

[27] R Auchmuty, 'The limits of marriage protection in property allocation when a relationship ends' (2016) 28(4) *Child and Family Law Quarterly* 303, 319–20.

[28] *Allan v Clibbery* [2002] EWCA Civ 45.

she was not a common law spouse, would far exceed that of a disappointed spouse realising the true extent of the sharing principle upon divorce. Misunderstanding as to the *extent* of protection is not the same as whether couples are protected in the first place.

ii. Opportunity to Self-regulate

Another obstacle to self-ordering is timing or, put differently, when the opportunity arises for couples to put their affairs in order. A dream home sourced and jointly purchased by the parties often will prompt contemporaneous discussions of joint tenancies and tenancies in common with a conveyancer. This sequence of events forces the couple to confront the question of legal and equitable ownership, and a failure by the conveyancing solicitor to advise accurately may even result in a claim in negligence.

We have seen an increased number of properties purchased in joint names, which ensures both parties have some form of legal entitlement, whether it be expressly declared or obtained via the operation of the presumption of beneficial joint tenancy.[29] But a cohabitant moving into another's already purchased property would find themselves in a difficult position. While they naturally should feel able to discuss with their partner what might happen if their relationship ends, there is unsurprisingly an optimism bias. Indeed, couples in love are less likely to act with the degree of legal rationality expected by the general law, as observed by Lord Justice Jacob in *Jones v Kernott*, when he noted that 'human emotional relationships simply do not operate as if they were commercial contracts and it is idle to wish that they did'.[30] Requesting joint legal ownership or an express declaration of trust requires a degree of knowledge of the law, cooperation of both parties, and resources. Without self-ordering, protection upon breakdown is dependent on establishing a trust interest in the home using principles that prioritise financial contribution, require unrealistic discussions as to party intentions, and have been roundly criticised as 'relationship blind'.[31]

iii. Structural Pressures

Even with both some degree of knowledge of the law and an opportunity to self-regulate, structural pressures exerted from outside the relationship can contribute to cohabitants' experience of relationship-generated disadvantage. Such pressures

[29] See R Probert, 'Trusts and the modern woman – establishing an interest in the family home' (2001) 13(3) *Child and Family Law Quarterly* 275; and R Probert, 'Equality in the family home?: *Stack v Dowden* [2007] UKHL 17' (2007) 15(3) *Feminist Legal Studies* 341.

[30] *Jones v Kernott* [2010] EWCA Civ 578 [90]. See also A Barlow, 'Legal Rationality and Family Property: What has love got to do with it?' in J Miles and R Probert (eds), *Sharing Lives, Dividing Assets: An Interdisciplinary Study* (Oxford, Hart Publishing, 2009) 303.

[31] A Bottomley, 'Women and Trust(s): Portraying the Family in the Gallery of Law' in S Bright and J Dewar (eds), *Land Law: Themes and Perspectives* (Oxford, Oxford University Press, 1998) 206.

often centre on gender roles and the provision of care for children.[32] We know that statistically, women still provide more childcare than men and are more likely to work part-time because of caring responsibilities, which in turn has a knock-on effect on their salaries and career progression.[33] Statistics published in 2022 revealed for the first time in decades an increase in the number of women leaving the workforce to look after children, and in particular there was an increase of 12.6 per cent for women aged 25–34.[34] And as a society, we are still also operating under gendered assumptions as to the provision of care. The 2019 British Social Attitudes Survey showed that 19 per cent believed women should stay at home to look after a child.[35]

These gendered assumptions of care and labour generate issues for cohabitants. Research by Heenan has shown that the 'division of childcare responsibilities has unequal financial consequences,' especially post-separation, and that women tend to view their own contributions to a relationship as less valuable than those of their male counterparts.[36] The general law reinforces that viewpoint too. Unlike in the context of divorce, where homemaker and breadwinner contributions are treated equally (or at least in theory they are), trusts law continues to prioritise financial over non-financial contributions. It has been argued that non-financial contributions can be commodified to render them quantifiable and, more importantly, valued by the law.[37] That step has not been taken and, at present, a clear hierarchy of contributions is maintained.

While it is also true, as Fisher and Low have shown, that married women struggle in post-divorce economic recovery, that outcome arises in a context where the other spouse may at least be subject to some form of financial liability based on party need.[38] Cohabitants left in such a position, especially those with children, have no equivalent protection and are instead subject to the discretion of the stronger party. Child support would be payable in those cases, but given the demographics of cohabitants, it is highly likely that schedule 1 to the Children Act 1989 would be out of reach for most, given that it tends to be used

[32] Religion plays a role too, especially in the context of religious-only marriages that are not legally recognised in England and Wales. See RC Akhtar, 'Religious-Only Marriages and Cohabitation: Deciphering Differences' in R Akhtar, P Nash and R Probert (eds), *Cohabitation and Religious Marriage: Status, Similarities and Solutions* (Bristol, Bristol University Press 2020) 69; and R Sandberg, *Religion and Marriage Law: The Need for Reform* (Bristol, Bristol University Press, 2021).

[33] Office for National Statistics, 'Women shoulder the responsibility of unpaid work' *ONS Digital* (10 November 2016).

[34] Office for National Statistics, *Labour market overview, UK: March 2023* (14 March 2023).

[35] J Curtice et al (eds), *British Social Attitudes 36* (The National Centre for Social Research, 11 July 2019).

[36] See Written Evidence submitted by Anna Heenan to the Women and Equalities Committee Inquiry, *The Rights of Cohabiting Partners* (2021).

[37] See, eg, S Bannister, 'Domestic contributions as unjust enrichments: commodifying love?' (2021) 33 *Child and Family Law Quarterly* 257.

[38] H Fisher and H Low, 'Who Wins, Who Loses and Who Recovers from Divorce?' in J Miles and R Probert (eds), *Sharing Lives, Dividing Assets: An Inter-Disciplinary Study* (Oxford, Hart Publishing, 2009) 254.

by wealthy cohabiting couples.[39] Any financial provision made under that regime is not destined for the partner themselves but rather for the child concerned. Here, the financial losses, disadvantages and sacrifices made by one partner can go unnoticed.

This discussion is not seeking to peddle a so-called 'atrocity tale', infantilise autonomous individuals about relationship choices or paint women as vulnerable supplicants.[40] Rather, what it reveals is that a range of different factors are operating simultaneously and that, when their effect is viewed cumulatively, they justify the need for cohabitation reform. Put differently, our current legal framework is difficult to navigate and hard to understand while the relationship is intact. That knowledge, distorted through the operation of the common law marriage myth, impacts the opportunity to self-regulate. In the event that the couple separate, disadvantage can arise owing to the way in which the couple structured their relationship, both purposefully and owing to societal pressures or expectations. As it stands, rather than the law providing a safety net, the way a cohabiting relationship was organised, and the labour divided by the couple, can then be exploited by the financially stronger party.

Without an appropriate legal framework mandating a measure of compensation for their work or recognition of their contributions, the economically weaker party in these circumstances is effectively dependent on the generosity of their former partner. Most likely the absence of liability on the economically stronger party will mean the other falls on the state for support. Self-ordering is not the solution, as it overlooks relational power dynamics – for that to work, we need equality of arms in an equal society. Similarly, this is not a hypothetical scenario or predicament faced by a handful of so-called 'hard' cases. In a poll of Resolution members in 2017, 98 per cent of respondents stated they were unable to help clients, owing to the lack of legal protections.[41]

III. The Reform Proposal and Justification

The proposal advanced in this chapter is for England and Wales to introduce an ability for a former cohabiting partner to bring a financial claim against their former partner upon relationship breakdown. The justification for such claim would be to remedy relationship-generated disadvantage that has arisen as a direct consequence of contributions made by the applicant to the relationship. This approach would be better than maintaining the status quo. Further developing property law through a process of familialisation of trust principles in this

[39] See Written Evidence submitted by Resolution to the Women and Equalities Committee Inquiry, *The Rights of Cohabiting Partners* (2021).

[40] See H Reece, 'Leaping Without Looking' in R Leckey (ed), *After Legal Equality: Family, Sex, Kinship* (Abingdon, Routledge, 2015) 115.

[41] See Written Evidence (n 39). A poll in 2019 gave similar results.

context is not the solution,[42] and the experience of other countries has shown that general law principles fail to effectively address the issues raised by cohabitation.[43] Instead, a bespoke family law remedy based on the fact of the relationship is needed.

Entitlement to bring an application would not be based on an act of formalisation. Rather, qualifying cohabiting couples who have lived together for a minimum duration period, or who have had a child together, will be able to apply. Before exploring how such claim might operate, this section will analyse why this model of reform would be the most appropriate in England and Wales.

A. The Method Used to Acquire Legal Protections

Comparative family law reveals a multitude of ways of giving legal recognition to cohabitants upon relationship breakdown.[44] It allows us to identify diverse strategies, reform initiatives and a range of different experiences as to the overall efficacy of the frameworks created.[45] At its core, policymakers contemplating any reform must answer several key questions. The first is whether any new law should be premised on an act of formalisation or should instead be ascriptive, that is ascribe certain rights and protections to qualifying relationships, notably based on their duration and the presence of children. Expressed differently, this is the question of whether the law should be 'opt-in' or instead 'opt-out'; that is default, but with a potential for couples to disapply its application.

Marriage and civil partnership are, of course, examples of opting-in, and proponents of this approach for cohabitants emphasise the value it has for respecting party choice, enhancing autonomy and providing certainty as to when legal entitlements arise or might end. Aloni has argued that a form of registered status offers flexibility and a pluralistic response, and may offer benefits to LGBT+ cohabiting couples who may have reservations about the institution of marriage, owing to its heteronormative and originally exclusionary foundations.[46]

While appreciating the autonomy-enhancing benefits of formalisation, this proposal does not favour an opt-in model for England and Wales. At present, couples can opt in to marriage or a civil partnership, and doing so will see the couple receive the full range of legal benefits and protections available. No significant legal distinctions exist between the two regimes, and the method of expressing a relationship is largely based on couple choice and perceptions of the two statuses.

[42] See A Hayward, 'Family Property and the Process of Familialisation of Property Law' (2012) 23(3) *Child and Family Law Quarterly* 284.

[43] See, eg, IM Ellman, '"Contract Thinking" Was Marvin's Fatal Flaw' (2001) 76 *Notre Dame Law Review* 1365.

[44] See, eg, M Allum et al, 'Cohabitation Rights in England and Wales, Scotland and Australia' (2023) 2 *Financial Remedies Journal* 135.

[45] J Miles, 'Unmarried Cohabitation in a European Perspective' in JM Scherpe (ed), *European Family Law*, vol III: *Family Law in a European Perspective* (Cheltenham, Edward Elgar Publishing, 2016) 82.

[46] E Aloni, 'Registering Relationships' (2013) 87 *Tulane Law Review* 573.

Cohabitants may wish to formalise via either of these routes, but claims made that civil partnerships are capable of protecting cohabitants, especially following their extension to mixed-sex couples in December 2019, are exaggerated.[47] Early indications reveal that a statistical minority of cohabiting couples are selecting civil partnerships, and even taking into account the impact of the Covid-19 pandemic on registration numbers, there has not been a statistically significant surge in terms of uptake.[48]

Therefore, the difficulty of opt-in regimes in the context of England and Wales is that a *third* method of formalisation would be required, offering cohabitants something distinct from both marriage and civil partnership. To create differentiation, it would also need to be capable of personalisation, as is possible under the French *pacte civil de solidarité* or the Belgian *cohabitation légale*, while at the same time being meaningful in terms of the range and intensity of the legal protections afforded. Weak remedies, for example those limited exclusively to ownership of the family home and excluding maintenance, may not provide the requisite safety net for applicants. This may mean, as we have seen in Scotland[49] and Belgium,[50] that further reforms are required to strengthen existing protections. Conversely, creating a range of strong remedies, potentially mimicking those conferred by marriage, may not have the desired results in terms of overall attractiveness. For example, research by Matsumura analysing Colorado's designated beneficiaries law allowing couples to confer benefits upon one another, revealed that, when faced with a choice, couples overwhelmingly chose marriage.[51] Indeed, Matsumura noted that only 672 couples in three populous counties used Colorado's designated beneficiary law, as compared to the 131,100 couples who married.

In addition, if a third opt-in regime were created in England and Wales, and leaving aside the potential for confusion among the public, we would encounter the fundamental problem that cohabitants might believe they are already protected as common law spouses, so do not take the step of formalising. Even if this myth did not exist, formalisation is not an option if one partner does not wish to formalise, perhaps being fully aware of the legal risks of doing so. These 'uneven' relationships pose a particular challenge for policymakers and again militate towards introducing an opt-out financial claim.[52] This claim shifts the power away from the party not wishing to formalise to the potentially economically weaker party instead.

[47] Hayward (n 16).

[48] Office for National Statistics, *Civil partnerships in England and Wales: 2021* (9 December 2022).

[49] See Scottish Law Commission, *Report on Cohabitation* (Scot Law Com No 261, 2022).

[50] See G Willems, 'Registered Partnerships in Belgium' in JM Scherpe and A Hayward (eds), *The Future of Registered Partnerships – Family Recognition Beyond Marriage?* (Cambridge, Intersentia, 2017).

[51] KT Matsumura, 'Consent to Intimate Regulation' (2018) 96 *North Carolina Law Review* 1013, 1018.

[52] A Barlow and J Smithson, 'Legal assumptions, cohabitants' talk and the rocky road to reform' (2010) 22(3) *Child and Family Law Quarterly* 328.

B. Equal Treatment with Spouses

Having accepted the need for opt-out provision, the next question becomes the intensity of the rights conferred or, as Scherpe observes, whether a scheme should 'keep [a] distance from marriage and if so, how much'.[53] Miles has termed this a question of whether the law should pursue an assimilationist or differential approach.[54] Certain jurisdictions, such as Australia and New Zealand, treat qualifying cohabitants in the same manner as spouses. For example, in Australia, a qualifying cohabitant who has lived together with their partner for two years, or if they have had a child together, would be treated as a de facto spouse.[55] The rationale for this is functional equivalence – having satisfied the statutory definition of a cohabitant, the relationship is deemed by the court to have the sufficient permanence and commitment to justify treatment as a spouse. This makes sense for many couples that function in an analogous way to spouses, through intertwining their lives, financial affairs and provision of care for children, without going one step further and formalising. Assimilation has multiple benefits, notably the ease of administration. Rather than operating two separate regimes for formalised and non-formalised couples, you have a single regime accessed via different entry points. This has been emphasised as a key benefit of the Australian regime, Young noting that the subsequent inclusion of de facto couples within an existing regime used by spouses was not that difficult to realise.[56] Similarly, while at face value this appears controversial, the experience in Australia and New Zealand shows that although there was initial opposition to reform, changes have broadly been welcomed.[57] Resistance, if it materialises, centres on conflating relationships that some consider to be fundamentally different in nature. The decision not to marry or register a civil partnership, whether fully appreciated or not, should be respected, and couples should not be converted to spouses ex post facto. More ideologically driven opposition focuses on how assimilation would diminish the value we place on marriage in society.

An alternative approach to reform is to maintain a distinction between marriage/civil partnership and cohabitation, by offering cohabitants a more limited menu of remedies that are distinct from those applicable upon divorce or dissolution. Such reform, introduced via a specific cohabitation statute, ensures a visible distinction is drawn between different types of relationship, emphasising

[53] Oral Evidence Session of the Women and Equalities Committee, *Rights of Cohabiting Partners Inquiry* (5 January 2022).

[54] Miles (n 45).

[55] See Family Law Act 1975 (Commonwealth); and Family Court Act 1997 and Interpretation Act 1984 (Western Australia).

[56] See, eg, L Young, 'Considering the broader implications of the law of termination of domestic partnerships: lessons from Australia' (2023) 35(4) *Child and Family Law Quarterly* 365.

[57] See, eg, M Briggs, 'Which Relationships Should be Included in a Property Sharing Scheme?' in J Palmer, N Peart and M Briggs (eds), *Law and Policy in Modern Family Finance* (Cambridge, Intersentia, 2017).

a policy position that cohabitants are not spouses and thus should not be treated as such. Using a restricted range of remedies has the benefit of tackling the most extreme instances of relationship-generated disadvantage, while at the same time remaining politically palatable for those wanting marriage to be privileged. Certain jurisdictions, such as Scotland[58] and Ireland,[59] have pursued this route.

There is certainly an argument to be made that England and Wales should pursue an assimilation policy and permit qualifying cohabitants access to the same protections as spouses upon divorce. This has been advocated by Barlow and Douglas, and is considered to be an approach especially justified where the couple concerned have children together.[60] Research in 2007 by Barlow, Burgoyne and Smithson found among respondents that 90 per cent felt cohabitants should have the same rights as married couples where they had a child together.[61] In their study, 85 per cent felt that cohabitants, whether or not they have children, should have the same rights as married couples after living together, but not as soon as they start living together (there was no consensus on how long the period should be).[62] However, that approach was rejected by the Law Commission in 2007 on the basis that cohabiting relationships vary widely and there may be 'significant public disquiet if cohabitants were to be treated similarly [to spouses],' given the controversy surrounding large divorce settlements.[63] That position was endorsed more recently, in 2022, by the Women and Equalities Committee Inquiry into the Rights of Cohabiting Partners.[64] Reflecting on the legal principles themselves might also give us pause for thought. The sharing principle used by spouses and civil partners could be viewed as overly generous and potentially inappropriate for cohabitants, especially in the context of short relationships. The principle of needs would likely be a much more appropriate standard to apply, but it could be criticised on the basis that cohabitants have not assumed the responsibility to cater for each other's needs in all circumstances. While assimilation is certainly tempting, a distinct claim is favoured in this chapter for several reasons.

First, at present there is considerable political opposition to reform, and one of the main counterarguments advanced is the eroding of the distinction between marriage and cohabitation. While family lawyers are virtually unanimously in favour of some form of cohabitation reform, the Government, at present, is not. Indeed, even the proposal for a low-level financial claim proposed by the Women

[58] See Family Law (Scotland) Act 2006, ss 25–31.

[59] See Civil Partnership and Certain Rights and Obligations of Cohabitants Act 2010.

[60] See Written Evidence submitted by Anne Barlow and Gillian Douglas to the Women and Equalities Committee Inquiry, *The Rights of Cohabiting Partners* (2021).

[61] A Barlow, C Burgoyne and J Smithson, 'The Living Together Campaign – The Impact on Cohabitants' [2007] *Family Law* 165, 166.

[62] ibid.

[63] Law Commission, *Cohabitation: The Financial Consequences of Relationship Breakdown* (Cm 7182, 2007) para 4.9.

[64] Women and Equalities Committee, *The Rights of Cohabiting Partners Report* (4 August 2022).

and Equalities Committee was rejected by the Government on the basis that a review of financial remedies needed to be completed before the issue of cohabitation could be addressed.[65] Thus, while there are certainly merits to assimilation, we must appreciate the specific context of England and Wales and acknowledge potential resistance to change. This may change, given the Labour Party's announcement in October 2023 that they plan to review this area with a view to introducing reform.[66] But at present, no further details are available as to Labour's reform strategy or model, and resistance in the Government remains.[67]

Second, key practitioner organisations such as Resolution and the Family Law Bar Association are not in favour of equalisation of treatment but strongly support the introduction of a bespoke opt-out reform.[68] As discussed in section IV, the key to success is the building of a reform movement by academics alongside practitioner organisations. Reform is contingent on a clear, harmonised position, political will and, potentially, proposals by individual Members of Parliament (MPs) for reform via Private Members' Bills.[69]

Third, the Government's current position is that a recently announced review of financial remedies, which currently excludes cohabitation from its remit, must be completed before the question of cohabitation reform can be considered.[70] Such focus on financial remedies stated in the Government's response to the Women and Equalities Committee Report is likely to be a tactic to prevent meaningful review of cohabitation. Even if there is little political appetite within the Government at present, advocating for a separate financial claim enables cohabitation reform efforts to be uncoupled from, and thus not interfere with, deliberations regarding financial remedies on divorce. As such, momentum for reform can be maintained, and this line of argument may be particularly useful when it is appreciated that reform of financial remedies is likely to take years to achieve.

C. The Parameters of the Financial Claim

Having selected an opt-out model that offers a claim distinct from that afforded to spouses or civil partners, this section will now detail more precisely the parameters

[65] Women and Equalities Committee, *The Rights of Cohabiting Partners: Government response to the Committee's Second Report* (1 November 2022).

[66] Emily Thornberry MP (Shadow Attorney-General), *Making the Law Work for Women* (Labour Party Conference Speech, 10 October 2023).

[67] See A Hayward, 'Cohabitation and Labour's Commitment to Changing the Law: What Reform Might Look Like' *Financial Remedies Journal* (23 November 2023).

[68] See Written Evidence submitted by Resolution and The Family Law Bar Association to the Women and Equalities Committee Inquiry, *The Rights of Cohabiting Partners* (2021). Resolution's position has softened and assimilation is not ruled out in its Vision for Family Justice 2023.

[69] As was the case with the Cohabitation (No 2) Bill (introduced in 2009 by Mary Creagh, MP), the Cohabitation Bill (introduced in 2008 by Lord Lester of Herne Hill) and the Cohabitation Rights Bill (introduced in 2015 by Lord Marks of Henley-on-Thames).

[70] Law Commission, *Financial Remedies on Divorce* (4 April 2023). Details available at www.lawcom.gov.uk/project/financial-remedies-on-divorce/.

of the application. The proposal draws upon the approach adopted by the Law Commission in 2007, which found favour in the Women and Equalities Committee Report, but it builds upon it using comparative family law insights to modify certain elements. In agreement with the findings of that Committee, there is no need to reinvent the wheel when creating a reform proposal, but we can update it, where needed, to acknowledge developments that have occurred in the 15 years since its creation. The following will identify core elements of the proposal, but space precludes a detailed articulation of all aspects.

i. Defining Cohabitation

The first question becomes who the beneficiaries of this claim are. To speak of cohabitants without any attempt at refinement will produce a scheme that is overly broad and imprecise. It should be remembered that spouses and civil partners are very often also cohabitants, and there are certain types of relationships where the individuals might cohabit but should be excluded from the remit of the scheme, such as siblings or caring relationships.

This proposal favours targeting intimate, committed and dyadic interpersonal relationships. While the term 'intimate' is used here to differentiate such couples from those prohibited by law, such as relatives and siblings, there is no requirement for sexual activity or conjugality per se. Cohabitants in this proposal are to be defined as 'a couple living together in an intimate, committed and enduring family relationship'. This formulation is favoured over that used by the Law Commission in 2007, namely, 'living together as a couple in a joint household', as the shift away from a shared household might embrace living-apart-together couples (LATs) who are in a relationship but live in two or more separate properties.[71] This aligns with the approach taken in other jurisdictions that permit cohabitation to be found despite the fact that the couple do not live together under the same roof, and thus might be more embracing of modern family arrangements.

In addition, the proposed definition rejects any marriage comparator, for example where cohabitants are defined as a 'couple living together as husband or wife', 'living together in a manner analogous to marriage' or 'in a marriage-like relationship'. As the rationale of the proposal is to provide a regime that is different from marriage, a couple's inclusion within such scheme should not be based on their relationship's similarity to marriage. To do so would indirectly promote marriage as the gold standard and potentially exclude meritorious relationships. The Scottish Law Commission's 2022 proposals favour amending their current definition, which includes a marriage comparator, and adopting instead one that

[71] See, eg, S Duncan et al, *Living Apart Together: Uncoupling Intimacy and Co-Residence* (London, NatCen, 2013); and A Reimondos, A Evans and E Gray, 'Living-Apart-Together (LAT) Relationships in Australia' (2011) 87 *Family Matters* 43, 45.

is neutral, namely, a shift from living together as husband and wife to 'living together as a couple in an enduring family relationship'.[72]

Unlike marriage, where the ceremony provides proof of its existence, cohabitation involves the 'gradual process of increasing enmeshment with one another over time'.[73] So, a key question is whether statutory guidance should be provided to judges to use when determining whether a qualifying cohabiting relationship exists. The Law Commission did not favour the use of a statutory checklist, because it was felt that the courts currently identify cohabitants without the assistance of a checklist and that consultees cautioned against rigidity and a 'box-ticking mentality'.[74] Similarly, practitioners have said such guidance may not necessarily be needed, as both practitioners and judges will 'know cohabitation when they see it'.[75] While this proposal favours an evolutive approach to be taken by the judiciary, it supports the inclusion of a statutory checklist of factors for judges to consider when determining whether a relationship qualifies. As there are no formalities, and thus no documented evidence of the existence of the relationship, the courts must adopt a functional approach, which has its own benefits and limitations.[76] This prompts the making of a value judgement as to when a relationship has matured into something justifying legal protection. Rather than leaving this exclusively to the viewpoint of an individual judge, who may or may not apply their own idiosyncratic standards, a list of factors would assist in shaping that deliberative exercise. Australia and New Zealand both use extensive statutory definitions. For example, under section 4AA(2) of the Family Law Act 1975, a judge in Australia may have regard, inter alia, to the duration of the relationship, financial dependence or interdependence, and the degree of mutual commitment to a shared life. However, despite listing nine factors, none are essential when determining as a matter of fact whether a de facto relationship exists, and the court may have regard to any matter it considers appropriate.[77] This proposal favours the creation of a shorter checklist of factors, directing a judge to consider relationship duration, ownership and use of property, and care of children. It would favour a list of considerations that are objectively verifiable rather than overtly subjective, such as the nature of the relationship or degree of commitment shown. A shift away from these subjective elements may avoid an intrusive dissection of the private lives of parties, which is often a key criticism of schemes based on functionality.[78]

[72] See Scottish Law Commission (n 49).

[73] P Parkinson, 'When All Roads Lead to Rome: The Problem of Treating De Facto Relationships as Marriages in Australia' (2022) 44 *Houston Journal of International Law* 253, 264.

[74] Law Commission (n 63) para 3.17.

[75] See Oral Evidence by Graeme Fraser to the Women and Equalities Committee Inquiry, *The Rights of Cohabiting Partners* (2021).

[76] See, eg, Notes, 'Looking for a Family Resemblance: The Limits of the Functional Approach to the Legal Definition of Family' (1990–1991) 104 *Harvard Law Review* 1640; and K Griffiths, 'From "Form" to Function and Back Again: a New Conceptual Basis for Developing Frameworks for the Legal Recognition of Adult Relationships' (2019) 31(3) *Child and Family Law Quarterly* 227.

[77] See s 4AA(3)–(4).

[78] See K O'Sullivan, 'Cohabitant Protection on Relationship Breakdown in Ireland: A Lesson in Illusory Justice?' (2023) 37(1) *International Journal of Law, Policy and the Family* 1.

A related and practical question is when a cohabiting relationship begins and ends. Owing to the absence of an act of formalisation, determining the start and end dates of a cohabiting relationship is a difficult exercise. Does it start when the couple move in together, have overnight stays, enter into property transactions or publicly acknowledge the relationship? Similar questions arise upon its end date – is it marked by moving out, or by severing financial ties or shared intentions? The use of the statutory checklist may be particularly helpful here to allow judges to develop principles to guide the exercise of discretion. In terms of separation, while there is no formal process for couples to undertake given the nature of the relationship, the statute could state that a couple's cohabitation is deemed to have ended if they no longer cohabit for three months or treat their relationship as over (which might be more applicable to LAT couples).

ii. Eligibility Criteria

Distinct from definition is the question of eligibility. Not all cohabiting relationships should be entitled to remedies under this scheme. For example, this proposal does not favour, as in the case of Scotland currently, the ability for couples to bring a financial claim immediately upon the commencement of their relationship. Rather, there will be an additional filter to ensure that the relationship meets a specific threshold of permanence to justify intervention.

Comparative family law reveals that jurisdictions using a standalone financial claim, like Ireland, or even the more far-reaching concept of de facto spouse as a gateway to spousal remedies, like Australia or New Zealand, stipulate the need for the relationship to subsist for a minimum duration period or for the couple to have a child together. In terms of the length of minimum duration periods, these average around two to three years, but some jurisdictions impose a longer period. For example, a childless cohabiting couple in Ireland must cohabit for a minimum of five years.[79] Virtually all jurisdictions with cohabitation regimes fast-track access when a couple have a child together, although in Ireland, having a child will not dispense with the minimum duration period completely but merely reduce it to two years.

Careful thought is needed as to the minimum duration period. If it were to be set too short, it would be criticised for collapsing the distinction between marriage and cohabitation, and for catching relationships that are undeserving or deemed transient. However, evidence from Scotland[80] and Canada[81] has shown that such criticism must be approached cautiously, given that generally only committed and relatively long relationships tended to litigate. Conversely, if the duration period

[79] See Civil Partnership and Certain Rights and Obligations of Cohabitants Act 2010, s 172(5).

[80] See F Wasoff, J Miles and E Mordaunt, *Legal Practitioners' Perspectives on the Cohabitation Provisions of the Family Law (Scotland) Act 2006* (Nuffield Foundation, 2010).

[81] R Leckey, 'Cohabitation, Law Reform, and the Litigants' (2017) 31(2) *International Journal of Law, Policy and the Family* 131.

were set too long, it would be criticised for failing to combat relationship-generated disadvantage. Duration periods can be also criticised from a different perspective, on the basis that they prompt litigation regarding the precise start and end dates and try to objectively quantify a relationship that arises incrementally based on the subjective perceptions of the parties.

It is envisaged that a period of two years would be in line with comparative family law experience, aligns with time frames used for existing claims upon death, and offers an effective compromise between accessibility and political acceptability. Of course, time periods will also prompt debates as to short relationships or breaks in continuity. The proposal supports insistence on compliance with the time period, with no discretion to dispense, albeit with careful consideration of the option for short relationships to be recognised as a standalone eligibility route if 'substantial contributions' were made to the relationship that it would be inequitable to disregard.[82] Similarly, a flexible approach to breaks is favoured, so that couples might satisfy the period cumulatively and without returning the clock to zero if they were to briefly separate. This approach, adopted in Australia, favours inclusivity and is less arbitrary.

Given the public opinion that cohabiting couples with children should be treated equally with spouses and civil partners, this proposal favours the presence of a child as constituting a means to automatic eligibility. As noted in section II, the division of labour within an interpersonal relationship often generates relationship-generated disadvantage and has a gendered impact. Priority should therefore be given to couples with children, even though other (less-used) routes to a remedy will continue to exist, such as claims under Schedule 1 of the Children Act 1989.

iii. The Rationale for Legal Intervention and the Range of Remedies Available

For a cohabitation regime to operate effectively, there must be a clear rationale justifying legal intervention, which is capable of consistent application by the judiciary and easily understood by members of the public to permit self-ordering. This was one of the resounding findings of the Scottish Law Commission in their review of the Family Law (Scotland) Act 2006. Comparative family law reveals multiple rationales. For the de facto regimes in Australia and New Zealand, qualifying cohabiting couples are exposed to the same methods of division of assets as spouses, thus equitable redistribution based on what is fair and rule-based sharing of relationship property, respectively. To transpose that model into the context of England and Wales, qualifying cohabitants would be granted access to part II of the Matrimonial Causes Act 1973 and be able to seek the full range of orders available. There is certainly an attractiveness to this approach, and it was considered,

[82] As is the case in Australia: see Family Law Act 1975, s 90SB.

albeit ultimately dismissed, by the Law Commission in 2007. Moreover, Miles notes it often is logical for a country operating equitable redistribution for spouses to align that model for cohabitants (rather than say rule-based sharing under a community of property for spouses and equitable redistribution for cohabitants, or vice versa).[83]

This proposal, however, does not favour this option. Rather, a more limited form of discretion will be advocated that offers an appropriate balance of rules and discretion. This is more consistent with the approaches adopted in Ireland and Scotland. Instead of using the rationales applicable under the Matrimonial Causes Act 1973, this proposal will seek to give legal recognition to the concept of relationship-generated disadvantage. This is a modification of the Law Commission's proposal that deployed specifically defined concepts of 'economic disadvantage' and 'retained benefit'. That proposal is commendable for its rigour, but it received criticism for potentially being too rigid in its operation and for being almost too intellectual, to the extent that it might struggle to be deployed in practice.[84] Probert noted that some of the principles surrounding contributions, such as failing to recognise the payment of bills or household expenses unless the other party could not otherwise have paid the mortgage, produced outcomes that were 'no more generous than the current law of property'.[85] There is also a feeling that the stated desire by the Law Commission to differentiate its regime from marriage, given fears of undermining it, rendered the scheme overly technical.

This proposal aims to take the compensatory essence of the Law Commission scheme but inject a degree of flexibility through explicit use of fairness and guiding principles. To qualify, the applicant must make qualifying contributions to the relationship. Such contributions would be broader than those capable of triggering an interest under the implied trusts to provide meaningful protection. Thus, contributions could be both financial and non-financial in nature, and would naturally include domestic contributions and giving up work to look after children. The court would then look at the overall economic position of the parties to determine whether a change has occurred. It must be demonstrated that these contributions have placed the applicant in a position of relationship-generated disadvantage and the respondent in a correlating position of economic advantage. Here, a causal connection between the contribution and position of the applicant must be demonstrated.

Once a change is found, judges would then be empowered to remedy such disadvantage by fairly compensating the other party and conversely reversing an advantage by fairly distributing it. This will be a holistic exercise that can consider the current financial circumstances of both parties and future considerations,

[83] Miles (n 45) 82.

[84] See D Hughes, M Davis and L Jacklin, 'Come live with me and be my love – a consideration of the 2007 Law Commission proposals on cohabitation breakdown' [2008] *Conveyancer and Property Lawyer* 197.

[85] R Probert, 'A Review of "Cohabitation: The Financial Consequences of Relationship Breakdown", Law Com No 307 (HMSO 2007)' (2007) 41(3) *Family Law Quarterly* 521, 529.

such as the reduced earning capacity of the applicant. Like the Law Commission's proposal, a truncated list of factors could be created to guide the exercise of discretion, with a particular emphasis placed on the needs of children and the resources of the parties, albeit without requiring the applicant to show financial dependency, which has overly restricted the effectiveness of the Irish regime.[86]

Space precludes a detailed articulation of all aspects of this proposal, but the sketch above should reveal that it is an amalgam of several proposals and existing regimes. It adopts at its core the principle of compensation deemed appropriate for cohabitants, but seeks to avoid the mathematical precision of the Law Commission's proposal by injecting a bounded and principle-guided discretion. This provides much-needed flexibility, but it would fall short of conferring an expansive discretion as seen, for example, in Lord Lester of Herne Hill's proposal from 2008. His Cohabitation Bill offered a limited financial claim like the Law Commission's, but it enabled judges to make orders whenever 'just and equitable to do so', having regard to a range of factors that were highly reminiscent of those applicable upon divorce, albeit with the controversial sharing principle expunged.

The remedies that could be awarded would include the full menu available under the Matrimonial Causes Act 1973 and include periodical payments (unlike the Law Commission's proposal that permitted them only in narrowly drawn circumstances). The justification for this approach is another finding of the Scottish Law Commission's consultation exercise that is now recommending an increase in the range of orders available to better provide flexibility and bespoke outcomes in the circumstances of the case.[87] However, there will be an emphasis placed on the need for clean break and the severing of financial ties. Open-ended maintenance orders, such as those without a term imposed, will not be available under this proposal, and a strong focus will be placed on facilitating financial independence through applicants' becoming self-supporting. Given the current controversy over the use of such orders upon divorce and dissolution, this proposal will adopt a cautious approach and require judges to offer cogent reasons for their use in the cohabitation context. It is anticipated that this regime will not produce headline-grabbing, windfall pay-outs or media narratives surrounding 'meal tickets for life', and instead will offer a safety net to cohabitants.

Blending rules with a bounded framework of discretion will mean there will be judicial evolution of principles. This is important, especially for out-of-court negotiation in the current context where legal aid has all but vanished. Reflecting on the extensive jurisprudence in Australia, Parkinson has noted the importance of this and remarked that today the 'challenge is how to bargain in the shadow of the law when the law casts very little shadow'.[88] Thus, courts will be required

[86] See, eg, J Mee, 'Cohabitation law reform in Ireland' (2011) 23(3) *Child and Family Law Quarterly* 323.

[87] See Scottish Law Commission (n 49) paras 5.71–5.79.

[88] Parkinson (n 73) 282.

to develop the understanding of key elements and concepts within the proposal to ensure the scheme is responsive and capable of tackling the core rationale of the regime, relationship-generated disadvantage. The understanding of that concept will be developed incrementally, with appellate courts able to restrain excessive or impermissible interpretations of the statutory provisions.[89]

iv. Rejection of the Scheme through an Opt-Out Agreement

As the scheme operates in a default manner, that is without couples' voluntarily entering into it, there must be an option for them to disapply the scheme or opt-out. This aspect is likely to be the most controversial, and careful thought is needed in terms of how it is articulated to the public. The potential for opposition stems from the belief that the imposition of remedies upon those who have not voluntarily assumed them violates couple autonomy, invades privacy and converts cohabiting relationships into marriages ex post facto.[90] It has also been criticised for failing to appreciate the diversity of cohabiting relationships. As Atwood and Cahn note:

> Any legal regime that forces these varied forms of nonmarital couplehood into a single prototype might provide simplicity and clarity but at the same time risks standardizing non-standard relationships based on a set of norms that may not be applicable.[91]

Moreover, a scheme based on ascription can involve an intrusive examination of a couple's life and may also generate outcomes that go against a couple's expectations of their relationship and its legal consequences.

This proposal must confront these arguments and offer an effective balance between protection from relationship-generated disadvantage and respect for autonomy. A key element to this would be for couples to disapply the scheme via an opt-out agreement. This would be a written and signed agreement by the parties that expresses a clear shared intention to disapply the scheme. Unlike the Law Commission's proposal, under this proposal there will be a requirement for couples to obtain separate legal advice to ensure a full appreciation of the implications of opting out.

If this proposal is enacted, there must be clear messaging about this function and the nature of the scheme. It must be noted that, even without an opt-out agreement, the imposition of remedies would be far from automatic. Entitlement would

[89] See, eg, P Parkinson, 'Why Are Decisions on Family Property So Inconsistent?' (2016) 90 *Australian Law Journal* 498.

[90] See, inter alia, R Deech, 'The Case against Legal Recognition of Cohabitation' (1980) 29 *International and Comparative Law Quarterly* 480; Auchmuty (n 27); and M Garrison, 'Is Consent Necessary? An Evaluation of the Emerging Law of Cohabitant Obligation' (2005) 52 *UCLA Law Review* 815.

[91] B Atwood and N Cahn, 'Nonmarital Cohabitants: The US Approach' (2022) 44 *Houston Journal of International Law* 191, 217. See also N Cahn and J Carbone, 'Blackstonian Marriage, Gender, and Cohabitation' (2019) 51 *Arizona State Law Journal* 1247.

not arise from the mere fact of the relationship's existence. Unlike the de facto regimes in New Zealand and Australia, which in effect treat qualifying couples identically to spouses, there are multiple hurdles for an applicant to surmount before they receive remedies. Not only must they satisfy the definition of cohabitant and eligibility criteria, but they must also evidence requisite contributions that justify the court's intervention.

Similarly, clear guidance must be provided about the default scheme itself, for couples to be aware that they must enter an agreement. Aloni's research on Canada is particularly insightful on this point, reporting that around one-third to one-half of interviewees did not know enough about the opt-out property-sharing regime in British Columbia to make informed decisions as to whether to disapply it.[92] This issue will need to be confronted when the parameters of the scheme are publicised.

IV. Securing Reform

Any proposed cohabitation reform needs to be evidence-based and grounded in empirical insights so that it can effectively tackle the specific issues faced by cohabitants in a particular jurisdiction. It must be viable in terms of having a strong likelihood of working well in practice. But equally important is the need for it not to be merely an academic thought experiment but something that actually reaches the statute book. It is all well and good for academics, practitioners and policy-makers to concoct reform proposals, but these need to leave the realm of fantasy family law and instead be translated into practice.

At present, there appears to be little political appetite for reform on the part of the Government, although positive signs are coming from the Labour Party. The Law Commission's review of financial remedies will see a considerable amount of the Commission's time and resources channelled towards that project, but cohabitation is excluded from the remit of that review.[93] A separate review by the Ministry of Justice or Government Equalities Office is conceivable but highly unlikely, given the Government's comprehensive rejection of recommendations made by the Women and Equalities Committee Inquiry. Moreover, while that response saw the Government back increased public awareness, it did not commit any funds to that activity. Even if such funding were available, such campaigns have been questioned in terms of their effectiveness.

What is needed instead is further strategising and activism to place cohabitation reform back on the political agenda. Raising awareness of the disadvantage faced by some cohabitants is one method, but this is difficult to do in an abstract sense. A high-profile case, equivalent to *Owens v Owens*, which provided impetus

[92] E Aloni, 'Compulsory Conjugality' (2021) 53(1) *Connecticut Law Review* 55.

[93] See Law Commission, 'Review to examine 50-year-old laws on finances after divorce and the ending of a civil partnership' (4 April 2023).

in the campaign for no-fault divorce, is one method of getting the issue recognised, but it is not without challenges.[94] Given the limited claims that cohabitants currently can bring, the potential route into court would be a dispute based on implied trusts or proprietary estoppel.[95] To evidence the injustice of the existing law, it would need to be a sole-legal-title dispute, where one party has failed to establish a beneficial interest despite making significant non-financial contributions (they would have to be non-financial, given that financial contributions would trigger a resulting or constructive trust). Litigating a modern-day 'Mrs Burns' scenario is further hampered by the risks associated with legal proceedings and the costs involved, although it is hoped that any legal representation would be offered on a pro bono basis.[96] Human rights litigation, as seen with cases such as *McLaughlin*[97] and *Brewster*,[98] might be another option for extending to cohabitants specific benefits presently reserved to spouses, but it may encounter resistance, especially considering prevailing human rights scepticism. There is no positive obligation on states to introduce cohabitation reform, and at present the United Kingdom exceeds the level of protections demanded by the European Convention on Human Rights and the Strasbourg Court.[99]

Even if such a case were found and media interest generated, careful thought is needed as to how its message is presented to the public. The language used to justify the case for cohabitation reform can sometimes risk alienating members of the public. While a poll of Resolution members in 2019 saw 63 per cent of respondents state that women are more likely to fare worse than men in these disputes, a narrative emphasising vulnerability, plight or a lack of autonomy will fail to allow individuals to identify with this issue (especially those who would dispute that characterisation).[100] Even the term 'safety net' can be criticised for suggesting that cohabitants must in some way be rescued or protected from the mistakes they might make. Nuance and legal accuracy might not sell newspapers, but equally, homogenising cohabitants or painting them as supplicants will likely fail to gain traction either. Instead, as this proposal advocates, reform should be grounded in more neutral terms like 'relationship-generated disadvantage'.

Other routes to securing reform would be for constituents to lobby their MPs. There may be support among MPs, and in 2013 a Resolution poll of MPs found

[94] *Owens v Owens* [2018] UKSC 41.

[95] Governed by principles expressed in *Lloyds Bank v Rosset* [1990] UKHL 14.

[96] See the well-known case of *Burns v Burns* [1984] Ch 317, discussed in A Hayward, '*Burns v Burns*: The Fable Forty Years On' in M Briggs and A Hayward, *Research Handbook on Family Property and the Law* (Cheltenham, Edward Elgar, 2024) 443.

[97] *In the matter of an application by Siobhan Mclaughlin for Judicial Review (Northern Ireland)* [2018] UKSC 48.

[98] *In the matter of an application by Denise Brewster for Judicial Review (Northern Ireland)* [2017] UKSC 8.

[99] See H Rodway, 'Invoking human rights to protect unmarried couples' (2022) 34(3) *Child and Family Law Quarterly* 221.

[100] See Resolution's Written Evidence to the Women and Equalities Committee.

60 per cent favouring greater legal protections for cohabitants upon separation. Although the political make-up of both Houses has changed since then, it is still hoped that the issue may be raised again in debates, and preferably through introduction of a Private Member's Bill. Engagement with MPs by practitioner organisations is of crucial importance too, as seen with the recent successful campaign for no-fault divorce.[101] Resolution, for example, runs a Cohabitation Awareness Week, and reform in this area is now considered the top priority in their latest Vision for Family Justice, launched in November 2023.[102]

V. Conclusion

Writing in 2014, former President of the Family Division of the High Court, Sir James Munby, remarked:

> Reform is desperately needed – has been desperately needed for at least forty years. The Law Commission has recommended reform. Thus far Governments have failed to act. Reform is inevitable. It is inconceivable that society will not right this injustice in due course.[103]

But a decade later, reforming legal protections for cohabitants remains a challenge in England and Wales. This fact is more striking when it is appreciated how far behind this jurisdiction is when compared to others. New South Wales in Australia introduced protections for de facto couples 40 years ago, which were extended to all at the federal level in Australia in 2008.[104] And closer to home, Scotland introduced protections in 2006, and is now in the enviable position of strengthening that earlier reform. We are not the only country pushing for reform either.

The need for change is fully understood by academics,[105] members of the judiciary[106] and practitioners. It currently represents the centrepiece of future reform priorities of practitioner organisations such as Resolution and the Family

[101] See G Fraser and A Hayward, 'Securing cohabitation reform: building a movement and why collaboration matters' (2023) 224 *Resolution – The Review* at https://resolution.org.uk/the-review/archive/the-review-issue-224/securing-cohabitation-reform-building-a-movement-and-why-collaboration-matters/.

[102] Resolution, *Vision for Family Justice* (November 2023) at https://resolution.org.uk/wp-content/uploads/2023/11/Resolution-Vision-for-Family-Justice-full-221123.pdf.

[103] Sir James Munby, '21st Century Family Law', *The 2014 Michael Farmer Memorial Lecture* (Bangor University, 2014) at https://www.judiciary.uk/wp-content/uploads/2014/10/munby-speech-bangor-10102014.pdf.

[104] See New South Wales: De Facto Relationships Act 1984 (later renamed the Property (Relationships) Act 1984 in 1999) and the Family Law Amendment (De Facto Financial Matters and Other Measures) Act 2008 (Commonwealth). See also the Family Court Act 1997 and the Interpretation Act 1984 (applicable in Western Australia).

[105] See Written Evidence submitted to the Women and Equalities Committee, *Rights of Cohabiting Partners Inquiry*.

[106] See *Burns v Burns* (n 96) (especially Fox and May LLJ); and *Gow v Grant* [2012] UKSC 29.

Law Bar Association. In addition, reform finds support among members of the public here, and the experience of other countries shows changes have been received 'with very little questioning or complaint'.[107]

So it is curious why proposals sharing similarities with the one advanced in this chapter have yet to be introduced; a fact that is even more surprising given the considerable amount of time that reform has been on the radar of policy makers and the Law Commission. In one sense, cohabitation reform could just be a matter of time as, previously, energy and resources were merely channelled elsewhere in the form of changes to civil partnerships and no-fault divorce. But it is argued that this not the only explanation, especially considering the experience of other jurisdictions. What is clear is that the prospect of change today still generates strong opinions, as seen from evidence submitted to the Women and Equalities Committee Inquiry. As Probert noted in her evidence to that inquiry, cohabitation reform now has the rather unusual ability to unite opponents of all political colours and persuasions, including *Daily Mail* readers, fearful that reform will undermine marriage, and *The Guardian* readers, concerned about an invasion of autonomy.[108]

As the chapters in this collection reveal, family-law reform is a process, rather than a single act, so these differing views and perspectives must form part of that conversation. This is key to ensuring that comprehensive support can be obtained, there is satisfaction with any law created, and that relationship-generated disadvantage can be tackled effectively in the unique context presented by England and Wales.

[107] Parkinson (n 73) 283.

[108] See Oral Evidence Transcript (22 September 2021) at https://committees.parliament.uk/oralevidence/2785/pdf/.

Response to Chapter 9

Cohabitation Reform in England and Wales: Time for Action

ROB GEORGE*

I. Introduction

While there remains a minority view within the family law academy and practitioner base that opposes any meaningful expansion of the rights of cohabitants in England and Wales, the clearly dominant view is that 'something must be done'. Andy Hayward's chapter sets out the compelling evidence as to why the argument for reform is so persuasive.

Demographics provide the underlying basis for change: the rise and rise of cohabitation shows no signs of abating, and (outside certain religious and cultural groups) there is no significant stigma attached to unmarried cohabitation, nor to having a child without being in a formalised relationship.

The existing law is also, evidently, unsatisfactory. The piecemeal approach to reform over the last 50 years has resulted in a hotch-potch of legal provisions that experienced lawyers struggle to catalogue, let alone apply. These provisions create arbitrary distinctions around eligibility and the scope of any available remedies, and the most valuable of them in many cases – schedule 1 to the Children Act 1989 – is widely misconceived as being 'law for the wealthy'; it is a failure of the collective imagination that schedule 1 applications are not as common as applications for financial remedies under the Matrimonial Causes Act (MCA) 1973. While cohabitants can, in theory, self-regulate with cohabitation contracts, the reality is that few do;[1] and the one thing they cannot contract into is the broad discretionary regime that applies to those who formalise their relationship.

At the same time, this unsatisfactory legal framework sits against a background of a widespread but seemingly unshakable popular belief that legal

* Professor of Law and Policy, University College London. I am grateful to Alison Diduck and Mavis Maclean for comments on an earlier draft of this chapter; as ever, the views and any errors remain my own.

[1] See discussion in E Sutherland, 'Unmarried Cohabitation' in J Eekelaar and R George (eds), *Routledge Handbook of Family Law and Policy*, 2nd edn (Abingdon, Routledge, 2021) 67.

remedies accrue to cohabitants on largely the same basis as for married couples and civil partners.[2] The lack of any legal remedy for cohabitants therefore comes as a surprise when the moment of need arises. (In the context of separation, it may be a welcome surprise for the more economically powerful partner; it will rarely be welcome in the event of death.)

It follows that I take no issue at all with the idea that there should be reform, and that this is a pressing priority. I also think that there is a pragmatism to Hayward's proposal: it builds on existing experience of our near-neighbours in Scotland and on the Law Commission's work in 2007, 'using comparative family law insights to modify certain elements'. This approach presents what may be a more palatable option for reform-minded politicians conscious of the need to avoid politically difficult positions, and aligns closely with the views of the Women and Equalities Committee in 2022 and of the professional groups represented by Resolution and the Family Law Bar Association. I agree that there is political opposition to significant reform (or possibly any reform), and so proposals need to be alive to that political reality; there is wisdom in seeking to capitalise on existing reformist agendas from respected bodies.

However, despite the merits of the argument, for me, this proposal is not the answer as a matter of principle. My view, as I will set out, is that the evidence supports a more extensive, but also far more straightforward, reform – the extension of the discretionary regime of the MCA 1973 to unmarried couples, as already happens in Australia, New Zealand and many jurisdictions in Canada.

II. Arguments of Principle

My first point is that I think there is a danger of underplaying concerns about power imbalances in relationships. This point is made in Hayward's chapter, noting as he does that there is potential for the current law to be exploited by a financially stronger party. But I think it goes further. I think we need to ask about the reasons why couples do and do not formalise their relationships. Some actively oppose the legal regime or state involvement in their personal lives;[3] some think that there is an inherent patriarchal or religious undertone to marriage,[4] though

[2] A Barlow et al, 'Cohabitation and the Law: Myths, Money and the Media' in A Park et al (eds), *British Social Attitudes: The 24th Report* (London, NatCen Social Research, 2008) 29.

[3] This view is central to the arguments against legal regulation of cohabitation put forward to Ruth Deech. See, eg, R Deech, *Cohabitation and the Law* (Gresham Lecture, 17 November 2009) at www.gresham.ac.uk/watch-now/cohabitation-and-law. It is unclear how widely held these views are in the general population.

[4] See the views expressed by the appellants in *R (Steinfeld and Keidan) v Secretary of State for International Development* [2018] UKSC 32, [2020] AC 1.

note Lady Hale's comment that this view is not really rational in the modern era;[5] many do not know that it matters, legally speaking;[6] and some intend to marry but do not because something comes up that disrupts their plans and they never get around to it.[7] But do we start with the assumption that these decisions are all made on the basis of an equality of bargaining power, by legally rational actors each able to look out for their own interests?[8] Jacob LJ puts is well in the comment quoted by Hayward in his chapter: 'human emotional relationships simply do not operate as if they were commercial contracts and it is idle to wish that they did'.[9] The same theme is apparent in Lady Hale's dissenting judgment in *Radmacher v Granatino*, where – this time in the context of the question of autonomy in 'choosing' to enter a nuptial agreement or not – she comments:

> Some may regard people who are about to marry as in all respects fully autonomous beings; others may wonder whether people who are typically (although not invariably) in love can be expected to make rational choices in the same way that businessmen can. Some may regard the recognition of these factual differences as patronising or paternalistic; others may regard them as sensible and realistic.[10]

People do not always have autonomous free choice about the status of their relationship. If you are in a relationship with someone who refuses to marry or enter a civil partnership, they have an absolute veto over that; your choice is to accept it and continue the relationship, or leave. But those are not always free choices. Those who have children, or who are pregnant, or who have a significant imbalance in financial resources, or whose immigration status is contingent on the continuation of their relationship (to take just a few examples) are not free 'just' to leave. The autonomy being promoted here is only really autonomy for one of the parties, inevitably the one in the stronger bargaining position.[11] So I do not doubt that there are some couples who both share a wish not to have any formalised aspect to their relationship, not to have it recognised by the state, not to have any legal rights or obligations towards one another; but I do not think that there is any

[5] B Hale, 'What is a 21st Century Family?' (Watford, International Centre for Law, Policy and Practice, 2019) at www.supremecourt.uk/docs/speech-190701.pdf. In this context, she notes that marriage has 'lost virtually all the legal trappings associated with the old patriarchal and dynastic system. But pure reason is not to be expected when it comes to personal relationships.'

[6] See Barlow et al (n 2); M Albakri et al, 'Relationships and Gender Identity: Public Attitudes within the Context of Legal Reform' in J Curtice et al (eds), *British Social Attitudes 36* (London, NatCen Social Research, 2019) 112.

[7] J Eekelaar and M Maclean, 'Marriage and the Moral Bases of Personal Relationships' (2004) 31(4) *Journal of Law and Society* 510; M Maclean and J Eekelaar, 'The Obligations and Expectations of Couples within Families: Three Modes of Interaction' (2004) 26(2) *Journal of Social Welfare and Family Law* 117.

[8] This seems to be Deech's view, maintained in her evidence to the Women and Equalities Committee, *The Rights of Cohabiting Partners, Second Report of Session 2022–23 HC 92* (2023–2022) para 44.

[9] *Jones v Kernott* [2010] EWCA Civ 578 [90].

[10] *Radmacher v Granatino* [2010] UKSC 42 [135].

[11] That is not necessarily to imply an intentional abuse of power in what Elaine Sutherland terms these 'asymmetrical couples': Sutherland (n 1) 66.

evidence to suggest that this approach is common. Indeed, the evidence suggests that a large majority of people think that there should be legal rights and responsibilities attached to cohabitation,[12] as I will come back to shortly.

Related to this is the argument about functional equivalence between couples who formalise their relationships and those who do not. Hayward describes the argument for equal legal treatment as 'mak[ing] sense for many couples *that function in an analogous way to spouses*, through intertwining their lives, financial affairs and provision of care for children' (emphasis added). Where I struggle with this argument is that there is an assumption that married couples have a default way of behaving, that there is a 'standard' model to which we can compare unmarried couples. I am not convinced that there is: in fact, I think there is huge variety under the umbrella of 'marriage' and civil partnership. Married couples may intertwine their finances to a greater extent or to a lesser extent (or not at all!);[13] they may share childcare or other caring responsibilities in more equal ways or in less equal ways (or one spouse may in reality do all of this work). The default assumptions about how a young(ish), first-time married couple behave (buying a property together if they can; having children together if they can) may or may not apply to an older, second- or third-time married couple with existing properties and teenage or adult children. Couples' approaches to money, both within and outside marriage, vary widely and change over time.[14] This huge variation is a large part of the reason why the bespoke financial remedies regime that we have on divorce or dissolution makes sense. Consequently, the argument that cohabiting couples somehow fail to 'match up' to what we expect of 'committed' (married) couples relies on assumptions about marriage that are, at best, a partial picture.

Hayward argues against complete assimilation of unmarried couples into the MCA regime on the basis that *sharing* of financial assets on separation 'could be viewed as overly generous and potentially inappropriate', particularly in the context of short relationships. However, the law will inevitably be setting a lower threshold for the duration of the relationship before which this regime will not apply at all; consequently, unlike in marriage and civil partnership cases, where financial remedies are available even if the marriage lasts only a single day,[15] the law will already be setting a minimum duration that is deemed necessary before a

[12] A Barlow, C Burgoyne and J Smithson, 'The Living Together Campaign – The Impact on Cohabitants' [2007] *Family Law* 165.

[13] C Vogler, 'Managing Money in Intimate Relationships: Similarities and Differences Between Cohabiting and Married Couples' in J Miles and R Probert (eds), *Sharing Lives, Dividing Assets: An Interdisciplinary Study* (Oxford, Hart Publishing, 2009) 61.

[14] See, eg, J Pahl, 'Individualisation in Couple Finances: Who Pays for the Children?' (2005) 4(4) *Social Policy and Society* 381; C Vogler, M Brockmann and R Wiggins, 'Intimate Relationships and Changing Patterns of Money Management at the Beginning of the Twenty-First Century' (2006) 57(3) *British Journal of Sociology* 455.

[15] There is a minimum period of time before either party can apply for divorce, but they can separate in practice immediately after the marriage ceremony.

claim can be brought. More generally, the law already accommodates this 'problem' within the post-divorce financial remedies system. *Miller v Miller* itself was such a case,[16] the marriage lasting less than three years: Mrs Miller received a total of £5m, amounting to less than one-sixth of the total assets, despite the fact that much of their value had been created during the subsistence of the marriage. The law can therefore demonstrably accommodate the need to account for short relationships in determining the fair allocation of resources.

While Hayward sees a focus on needs as 'much more appropriate', he suggests that it will be criticised because 'cohabitants have not assumed the responsibility to cater for each other's needs in all circumstances'. However, that claim is not actually straightforward. Of course, most unmarried cohabitants have not taken vows and thereby positively accepted that they should be responsible for each other, 'for richer, for poorer' and so on (though it is worth noting that those in religious marriages with non-qualifying ceremonies have positively done this, just not in a way that marriage law recognises). But in a great many contexts, the law recognises and enforces obligations based not on positive assertion by the respondent, but on the parties' actions. The administrative law concept of legitimate expectation and even more so tort law's *assumption of responsibility* for the financial losses of another are obvious examples. The law does not therefore need a positive, explicit acceptance of responsibility for it to be imposed based on that party's behaviour. Indeed, we see this already in family law: child support liability is based on the mere fact of being a legal parent, irrespective of the circumstances by which that came about, and indeed even if the father has good moral reasons not to be liable.[17] The empirical evidence is that cohabiting couples 'show just as much commitment to their partnership when compared like for like, as married people'.[18]

III. Arguments of Practice

The second limb of my argument relates to the practical realities of the various options.

One of the major advantages of the assimilation route is that the law is already there, well understood. One of the benefits of the MCA scheme (though I accept that not everyone sees this as an advantage) is that it is bespoke. Judges are used

[16] *Miller v Miller* [2006] UKHL 24, [2006] 2 AC 618.

[17] See, eg, the much-publicised cases of sperm donors: R Williams, 'Sperm donor to lesbian couple forced to pay child support' *The Guardian* (4 December 2007) at www.theguardian.com/politics/2007/dec/04/gayrights.immigrationpolicy; and M Brignall, 'Gay sperm donor told to pay child maintenance for "his" two children' *The Guardian* (26 October 2012) at www.theguardian.com/money/2012/oct/26/gay-sperm-donor-pay-child-support-maintenance.

[18] A Barlow et al, *Cohabitation, Marriage and the Law: Social Change and Legal Reform in the 21st Century* (Oxford, Hart Publishing, 2005) 74; Eekelaar and Maclean (n 7) 538.

to deciding cases based on the specific nuances of the facts, and lawyers are used to advising about them, with a strong track record of successful negotiation before and during litigation.[19] Just as the MCA scheme can account for short marriages, different ways of holding assets within a family or specific agreements reached by the parties before, during or after the formalisation of their relationship, the fact that the relationship was never formalised and, more importantly, some understanding of the particular reasons *why* it was not formalised could be accommodated by the scheme. In some cases, the financial order would be identical and the fact of marriage or not might prove to be irrelevant; more often, I suspect, that would not be the case.

One concern that arises in the context of the assimilationist reform that I favour is the 'public disquiet' (as the Law Commission termed it[20]) if cohabitants were to be treated the same as married couples. The evidential basis for this concern is unclear to me. Research in 2007, at the same time as the Law Commission's work, showed overwhelming support for precisely this arrangement: 90 per cent of respondents said that cohabitants with children should have the same rights as married couples, and 85 per cent still thought that in cases with no children.[21] The better part of 20 years later, with unmarried cohabitation rates having increased[22] and a majority of children now born outside marriage,[23] there is reason to think that, if anything, those view will have strengthened. So I am unclear why there would be 'public disquiet'. The Law Commission appeared to base its view on the fact that the MCA 1973 'may generate enormous awards even after very short marriages'.[24] Well, it *may*, but it almost always does not; every case is different, and outcomes are explained and justified on the facts by the judges deciding them. There are two things to say about this argument. The first is that making general rules based on exceptional cases is, in my view, a flawed approach to policy. The courts should be trusted to make appropriate decisions on the particular facts of the cases. We know that everyday financial remedy cases bear little resemblance to the headline-grabbing high net-worth cases heard in the High Court,[25] so these cases provide no guide to what would happen in the vast

[19] See, eg, J Eekelaar, M Maclean and S Beinart, *Family Lawyers: The Divorce Work of Solicitors* (Oxford, Hart Publishing, 2000).

[20] *Cohabitation: The Financial Consequences of Relationship Breakdown* (Law Com No 307, 2007) para 4.9.

[21] Barlow, Burgoyne and Smithson (n 12).

[22] In 2007 there were an estimated 3.56m unmarried cohabiting couples, which increased to 5.08m couples by 2020. See Office for National Statistics, *Population estimates by marital status and living arrangements, England and Wales, 2002 to 2020* (London, ONS, 2021) Table 4. Census data show the proportion of people who live in a couple who are cohabiting outside marriage/civil partnership increasing from 20.6% in 2011 to 24.3% in 2021: Office for National Statistics, *People's living arrangements in England and Wales: Census 2021* (London, ONS, 2023).

[23] 51.4% of births are outside marriage or civil partnership: Office for National Statistics, *Births in England and Wales 2022* (London, ONS, 2023) 3.

[24] *Cohabitation: The Financial Consequences of Relationship Breakdown* (n 20) para 4.9.

[25] See, eg, E Hitchings et al, *Fair Shares? Sorting Out Money and Property on Divorce* (Bristol, University of Bristol, Nuffield Foundation and Bryson Purdon Social Research, 2023); J Miles and

majority of cohabitation cases either. My second concern is that this discussion about 'enormous awards', as the Law Commission termed them, may be a form of sexism. Even the term 'award' suggests some kind of prize or benevolence that is being bestowed, whereas the order is, to the contrary, an entitlement, a reflection of what is *owed*.[26] The wife (usually) is not a supplicant, nor is she seeking to win something akin to the lottery; the argument reminds me uncomfortably of *Daily Mail*-style headlines, where the wife is invariably presented as 'winning', as if she had entered a competition.[27]

My final issue is the complexity of the proposal, which was also a difficulty that I had with the Law Commission's proposals in 2007. While the MCA scheme does rely on a reasonably detailed understanding of the parties' financial positions, the approach uses broad brushstrokes that allow an overall 'fair' outcome to be reached. By contrast, the model proposed for cohabitants requires individuals to be able to identify and quantify the benefits and burdens that they each claim have resulted from their relationship (issues which will often be disputed between them). There is a danger that, just as successful examples of 'compensation' claims in MCA cases are vanishingly rare,[28] so too applicants under the new scheme might find the court reluctant to recognise their entitlements, such that the reform does little to improve outcomes in many cases. The complexity of the scheme does not encourage settlements, and there are potentially endless permutations about what 'counts' and does not count as a relevant change of circumstances. It is said that a 'causal connection' will be required, but existing cases show us that causal connections in the context of family decisions are in the eye of the beholder.[29] I am unclear how the 'holistic exercise' will then work, since it is expressly not the same process as under the MCA 1973.

IV. Concluding Thoughts

I would not want to give any impression that I am opposed to the reform that Hayward has proposed. As I set out at the start, I think that there are strong

E Hitchings, 'Financial Remedy Outcomes in England and Wales: Not a Meal Ticket for Life' (2018) 32 *Australian Journal of Family Law* 43; E Hitchings, 'Chaos or Consistency? Ancillary Relief in the "Everyday" case' in J Miles and R Probert (eds), *Sharing Lives, Dividing Assets: An Interdisciplinary Study* (Oxford, Hart Publishing, 2009) 185.

[26] See, eg, *Miller v Miller; McFarlane v McFarlane* [2006] UKHL 24, [2006] 2 AC 618 [9]: 'The claimant is not a supplicant. Each party to a marriage is *entitled* to a *fair* share of the available property' (per Lord Nicholls, original emphasis).

[27] A smattering of examples (italic emphasis added): 'Beauty Queen Kirsty Bertarelli *wins* Britain's biggest split settlement …'; 'Britain's biggest-EVER divorce settlement *awarded* to ex-wife …'; 'Wife *wins* £4.25m divorce payout …'; 'Entrepreneur's ex-wife *wins* £1m boost to her divorce payout'.

[28] *RC v JC* [2020] EWHC 466 (Fam) [72]: 'very much the exception'; 'rare'.

[29] I am thinking of *Radmacher* (n 10) again, where Mr Granatino's decision to leave his City job and do a PhD was seen as being for the benefit of the family by Lady Hale, and as only for his own benefit by the majority of the court.

arguments for taking a pragmatic approach and getting something done, and in the present political environment it may well be that Hayward's proposal has a greater likelihood of being accepted than any other. If that reform could be achieved, it would be a major step forward and one that would significantly improve the lives of a great many people. But it is not a reform that excites me. Perhaps the focus should be on doing what we can: doing something is, in this context, far better than doing nothing. I hope, though, that we might be able to do more.

My view is that we are trying to reinvent the wheel to accommodate outdated sensibilities that are held by significant numbers of policy makers (including MPs and Peers) but by very few members of the population more generally. Far easier, and far more appropriate, simply to use the existing MCA scheme.

10

Nullity Reform: Redefining Marriage

ALEXANDER MAINE

I. Introduction

Marriage is arguably in a time of transition, at once more inclusive and welcoming than ever but declining in significance for many. Marriage has evolved considerably in the last two decades. New avenues of relationship recognition were created and then expanded in the introduction of civil partnership for same-sex couples in 2004 and the inclusion of different-sex couples in 2019.[1] Same-sex marriage then built on the progress of civil partnerships in 2013, redefining marriage to include gay and lesbian relationships.[2] The procedure for divorce has been simplified, allowing couples to end their marriage in a way that is intended to minimise costs and acrimony.[3] The vast changes that have occurred to marriage processes, cultures and practices tell us about the changing shape of society and the increasing liberalisation of relationship norms and growing acceptance of a diversity of families. Marriage remains an integral feature of society, and continues to occupy a central space in the UK's social imagination, being widely celebrated, popular and contributing to the economy,[4] while celebrity and royal weddings continue to capture the imagination of the UK and other countries around the world.[5]

[1] Civil Partnership Act 2004; Civil Partnership, Marriages and Deaths (Registration etc) Act 2019.

[2] Marriage (Same-Sex Couples) Act 2013; see A Maine, 'The Hierarchy of Marriage and Civil Partnerships: Diversifying Relationship Recognition' in F Hamilton and G Noto La Diega (eds), *Same-Sex Relationships, Law and Social Change* (London, Routledge, 2020) 209, 212.

[3] Divorce, Dissolution and Separation Act 2020.

[4] The average wedding costs £18,000 and the wedding industry as a whole is worth £14.7 billion: Sonas, 'An Overview of the Wedding Industry' at www.sonas.events/blog/an-overview-of-the-uk-wedding-industry/#:~:text=The%20UK%20wedding%20industry%20is,has%20needed%20to%20adapt%20quickly (accessed 5 June 2023); see also at www.hitched.co.uk/wedding-planning/organising-and-planning/the-average-wedding-cost-in-the-uk-revealed/ (accessed 5 June 2023).

[5] On 19 May 2018, an estimated 29.2 million people viewed the Royal Wedding of Prince Harry of Wales and Meghan Markle, later the Duke and Duchess of Sussex, which took place at Windsor Castle in England. See at www.nielsen.com/insights/2018/over-29-million-viewers-watch-prince-harry-and-meghan-markles-wedding/#:~:text=Television%20Audience%20Estimates,at%20Windsor%20Castle%20in%20England (accessed 5 June 2023).

Marriage rates have continued to fall since the 1970s, while more couples continue to cohabit.[6] Despite the advent of same-sex marriage, and the inclusion of a new demographic able to form marital relationships, marriage is of decreasing significance: marriage may not accurately reflect the relationship forms that exist, while for some it actively discriminates against certain relationship forms, such as non-monogamy, polyamory and political aversions to marriage formed in feminist and queer thought. The exclusionary nature of marriage stems from the provisions related to its formation, particularly nullity provisions. Nullity provisions insist that only certain couples may marry and that only certain types of marital relationships are deemed legitimate. These are, by definition, exclusionary, maintaining standards of recognition for couples. Some of these standards are necessary from a safeguarding perspective, particularly age and capacity, while some bar non-conventional relationship forms from marriage. An example of the beneficial approach to reforming these discriminatory standards can be seen in the creation of same-sex marriage, amending nullity provisions that required a marriage to be between two people of the opposite sex.[7]

Nullity and the process of annulment refer to the declaration of an act or thing that is legally void. In reference to marriage, a decree of nullity, or the annulment of marriage, means that the marriage is void, therefore legally never having existed, thus not having any legal effect. The process of annulment and the declaration of a marriage as void is not always strictly necessary, but even when not necessary may be desirable in providing clarity and certainty that a marriage contains no legal consequences and that the parties are not married. A decree of nullity, though declaring a marriage to have never legally existed, does enable parties to bring claims for financial relief.

Nullity is a doctrine of marriage that upholds retained discriminatory and exclusionary standards of marriage. Nullity exists to provide a means of relationship breakdown, separate from divorce, enabling courts to distinguish between a validly formed marriage and one that has a flaw in its creation. It is distinct from divorce, which ends a validly formed marriage. Nullity provides a definition of what a marriage should be, how it should be created and celebrated, and how couples should co-exist as partners. It does this by stipulating the parameters of relationships that may marry and establishing the grounds on which a marriage may be declared invalid if it is voidable. Nullity is useful in telling us what a valid marriage is, but we can question such validity as being reliant on outdated

[6] The proportion of people who live in a couple that are cohabiting (not in a marriage or civil partnership) has increased from 20.6% in 2011 to 24.3% in 2021, an increase across all age groups aged under 85 years. Office for National Statistics at www.ons.gov.uk/peoplepopulationandcommunity/householdcharacteristics/homeinternetandsocialmediausage/articles/livingarrangementsofpeopleinenglandandwales/census2021#:~:text=1.-,Main%20points,groups%20aged%20under%2085%20years (accessed 5 June 2023). See also HC Women and Equalities Committee, 'The rights of cohabiting partners: Government response to the Committee's Second Report' (2022).

[7] Section 11(c) of the Matrimonial Causes Act 1973 omitted by virtue of the Marriage (Same Sex Couples) Act 2013, s 21(3), sch 7, para 27.

standards, as was done in the redefinition of marriage to include same-sex couples. These standards rely on the construction of the legally valid couple, which 'still retains substantial normative influence on the legal understanding of family'.[8]

It is against this backdrop that we will consider further reform of marriage in order to abandon some of its traditional legal features that may be deemed exclusionary, restrictive or discriminatory. First, this chapter will examine void marriages, considering the grounds on which a marriage may be declared void and what may replace, or be retained of, these grounds. Second, we will turn to voidable marriages, and similarly consider the reform or repeal of certain provisions within section 12 of the Matrimonial Causes Act (MCA) 1973. This will then lead into discussion of the possible new frameworks that can exist, particularly with the integration of no-fault divorce and those elements of nullity that should be retained. Finally, we will summarise the relevant changes to law that are needed and the means that should be taken to achieve them. Ultimately, this chapter will conclude that, in an age of more pluralised relationship recognition and facilitative family law in personal lives,[9] the validity requirements of marriage set in the 1970s are no longer appropriate for an institution that finds itself in decline. This chapter seeks to modernise the institution and make it more amenable and relevant to more couples.

II. The Context of Nullity

While the 'sexual apartheid'[10] of restricting marriage between same-sex couples has now ended, there remain provisions in nullity that preserve inequalities. Section 11 of the MCA 1973 stipulates the grounds on which a marriage is void due to a flaw in its creation. Section 12 of the 1973 Act stipulates the grounds on which a marriage may be voidable due to some defect in its operation, and therefore vulnerable to a decree of nullity. These categories render marriage problematic, in the imposing of discriminatory standards that give a party an 'out' to marriage if their partner does not fit within the traditional mononormative[11] and cisnormative[12] roles of marriage. If their new wife is pregnant by someone else, or if the new husband has a communicable venereal disease, or if their partner

[8] A Brown, *What is the Family of Law?* (Oxford, Hart Publishing, 2019) 89.

[9] J Eekelaar, Family Law and Personal Life, 2nd edn (Oxford, Oxford University Press, 2017).

[10] G Rubin, 'Thinking Sex: Notes for a Radical Theory of the Politics of Sexuality' in CS Vance (ed), *Pleasure and Danger: Exploring Female Sexuality* (London, Routledge, 1984) 159.

[11] 'Mononormativity' refers to normative expectations of monogamy that delegitimise non-monogamous or polyamorous relationships: R Bauer, 'Non-Monogamy in Queer BDSM Communities: Putting the Sex Back into Alternative Relationship Practices and Discourse' in M Barker and D Langdridge (eds), *Understanding Non-Monogamies* (London, Routledge 2010) 144.

[12] 'Cisnormativity' refers to a normative positioning of gender, which assumes that all people identify as the gender to which they were assigned at birth, to which being transgender is a disruption.

is transgender, a marriage is vulnerable to a decree of nullity due to the deeming of the marriage as voidable. If married heterosexual partners do not have a sexual relationship, their marriage is vulnerable to a decree of nullity, as it may again be deemed voidable, but a sexless same-sex marriage would not be. As the Law Commission has stated, 'our law of marriage was designed in and for another age'.[13]

Nullity is an ancient process and is tied to the conjugal nature of marriage.[14] Nullity historically existed as a way of declaring a marriage as illegitimate that would preserve the sanctity of marriage, as opposed to terminating a legally valid marriage. As Monk has stated, the famous marriages of Henry VIII were not, in fact, terminated through divorce:

> Despite the catchy rhyme, Henry VIII was never divorced: his first and fourth marriages to Catherine of Aragon and Anne of Cleves were in fact both annulled – that is, declared never to have existed in the first place. To a certain extent, the confusion is understandable: Catherine of Aragon's statement in her trial refers to 'divortium inter nos fieri'. But 'divortium' at that time referred to annulment or legal separation, and not to divorce in the modern sense of terminating a valid marriage.[15]

Annulment may ease the anxiety that exists towards divorce, particularly from a religious perspective. Divorce remains a discouraged practice in some religions,[16] and there are contentious issues regarding Islamic marriages and their legal recognition.[17] Probert has discussed the oft-mentioned definition of marriage in *Hyde v Hyde*, in which Lord Hobhouse described marriage as the 'voluntary union for life of one man and one woman to the exclusion of all others'.[18] Probert argues that a more meaningful definition of marriage was advanced in *Bellinger v Bellinger*,[19] in which it was suggested that marriage should be 'a contract for which the parties elect but which is regulated by the state, both in its formation and in its termination by divorce, because it affects status upon which depend a variety of entitlements, benefits and obligations'.[20] Probert argues that such a definition should be 'aspirational in one sense, in that it looks forward to a time when marriage can be defined in gender-neutral terms. It may yet become an accurate definition of marriage in the twenty-first century.'[21]

[13] Law Commission, *Getting Married: A Scoping Paper* (17 December 2015) 31.

[14] R Probert, 'Hyde v Hyde: Defining or Defending. Marriage?' (2007) 19 *Child and Family Law Quarterly* 322; G Douglas, *Obligation and Commitment in Family Law* (Oxford, Hart Publishing, 2018).

[15] D Monk, 'Royal Divorces and the Remaking of Marriage and Monarchy' in J Miles, D Monk, and R Probert, *Fifty Years of the Divorce Reform Act 1969* (London, Bloomsbury, 2022) 201.

[16] For instance Catholicism, in which divorced people face religious sanctions and cannot remarry in a Catholic fashion.

[17] R Probert and S Saleem, 'The Legal Treatment of Islamic Marriage Ceremonies' (2018) 7 *Oxford Journal of Law and Religion* 376.

[18] *Hyde v Hyde* (1866) LR 1 P&D 130.

[19] *Bellinger v Bellinger* [2001] EWCA Civ 1140, [2001] 2 FLR 1048.

[20] ibid [128] per Thorpe LJ.

[21] Probert (n 14) 336.

III. Void Marriages

Section 11 of the MCA 1973 establishes the grounds that would determine whether a marriage was *void ab initio*. This means that it is so flawed in its creation that it is to be treated as it if has never legally existed. A decree of nullity can be sought in order to provide legal certainty of the void marriage and allows for financial arrangements to be made for the parties. Similarly, a decree of nullity issued for parties to a void marriage would allow either party to marry again, without risk of criminal proceedings being brought for a polygamous marriage. These grounds will be analysed in order to make clear the need for reform in order to modernise and pluralise marriage, to be fit for the range of modern relationships, while also being capable of providing the clarity needed in order to recognise validly formed relationships and withhold recognition from those relationships that do not reach a threshold supportive of safeguarding measures. Some elements of section 11 should be retained in order to maintain a threshold of safeguarding measures, in order to prevent those incapable of marrying from doing so.

A. Prohibited Degrees of Relationship

Section 11(a)(i) of the MCA 1973 concerns prohibited degrees of relationships and serves to prevent people who have certain familial relationships, whether blood relatives or marital relatives, from marrying, to prevent incestual relationships for biological and social reasons. Incestuous relationships are a criminal offence,[22] and any marriage between two people within the prohibited consanguineous relationships is automatically void: the prohibited degrees are any parent/child relationship, grandparent/grandchild relationship or sibling relationships. Cousin-marriages are not automatically void, nor are they a criminal offence. Affinity relationships between those who are related through marriage (for instance a step-parent and step-child, step-grandparents/step-grandchild) and between adoptive parents and children are regulated further through the Marriage (Prohibited Degrees of Relationship) Act 1986. This Act establishes that certain affinity relationships (such as former step-parent and child relationships) do not automatically fall within the remit of section 11 of the 1973 Act, as long as the 'child' has reached the age of 21. In *B and L v United Kingdom*,[23] the European Court of Human Rights (EctHR) held that the right to marry was breached in the case of a father-in-law and daughter-in-law whose previous relationships had broken down and who were living together. They wished to marry but were unable to, because although both were above the age of 21, one of their respective original partners still lived. This amounted to a breach of Article 12 of the European Convention on Human Rights (ECHR) because the rationale behind such provisions was neither rational nor

[22] Sexual Offences Act 1956, ss 10 and 11.
[23] *B and L v United Kingdom* App no 36536/02, [2005] 3 FCR 353.

logical and served no useful purpose of public policy. Since this case, the law has been changed to remove a requirement that both former spouses should be dead. The prohibited degrees of relationship are therefore effective in providing another form of preventing incestuous relationships that may be deemed harmful, but the law has adapted to restrictions on marriage that may be deemed irrational.[24]

It is therefore important that safeguarding is in place in order to prevent harmful marriages, including incestuous marriages. Such safeguarding is necessary in order to prevent marriages for those who should not marry, such as those under a certain age.

B. Age

The age at which parties may enter a marriage has changed very recently. While the age of marriage previously mirrored the age of consent to sexual relations (16 years old), the Marriage and Civil Partnership (Minimum Age) Act 2022 has raised the marriage age to 18. This means that any marriage between two persons where one party is below the age of 18 is void, and that it is a criminal offence to cause a child (someone under the age of 18) to marry. The piece of legislation was brought in to prevent forced religious marriages. This reform arguably may lead to some peculiar and discriminatory outcomes. For example, a religious person for whom marriage before sex is important cannot legally enter into such a relationship until the age of 18, but someone for whom marriage is unimportant can have a sexual relationship at 16. The inconsistency between the age of sexual consent and the age of marriage is of concern, and is criticised by Clucas as unfairly restricting young peoples' autonomy while conflating forced marriages with consensual marriages between young people.[25] Consistency and equality should be maintained, therefore this reform should be reversed.

C. Parties Have Intermarried in Disregard of Certain Requirements as to the Formation of Marriage

The requirements specified in the Marriage Act 1949 state that parties must marry according to certain formalities that vary for both civil and religious marriages. The Law Commission, in its 2022 report, has written:

> The law is ancient and has developed incrementally over time to cater for weddings by different groups. Like a house that has been repeatedly extended, a scheme originally

[24] L Schäfer, 'Marrying an in-law? The future of prohibited degrees of affinity and consanguinity in English Law (2008) 20(2) *Child and Family Law Quarterly* 219.

[25] R Clucas, 'Early marriage: any need for action? (2023) 68(11) *The Journal of the Law Society of Scotland* at https://napier-repository.worktribe.com/output/3373616/early-marriage-any-need-for-action (accessed 21 May 2024).

> designed for a particular type of wedding has expanded over the last 250 years to cover a variety of other situations, resulting in an array of mismatched rules. The result is a law that is inconsistent and complicated, inefficient, unfair, and needlessly restrictive.[26]

As the Commission has so recently and extensively reported on its suggestions for reform of the process of marrying as specified under the 1949 legislation, it is also outside of the scope of this chapter to further argue for reform of this area, despite such reform's being necessary in line with the Law Commission's recommendations.

D. Polyamorous or Multi-Partner Marriage

Marriage need no longer be strictly dyadic. Recent reform, in the shape of the introduction of no-fault divorce and the omission of 'adultery' from same-sex marriage, has begun to suggest a process of disestablishing monogamy as a strict feature within marriage. As I have previously argued in the context of same-sex marriage, sex is no longer a 'deal-breaker' in the same way that consummation is no longer a 'deal-maker'.[27] Since the advent of the Divorce, Dissolution and Separation Act 2020, sex is also no longer a 'deal-breaker' in different-sex marriages, as it is no longer a factor contributing to the breakdown of the marriage. Moving beyond 'adultery' and the possibility of non-monogamy in marriage, I argue for a bolder iteration of marriage, in the possibility of extending marriage to polyamorous groupings. I argue that a marriage between two people where one or more party is already married should no longer be automatically void.

As stated in the Home Office's 2023 briefing, there is no formal assessment of the number of polyamorous households in the United Kingdom (UK). The Home Office admits in its briefing that

> [p]arties to these relationships do not have the same rights as legally married couples, such as access to financial remedies on divorce or automatic inheritance rights on the death of one of the parties. Calls have been made for all marriages taking place in England and Wales to be registered as a way of addressing this issue – it would not be possible to register a polygamous marriage.[28]

In some religious settings, polygamy is practised, and it may be recognised in the UK if the marriages took place in a jurisdiction where it is legal. Additionally, some queer relationships feature polyamory, that is, the practice of 'throuples' (a tri-partner relationship).[29]

[26] *Celebrating Marriage: A New Weddings Law* (Law Com No 408, 2022).

[27] A Maine, Queer(y)ing Consummation: An Empirical Reflection on the Marriage (Same Sex Couples) Act 2013 and the role of Consummation (2021) 33(2) *Child and Family Law Quarterly* 143; A Maine, 'Queering Marriage: The Homoradical and Anti-Normativity' (2021) 11(1) *Laws* 1.

[28] *Polygamy*, Commons Library Research Briefing no 05051, 1 February 2023.

[29] J Haritaworn, C Lin and C Klesse, 'Poly/logue: A Critical Introduction to Polyamory' (2006) 9 *Sexualities* 515, 518.

Section 11(b) of the MCA 1973 states that a marriage should be void if 'at the time of the marriage either party was already lawfully married or a civil partner.' Bigamy is a criminal offence.[30] The reform proposed would also require criminal law reform. In allowing polyamorous relationships to be legally recognised, parties must freely consent and wish to register their relationship outside of the dyadic structure currently inherent to marriage. As we know from literature,[31] marriage is no longer strictly monogamous nor is there any legal consequence for breaching monogamy within marriage. This development is significant and, as the Home Office reports,[32] many in polyamorous relationships are at risk of missing out on pensions and certain benefits as they do not have recognition for their relationships.[33] The reform of marriage to include polyamorous relationships could resolve this issue. The same could be said for a cohabitation framework, stopping short of marriage reform. For the purposes of this chapter, I will focus on the reform of nullity provisions.

The ECtHR has not interpreted the right to marry as including a right to polyamorous marriages. In 1987, the Court held that 'a Contracting State cannot be required under the Convention to give full recognition to polygamous marriages which are in conflict with their own *ordre public*'.[34] However, in order to recognise a greater variety of relationships, nullity provisions should be reformed. Polyamory, literally 'many love', is the practice of maintaining multiple sexual and emotional relationships. Marriage, as a heteronormative model, fails to recognise or provide for such relations. It is likely that LGBTQ populations deviate from the heteronormative and mono-normative model more than their different-sex counterparts. As such, same-sex marriage that is predicated on coupled legal monogamy fails to adequately provide any recognition or security for polyamorous relationships, which may take many forms. It can be said that those relationships that exist outside of the realm of state recognition can be classed as sex-radical, and therefore as rejecting and resisting mononormative state interference. To achieve recognition for such relationships, marriages should no longer be automatically void if a party is already married. The author argues that if parties enter into a marriage when they are already married, then both marriages should be made

[30] Offences against the Person Act 1861, s 57.

[31] B Heaphy, C Smart and A Einarsdottir, *Same-Sex Marriages: New Generations, New Relationships* (London, Palgrave Macmillan 2013) 82; E Sheff, 'Polyamorous Families, Same-Sex Marriage, and the Slippery Slope' (2011) 40 *Journal of Contemporary Ethnography* 510; M Barker, '"This Is My Partner, and This Is My … Partner's Partner": Constructing a Polyamorous Identity in a Monogamous World' (2004) 18 *Journal of Constructivist Psychology* 75; J Haritaworn, C Lin and C Klesse, 'Poly/logue: A Critical Introduction to Polyamory' (2006) 9 *Sexualities* 515, 518; C Klesse, 'Polyamory and Its "Others": Contesting the Terms of Non-Monogamy' (2006) 9 *Sexualities* 569; R Bauer, 'Non-Monogamy in Queer BDSM Communities: Putting the Sex Back into Alternative Relationship Practices and Discourse' in M Barker and D Langdridge (eds), *Understanding Non-Monogamies* (London, Routledge 2010) 142.

[32] *Polygamy* (n 28) 4.

[33] ibid 12.

[34] *M and OM v the Netherlands* App no 12139/86 (ECtHR, 5 October 1987). See C Draghici, *ECHR: Right to Marry* (London, Insight, 2015).

voidable. Consent to such a marriage would be key: if parties had consented to such a union, in the event of relationship breakdown between consenting polyamorous marriages, divorce would be a more appropriate legal dissolution, rather than annulment. Polyamorous marriages where each party had entered into the relationship consensually would only be eligible for divorce proceedings where, if there was evidence to suggest that the marriage was not consensual, nullity would remain a valid option. This reform would simply entail removing section 11(b) of the 1973 Act and replacing the provisions within section 12, entailing that a marriage where either party was already lawfully married could become voidable if not consented to.

This indicates that there is an option to end the marriages through the process of nullity, while the process of divorce would still be available. However, this would also mean that multi-partner marriages would be possible, for instance if two married partners each married another partner.

In this section of the chapter, the author has argued that section 11 of the MCA 1973 should be amended in order to enable polyamorous relationships to be recognised, and advocated for a return to equal ages of marriage and consent, while still maintaining safeguarding measures to prevent the marriage of related individuals. Next, the grounds set out in section 12 of the Act will be analysed.

IV. Voidable Marriage

Lasok has stated that as long as a voidable (or defective) marriage exists, 'nullity hangs over [the married parties'] heads like the sword of Damocles but falls down immediately should a whim or a long-harboured grudge put the law into motion'.[35] A voidable marriage is one that contains some defect as to its operation and may be vulnerable to a decree of nullity, though it remains valid until declared annulled. It is thus distinct from a void marriage, which is flawed from its creation. It is not the intention of this chapter to remove voidable marriages; as already stated, they can be a useful tool, particularly for a non-consensual polyamorous marriage. However, this chapter argues for reform of voidable grounds, in order to remove the discriminatory and stigmatising elements. Section 12 of the MCA 1973 states the grounds on which a marriage may be voidable, namely: that a marriage has not been consummated owing to lack of capacity or refusal; a lack of consent to marry; that either party was suffering from venereal disease; or that a party to the marriage was pregnant. This chapter will establish the rationale on which the grounds should be reformed, in order to determine a more appropriate model for relationship recognition, removing outdated provisions but maintaining the section 11 process where useful. Going forward, it will focus on the grounds of consummation, venereal disease, and pregnancy.

[35] D Lasok, 'Approbation of Marriage in English Law and the Doctrine of Validation' (1963) 26 *MLR* 251, 250.

A. Lack of Consummation

Section 12(1)(a) and (b) of the MCA 1973 stipulate the ground on which a marriage may be voidable owing to a lack of consummation, caused by either lacking capacity or wilfully refusing to consummate the marriage. I have already discussed the fact that this ground is discriminatory and should be removed, contributing to a range of literature that discusses the same issue.[36] A key point in this argument is the fact that this ground is only applicable to different-sex marriages, as consummation is defined exclusively in heterosexual terms. Consummation is described by Brook as 'performative', amounting to *copula vera* (meaning the true conjunction of bodies). As such the nature of consummation, as an act of sexuality that can only be performed by heterosexual bodies, that is only included in different-sex marriage, facilities the heteronormative nature of marriage.[37]

This means that same-sex marriages are not afforded the same rights to nullity as different-sex marriages. As I have previously argued, consummation should be removed as a ground for nullity owing to the inequality it represents and the lack of a legal definition of sexual intercourse that is not solely grounded in heteronormativity:

> [R]emoving consummation from the law entirely (much as adultery has been removed by the advent of notification-based divorce) would also serve the equality objective, while avoiding the practical problems inherent in defining same-sex consummation. While this would preclude any express, symbolic validation of same-sex intercourse, not doing so can be justified on the basis that the state has no interest in any spouses' consensual sexual activities, especially non-procreative activities. Moreover, given the religious foundation of different-sex consummation, there can clearly be no logical counterpart for same-sex relationships, and so a further argument for the abolition of consummation is that a religiously grounded notion has no place in contemporary secular law in any event.[38]

Turning to a lack of consummation owing to a lack of capacity, we once again see the issue of defining marriage by reference to a negative omission, rather than a positive duty. In defining it as such, 'the law's ongoing recognition of sexual intercourse as important tells us not only that sex is significant, but that some types of

[36] Maine, 'Queer(y)ing Consummation' (n 27); A Maine, 'Consummating in Court' in R Probert and S Thompson, *Research Handbook on Marriage and Cohabitation* (Cheltenham, Edward Elgar, forthcoming); H Brook, 'Zombie Law: Conjugality, Annulment, and the (Married) Living Dead' (2014) 22 *Feminist Legal Studies* 49; J Herring, 'Why Marriage Needs to be Less Sexy' in J Miles, P Mody and R Probert (eds), Marriage Rites and Rights (Oxford, Hart Publishing, 2015); G Black, 'Adult Relationships and the Ongoing Legal Significance of Sexual Intimacy' in J Scherpe and S Gilmore (eds), *Family Matters: Essays in Honour of John Eekelaar* (Cambridge, Intersentia, 2022) 1, 13; D Sanyal and A Ghosh, 'Abolishing consummation: the need to de-essentialise sex within marriage' (2022) 6(3) *Indian Law Review* 331; S Beresford, 'We're All Same (Sex) Now?: Lesbian (Same) Sex; Consummation; Adultery and Marriage' (2016) 12(5) *Journal of GLBT Family Studies* 468.

[37] Brook (n 36).

[38] Maine, 'Queer(y)ing Consummation' (n 27) 160.

sexual activity are more relevant than others. It also potentially indicates that other non-sexual activities are not legally or socially meaningful.'[39]

To lack capacity for a sexual relationship means lacking capacity to marry. Munby J stated in *Sheffield City Council v E*[40] that this was a deliberately low threshold for marriage, because there are people in society who may be of limited or borderline capacity but who still have a right to marry. Such an approach has been confirmed in subsequent cases,[41] but an understanding of the broader issues of consent and risk of disease and pregnancy were deemed important elements. Even in this instance of consent and mental unsoundness, the court has placed a sexual component in marriage, and it was held that an individual would only have the capacity to marry if they understood the obligation, inter alia, 'to love each other as husband and wife to the exclusion of all others'.[42] As such, the consummation requirements, as the author has argued elsewhere,[43] only serve to contribute to discriminatory and illogical applications of the law.

In order to remove consummation from marriage, sections 12(1)(a) and 12(1)(b) should be omitted from the MCA 1973. This is simple legislative reform that would follow from the omission of consummation from the Marriage (Same-Sex Couples) Act 2013.[44]

B. Lack of Consent and Unfit for Marriage Due to Mental Ill-Health

As noted in section IV.A, to lack capacity for sexual intercourse similarly entails the lack of consent to marry. This understanding of marriage as a serious and significant legal institution is important, and with that understanding is an explicit requirement that both parties consent to that marriage. In order to maintain safeguarding, particularly for vulnerable parties to a marriage in order to ensure consensual marital relationships, consent will remain an integral feature of marriage. Therefore, the requirements for consensual marriage, and the nullification of a marriage that has been formed owing to mistake or duress, will remain as factors in the reformed nullity proceedings.

With regard to those who are unfit for marriage due to mental ill-health, as with consent, there should be safeguarding measures in place; under these reforms, the grounds relating to mental ill-health would not change and would remain voidable.

[39] Black (n 36) 4.
[40] *Sheffield City Council v E* [2004] EWHC 2808 (Fam), [2005] Fam 326.
[41] *KC and NNC v City of Westminster Social and Community Services Department* [2008] EWCA Civ 198, 220; *D Borough Council v B* [2011] EWHC 101 (Fam), [2012] Fam 36.
[42] *Sheffield City Council v E* (n 40). Maine, 'Consummating in Court' (n 36).
[43] Maine, 'Queer(y)ing Consummation' (n 27); Maine, 'Consummating in Court' (n 36).
[44] Marriage (Same-Sex Couples) Act 2013, sch 4, pt 3.

C. Venereal Disease in a Communicable Form

The third ground, related to the suffering of a venereal disease in a communicable form (sexually transmitted infection (STI)), relies on problematic assumptions and should serve no basis for whether a marriage is functioning appropriately. The ground is applicable within the first three years of a marriage and the petitioner must not have been aware of the respondent's STI status prior to the marriage.[45] This ground was introduced at a time when treatments for STIs were not as advanced as they are today, particularly as regards antibiotic treatment. Maintaining this as a reason to annul a marriage puts a mononormative imperative on marriage. This can be attributed to the belief that if a person has an STI then they are not suitably married and have committed a deception. The ground also stigmatises those living with incurable but treatable STIs.

Most STIs can be treated within one to two weeks with antibiotics provided by sexual health services. The treatment of human immunodeficiency virus (HIV) now means that people living with HIV cannot pass on the virus to their sexual partners when they are on medication,[46] while they have the same life expectancy as people who are not living with HIV. However, if a person living with HIV were to marry, their marriage would currently be vulnerable to a decree of nullity, owing to their HIV status, if their partner was unaware and they were not taking medication. In such a situation, a spouse should not be able to annul their marriage but may use the divorce process instead.

Thus, there is an implication within the law that people with STIs are a cause to question the validity of a marriage. This is ultimately stigmatising and should be reformed. Not only this, but the ground solely applies to marriage and not to civil partnerships. Again, there is an suggestion here that same-sex couples may be more likely to live with STIs, particularly HIV. The most recent UK-wide estimate is that 106,890 people were living with HIV in the UK in 2019. The more recent estimate for England (not the whole UK) is that there were 95,900 people living with HIV in England in 2021; of these, around 4,400 were undiagnosed and do not know they are HIV positive. In England, 2,692 people were diagnosed with HIV in 2021; 218 in Scotland; and 60 in Wales. Anyone can get HIV, but people from some groups or parts of the world are more likely to be affected. In particular, men who have sex with men and Black African people are disproportionately affected.

[45] MCA 1973, s 12(1)(e).

[46] People on effective HIV medication cannot pass on the virus and have an undetectable viral load, having the moniker 'U = U' (undetectable = untransmittable). See M Weait, 'The Healthcare Rights of People Living with HIV and AIDS' in C Ashford and A Maine (eds), *Research Handbook on Gender, Sexuality and the Law* (Cheltenham, Edward Elgar, 2020); A Maine, 'Bareback Sex, PrEP, National AIDS Trust v NHS England and the Reality of Gay Sex' (2020) 23(8) *Sexualities* 1362; C Ashford, M Morris and A Powell, 'Bareback sex in the age of preventative medication: Rethinking the "harms" of HIV transmission' (2020) 84(6) *Journal of Criminal Law* 596; C Giles, 'A Sexual Harm? HIV Transmission, "Biological" GBH and Ancillary Sentencing Provisions in England and Wale' (2021) 85(2) *Journal of Criminal Law* 209.

People who inject drugs are also at increased risk of HIV transmission. Of the 2,023 people diagnosed with HIV in England in 2021, 36 per cent were gay, bisexual or other men who have sex with men. Of the 798 heterosexual people diagnosed with HIV in England in 2021, 37 per cent were of Black African ethnicity.[47] This is significant, as many venereal diseases, particularly HIV, have a higher infection rates amongst minority groups, therefore putting them at greater risk of a decree of nullity than other demographic groups. In 2004, during the passage of the Civil Partnership Act, the Government was aware of the inconsistency and illogical nature of such provisions, labelling them a 'provision from a bygone age' that suggested that sexually transmitted infections needed to be treated differently from any other communicable disease, which was counterproductive to the overall goal of improved sexual health.[48]

Maintaining this ground while civil partnerships would have to seek dissolution in the same circumstances (if a partner took issue with their partner's sexual health status) demonstrates the illogical and discriminatory nature of such a ground such that it should be removed. Marriage should not be vulnerable to a decree of nullity because of a person's sexual health history. As with removing consummation from marriage, it is argued here that section 12(1)(e) should be omitted from the MCA 1973.

D. The Respondent was Pregnant by Some Person Other than the Petitioner

One of the clearest examples of the outdated nature of nullity is the ground under which a husband may nullify his marriage if his wife is pregnant with another man's child.[49] Some may argue that this ground is justified, on the basis that the wife had been unfaithful or deceitful, and that the pregnancy would mean that the husband may be 'duped' into raising another man's child.[50] However, none of these arguments justifies a specific ground for nullity when no-fault divorce is a possibility. This ground may only be relied upon by the petitioner who is not pregnant: in *most* marriages, this means that the husband has a way of nullifying a marriage that is not available to the wife. When marrying a pregnant woman, the husband will assume parental responsibility and fatherhood when the child is born, the child therefore becoming 'his' child.

Again, the author does not believe that such concerns merit a ground for nullification, as that would imply that the marriage is *defective*, owing to women's

[47] See at www.tht.org.uk/hiv-and-sexual-health/about-hiv/hiv-statistics#:~:text=The%20more%20recent%20estimate%20for,Scotland%20and%2060%20in%20Wales (accessed 27 July 2023).

[48] *Hansard*, Official Report – Civil Partnership Bill Debates, HC Standing Committee D, col 162, 26 October 2004.

[49] MCA 1973, s 12(1)(f).

[50] A man who is married to a woman who has given birth automatically gains parental responsibility as a father, in accordance with s 2(1) of the Children Act 1989.

autonomous exercise of their sexuality. There is no ground for nullification if the husband has made a third partner pregnant at the time of the wedding, an inequality that offers men greater recourse to legal process than women. Nor is there any such ground on the basis that the husband has committed any other sexual act with other third parties, consensual or not, as 'adultery' is no longer a factor in determining divorce under the Divorce, Dissolution and Separation Act 2020.

Brook notes that the requirements surrounding nullity concern a form of failure in a marriage, and that pregnancy falls within a failure of disclosure, meaning that a marriage is so flawed on the basis of a deception:

> In its construction as certifiably 'clean', marriage is set up in opposition to 'perversion', and bears the discursive weight of 'healthy' intimacy, whether or not health and well-being are necessary corollaries to marriage.[51]

The unequal application of such a ground, and the lack of remedy for a wife whose husband has impregnated someone else, calls into question the validity of such a ground, particularly when no-fault divorce gives a better option for the dissolution of a marriage.

Accordingly, section 12(1)(f) should also be removed as a ground contributing to the nullification of a voidable marriage.

E. Grounds Relating to Gender Recognition

The final two grounds for a voidable marriage relate to gender identity and the specific provisions of the Gender Recognition Act 2004. Despite the introduction of same-sex marriage, sex and gender still remain contentious issues, and parties to a marriage with a transgender person may have an 'out' to a marriage based on their partner's gender transition. Although legislatively we have moved on from the decision in *Corbett v Corbett*,[52] there remain difficult issues with regard to trans people's marriages.

Section 12(1)(g) of the MCA 1973 provides that a marriage is voidable because an interim gender-recognition certificate has been issued to either party to the marriage. This means that if a party to a marriage does not consent to their partner's transition, they may end the marriage owing to this transition. Section 12(1)(h) means that a person's gender history must be disclosed to their partner, otherwise the partner may again nullify the marriage owing to their spouse's gender status. As Brook states, where a 'transsexual person marries in their "new" sex

[51] Brook (n 36) 57.

[52] *Corbett v Corbett* [1971] P 83. For commentary, see A Sharpe, 'English Transgender Law Reform and the Spectre of *Corbett*' (2002) 10(1) *Feminist Legal Studies* 65, 68; R Collier, *Masculinity, Law and the Family* (London, Routledge 1995); K O'Donovan, *Family Law Matters* (London, Pluto, 1995); S Gilmore, '*Corbett v Corbett*: Once a Man, Always a Man?' in S Gilmore, J Herring and R Probert (eds), *Landmark Cases in Family Law* (London, Bloomsbury, 2016); R Probert, 'How would *Corbett* be decided today?' (2005) 35 *Family Law* 382.

without first confessing their history of sexual identity to their spouse, they risk contracting a voidable marriage'.[53] Further, we can question the necessity for such provisions: a partner with a rape, violent crime or murder conviction would not have the same effect on the marriage as being trans would. We can question the emphasis this places specifically on trans peoples' histories and marriage.

Sharpe has argued that this provision is discriminatory, particularly targeting trans people's ECHR right to respect for private and family life, and the right to marry. Nor does the provision impose any corresponding obligation on a cisgender person to disclose their gender history.[54] As Sharpe states, the provisions of the law are dubious, and may potentially violate the human rights of married trans people, particularly highlighting tensions with Articles 8 and 12 ECHR, while contributing to feelings of exclusion and suspicion towards them. In the current climate of increased prejudice and transphobia, it is important that legal structures contributing to the instability of trans people's marriages should be removed. Furthermore, the issue of consummation may affect the validity of a trans person's marriage; as Probert notes, the Gender Recognition Act 2004 is silent on consummation[55] and may lead to a situation where,

> [e]ven after a person has undergone gender reassignment surgery, and has had their reassignment legally recognized under the Gender Recognition Act, it is possible that his or her marriage could be annulled on a ground first devised by medieval canonists. Even if this is no more than a theoretical possibility, this is hardly satisfactory.[56]

Therefore, the provisions relating to gender recognition within the MCA 1973 are discriminatory and are in need of reform. As no-fault divorce is available, parties to a marriage who wish to separate can legally do so with little acrimony, without the need to apportion blame. This means that the provisions regarding trans nullity are no longer needed. By omitting sections 12(1)(g) and 12(1)(h) from the 1973 Act, the uncomfortable legal situation faced by married trans people would be removed.

V. Suggested Amendments to Legislation

Ultimately, the reforms that the author suggests maintain nullity as a function of marriage, and recognise that it is a useful tool in defining what a marriage is or should be. Cases of annulments have decreased, from 297 in 2019, to 257 in 2020,

[53] Brook (n 36) 58.

[54] A Sharpe, 'Transgender Marriage and the Legal Obligation to Disclose Gender History' (2012) 75(1) *MLR* 33, 52.

[55] Probert (n 52) 385.

[56] ibid 389.

and down to 231 in 2021.[57] The low numbers of nullity applications each year would seem to indicate that in practical terms, annulment is not significant as a means to terminate a relationship but tells us more about how the law perceives marriage, its boundaries and what is seen as a 'normal' marital relationship, as well as safeguarding vulnerable people due to age or capacity. The law further maintains nullity for those who may wish to avoid divorce, if and where appropriate, but it remains clear that certain outdated grounds of nullity should be removed in order to modernise the process.

This chapter calls for the reclassification of section 11(b) of the MCA 1973 as a section 12 ground for voidable marriage. This means that marriages between those who are already married would not automatically be void but voidable, raising the possibility of polyamorous marriages, particularly appropriate for those that were entered into non-consensually, while divorce would be the preferred form of dissolution for consensual polyamorous marriages. This would also entail the repeal of section 57 of the Offences against the Person Act 1861.

Further, it calls for the removal of section 12(1)(a) and (b), the provisions relating to consummation. The result of this would be that lack of consummation would no longer mean that a marriage is voidable, and it would also break the link between law and normative perceptions of sexuality.[58]

Section 12(1)(e), (f), (g) and (h) should all be repealed, removing the provisions relating to venereal disease, pregnancy and trans people's marriages.

Marriages will still be required to be between parties who are over the age of 18 and not related by affinity or blood. Marriages must be consensual, and safeguarding will remain in place for those who are living with mental ill-health. There would be no requirement for consummation, and no provisions for disease, pregnancy or in relation to transgender marriages. Marriages could be polyamorous.

VI. Conclusion

While some may argue that nullity is no longer necessary in the age of no-fault divorce, it still serves an important purpose in the definition of what a valid marriage is, as opposed to those that are void or voidable. By altering the specific grounds on which an annulment is available, the discriminatory nature of these provisions on marriage will be removed. These categories render marriage problematic by the imposing of discriminatory standards that give a party an 'out' to marriage if their partner does not fit within the traditional mononormative and cisnormative roles of marriage.

[57] Office for National Statistics, Divorces in England and Wales: 2021 at www.ons.gov.uk/peoplepopulationandcommunity/birthsdeathsandmarriages/divorce/bulletins/divorcesinenglandandwales/2021 (accessed 6 February 2024).

[58] Maine, 'Queering Marriage' (n 27); Maine, 'Queer(y)ing Consummation' (n 27).

In sum, these provisions would mean that fewer couples would obtain an annulment: the implementation of no-fault divorce would gain even more salience as the simpler and more streamlined way of ending a marriage. Given that there are only around 300 annulments each year, this area of reform pertains to the nature of marriage, going beyond the reform of the 2013 same-sex marriage legislation in order to remove some of the discriminatory, monormative and cisnormative standards retained by the law.

Response to Chapter 10

Nullity Reform: Redefining Marriage

GILLIAN BLACK*

I. Introduction

As Alex Maine notes at the very start of chapter 10, marriage is in a time of transition. In the last 20 years, the legal recognition of adult relationships has become 'more inclusive and welcoming than ever',[1] with the introduction of same-sex civil partnership, same-sex marriage and different-sex civil partnership. Since 2006, Scotland has also recognised cohabitation in law, making provision for one partner to seek a financial award at the end of a cohabiting relationship to reflect any economic disadvantage suffered as a result of that cohabitation.[2] Most recently, in England and Wales (but not in Scotland), a wholly no-fault route to divorce and dissolution has been introduced.[3] The law generally is moving towards a more supportive framework, reflecting the needs of adults entering into and exiting a range of relationships, rather than trying to use family law to shape family forms by promoting different-sex marriage to the exclusion of all else. But while progress has been made, there remain corners of the law that still reflect historical beliefs and attitudes – and arguably this is clearest when one examines the doctrine of nullity of marriage, and specifically voidable marriage.

At the outset, it is important to draw a clear distinction between those factors that render a marriage void, so that it has never existed at all, and those that result in a voidable marriage, that is one which is legal and binding unless successfully challenged in court. One critical difference is that a void marriage does not technically need a court decree to recognise the marriage as null: it just never existed. However, as acknowledged by Clive in Scotland and Herring in England,

* I wish to thank Dr Lesley-Anne Barnes-Macfarlane and Dr Rob Clucas for their very helpful comments on an early draft of this response: all errors remain my own, despite their best efforts.

[1] Maine, ch 10 in this volume, section I.

[2] Family Law (Scotland) Act 2006. See also recommendations for further law reform in this area in: Scottish Law Commission, *Report on Cohabitation* (Scot Law Com No 261, 2022).

[3] Divorce, Dissolution and Separation Act 2020. The Divorce (Scotland) Act 1976 retains fault-based behaviours for divorce, namely, adultery and 'unreasonable behaviour' in s 1(2)(a) and (b).

a decree is often desirable, to provide certainty and resolve any financial issues.[4] Such a decree of nullity can be sought by *any* party with a legitimate interest.[5] In contrast, a voidable marriage is legally binding unless and until one party to the marriage challenges it – one immediate point of difference being the fact that only the parties to the marriage have title to seek a decree of nullity. This reflects one of the distinctions between void and voidable marriages: marriages that are void *ab initio* tend to be void on grounds of public policy, reflecting the state's interest in regulating who gets married; while the grounds for rendering a marriage voidable are typically personal to the parties themselves.

In this response to Maine's chapter, I wish to draw out the differences between the English law of nullity and that of Scotland. These are reflected in one stark statistic: whereas England and Wales sees just over 200 annulments per year,[6] in Scotland, there have been *nine* decrees of nullity in the course of the 10-year period from 2009–19.[7] This considerable disparity suggests a fundamental difference in the legal and social relevance of nullity north and south of the Border, and by identifying possible reasons for these differences, we can assess what reform, if any, is required. This also picks up Maine's analysis of the discriminatory impact of voidable marriages, in section 12 of the Matrimonial Causes Act 1973 (the '1973 Act' or 'MCA 1973'). Do any justifications suffice to outweigh the exclusionary and damaging impact of the grounds for voidable marriages? How best can we accommodate those grounds that continue to serve a useful function?

II. Scotland and England: Different Theory, Similar Results?

The grounds for voidable marriages in England and Wales are set out in section 12(1) of the 1973 Act, and Maine provides a detailed account of the eight bases: non-consummation due to incapacity; non-consummation due to wilful refusal; that either party did not validly consent; that either party was suffering from mental disorder so as to be unfitted for marriage; the respondent was suffering from a communicable venereal disease or was pregnant by another man at the time of the marriage; that an interim gender recognition certificate is issued after the date of the marriage; or that at the time of the marriage the respondent had acquired their

[4] EM Clive, *The Law of Husband and Wife in Scotland*, 4th edn (Edinburgh, SULI, 1997) para 7.004; J Herring, *Family Law*, 11th edn (London, Pearson, 2023) ch 3, 198, section C.

[5] Clive (n 4) para 7.005.

[6] Maine (n 1) suggested amendments to legislation, citing the 2021 ONS Census data: Office for National Statistics, *Divorces in England and Wales: 2021* (ONS, 2 November 2022) at www.ons.gov.uk/peoplepopulationandcommunity/birthsdeathsandmarriages/divorce/bulletins/divorcesinenglandandwales/2021.

[7] Scottish Civil Justice Statistics, published for 2018–19 at www.gov.scot/publications/civil-justice-statistics-scotland-2018-19/pages/12/. Since 2019, these data have not been disaggregated.

gender under the Gender Recognition Act 2004. Two further points are worth emphasising: (i) the non-consummation bases are specifically excluded for same-sex marriages, under section 12(2) of the 1973 Act;[8] and (ii) section 13 of the 1973 Act provides for certain bars to seeking a declarator of nullity on these grounds, to protect the parties from the perpetual uncertainty of a future claim – for example, a declarator of nullity in relation to consent or pregnancy must be raised within three years.[9] There is therefore a limit to when the 'sword of Damocles' might fall.[10]

By contrast, in Scotland there is only one ground for a voidable marriage: 'if and only if, one of the parties is at the time of the marriage permanently and incurably impotent in relation to the other spouse'.[11] Impotence means an inability to have sexual intercourse – defined, as in England and Wales, as penetration of the vagina by the penis. It is therefore heteronormative and phallocentric, and it does not trouble same-sex marriage.[12] The only ground of voidability in Scots law is therefore immediately discriminatory, as it is only available to those in a different-sex marriage.[13] To this extent, impotence is comparable to non-consummation in England and Wales. However, in Scotland, the impotence must be due to physical or psychological causes:[14] wilful refusal does not suffice, although older case law has accepted that women may be impotent by virtue of their 'invincible repugnance' or 'repulsion' to sex,[15] such that the Court has concluded it was 'entitled to draw the inference that there was a practical incapacity on the part of the wife'.[16]

It would seem at first sight that Scottish spouses are ill-served when it comes to avoiding a marriage, being able to rely only one ground, and even then there must be a genuine incapacity to consummate the marriage, rather than a refusal to do so. Of course, one response might be that Scottish spouses are consequently spared those bases in section 12 that Maine rightly criticises as discriminatory and stigmatising,[17] derived from out-dated and inappropriate ideals. This is certainly the case in relation to (i) avoiding the marriage due to sexually transmitted infections; (ii) pregnancy; and (iii) full gender-recognition certificates: these would be legally irrelevant circumstances in Scots law.

[8] See Maine, ch 10 in this volume, section IV.A, 'Lack of Consummation'.

[9] See the various bars set out in s 13.

[10] See Maine, ch 10 in this volume, section IV, quoting Lasok.

[11] Clive (n 4) para 7.063. Note that Clive does also seem to hint that lack of capacity could result in a voidable marriage, if it does not suffice to make the marriage void, see ibid para 7.030.

[12] For a further discussion of the problems with impotence and non-consummation, see G Black, 'Adult relationships and the ongoing legal significance of sexual intimacy' in JM Scherpe and S Gilmore (eds), *Family Matters: Essays in Honour of John Eekelaar* (Cambridge, Intersentia, 2022) 309; and A Maine, 'Queer(y)ing consummation: an empirical reflection on the Marriage (Same Sex Couples) Act 2013 and the role of consummation' (2021) 33(2) *Child and Family Law Quarterly* 143.

[13] It is not relevant for civil partnerships at all.

[14] Clive (n 4) para 7.064.

[15] *G v G* 1924 SC (HL) 42.

[16] *AB v CB* [1906] SLC 43_411, 416 per the Lord President.

[17] Maine (n 10).

However, the other bases for avoiding a marriage in section 12 of the 1973 Act do have a place in Scots law, and are actually elevated to more fundamental conditions for marriage: failure to give genuine consent[18] and lack of capacity to consent[19] are both bases for a void marriage in Scotland, together with two further grounds, which also give rise to a void marriage in England and Wales: non-age (currently 16 in Scots law[20]), or being within the prohibited degrees of relationship.[21] Thus, a marriage formed under Scots law is void if one of the parties did not give consent, or lacked capacity, and these obstacles can be raised by any party with an interest: it is not the case that the marriage is voidable and will subsist until challenged. The grounds for a void marriage in Scotland reflect the fundamental conditions for marriage – age, consent, capacity – so that if any one is lacking, there is a public policy basis for not recognising the marriage at all. In respect of the voidable ground in English law, the grant of an interim gender-recognition certificate after the date of the marriage,[22] this finds an equivalent in section 1(1)(b) of the Divorce (Scotland) Act 1976, as one of the two grounds for divorce in Scots law (the other being the irretrievable breakdown of the marriage). Thus, spouses north and south of the Border have a route to exit the marriage based on largely the same factors, albeit they are not always categorised in the same way.

One possible reason for the difference in approach could be found in the differing availability of divorce in Scotland and in England, historically. Nullity, whether for void or voidable marriage, can be seen as a socially-sanctioned alternative to divorce, in an era when divorce was either not available, or carried heavy social and religious penalties. It is therefore of greater significance where divorce laws are more restrictive. In the period from 1560 until 1938,[23] divorce was available to any spouse in Scotland on one of two grounds: adultery[24] and desertion.[25] South of the border, however, divorce was more restricted for much of this period, being available (typically to the wealthy elite) only by way of a private Act of Parliament until the Matrimonial Causes Act 1857. This Act did introduce divorce as a general legal right, but it was available only for adultery, and very unequally: men simply had to show that their wives had had an adulterous relationship, while women had to show not merely adultery on the part of their husband but also some further harm, such as incest, bigamy or cruelty. Conditions that allowed a spouse to seek

[18] Marriage (Scotland) Act 1977, s 20A(2).

[19] Marriage (Scotland) Act 1977, s 20A(3).

[20] Marriage (Scotland) Act 1977, s 1. It is 18 in England and Wales, and is listed as a basis for a void marriage in s 11(a)(ii) of the Matrimonial Causes Act 1973.

[21] Marriage (Scotland) Act 1977, s 2 and sch 1; MCA 1973, s 11(a)(i).

[22] MCA 1973, s12(1)(g).

[23] In 1938, the Divorce (Scotland) Act introduced cruelty, incurable insanity, sodomy and bestiality as alternative grounds for divorce. As a result of the Divorce (Scotland) Act 1976, the sole ground for divorce is the irretrievable breakdown of the marriage, which can be evidenced through non-cohabitation for a period of one or two years, or adultery or 'unreasonable behaviour'.

[24] EM Clive and JG Wilson, *The Law of Husband and Wife in Scotland* (Edinburgh, SULI, 1974) 440.

[25] Act concerning Divorce for Desertion 1573, c 55; see: Clive and Wilson (n 24) 440.

a declarator of nullity were therefore of considerable importance. In an era of no-fault divorce, which England now enjoys, are the grounds of voidable marriage still required?

III. Justifications for Voidable Marriage: Religion and Deceit

One justification that is often advanced in favour of retaining voidable marriage, and which Maine explores, is the continuing need to allow an exit-route from marriage for those whose religious beliefs preclude divorce: 'Annulment may ease the anxiety that exists towards divorce, particularly from a religious perspective. Divorce remains a discouraged practice in some religions …'[26] The Law Commission of England and Wales supported the retention of voidable marriages, rather than relying on divorce, in part for religious reasons, in its 1970 Report, *Family Law: Nullity of Marriage*.[27] However, in 1992, the Scottish Law Commission reached a different conclusion, as part of its review of family law, recommending that there should be no role for impotence in Scots law and that religion did not offer a compelling justification:

> We do not believe, however, that the ordinary law of the land on the remedies available to all, for purely civil purposes, in cases of marriage breakdown ought to be determined by the views of any particular religion.[28]

Clive also argues (at least in Scotland) that the belief that nullity is required as a remedy for religious reasons is mistaken: a civil declarator of nullity is no better than a civil divorce for religious purposes, as 'the Canon law does not recognise the competence of the civil courts in relation to the religious effects of marriage'.[29] Ultimately, I would contend that religious beliefs should not operate to shore up bases of voidability that are so flawed: as Maine has argued elsewhere in respect of non-consummation, 'establishing the legitimacy of marriage on the basis of a sexual act is a peculiarly reductive endeavour, going against the notion that marriage is essentially a caring and mutual relationship'.[30]

Is there any other rationale for maintaining voidable marriage for personal 'traits' such as non-consummation or impotence, pregnancy or a sexually transmitted infection? One argument could be that allowing one party to avoid a marriage because of impotence/non-consummation, or for any of the section 12

[26] Maine, ch 10 in this volume, section II.

[27] Law Commission, *Family Law: Nullity of Marriage* (Law Com No 33, 1970). Religious concerns and the views of the Church were considered at para 24. The draft Nullity of Marriage Bill appended to the Report was never enacted, but the individual clauses can be found in the MCA 1973. For example, cls 1 and 2 map onto ss 11 and 12 of the 1973 Act.

[28] Scottish Law Commission, *Report on Family Law* (Scot Law Com, No 135, 1992) para 8.28.

[29] Clive (n 4) para 07.063.

[30] Maine (n 12) 159.

grounds, has an important value in exposing the lie or deception at the heart of the marriage. In these cases, the person seeking the decree of nullity is saying that they were deceived as to some aspect of the person they married: that deceit should be exposed through judicial recognition and a declarator of nullity. The significance of intimate deception has been explored by Kennedy[31] and by Hasday.[32] If a marriage cannot be annulled because of the section 12 grounds, so that the marriage is considered entirely valid, then the law is failing to protect innocent parties where there has been deception, and failing to provide an incentive for openness and honesty in intimate relationships.[33] However, Hasday also points to the (many) deceitful situations where the courts have declined to annul a marriage, illustrating that deceit alone does not routinely operate as a basis for avoiding a marriage.[34]

Using legal routes to seek exposure of or catharsis for wrongs in intimate relationships is not always helpful – and it is certainly an expensive, sometimes uncertain and often public means of doing so. Exiting from a marriage swiftly and cleanly will generally be the most constructive way forward for parties who find themselves married to someone who, deceptively or otherwise, does not meet their expectations: no-fault divorce offers this, and also avoids the discrimination and historical baggage that undoubtedly attaches to the current law of voidable marriage. Moreover, voidability (unlike fault-based divorce) can in some cases[35] be sought by the very person who gives rise to the claim: in which case, it does not help the 'innocent' party to seek redress for the 'deceitful' conduct if the declarator of nullity is sought by the party who is impotent or lacks capacity.

IV. Polyamory and Polygamy

Although my focus has been primarily on the voidable grounds in section 12 of the 1973 Act, I want to reflect on the reform proposed by Maine in relation to a section 11 void ground. He argues for a 'bolder iteration of marriage'[36] through extending marriage to polyamorous couples. This could be achieved by reclassifying section 11(b), which states that a marriage is void where either party to it is already married, from a void to a voidable ground.[37] This would allow people to enter into multiple marriages if they wished, recognising polygamy as legal in

[31] C Kennedy, *Inducing Intimacy: Deception, Consent and the Law* (Cambridge, Cambridge University Press, forthcoming).

[32] JE Hasday, *Intimate Lies and the Law* (Oxford, Oxford University Press, 2021).

[33] ibid 156.

[34] ibid 160–63.

[35] Thus, a person can rely on their own impotence/non-consummation to seek to avoid the marriage. However, s 12 of the 1973 Act confirms that only the other party can seek to avoid the marriage for venereal disease, pregnancy, or a full gender recognition certificate: s 12(e), (f) and (h).

[36] Maine, ch 10 in this volume, section III.D.

[37] In Scotland, s 5(4) of the Marriage (Scotland) Act 1977 states it is a legal impediment to marriage if one or both parties is already married or in a civil partnership, while s 24 makes it an offence for a person to enter into a marriage if they are already in a marriage or civil partnership.

England and Wales, while allowing either or both the marriages to subsist or to be brought to an end. The voidability provision would avoid one spouse's taking advantage of the other. Maine rightly notes the need for openness and consent to a polygamous marriage,[38] so that a party who agrees to enter into one could not then rely on the voidable provisions to bring it to an end: their only exit route would be divorce.[39] This helps mitigate the risks of deception in multiple-partner marriages,[40] although how this consent to a polygamous marriage (separate to consent to marriage *per se*) would be legally evidenced remains to be seen. Moreover, the consent to a polygamous marriage would only be relevant at the point of entering into the second or subsequent marriage: it could not apply or be evidenced when the first marriage was entered into, which (by definition) would not at that stage be polygamous.

Putting the practicalities to one side, the question remains whether we should move towards recognising formalised polyamorous relationships. As Sutherland asks, should our legal system 'abandon its attachment to mononormativity [and] respect freedom of choice' by recognising polygamous marriage?[41] While polyamorous relationships are growing in open recognition, and marriage is no longer legally monogamous,[42] facilitating polygamy requires very careful consideration, to ensure that women, in particular, are not exposed to an exploitative or subservient relationship.[43] The risk of exploitation and oppression in polygamy is not inevitable of course – and indeed it is arguably potentially present in any marriage: 'It is quite possible to imagine a version of polygamy, open to men and women equally and in whatever gender combination the parties choose, that is no more or less oppressive than any other kind of marriage.'[44] Nevertheless, reclassifying polygamous marriage from void to voidable would require us to tread very carefully, to ensure we avoid that peril of all law-reform projects, the unintended consequence.

V. Conclusion

To echo Maine's conclusion, modernising nullity and removing outdated grounds are essential. We agree that there is no role in the twenty-first century

[38] Maine refers to them as 'polyamorous marriages' but I have chosen to use 'polygamous': a marriage at present could be polyamorous, where two spouses agree to have an open marriage and (non-formalised) relationships with other people. The specific nature of formalised multiple-partner marriage is therefore more accurately referred to as polygamous marriage.

[39] Maine (n 36).

[40] Hasday discusses the legal regulation of bigamy, and notes that men constitute almost all bigamy defendants, revealing a deeply troubling gendered aspect to deceptive marriage practices: Hasday (n 32) 163.

[41] E Sutherland, 'Scots child and family law: liberty, equality and protection revisited' (2019) 33 *Juridical Review* 41.

[42] Maine (n 36).

[43] J Herring, *Family Law: A Very Short Introduction* (Oxford, Oxford University Press, 2014) 11–12.

[44] Sutherland (n 41) 41.

for non-consummation, or impotence in Scotland, together with the grounds of venereal disease, pregnancy or interim/full gender-recognition certificates. Sections 12(1)(a), (b), (e), (f), (g) and (h) of the 1973 Act should be repealed, along with the abolition of the common law doctrine of impotence in Scotland. (Divorce law in Scotland would also benefit from reform, to introduce no-fault divorce.) Such reform would bring both jurisdictions into alignment. Where we diverge is as to the two remaining section 12 grounds: consent or incapacity (in section 12(1)(c) and (d)). While Maine favours keeping those as grounds for avoiding a marriage, I would argue that consent and capacity to consent to marriage are so fundamentally important that lack of consent or capacity should render the marriage void.[45] Thus, these section 12 grounds should be relocated to section 11, to place them at the heart of marriage. Such a package of reforms would ensure that the legal definition of marriage moves away from its current discriminatory standards,[46] to a more equal and inclusive institution.

[45] I note that the Law Commission of England and Wales favoured keeping them as voidable grounds: Law Commission (n 27) paras 11–15.

[46] Maine, ch 10 in this volume, section VI.

Conclusion

JOE AILION

I. The Importance of Family Reform

For family law practitioners, reform is inconvenient.

I accept that this is a peculiar start to the concluding comment of a book containing a collection of proposals for reform. However, I believe that it is an unfortunate truth. Practitioners are creatures of habit. We often work in the way that we were trained. We reach for familiar advice, style and procedure. Reform requires re-think. Re-think is not always convenient, nor is it easy when it deals with such deeply emotive and often conflicting considerations.

This inconvenience may be mundane: in February 2022, some family practitioners might have bemoaned the added administrative burden required by the new form of information in support of a financial consent order, in comparison to the briefer document that had been used for the last decade, even if the merits of the more thorough new document were fairly clear.[1]

Alternatively, the inconvenience may be strategic: it might previously have been a routine task for an experienced practitioner to prepare a schedule of allegations of domestic abuse. However, some more recently might have scratched their heads whilst considering the best way to draft pleadings dealing with allegations of controlling and coercive behaviour consisting of a large number of 'smaller' incidents as a pattern of behaviour, given the Court's comments in *Re H-N and Others (Children) (domestic abuse: finding of fact hearings)*.[2]

It may even be profound: on 14 October 1991, the Children Act 1989 came into force and family lawyers will have needed to rip up everything they had known about the subject and re-learn an entire body of law. On 26 October 2000, the House of Lords made its seminal decision in *White v White*.[3] It created the 'yardstick of equality' in financial remedy proceedings following a divorce, a principle that forced a change in the advice that would be dispensed by practitioners by habit in almost every client meeting, and which has subsisted ever since.

[1] 'Notice from the Financial Remedies Court: D81' (Courts and Tribunals Judiciary, 2022) at www.judiciary.uk/guidance-and-resources/notice-from-the-financial-remedies-court-3/.

[2] *Re H-N and Others (Children) (domestic abuse: finding of fact hearings)* [2021] EWCA Civ 448.

[3] *White v White* [2000] UKHL 54.

I do not profess to have been in practice at the time of those profound changes, but they essentially created fundamental features of the law within which I work daily.

In a similar way to my colleagues at the time, I may shortly have to rip up what I have learned about representing clients seeking a parental order following a surrogacy arrangement, if new reforming legislation is soon introduced as proposed by the Law Commission.[4]

I expect that my strategic advice on financial disputes may, in the future, shift fundamentally should the nature of pre- or post-nuptial agreements follow possible trajectories towards the regime in various other jurisdictions. That is, by moving from effectively enforceable with creative application of the current law, to nearing impossible to challenge when done properly (again, as effectively proposed by the Law Commission).[5]

From the mundane to the profound: change creates effort and uncertainty for practitioners on the ground. A reluctance to embrace it, therefore, would be entirely understandable for the following reasons. First, consider the climate within which we operate. Family practitioners are tasked with navigating clients (and their most emotive and personal issues) through a creaking system. In a world after the Legal Aid, Sentencing and Punishment of Offenders Act (LASPO) 2012, the Court, CAFCASS and local authorities are chronically overburdened and under-funded. As a result of the near elimination of legal aid in private disputes, a large proportion of cases now involve litigants in person, either struggling to do their best with obvious difficulty or, in some cases, deliberately being obstructive at no cost to themselves.[6] further, those still working within the surviving scraps of the legal aid system, often dealing with the most complex child welfare or international matters, must do so whilst being equally overburdened and underpaid.

Then, consider whether it is this sort of climate that is conducive to innovation and an openness to change. A resistance to reform, and all of its consequent headaches and extra work, would be an obvious and fair reaction.

Nonetheless, family practitioners must (and do) seek innovation.

Why? Constant evolution of family law is so fundamentally, uncompromisingly important. For the vast majority of society, the family is probably the most important part of one's life. Family is central to the fabric of society. Our modern society progresses at pace. The law, unfortunately, does not. The lag between the reality of the family and the laws that govern it often creates unconscionable real-world problems.

[4] *Building Families Through Surrogacy: A New Law* (Law Com No 411 and Scot Law Com No 262, vol 2, 2023).

[5] See *Radmacher v Granatino* [2010] UKSC 42; *Matrimonial Property, Needs and Agreements* (Law Com No 343, 2014).

[6] The Ministry of Justice's *Family Court Statistics Quarterly* published in September 2023 sets out that, of 22,482 parties to private law children proceedings within the first quarter of 2023, 16,058 of them were unrepresented. See *Family Court Statistics Quarterly: April to June 2023* (Ministry of Justice, 2023) at www.gov.uk/government/statistics/family-court-statistics-quarterly-april-to-june-2023.

For example, throughout the 1980s, Parliament hurriedly sought to respond to the emerging method of family creation in surrogacy by creating a thrown-together legal system in a reactive sequence of legislation that largely remains in force. It is nearly unanimous amongst fertility law practitioners (and indeed the Law Commission) that surrogacy law is terribly out-of-date. The result is qualifying criteria for parental orders that are, in parts, arbitrary and, in others, virtually obsolete.[7]

The Court has been creative to solve this where it can. For example, the law requires that applications for a parental order must be made within six months of the child's birth. On a strict reading of the legislation, that is an absolute bar.[8] There can be no real reason for this. Why should a child be kept in legal uncertainty, and a surrogate remain unwillingly connected to a child she has no intention of raising, because the intended parents perhaps forgot, or were not aware of, a deadline for an application? In *Re X (A Child) (Surrogacy: Time Limit)*,[9] the Court found that it had its own discretion to make parental orders that were clearly in the children's best interests (regardless of a missed arbitrary deadline) and that legislation can be read down in a way that enables a 'sensible result'. The legislation also strictly prohibits payments for surrogacy that go beyond 'reasonable expenses' (which goes undefined).[10] However, what about the child's welfare in the event that intended parents had made such payments in good faith, complying with the law in a different country where it is entirely legal to make payments to a surrogate? The child was not an accessory to that process. Is it fair for their legal status to remain uncertain as a result? In *Re X & Y (Foreign Surrogacy)*,[11] the Court confirmed that payments exceeding 'reasonable expenses' can retrospectively be authorised before making the parental order. There has been no known case since in which a parental order has not been granted because payments made could not be retrospectively authorised. Indeed, it is now common practice, especially where payments were made in a jurisdiction in which commercial surrogacy arrangements are legal and no public policy or exploitation issues have been identified. With other, similar cases, slowly the 'mandatory' checklist was softened and refined.

However, the Court's flexible application of the law can only bend so far before it risks a snap. For example, until 2019, parental orders were only available to couples (by contrast, adoption has long been available to single individuals). In *Re Z (A child) (No 2)*,[12] the Court was faced with an application by an individual father who had a child through surrogacy in the USA. It did not feel able to apply judicial creativity to solve such an explicit problem in law, and was forced to make a declaration of incompatibility between the law in its form at the time

[7] See *Building Families Through Surrogacy* (n 4).
[8] Human Fertilisation and Embryology Act 2008, s 54(3).
[9] *Re X (A Child) (Surrogacy: Time Limit)* [2014] EWHC 3135 (Fam).
[10] Human Fertilisation and Embryology Act 2008, s 54(8).
[11] *Re X & Y (Foreign Surrogacy)* [2008] EWHC 3030 (Fam).
[12] *Re Z (A child) (No 2)* [2016] EWHC 1191 (Fam).

and the human rights of the father and child. Consequently, the law was amended by Parliament.[13] However, that particular applicant, and his child, were left in the unenviable position of having to wait for Westminster to clear up the legal limbo in which his family had found itself.

It is a perfect illustration of the problems facing real people in the real world, when the law is out of pace with the way in which family lives are being lived.

II. The Role of Practitioners to Reform

This collection has been commissioned and edited by the Family Law Reform Now Network – a group led by specialist family law academics. Academics, of course, are well acclimatised to thought leadership. Academics have freedom for 'blue-sky thinking' as to what *could* be. Practitioners, by contrast, are stronger on (or perhaps restrained by) 'nuts-and-bolts' practical application and understanding of the law as it stands. The Network, however, still extends to practitioners in recognition of the importance of their role in this discourse. The essence of the Network is this: academics and practitioners can best drive the changes we need when working together.

This relies on practitioners' recognition of the significance of the role we play. In delivering services to clients and families, we are the eyes and ears on the ground as to what is happening within our system. We are the first ports of call to hear of tricky issues that ultimately need to be brought to the Court for guidance and precedent, ultimately creating necessary case law.

Practitioners' submissions in bringing those cases can be supported by well-researched studies and thought leadership from our academic colleagues, but the actual movement of cases through the Court system relies on our hands on deck. In turn, academic discourse will assist us most if we cooperate in dialogue, to ensure that research efforts are directed towards the matters that we encounter in practice.

Given the challenges facing the family law sphere in the current climate, there are now fewer lawyers working on fewer cases.[14] This creates a duty, in my view, to those remaining, to be pro-active in driving change when we have the opportunity to do so.

The use of the word 'duty' here is deliberate. A fundamental principle of the Solicitors Regulatory Authority is the duty to act in the best interests of each client. The principles elaborate further that 'client' includes prospective clients.[15] Perhaps it is a reach in interpretation of our regulatory duties, but I choose to accept this as

[13] The Human Fertilisation and Embryology Act 2008 (Remedial) Order 2018 (SI 2018/1413).

[14] See *Family Court Statistics Quarterly* (n 6).

[15] See Principle 7 of 'SRA Principles' (Solicitors Regulation Authority, 2019) at www.sra.org.uk/solicitors/standards-regulations/principles/.

a duty to those who may need to access family justice in the future. That is, a duty to do our bit in ensuring that the system and law are fit for purpose.

III. Taking Inspiration from Innovators

We are fortunate as family lawyers that we do not have to search very far to find colleagues who have carried the torch for reform. The history of our field is populated with innovators who will not take 'no' for an answer.

I immediately think of the late Anne-Marie Hutchinson of Dawson Cornwell. She was a leader in almost all fields of family law, but perhaps most renowned for pioneering modernisation of the law on forced marriage and child abduction. She helped a great number of vulnerable children and adults at risk of this harm, including in a number of cases that established principles that would go on to be used for their protection.

Prior to 2007, there was no specific legislation addressing forced marriage, and she and her colleagues managed this, therefore, by creative application of existing doctrines, such as wardship, injunctive powers or voidable marriage, to achieve that protection.[16] Her experience in these cases led to her advice to Parliament in the drafting of Forced Marriage (Civil Protection) Act 2007. It was this Act that created the forced marriage protection order – the power for the Court to make any provision it considers appropriate to prevent a forced marriage, or the harm it could cause. Anne-Marie, together with her colleagues Henry Setright KC, Teertha Gupta KC and James Turner KC, were thanked in Parliament for their contributions to the Act, including in respect of ensuring adequate access to legal aid and the ability of properly interested third parties to apply for protective orders on behalf of a potential victim.[17]

Further, there are few more decorated family lawyers than Lady Hale. She is widely and deservedly celebrated as a heroine of the profession. I am aware of colleagues in the profession who wear t-shirts with her portrait on them with inspirational, Barack Obama campaign-style branding. As with Anne-Marie Hutchinson, her contributions cannot be fairly distilled into a few paragraphs of this concluding chapter. She has, however, directly contributed to some of the most important progressions of family law that have taken place in the past 40 years. Her work at the Law Commission led to the introduction of the Children Act 1989. As mentioned in section I, this was a seismic shift forward for the welfare of children. Her work also contributed to the introduction of the Family Law Act 1996 – an Act specifically designed to modernise the law, protect property rights of spouses currently at risk of unfairness and establish much-needed civil

[16] See, eg, *Re KR (Abduction: Forcible Removal by Parents)* [1999] 2 FLR 542; and *NS v MI* [2006] EWHC 1646 (Fam)).

[17] See the Forced Marriage (Civil Protection) Bill: HC Deb 26 January 2007, vol 688, col 1320.

protections for those at risk of domestic abuse. That Act was also a forerunner in aspiring to bring reform to the fault-based divorce system[18] of the time, which, as is explored in section V, only gained real momentum some 20 years later.

This momentum continued within her eminent judicial career. Lady Hale can be credited with progressing the way in which children's voices are heard in the Family Court.[19] She has done what she can, within the confines of the legislation, to protect the rights of unmarried couples by applying old doctrines of constructive and resulting trusts to the modern world in which marriage is no longer a universal norm.[20] This amongst innumerable other contributions to the protections of rights and interests of the vulnerable within family law and beyond.

Perhaps it is no coincidence that Lady Hale spent much of her pre-judicial career straddling academia and the Family Bar. A perfect illustration of the potential that can be realised with academia's imagination and practitioners' 'boots on the ground' application.

That is consistent with the comments of Lady Justice Carr in the University of Oxford's Harris Society Annual Lecture. In that address, the learned Judge references Lady Hale's contribution specifically in support of her argument that judges and academics are a 'marriage of true minds' – their constructive dialogue largely contributing to a law that is 'conceptually, morally and legally sound'.[21] It is, I hope, clear from the key message of this chapter that I would – very, *very* humbly – ask Her Ladyship to extend this to include solicitors and barristers. Between us all, we make a system that, if we work together, can achieve optimal progression in our field.

IV. Current Conversations

It is to be celebrated that family lawyers remain motivated and driven professionals. Despite the pressures on our arena, there remains fervent, passionate and diverse debate within the profession. Indeed, this book contains a number of conversations of such topical matters (although it is not my intention to speak over the expert and eloquent words of the contributors).

As society evolves, so too will the conversation amongst the profession about what needs to change to ensure the law stays relevant and fit for purpose. There are numerous topics that are currently being grappled with, in the pursuit of positive reform.

[18] Family Law Act 1996, pt 2 – later repealed. See C Fairbairn and C Barton, 'No-fault divorce' (Research Briefing Paper No 01409, House of Commons Library, 2019).

[19] See *Re D (Abduction: Rights of Custody)* [2006] UKHL 51; and *Re W (Children) (Abuse: Oral Evidence)* [2010] 1 WLR 701.

[20] See *Stack v Dowden* [2007] UKHL 17; and *Jones v Kernott* [2011] UKSC 53.

[21] S Carr, 'Harris Society Annual Lecture: "Delicate Plants", "Loose Cannons" or "A Marriage of True Minds"? The Role of Academic Literature in Judicial Decision-Making' (16 May 2023) https://www.judiciary.uk/harris-society-annual-lecture-lady-justice-carr/.

One example of a current conversation amongst the profession is Family Court transparency. The President of the Family Division recently established, and now leads, the Family Transparency Implementation Group. The Group comprises various eminent practitioners, as well as representatives from academia and think-tanks.[22] Since its formation in 2021, the Group has already published a 164-page report with guidance for transparency and reporting in the Financial Remedy Court.[23]

Another example, and one that has arguably produced the most dynamic movement within the profession, is the push towards more conciliatory forms of resolving disputes within family law. This has always been the modus operandi of Resolution – a membership group of family lawyers committed to lessening conflict in family law resolution, and which has grown to the extent that it can be considered now to effectively represent the family law profession.

Resolution's efforts in advocating for a 'better way' have picked up significant traction, including with policy makers. The Ministry of Justice recently launched a (now abandoned) consultation on a proposal to enforce mandatory mediation within private Family Court disputes, with risk of possible costs sanctions for failure to engage.[24] The feasibility of such a reform was suspect and the resultant objections from practitioners might well have contributed to the change in policy that led to its being shelved. More recently, the Family Procedure Rules have been amended to include a requirement for litigants to have explored non-Court dispute resolution before and during Court proceedings, with the Court having powers to adjourn proceedings or sanction those who fail to do so.[25] It is perhaps a 'softer' duty than the Ministry of Justice under Dominic Raab might have intended, but is still indicative of the shift towards alternative dispute resolution (ADR) and how seriously it is to be taken at all levels.

A cynic might say that a push towards private methods of ADR presents a convenient escape route for a government unwilling or unable (depending on one's political views) to direct adequate resources towards the Family Court system. I would argue that this is unfair. The merits of offering collaborative ways for families to resolve their disputes are obvious and wide-reaching, though of course they must sit alongside, and not in replacement of, a functioning judicial system.

Resolution and other professionals interested in 'constructive conflict resolution' are arguably becoming more confident and radical with this growth. In recent years, momentum has been building behind an emerging 'One Lawyer'

[22] 'Membership announcement for the Family Transparency Implementation Group (TIG)' (Courts and Tribunals Judiciary, 2021) at www.judiciary.uk/guidance-and-resources/membership-announcement-for-the-family-transparency-implementation-group-tig/.

[23] Transparency in the Financial Remedies Court, *The Final Report of the Financial Remedies Sub-Group of the Transparency Implementation Group* (London, Transparency in the Financial Remedies Court, 2023).

[24] *Supporting earlier resolution of private family law arrangements: A consultation on resolving private family disputes earlier through family mediation* (Ministry of Justice, CP No 824, 2023).

[25] Family Procedure (Amendment No 2) Rules 2023 (SI 2023/1324).

model, in which divorcing couples can choose to be represented jointly by a single practitioner.[26] The theory is clear – if spouses accept a shared interest in a settlement that is fair for both of them, no conflict of those interests arises. It is a pioneering step beyond a previous regulatory framework that is entrenched in a contentious system. I confess, it still instils nervousness in me and many of my colleagues, due to our traditional and familiar understanding of competing conflicts of interest. Credit therefore goes to the bravery and commitment of those driving the concept forward.

Generally speaking, family law attracts practitioners of an empathetic nature. We see first-hand the emotional toll that a primarily contentious system can take on our clients and their families. These are people we invariably come to care about. However, perhaps the profession's conviction and commitment to this particular issue would be dampened if it were not for the weight of academic support for it.

The Family Mediation Task Force was commissioned by the Ministry of Justice and consisted of a number of prominent family law academics. It published a leading report in June 2014, in response to the impact of LASPO 2012, which reiterates the consensus on the importance of mediation and makes recommendations to address the drop in publicly-funded mediation at that time.[27] Much of the more recent high-profile academic work considering mediation similarly appears to roundly accept its fundamental value. Discourse is consequently geared towards addressing its limitations or challenges to best harness its potential.[28]

These practically minded, problem-solving studies can provide mediation practitioners solutions to their obstacles, in turn improving that system. Thus, here we land once more at the essential message running through this piece. Practitioners are enabled and emboldened to 'do the right thing' when academia supports us.

V. A Case Study: 'No Fault Divorce'

Beyond ADR, Resolution – as a leading representative of the family law profession – has also positioned itself squarely on the front line of the campaign towards possibly the most seismic change in family law within the past 30 years.

On 6 April 2022, the notion of 'fault' was removed from divorce.[29] That a divorce was the fault of one party had been a feature of English law since the 1600s.[30]

[26] 'Resolution reveals innovative new model to help couples divorce amicably with just one lawyer' *Resolution* (1 August 2022) at resolution.org.uk/news/resolution-reveals-innovative-new-model-to-help-couples-divorce-amicably-with-just-one-lawyer/.

[27] *Report of the Family Mediation Task Force* (London, Ministry of Justice, Family Mediation Task Force, 2014).

[28] R Blakey, '"Mediators Mediating Themselves": Tensions Within the Family Mediator Profession' (2023) 43(1) *Legal Studies* 139; and A Barlow et al, *Creating Paths to Family Justice: Briefing Paper & Report on Key Findings* (University of Exeter, 2017).

[29] Divorce, Dissolution and Separation Act 2020.

[30] 'University of Exeter research leads to historic introduction of no fault divorce in England' (University of Exeter, 2020) at news-archive.exeter.ac.uk/homepage/title_801911_en.html.

Even in 'modern' times (by which I mean post-Matrimonial Causes Act 1973), 'fault' was necessary within divorce, unless spouses were to wait at least two years. It had long been the view of practitioners, including those campaigning through Resolution, that it was an unhelpful status quo. It forced divorcing couples into the language of adversaries. Even in 'no-fault' divorces based on a separated period of time, 'to divorce' was still necessarily an action that one spouse had to do to the other. Practitioners would have to help their clients through the childcare, financial disputes and uncertainty that followed divorce, and it was hardly a helpful tone to set for those already emotionally charged discussions. Practitioners did this, largely, by clever drafting of divorce petitions, which required the listing of behaviour that could be considered unreasonable – so as to walk the tightrope between wording anodyne enough to avoid controversy, yet sufficient enough to cross the threshold of seriousness to satisfy the Court that the marriage had indeed broken down irretrievably.[31] Sometimes, even the most acrobatic of lawyers could fall either side of that tightrope. In the emotional tinderbox of a divorce, even innocuous allegations are enough to cause conflict. To avoid it, lawyers might find themselves having to rely on facts so gentle that they might move a judge to conclude that the spouses asking for a divorce had, in fact, only had a tiff that could, with effort, be reconciled. I address that particular dynamic in more detail below.

Resolution was a very active campaigner to change this outdated system. It was, indeed, in good company. Simultaneously with Resolution's efforts, parallel conversations were taking place in academia. Professor Liz Trinder of the University of Exeter was funded by the Nuffield Foundation in her research and report, which concluded that 'fault' is an out-dated feature of the law that stoked confusion, tension and negatively impacted the children of divorcing parents. Trinder's report was launched in 2017[32] at an event in the House of Lords hosted by Baroness Butler-Sloss. It was well-publicised in the national press. It could be seen as the turning point between this being a niche concern, spoken about within the family law echo chamber, and a matter of national agenda.

Trinder's report was so compelling, perhaps in part because of its synergy with the efforts of practitioners. Her research consulted practitioners in order to establish the way in which the problems were being managed on the ground. It exposed a lack of clear certainty, even amongst experienced practitioners, as to where the 'threshold' of behaviour was so as to justify a fault-based divorce. It identified a tendency of lawyers to 'overshoot' allegations in order to provide their clients with certainty that the divorce would move forward. It further identified the tension between this and the professional guidance to keep particulars 'brief' and 'mild',

[31] Resolution, *Resolution Guide to Good Practice Guiding Note: Drafting documents* (London, Resolution, December 2022) at resolution.org.uk/good-practice-guides-and-guidance-notes/.

[32] L Trinder et al, *Finding Fault? Divorce Law and Practice in England and Wales* (London, Nuffield Foundation, 2017).

contained within Resolution's *Guide to Good Practice on Draft Documents*,[33] to which most family solicitors subscribe. It shared the challenge faced by practitioners in having to 'sell' a 'mild' petition to a potentially hurt or angry spouse who wanted to feel vindicated and heard by their representatives. Trinder's work, I would argue, helped to tie together the practical issues facing litigants and professionals in almost every case. The situation was a mess – and family law academia and practice agreed.

Whilst these impassioned discussions were taking place in family-law circles, one Mrs Tini Owens had fallen out of love with her husband, Hugh. She reached the view that her marriage with him had broken down irretrievably. She instructed solicitors to pursue a divorce and, entirely in keeping with the legal culture of tight-rope-walking at the time, the solicitors prepared a brief divorce petition based on a few examples of Hugh's behaviour, which, Tini said, had been such that it would be unreasonable to expect her to continue to live with him. Hugh did not agree that the marriage had broken down irretrievably on the basis of the behaviour described and defended the application. Tini's petition was rejected by the Court as being insufficient to demonstrate the irretrievable breakdown of the marriage. Tini's solicitors amended her petition to refer to 27 such allegations. At trial, the Court found the revised allegations were 'flimsy and exaggerated', and even if the marriage had broken down, the statutory test for a divorce on the basis of such a petition had not been met. Tini pursued the matter to the Court of Appeal and then the Supreme Court, though both tribunals found that the judge had not erred in his legal analysis and application of the test. The decision was upheld. Tini would, in the words of the Court, have to 'remain married for the time being'.

One might sympathise with Tini for feeling she was between a rock and a hard place. Indeed, the Court did. In delivering the majority judgment, Lord Wilson described the 'uneasy feelings' that came with the decision. His concluding sentence was understated yet influential: 'Parliament may wish to consider whether to replace a law which denies to Mrs Owens any present entitlement to a divorce in the above circumstances.'

The Court could clearly see the problem, and it needed Parliament to fix it. Resolution, as a representative of interested practitioners, and Professor Trinder were powerful advocates for that fact. It is clear that the Court heard those voices. Resolution intervened in the proceedings so that it might express the extent of practitioners' concerns about the problem. The Court, whilst not accepting Resolution's proposed interpretation of the statute, respectfully acknowledged its contribution to the discussion. Professor Trinder's reports were cited in the judgment in contemplation of the problem, her summary of the Court's approach described as 'admirable'.

[33] See Resolution (n 29).

Owens v Owens attracted nationwide headline press attention.[34] Sometimes, a case strikes a chord with wider society and the public, who might be forgiven for struggling to reconcile how out of step the law had become with the way in which modern life is lived. This issue found itself as one of national concern and public interest.

'No-fault divorce' progressed through the legislative agenda, driven in the first instance in the House of Lords by Baroness Butler-Sloss – the aforementioned host of the launch of Professor Trinder's research. The upshot was the Divorce, Dissolution and Separation Act 2020, which came into effect in April 2022. This legislation eradicated the concept of fault in divorce. There is now one singular basis for divorce – that one party (or both parties) considered the marriage to have broken down irretrievably. Resolution continued to work closely with Parliament and the Ministry of Justice to drive the legislation. Professor Trinder's research was cited and credited within Parliamentary debate.

A job, in my view, well done.

VI. Conclusion

There is an immense concentration of intelligence and talent in family law academia and practice. The progress towards 'no-fault divorce' described in section V is the proof of that pudding. Practitioners informed academia; academia emboldened practitioners. The matter came to a head in a test case in which both voices were heard in tandem. The result was legislative change and a huge and long-awaited step forward for family justice in England and Wales. This, I would argue, is a clear example for practitioners and academics to follow and is a development to be celebrated.

Keeping enthusiasm in check for a moment, the 'no-fault divorce' case study also helps to identify four strands that realistically need to be braided together to effect genuine change, not all of which are within the control of family lawyers (academic or practising).

First, of course we need practitioners to be pro-active, engaged and vocal in addressing the issues in need of change as they pass our desks. Those arguments need to be advanced in test cases when the opportunity arises. Where change is required, the Court ought to be told so. It is questionable whether 'no-fault divorce' would have happened were it not for the Owens family's litigation, for example.

Second, we need academia to add weight and support to practice. Change is only attractive when supported by persuasiveness. Persuasiveness is built through diligent research and creative thought-leadership. Academic innovation enables practitioners to find solutions to real-world problems as they arise.

[34] *Owens v Owens* [2018] UKSC 41.

Third, however, proposed reforms need to attract public interest and public sympathy. The *Owens* case clearly appealed to the public sense of injustice that people might find themselves matrimonially trapped due to a legal relic. Less widely relatable issues, although perhaps no less important, might struggle to pick up quite the same pace.

Fourth, perhaps the biggest reality check is that real change often relies upon political interest. Recent parliamentary discourse has been dominated by generational issues such as Brexit, COVID-19 and the cost-of-living crisis. It would be naive to suggest that legislative reform would happen easily if it were not politically convenient enough to force its way on to the agenda. This will often come with publicity,[35] political pressure[36] *or* simply political convenience.[37] Either way, change in the law often lies in the hands of those who make it. Consider, for example, the breadth of research that supports cohabitee rights and the broad agreement in practice in that regard. However, political will appears to have been lacking, leading to the need for passionate academics and practitioners to wait decades for their campaign to lift off in Parliament. Consider also the contradictions and debates within research on polarising topics such as pre-nuptial agreements, polygamy, religious marriage or the legal construction of parenthood, all of which have produced entire bodies of literature. Such literature has often generated intense debates amongst law students across the country, but without political will, progress on these issues remains slow.

Without each of these four factors, change is difficult. That is a challenge, because each factor, in its own right, is difficult to come by.

To use our efforts most effectively, we must acknowledge our limitations. Neither practitioners nor academics can control which matters strike the public's imagination. Likewise, we are not politicians and do not set the legislative agenda.

Consequently, let us focus on what is in our gift. We can control the extent to which we cooperate. The push for better outcomes for individuals and society is a duty for practitioners and a common motivator for many in academia. We share an interest here. I would suggest that there was good cross-disciplinary collaboration in the lead up to the 'no-fault divorce' reforms. Perhaps without it, the sails would not have caught the wind in the same way when the other non-controllable factors presented themselves. If we are serious about reform, there is therefore a shared endeavour.

Consider the consequences of failure in that endeavour. Earlier, I referenced, briefly, my view on the trajectory of pre- and post-nuptial agreements, in that they are becoming increasingly influential, even if not binding. That does not come without concern within academic circles. It has been well argued that the emotional pressure on financially weaker parties to a nuptial agreement to prove

[35] See ibid.
[36] See human rights arguments in *Re Z (A child) (No 2)* [2016] EWHC 1191 (Fam).
[37] See *Supporting earlier resolution of private family law arrangements* (n 23).

that the marriage is an endeavour of love not financial gain can override the persuasiveness of, and adherence to, one's legal advice. This is especially the case if a nuptial agreement reflects terms that are different from those a court would realistically order in the absence of that document.[38] Practitioners and judges would surely be well advised to keep these thoughts in mind, so as to ensure that the law does not move too far in a direction that leaves some individuals vulnerable and exploited. That enables us to harness the benefits that make them popular, in terms of personal autonomy and certainty, without risk of harm. The industry would be well assisted by collaborative study between academics and practitioners to ensure that the current safeguards are sufficient, a subject, perhaps, for another edition of this book. More positively, consider the untapped potential within the mission for collaborative reform. With rigorous debate and open-minded creativity, we maximise the chance of reaching the right answers. Indeed, consider the progress that has been made when there was collaboration, like in 'no-fault divorce'.

I repeat the sentence at the start of this section: 'There is an immense concentration of intelligence and talent in family law academia and practice.' This book aims to play its own part in harnessing it. It aims to be a blueprint for collaboration to create an innovative area of law that catches up and keeps pace with the way people live their lives.

[38] S Thompson, 'In Defence of the "Gold-Digger"' (2016) 6(6) *Onati Socio-Legal Series* 1225.

INDEX

www.ingramcontent.com/pod-product-compliance
Ingram Content Group UK Ltd.
Pitfield, Milton Keynes, MK11 3LW, UK
UKHW020236290926
15470UKWH00002B/572

9 781509 962181